SAGE BIOGRAPHICAL RESEARCH

SAGE LIBRARY OF RESEARCH METHODS

SAGE BIOGRAPHICAL RESEARCH

VOLUME IV

Other Documents of Life: Photographs, Cyber Documents and Ephemera

Edited by

John Goodwin

Los Angeles | London | New Delhi
Singapore | Washington DC

Los Angeles | London | New Delhi
Singapore | Washington DC

SAGE Publications Ltd
1 Oliver's Yard
55 City Road
London EC1Y 1SP

SAGE Publications Inc.
2455 Teller Road
Thousand Oaks, California 91320

SAGE Publications India Pvt Ltd
B 1/I 1, Mohan Cooperative Industrial Area
Mathura Road
New Delhi 110 044

SAGE Publications Asia-Pacific Pte Ltd
3 Church Street
#10-04 Samsung Hub
Singapore 049483

© Introduction and editorial arrangement by
John Goodwin, 2012

First published 2012

Typeset by Star Compugraphics
Private Limited, Delhi

Printed on paper from sustainable resources

Printed and bound in Great Britain by
TJ International Ltd, Padstow, Cornwall

Library of Congress Control Number: 2011941786

British Library Cataloguing in Publication Data

A catalogue record for this book is available from the
British Library

ISBN: 978-1-4462-4691-7 (set of four volumes)

Contents

Volume IV: Other Documents of Life – Photographs, Cyber Documents and Ephemera

Families, Secrets and Memories

Carol Smart

Introduction

It is a conventional wisdom that all families have secrets. It is of course impossible to find out whether this is so or not, but the belief itself is interesting. It suggests that there is a cultural tolerance for secrets, at least to some degree, and also that there is an understanding of the need to keep secrets. To suggest that all families have secrets also implies that families present a specific 'face' to the world and that this appearance will not be the full story of the kinds and quality of relationships going on behind the facade (Finch, 2007). Some research and exploration has been carried out on family secrets (Davidoff et al., 1999; Kuhn, 1995; Smart, 2007) but it is extremely hard to enquire into family secrets because of their sensitive nature, because of the reluctance to reveal one's own secrets (especially if they are still secret), and because of a sense of loyalty or decency that stops people revealing the secrets of others. This poses a problem for research into secrets because it appears that one is confounded by ethical dilemmas even before the start. And although it is possible to find out about some secrets in an 'objective' fashion, for example by studying official birth, marriage and death certificates, if we want to understand the impact of secrets on people's family lives and relationships more is clearly needed. In this article I do not overcome all these problems but I was fortunate to find an archive of data on family secrets which I describe below. These data allowed me to start a sociological enquiry into family secrets which leads me to an argument that secrets in families may be a way of sustaining kinship relationships. In what

Source: *Sociology*, 45(4) (2011): 539–553.

follows I explain the nature of the archive and the data deposited there, and I go on to discuss the kinds of secrets that the respondents wrote about. I argue that the telling of family secrets is tied into the workings of family memories and that the accounts that people provide cannot be regarded as simple factual accounts. Rather they are amongst the kinds of stories that people tell of families as part of the constitution of 'the family' and its past (Fivush, 2008). I will focus primarily on reproductive secrets but also discuss the consequences of dealing with secrets once they are uncovered.

Sociology and the Significance of Family Secrets

Although there is a growing popular interest in family secrets fuelled in particular by the expanding industry in genealogy and tracing family roots (Kramer, 2011a), there is a sociological significance to exploring both the existence and the workings of such secrecy. This significance has at least three dimensions. The first and most overarching concerns the workings of power which are, in turn, multidirectional. By this I mean that family secrets operate to defend a family against forms of governance from outside the family (Rose, 1989, 1999). Thus keeping illegitimacy secret could be a means of defending from outside scrutiny and adverse judgement (see Laslett, 1977, on illegitimacy, and Sayer, 2005, on shame). But equally this power works within the family, between family members. Hence the telling or not telling of secrets can defend an individual against other family members, or it can empower some members against the interests of weaker members. In these ways we can see both the micro workings of power (e.g. keeping secret one's sexual orientation in order to main relationships; Ponse, 1976; Valentine et al., 2003), but also the macro context in which the micro struggles are located (e.g. the State's criminalization or condemnation of homosexual practices, Weeks, 1991). The second realm of significance relates to the conceptual reconfiguration of 'the family' from a social institution into a set of practices (Morgan, 1996). This reconceptualization has given rise to a wave of enquiry into understanding family practices and has generated a renewed interest into the everyday workings of family life. In this context family secrets take on a particular salience because the keeping (and breaking) of secrets appears to be a core activity in both bonding members together and in excluding – or othering – other members. The workings of family secrets can be analysed in terms of how they both bond and exclude, whilst maintaining an apparent integrity to the naturalness of family unity. This is linked to the third dimension of sociological significance, namely what Gillis (1996) has referred to as the families we live by. Gillis makes the distinction between the families we live 'with' (i.e. our actual kin in an existing household) and families we live 'by' which are the idealized version of loving families which inhabit our cultural imaginations notwithstanding the fact that our actual families may be unhappy, conflict-ridden places. I suggest that family secrets are often a practical bridge between the families we live with, and those we live by. The operations of the secrets allow us to create a family story through which actual families come to appear more like the ideal or mythical family. In this sense family secrets are part of the arsenal of the wider family story which produces a sense of (respectable) heritage and creates such a large place both in personal memory and in cultural imaginings.

The focus on family secrets is therefore a conceptual window on everyday family life which can be read at a number of levels. One level is the micro workings of power on an everyday basis, and this is the level I concentrate on in this article. But this can be woven into a much bigger 'story' about historical change, law and governance, and transformations in family life (see Smart, 2009, 2010, for examples).

Mass Observation and Family Secrets

The Mass Observation Project (MOP) is an archive based at the University of Sussex which collects written narratives from a panel of regular writers who are invited to respond three times a year to a set of questions – known as Directives – on a diverse range of themes from royal weddings to friendship. The archive was originally founded in the 1930s (Jeffrey, 1999) and contains a great deal of material regularly used by historians researching everyday life during the war years. Until recently it was not used much by sociologists because of the strength of the positivist tradition which held that the panellists could not remotely be regarded as statistically representative of British society and because the free way in which they wrote was not regarded as sufficiently rigorous for sociological analysis (see Hubble, 2006, and Sheridan et al., 2000, for debates on these themes). More recently, however, sociologists using more qualitative or mixed methods approaches have begun to appreciate the value of the archive; in particular, they have started to commission new Directives as well as analysing existing data (Kramer, 2011b, 2011c; McGhee and Harrison, 2003; Savage, 2007). The archive is therefore becoming more of a sociological resource, particularly where the MOP data are situated alongside data generated in more conventional ways. Its value is often found in the richness and depth of the narratives that many panellists provide, arising from the policy of the MOP to encourage people to write about actual experiences and real events, rather than offering opinions and attitudes.

In 2000 a Directive was sent out to the panel asking them to write about their experiences of family life and family relationships. This Directive included questions on the history of their families but it also enquired specifically about family secrets and about gays and lesbians in the family. Replies were received from 168 women and 50 men, some writing at considerable length. Some panellists chose not to reveal any secrets and a few actually objected to being asked for such personal information. However, most writers seemed willing to reveal or uncover secrets and many wrote of quite delicate matters which might have been too sensitive to share in a face-to-face interview. The writers were not given a definition of 'family secret' and it was left to them to decide what they thought was relevant based on their own experiences. Most responded with apparent ease as if they had no trouble in identifying what a family secret was. But of course the reader has no idea how the respondents selected the particular secrets they wrote about, nor whether only some types of secret were chosen, nor indeed whether some types of secrets were regarded as too shameful to write about (McGhee and Harrison, 2003). It was interesting that the majority of respondents wrote mostly about secrets which occurred in their grandparents' or sometimes their parents' lifetimes. It was much less common for people to write about contemporary or ongoing secrets, or to write about secrets that they were themselves cultivating or guarding.

I have grouped the stories told by the respondents into five broad types. The first is the virtual myth, which took the form of a well-rehearsed account, such as the one focussing on a distant uncle running away with a circus entertainer or being related to royalty. The colourful story does not have to be totally mythical, but it offers a strong narrative about the qualities of ancestors whose exploits somehow lend substance to the family lineage. The second type was the shameful illness, which included mental illness but could also be about physical disability. In these cases the person concerned was often hidden away from sight.

> I had a cousin [. . .] who had what was then called a nervous breakdown at the age of about 21. My uncle and aunt, certainly from the best of motives, but most misguidedly, didn't get any help after she refused to see a doctor herself. They kept up the pretence that B was not very well and she lived in her room at their bungalow for perhaps 30 years. [. . .] One February day she was found dead in the river. [. . .] no-one falls into that river in daylight. (H2637, female aged 61, information officer)

The third type, the personal grievance, was usually over some shady misdemeanour concerning inheritance rights (and wrongs) or the swindling of money. The fourth type, the reproductive secret, constituted the largest single group and covered premarital conception and birth, illegitimacy, secret adoptions, paternity uncertainty, affairs leading to additional children, and, more latterly, matters of assisted reproduction. Finally, there was homosexuality which, because it was a separate question in the 2000 Directive, was not always discussed in relation to being a family secret. However, the responses on this question often fitted into the secrecy fold because panellists wrote a great deal about their suspicions and the hushed nature of any suggestion of homosexuality in the family, and some openly said that they were the family secret because of their sexual orientation.

> And then of course there's my husband's Uncle T. whom I've never met [. . .] The Uncle T. in question was very well dressed, and theatrical and was 'sent away to America' [in the 1950s], so the only conclusion to be drawn was that he was gay. And although there were lots of whispers, nobody ever actually mentioned the word homosexual. (We're talking church family here). (A1706, female aged 54)

I return to some of these types of secrets when I discuss three specific narratives, but before exploring the ways in which the respondents wrote about their secrets, it is important to consider the role of memory in the recounting of such matters.

Families and Memories

Families, it may be said, are as much collections of memories as they are of actual related people and kin (Misztal, 2003: 82). It is impossible to imagine a family without the sense that it is part of a lineage; that the people who are the current parent generation are the children of the previous generation and that they carry with them some sense or aura (not to mention genes) of those who have gone before. Being part of a lineage carries with it echoes of the past, plus an embeddedness in what went (or who went) before. The past and the present are therefore intertwined and each gives meaning to the other (Smart, 2007).

Misztal (2003) has argued that without memory there can be no sense of identity and that it is the ability to remember one's past that gives a person a sense of self which continues even though everything else changes and even becomes unrecognizable. So, it follows that the memories associated with families – those that we inherit as well as those deriving from our own direct experiences – are particularly potent because they constitute a 'specialised circle of memory' (2003: 95). By this it is meant that it is (usually) in families where one develops one's first memories but it is also in the relational context of family within which one goes on collecting memories over many years (Fivush, 2008; Miller, 1994). These memories are specialized because they are created around a small group of individuals who relate to one another over many years. Some of these memories will take the form of narratives (one's own and those of other family members) which can be later rehearsed and refreshed and, of course, modified. Hence the importance of family stories which carry these rehearsed narratives across the generations. I argue above that family secrets are embedded in these family stories and that through this process they import a sociological significance. But through the work of

Misztal we can also grasp the personal significance of such stories as part of the construction of identities of both families and individuals in families. This means that where family stories and memories are 'fictitious' there can be important social and personal ramifications arising from exposure. Of course, in considering family secrets and memory there is a problem because secrets are not typically thought of as being rehearsed and refreshed. Secrets, it is assumed, are just buried and forgotten. I found evidence of this practice in the MOP narratives because a lot of writers who were embarking on family genealogy were discovering forgotten or well-buried secrets. But it is equally likely in families that secrets can be kept alive by innuendo, palpable silences, evasions and rumour. Sometimes respondents to the Directive knew there was a problem area or were aware that there were questions they should not ask and they may never have found out what the secret was. But, for others, they did find out about the secret which, in effect, had been kept alive by the multiple acts of silence.

Memories about secrets are incredibly complex. Memory is chameleon in nature (Blokland, 2005). It changes over time, it ebbs and flows, it changes in significance and it meshes together adult memory and sensibilities with childhood memory and forms of understanding. Where secrets are concerned we must also consider the ways in which family members seek deliberately to deceive and fabricate events and chronologies. To add to this, where secrets have caused family division, memories and counter memories may both be available. Counter memories do not just tell another story but they construct the family, and the characters in it, in completely different ways which can lead to surprising re-evaluations of kith and kin when these alternative accounts become known. Secrets too can, of course, be complete fabrications rather than hidden 'truths'.

The writers in the MOP were also often well aware of these complex dimensions of family secrets:

> These are not really secrets though, more part of the mythology that accompanies old photographs. I wonder whether there are secrets and we just don't talk about them. (B2728, female aged 45, local government officer)

Thus, in writing about their family's secrets, these respondents were able to reflect on the status of their stories rather than just repeating them innocently as if they were self-evident historical facts. Several too mused upon the fact that they did not know any secrets and this might be because they were the ones in their family who could or would not be told such things. They were thus aware that not everyone in a family had the same privileged access to secrets and in this way they often seemed aware of the relationship between secrets and the workings of micro-power. Moreover, as with the writer above, there was an awareness that the open secrets or myths might have been a shield behind which could cluster the darker secrets that no one ever mentioned. The processes of keeping alive and also burying secrets could therefore occur simultaneously in the same family.

Exploring Family Secrets

Exploring family secrets does have its dangers precisely because the discovery of such things as adoption, premarital sex and even criminality can lead to a rewriting of the family story. The respectable image of ancestors can be shattered and the moral values, which were presumed to reflect the character of a particular family and its lineage, can be reinterpreted as mere hypocrisy. This in turn can impact on the reflexive construction of the 'self' or identity because, as I argue above, memory is part of this construction and family memories can be particularly powerful in this process. Of course the re-evaluation of self which may occur can be either positive or negative (and many shades in between). So, for example, for the young lesbian who wrote in the MOP that she had found that a great aunt had been a lesbian too, the discovery was entirely positive and made her feel she was not alone in her family. Others, however, could feel they had been 'short changed' or married in some way. For some, for example, the simple question about whether they knew of any gays or lesbians in their families brought out complete denials of the possibility. It was as if the mere thought of such a stain on the character of their family sent them reeling into ontological confusion. It is, therefore, little wonder that, once found, some secrets are buried again or that there is resistance even to speculating about them.

Discussions of secrecy can produce strong reactions (e.g. secrets are wrong/prying is wrong) or a complex ambivalence (e.g. secrecy is bad/privacy is good). The following remark seems to capture this ambivalence perfectly:

> I do not like secrets and like everything out in the open. There are things that happen that sometimes are better kept to oneself. (R860, female aged 53, retired lecturer)

In these two short sentences this writer captures the moral quagmire that can engulf matters of family secrecy. The shading of privacy into secrecy is subtle and the blurred boundaries are not stable but shift with the passage of time, the characters involved and the prevailing (local) normative framework. In this way it becomes possible to condone the keeping of secrets while publically adhering to principles of openness and transparency.

In what follows I have selected for more detailed discussion three of the stories narrated by MOP respondents. These have been selected because they reveal and/or demonstrate a number of the issues I have outlined above. I have reproduced sections of the writing exactly as they appeared in the archive and, where necessary, have explained the background in order that the story is as clear as possible.

Case 1: The Virtual Secret

By luck the first narrative in the MOP that I read proved to be what I came to realize was a classic account both in terms of the workings of memory and in terms of revealing the complex nature of family secrets. In this account the writer starts by denying the possibility of there being any secrets in her family's history. She states that this is because they were a 'respectable' family. However, she goes on to a powerful secret which could have been quite devastating to the family's respectability had it been revealed during the era in which it occurred (e.g. around the 1920s and 1930s). The account of the first secret begins thus:

> There have been no family secrets in the sense that you mean, as I belong to a very respectable family. There really were no secrets at all, but I suppose that the closest my family came to having a secret was that my father had a younger brother and sister who were hidden away until they died, and it was never openly spoken of in the family, and never mentioned at all by my father. (A2212, female aged 44, author)

This story is described as being 'close' to a family secret but not an actual secret – yet it becomes clear as the story unfolds that the two children concerned were kept hidden, they were hardly ever spoken of, and the author's father who was 15 years of age when his siblings died apparently never once mentioned them.

The author continues her story by recreating, in what appears to be a verbatim form, snatches of conversation that she overheard as a child. This form of storytelling is very powerful and gives a kind of veracity to the story even if it is unlikely that she can accurately remember what was said.

> The first I ever knew of this was when I was a child of about seven, and my paternal grandmother said to me, in a sad and rather wistful way, 'I had a little girl once, but she died'. I did not really know what to make of it. It seemed to me to refer to something that happened about forty years earlier when, as far as I was concerned, anything might have happened. It was just one of those things that adults said that was vaguely interesting but also incomprehensible. I know that my mother had had a baby sister who had died because we visited her grave from time to time, and I suppose I thought it was a similar situation, and that children had died more frequently in the past, and that maybe a lot of people of that age had had brothers and sisters who had died young. [. . .]

> Some years later when I was about fourteen, I overheard my first cousin once removed having a whispered conversation with my mother, which went something like this: 'I saw him once. He was just lying there and didn't respond. They carried him like a baby, but he was much older than that. He was about six or seven. He couldn't walk or talk. I don't know if he was blind.'

She continues with the explanation that her own mother gave to her:

> It had not been known what had actually caused their disabilities. My grandmother, she said, had always put it down to having been frightened by a sheep when she was pregnant, which would not explain why they were both disabled. My mother said that she suspected that my grandfather had caught a tropical disease when he was in the army in India, about the time of the First World War. My father had been born before his father went to India, and then the two other children had been born after he came back.

What is so interesting about this family secret is the way in which the writer reveals the workings of partial knowledge, memory, the passing down of accounts, the role of superstition and all these things combined with bits of factual genealogy (e.g. my first cousin once removed). The author herself accepts the account that her mother gave her which is perhaps why she describes this as only 'almost' a secret and also why she feels she can start her account with an assertion about the respectability of her family – her grandfather it seems became a lay preacher and her grandmother was very religious. The apparent underlying secret still tangled up in this story does not appear to reveal itself to the author. She seems to accept what she was told about 'a tropical disease'. She continues, however, by explaining that her sister did try to find out what was wrong with the prematurely deceased aunt and uncle because she feared there might be an inheritable genetic problem in the family line. But the author does not know what her sister found out and remained apparently incurious on her own behalf.

From the vivid descriptions of the physical conditions of the two short-lived children born after the First World War, combined with the reference to a 'tropical disease', it seems almost certain that the grandfather returned from the war with a venereal disease and that the children born subsequently would have suffered from congenital syphilis (Lancaster, 1990: 188). Of course, it is quite possible that the grandmother never understood why two of her children were born disabled and so, in this sense, she may not have been keeping secrets. However, the medical profession would have been familiar with congenital syphilis which was common at this time,[1] and it is also quite likely that the grandfather knew what had happened. The fact that the children were kept hidden is suggestive of the shame that threatened this middle-class family if knowledge or suspicion of the condition of the children spread. Given that disability alone was shameful at this time, apparently casting a shadow over a whole family, the possibility that an adulterous liaison had been the cause would have generated unbearable shame.

This family secret is a particularly interesting one because the author of the account seems entirely innocent of the extent to which this is a story still with the power to shock (Welzer, 2010). It does not lead her to re-evaluate her grandfather because she sees the tragedy as a kind of cosmic accident.

Nor does she seem particularly troubled by her own father's virtual amnesia on the topic of his two siblings. His complete silence on the matter suggests that he ingested fully the responsibility not to reveal anything of that history of his family. She refers to the discovery of her grandfather's will in which he wrote of the great suffering that he, and his wife, endured and how the grandmother's faith had sustained her. So there was clearly a great deal of misery surrounding the lives of these children and the secret would maybe have died with them had not the grandmother's sadness leaked out into little comments that kept their memory alive.

Case 2: The Family Joke

This story is about paternity and fits into the largest category of secrets discussed, namely reproductive secrets. It may be that one of the reasons why secrets about premarital conceptions, paternity uncertainty, adoptions and so on were so common in the MOP accounts was related to the growing interest in family genealogy and the ready (on-line) availability of official data such as birth, death and marriage certificates. I cannot be sure that these are the most common family secrets in general but, as I argue above, because of the long history of shame and disgrace associated with matter of sex and reproduction in the UK, it is not unlikely that reproductive issues have always had a tendency to operate within fields of secrecy.

The story that follows was not revealed as a consequence of genealogical research however.

> This family secret concerned my middle sister who had always secretly thought she had a different dad to myself and our two brothers as she was taller and didn't look like any of the rest of us, although to be honest none of us really look much like each other. However whenever she used to say to my mum, 'I think I must have a different dad to our so and so 'cause I don't look like any of the others', my mum used to look horrified and say 'Oh, our so and so, how can you say that, of course you haven't got a different dad!' We used to laugh at her scandalised expression. She was such a moral and upright woman that the very thought was fantastic.

> . . . She was laying on her deathbed aged 85 and the sister concerned was sat by her side when suddenly mum piped up with the fact that yes she has got a different dad but he died at Anzio in the second world war and if he hadn't have got killed then she would have left my dad and married this man. She knew he was the father because of the dimple and the date of her birth. [. . .] It was a burden she had carried round for most of her life and now that she had told my sister the truth, she didn't want to talk about it anymore and that was the last she said on the matter. (H1703, female aged 53, administrator)

In this case it transpired that the mother had travelled to Ireland to visit her husband who was stationed there the moment she realized she was pregnant by her lover. In this way she had avoided all suspicion about paternity, at least until her daughter began to suspect she had a different father because of her dissimilar appearance. The story about the suspicions becoming a family joke is intriguing because although the misgivings were strong, the belief that it was impossible for their mother to have had an affair was even stronger. Their whole view of their mother as such a moral and upright woman was unshakeable and so the children simply absorbed and lived with the contradiction in their lives. Moreover, the mother kept the secret until the very last minute even in the face of some incredulity. A lot was at stake for her. The revelation might well have destroyed her marriage; in the UK in the 1950s and 1960s she might even have lost her legitimate children had her husband wanted custody. Her second daughter would have been deemed illegitimate, which then carried serious legal consequences, and she would not have been able to rely on anyone to support her given that the father of the child was dead. As the daughter writing for the MOP remarks, her mother carried this burden throughout her life. What is more, although she ultimately confided the truth of paternity to the daughter concerned, she would not provide sufficient information to allow her to trace her father and possibly other biological kin. So she bequeathed her daughter an unsolvable mystery and, in effect, a different kind of burden. In this way the secret became unfinished business across the generations and, although in this case the writer does not report any sense of bitterness, in some cases the discovery of such secrets did lead to anger and festering resentments.

Case 3: Deepening Resentments

In this account a retired teacher wrote about how her parents kept lots of secrets. In particular there was a mystery about her birth, as different siblings were told different things. At times she was described as premature, sometimes her birth was said to be two weeks late, at other times her father was said to be 17 or maybe 18 years old when she was born; or it was said that they were married for one year, then two years, before she was born. So the narrator acquired her birth certificate and her parents' marriage certificate and found out that she was 14 months old when her parents actually married.

> Some time in the Eighties when my parents had gone through a phase of particular nastiness towards my sister and I happened to be working on the family tree, I decided to find out what they'd been hiding. I wrote to the Public Record Office for my full birth certificate and my parents' marriage certificate. What I discovered really shocked me because it turned out that my parents hadn't got married until I was fourteen months old. Suddenly it all became clear. All that control over their children, all that suspicion, nastiness and stifling over-protection was because they didn't want us to turn out like them. They had made the mistake of producing an illegitimate child in an era when such a thing brought disgrace and it seems to my

siblings and me that all our lives we'd been made to pay for that mistake. (W1813, female aged 50, teacher)

In this account the discovery of the secret 'explains everything' to the narrator. She describes what miserable childhoods the siblings had endured and how incredibly strict her parents had been. They had all longed to escape and felt little affection for the parents. From her account it is clear that the narrator understands the issue of shame and how her parents had had to endure disgrace. However, she is not prepared to forgive them for inflicting a miserable childhood on them all in order to make up for their own mistakes. She remarks, 'it's taken my siblings and me years to work out the games they've been playing with our lives'.

In this case too it is possible to see the intergenerational legacy of family secrets. In this instance, the parents were reacting to the shame they had endured and had created a fabricated and fragile account of their eldest daughter's birth which presumably they imagined they could sustain forever. However, the fluctuating account merely increased curiosity and led to the revelation. In this family the secret then becomes the defining feature of their dysfunction. It becomes a way of explaining the poor quality of their relationships, but it also appears to give the adult children 'closure' because they have acquired the key to the puzzle. The family's history becomes defined by this specific epiphanal event.

Narratives of Avoidance

In this penultimate section I explore the idea that the ways in which secrets are handled (or mishandled) may be culturally significant. The way in which secrets and secrecy are managed is a way of understanding family practices and a reflection on how families imagine they should conduct themselves. So while the substance of secrets is interesting and revealing of cultural norms and practices, another micro level of sociological analysis is available. This pertains to how families approach matters which are shameful and embarrassing and how they manage the flow of knowledge and understanding across generations and kin. The two axes which appear to determine how secrets are managed are 'respectability and uprightness of character' and 'discretion and active not-knowing'. The concept of 'active not-knowing' is discussed by Konrad (2005) who suggests that, from an anthropological perspective, people are engaged in practices of active not-knowing around family matters that are potentially disruptive. Part of growing up or simply relating to others may be learning what 'not to know'. And for parents or those at the centre of some particular family secret, active not-knowing is a way of keeping perceived problems at bay while also being part of the operations of micro-power. So there is a subtle choreography of secrecy management where some people learn not to ask, others create veils of confusion or are simply economical with the truth. It would seem that the majority of the writers in the MOP were well aware of this delicate set of balances and spoke of them as a defining feature of their family (and sometimes most families). Hence:

> I've always had a feeling as a child that there were things I was not to know – but if so they never came to light later on! Certain topics were discouraged from being mentioned – divorce for example, and there were mentions of black sheep – presumably those who had 'married out' of the faith (Jewish). (B2197, female aged 46, library volunteer)

The familiar strategy was simply to remain quiet about difficult matters, yet at the same time an aura could be created which kept the issue hanging in the air. Many families seem to realize that the only way to keep relationships going is to ignore the very thing which would make it impossible to sustain bonds of affection or filiation. This strategy was particularly evident over matters of homosexuality where a 'don't ask/don't tell' policy seemed particularly prevalent (Ponse, 1976). For example, one woman wrote about her lesbianism and said she had never come out to her parents even though she was 66 years of age and had been living with her partner for 30 years:

> I don't think they would have been pleased. They may have guessed, and preferred not to talk about it. (B1665, female aged 66, retired clerk)

This silence over matters regarded as awkward or uncomfortable was a way of accommodating conflicting values. In this context children were often the most powerless family members, becoming bewildered, especially as they started to be aware of the silences, the differences and sometimes the awkwardnesses. There were also recollections from childhood about how a matter might have been openly spoken of, so that family members knew about the issue, only to realize that a gradual veil had been drawn over the event and that progressively it was no longer mentioned so that it sank into becoming a family secret. The process was hard to define or pin down, but somehow it became absorbed into the normative expectations of a family that some things were no longer open for discussion. This is a kind of governance by silence in which no clear responsibility can be attributed to specific family members because control over knowledge is acquired through intangible inaction and unremarkable acquiescence.

What follows is an example of how members of a family knew about a reproductive secret (in this case an adoption) but how the child in question was never told. This means that all of the older generation, and possibly some of their children, had the knowledge but one person alone did not.

> They never told the adopted son who is now in his fifties and a granddad and I am always on edge when I meet him in case someone inadvertently mentions it. He is a devoted family man and I know he will be devastated if he ever finds out how deceitful we have all been. I am surprised the

secret has been kept from him for such a long time but I cannot see him
going through life without eventually finding out. (H180, male aged 75,
retired typesetter)

The strategy of avoidance comes therefore with a strong undertow. Everyone has to subscribe to the silence and to engage in what Konrad (2005) refers
to above as 'active not-knowing'. In other words the secret is not forgotten
but has to be suppressed over and over again.

Concluding Remarks

The anthropologist Marilyn Strathern (1999) has written about the ways in
which relationships between kin, particularly in the context of Euro-American
kinship, are profoundly affected by what is known about biological or genetic
connection. She argues that knowing about genetic connection is not simply
a matter of information but a form of knowledge that is constitutive of relationships. So, for example, knowing that one's niece is not the child of one's
brother has profound effects, it is not just a factual piece of information.
Reproductive secrets in families have the power to be disruptive and dangerous because, once revealed, they will always alter relationships. Other kinds
of secrets may alter how a person views their relatives, but reproductive
secrets may mean that a relative is not actually kin any more. Strathern argues
that this is because understanding of Euro-American kinship is based not on
caring and quality of relationships, but on biological or genetic 'fact'. This argument has been contested (Edwards, 2000; Finch and Mason, 1993) because it
is clear that family and kinship can be formed independently of genetic connection. However, Strathern's point remains a powerful one and it offers a
deeper explanation for the keeping of family secrets beyond simply ideas of
family respectability and shame. She argues:

> But we shall not understand the converse, people's reluctance, or their
> desire to not-know, or anxieties about where information will lead, unless
> we realise that kinship knowledge has certain built-in effects. (1999: 69)

From this we can conclude that although all forms of family secrets have effects
on relationships, secrets concerning sexuality and reproduction have the power
to reconfigure families altogether. This power to reconfigure families is an
example of the operations of micro-power discussed at the start of this article, but Strathern's insights add extra weight to the specific power of secrets
around reproductive matters because she points so cogently to what can be at
stake. The three case studies I use above are deployed precisely because it is
possible to see, through them, the workings of these risks and the things that
are at stake. These workings include mechanisms of everyday memory making,
identity constructions, bondings and otherings, and also the wider governance

of family life. Each story can be taken as a starting point to disentangle how families work, how they present themselves to the world, how they manage their weaker members, how they control knowledge, and how they construct their heritage and aura. The study of family secrets can be seen as an investigative approach which troubles the smooth facade of ordinary family life – not in order to decry family life as if some other form would be above such practices – but in order to demonstrate how complex family practices can be and how entangled they are with matters as conceptually distinct as public values and the personal construction of the self. Tracking family secrets sociologically is a method of linking the personal and the cultural, the historical, and the social. It is an enquiry which takes one immediately into the realms of memory, myth and the extra-literal, and which therefore requires a cautious reflexive approach, while simultaneously demanding grounded knowledge of cultural, historical and social context, plus a sensitivity to the important fact that real lives are involved and often marred by such secrets. Family secrets may be seen as a key to unlock otherwise obscure practices and invisible mechanisms; they are not simple lies or mere historical curiosities, rather they are part of the fabric of everyday family life.

Note

1. Statistics on the prevalence of congenital syphilis in England during this period are very sketchy. Children would not have been presented for treatment because patients had to pay for medical care, but also because of the stigma attached to venereal diseases. Lancaster (1990) refers to a report in 1923 which suggested that 8 per cent of 1000 school children in Plymouth, England, exhibited signs of the disease. Plymouth was a poor naval city where the incidence of venereal diseases might have been particularly high. Death certificates did not always provide accurate causes of death in these cases.

References

Blokland T (2005) Memory magic: How a working-class neighbourhood became an imagined community and class started to matter when it lost its base. In: Devine F et al. (eds) *Rethinking Class*. Basingstoke: Palgrave Macmillan.

Davidoff L, Doolittle M, Fink J and Holden K (1999) *The Family Story: Blood, Contract and Intimacy 1830–1960*. London: Longman.

Edwards J (2000) *Born and Bred*. Oxford: Oxford University Press.

Finch J (2007) Displaying families. *Sociology* 41(1): 65–81.

Finch J and Mason J (1993) *Negotiating Family Responsibilities*. London: Tavistock/ Routledge.

Fivush R (2008) Remembering and reminiscing: How individual lives are constructed in family narratives. *Memory Studies* 1(1): 49–58.

Gillis J (1996) *A World of Their Own Making*. Boston, MA: Harvard University Press.

Hubble N (2006) *Mass Observation and Everyday Life: Theory, Culture, History*. Basingstoke: Palgrave Macmillan.

Jeffrey T (1999) *Mass-Observation: A Short History*. Mass-Observation Archive Occasional Paper No. 10. Brighton: University of Sussex Library.

Konrad M (2005) *Nameless Relations*. Oxford: Berghahn Books.

Kramer A-M (forthcoming 2011a) Kinship, affinity and connectedness: Exploring the role of genealogy in personal lives. *Sociology*.

Kramer A-M (forthcoming 2011b) *Kinship and Genealogy*. Basingstoke: Palgrave Macmillan.

Kramer A-M (forthcoming 2011c) Mediat[is]ing memory: History, affect and identity in Who *Do You Think You Are?* Special Issue on 'Cultural Memory and Identity'. *European Journal of Cultural Studies* 14: 3.

Kuhn A (1995) *Family Secrets: Acts of Memory and Imagination*. London: Verso.

Lancaster HO (1990) *Expectations of Life: A Study in the Demography, Statistics and History of World Mortality*. New York: Springer-Verlag.

Laslett P (1977) *Family Life and Illicit Love in Earlier Generations*. Cambridge: Cambridge University Press.

McGhee D and Harrison K (2003) Reading and writing family secrets. *Auto/biography* 11(1–2): 25–36.

Miller PJ (1994) Narrative practices: Their role in socialization and self-construction. In: Neisser U and Fivush R (eds) *The Remembering Self*. New York: Cambridge University Press.

Misztal B (2003) *Theories of Social Remembering*. Milton Keynes: Open University Press.

Morgan D (1996) *Family Connections*. Cambridge: Polity.

Ponse B (1976) Secrecy in the lesbian world. *Journal of Contemporary Ethnography* 5(3): 313–38.

Rose N (1989) *Governing the Soul: The Shaping of the Private Self*. London: Routledge.

Rose N (1999) *Powers of Freedom: Reframing Political Thought*. Cambridge: Cambridge University Press.

Savage M (2007) Changing social class identities in post-war Britain: Perspectives from Mass Observation. *Sociological Research Online* 12(3). Available at: http://www.socresonline.org.uk/12/3/6.html

Sayer A (2005) *The Moral Significance of Class*. Cambridge: Cambridge University Press.

Sheridan D, Street B and Bloome D (2000) *Writing Ourselves: Mass-Observation and Literacy Practices*. Cresskill, NJ: Hampton Press.

Smart C (2007) *Personal Life*. Cambridge: Polity.

Smart C (2009) Family secrets: Law and understandings of openness in everyday relationships. *Journal of Social Policy* 38(4): 551–67.

Smart C (2010) Law and the regulation of family secrets. *International Journal of Law, Policy and the Family* 24(3): 397–413.

Strathern M (1999) *Property, Substance and Effect: Anthropological Essays on Persons and Things*. London: The Athlone Press.

Valentine G et al. (2003) Coming out and outcomes: Negotiation lesbian and gay identities with, and in, the family. *Society and Space* 21(4): 479–99.

Weeks J (1991) Pretended family relationships. In: Clarke D (ed.) *Marriage, Domestic Life and Social Change*. London: Routledge.

Welzer H (2010) Re-narrations: How pasts change in conversational remembering. *Memory Studies* 3(1): 5–17.

59

Accessories to a Life Story: From Written Diaries to Video Diaries

Ken Plummer

I have often thought that there has rarely passed a life of which a judicious and faithful narrative would not be useful.

(Samuel Johnson, 1750)

It is perhaps as difficult to write a good life as to live one.

(Lytton Strachey, 1880–1932)

Miss Prism You must put away your diary, Cecily. I really don't see why you should keep a diary at all.

Cecily: I keep a diary in order to enter the wonderful secrets of my life. If I didn't write them all down, I should probably forget all about them.

(Oscar Wilde, 1895, *The Importance of Being Earnest*, Act II)

Every person their own methodologist! Methodologists get to work!

(Mills, 1970: 137)

Having seen something of the standard range of life stories, this chapter goes on a whirlwind tour of ways of adding to them. Although the most standard approach has been to take a life story through an interview, there are many other 'tools' that can be employed – from simple diary keeping to more elaborate video diaries. In this chapter, once again, the the aim is fairly basic: to provide illustrations of these allied methods and hopefully to encourage their use.

Source: *Documents of Life 2* (London: SAGE, 2001), pp. 48–74.

Diaries

For Gordon Allport (1942: 95), the diary is the document of life *par excellence*, chronicling as it does the immediately contemporaneous flow of public and private events that are significant to the diarist. The word 'contemporary' is very crucial here, for each diary entry – unlike life histories – is sedimented into a particular moment in time: they do not emerge 'all at once' as reflections on the past, but day by day strive to record an ever-changing present. Every diary entry declares, ? am here, and it is exactly now' (Fothergill, 1974: 9). Yet whilst this is true it would also be naive to believe that each day's entry is that alone: for at least in sustained diary keeping, the diarist will eventually come to perceive the diary as a whole and to plan a selection of entries according to this plan. Indeed, as Fothergill comments:

> . . . As a diary grows to a certain length and substance, it impresses upon the mind of its writer a conception of the completed book that it might ultimately be, if sustained with sufficient dedication and vitality. If, having written regularly and fully for, let us say, several months, (s)he were to abandon the habit, (s)he would be leaving unwritten a book whose character and conventions had been established and whose final form is the shape of his life. (Fothergill, 1974: 44)

Such an issue is clearly raised by the most famous diaries of all: those of Samuel Pepys. There was little of significance before his daily nine-year venture, which led to 1,250,000 words in some 3,100 pages, and today it is generally deemed to 'fulfil all the conditions of what a diary should be' (Ponsonby, 1923: 82). Yet whilst it is common to believe that Pepys simply 'sat down every night for nine years just scribbling with effortless frankness the little incidents which [he was] honest enough to record as having caught [his] attention at the moment' (Fothergill, 1974: 42), it becomes clear from the new revised Latham-Matthews edition that the diary was not produced daily, but rather evolved: 'a product fashioned with some care, both in its matter and style' (Pepys, 1970: ciii). Diaries, then, are certainly valuable in talking to the subjectivity of a particular moment; but they usually will go beyond this to a conception of some whole.

Whilst there are a good number of literary diaries – see the classic studies by Ponsonby (1923) and Fothergill (1974) – there is little sociological usage. Park employed them in his Race Relations Survey in the 1920s (cf. Bogardus, 1926) and Palmer's research text *Field Studies in Sociology* (1928) can cite two other studies – Cavan's (1928) analysis of two suicide diaries and Mowrer's (1927) case study of Miriam Donaven, a young woman whose marriage gradually fell apart. Both these studies involve the use of diaries in only a very limited way, and subsequent reviews have hardly been able to depict any sustained refinement of the method (cf. Allport, 1942: ch. 8; Denzin, 1978a: 223–6), not least perhaps because the diary as a form of writing seems to be going out of fashion. Yet 'diaries' may still be one of the better tools for getting at the day-to-day experiences of a personal life; and some (often feminist) social scientists have tried to resurrect their importance (e.g. Bell, 1998).

Four apparent forms of diary research stand out. (See Allport's discussion of the intimate journal, the log and the memoir (1942) for a slightly different classification.) The first is simply where *informants keep diaries*. The anthropologist Pat Caplan, for instance, asked her key Tanzanian informant Mohammed to keep a diary as well as keeping one herself, and they serve as a core organizing device for the book *African Voices, African Lives* (1997), organized through themes such as 'marriage', 'puberty rites', 'the land', 'the sea' and 'being an ancestor'. Another study, by Maas and Kuypers (1974) of adjustments to old age in the lives of 142 upper class San Franciscans, asked a number of their respondents to keep diaries for a week. The subjects were given booklets with a day allocated to each page (each page subdivided into morning, afternoon and evening) and were given the following instructions:

> We would like you to keep a daily diary to help us get some idea of how you spend your time during a typical week. We are especially interested in the kinds of things you do, when you do them, for how long and whether you do them with other people. As you write your diary, be sure to include the time of the day when you get up, have your meals, go out of the house, and any other major activity. Also be sure to include whom you met, what you did with them. You may also want to include some of the thoughts and feelings that you had during the day. At the end of the week, look over the diary to see if you have described a pretty typical seven days. Make any comment you want about what you have written . . . (Maas and Kuypers, 1974: 218)

Their study is subsequently richly documented with extracts from these diaries. In their instructions the authors have attempted to get round two central weaknesses – *selectivity* (by indicating what should be included) and *typicality* (by asking their respondents to comment upon this) – but it is essentially a somewhat flat method, for their concern was more with creating ideal types and statistical probabilities than with insights into specific lives.

This method has recently been applied in the pandemic of AIDS to look at men's sexual lives. In what Anthony P.M. Coxon (1996) and his colleagues at Project Sigma call '*the sexual diary*', men are asked to keep a regular diary of their sexual encounters – usually for a month or so. They are asked to log in – on a daily basis – a record of their partners, activities, days, times and setting in which various sexual activities occurred (from a long and interesting list of various sexual practices!), adding in comments on ejaculations, roles played and the like. Their 'sexual diary analysis' has led to a significant database logging on over 50,000 sexual acts in 25,000 sexual sessions, by 1,035 individuals. In the end, however, this style of research once again does move more and more towards a quantitative study of 'events' rather than an interpretive study of lives. The same can be true of much of the work which adopts time '*logs*' and '*time budgets*'. Sorokin pioneered this method when he asked informants to keep detailed 'time-budget schedules' showing just how they allocated their time during a day (Sorokin and Berger, 1938) and others have used similar approaches in documenting the events of 'One Boy's Day' (Barker and Wright, 1951) (cf. Gershuny and Sullivan, 1998).

Perhaps the most celebrated use is that of Oscar Lewis. Lewis's particular method focused on a few specific families in Mexico, and the analysis of a 'day' in each of their lives. Of course his actual familiarity with each family was in no way limited to a day – nothing of value could possibly be gained from that. He 'spent hundreds of hours with them in their homes, ate with them, joined in their fiestas and dances, listened to their troubles, and discussed with them the history of their lives' (Lewis, 1959: 5). But in the end he decided that it would be analytically more valuable, for both humanistic and scientific purposes, to focus upon 'the day' as a unit of study. Thus each family – Martinez, Gomez, Gutierez, Sanchez and Castro – is first presented as a 'cast of characters' and then followed through one arbitrarily chosen but not untypical day of their life. Lewis believed that a study of a day had at least a threefold value: practically, it was small enough to allow for intensive observation, quantitatively it permitted controlled comparisons across family units, and qualitatively it encouraged a sensitivity to the subtlety, immediacy and wholeness of life.

A third type of diary study has been called '*the diary diary-interview method*'. Here, Don Zimmerman and Laurence Wieder were involved in examining the Californian counter-culture and found considerable difficulties in observing the full daily pattern of activities of their subjects. In place of observation they instituted a method in which respondents were paid a fee of $10 to keep a full diary for seven days. As they comment:

> The diary writer was asked to record in chronological order the activities in which he or she engaged over the course of seven days. We provided the formula: Who/What/When/Where/How? We asked them to report the identity of the participants in the activities described not by name, of course, but by relationship to the writer – e.g. room-mate, lover and so on – using initials to differentiate individuals and noting the sex of those involved. The 'What?' involved a description of the activity or discussion recorded in the diarists' own categories. 'When?' involved reference to the timing of the activity, with special attention to recording the actual sequence of events. 'Where?' involved a designation of the location of the activity, suitably coded to prevent identification of individuals or place. The 'How?' involved a description of what ever logistics were entailed by the activity, e.g. how transport was secured, how marijuana was obtained. (Zimmerman and Wieder, 1977: 486)

Of particular interest in their method is not just the rich documentation they gained about seven days of a person's life, but the fact that the person is subsequently interviewed step by step on each facet of the diary that has been presented.

The above three forms of diary research – the requested, the log and the 'diary diary-interview' – all entail the social scientist soliciting diaries and are comparable to the social scientist soliciting life histories. But there is a fourth type which depends on applying pre-existing diaries. Just as the life historian could also turn to pre-existing biographies to analyse, so the diary researcher could examine the plethora of pre-existing diaries. Many people publish 'diaries', from the lowly to the famous. And they can become a wonderful resource for analysis. But there are also many contemporary examples of this writing – as is seen in the outporing of AIDS diaries, capturing the illness, the stigma and the dying (e.g. Chambers, 1998; Monette, 1992). In each case an original subjective story is told from which the social scientists could start to learn a great deal. Thus, two much discussed and celebrated diaries are those of Arthur Munby and Hannah Cullwick, where a working class 'servant girl' reveals her day-to-day curious relationship with her middle class employer, as he reveals his. It has been the subject of many re-readings and reflections on gender and class in Victorian times (Davidoff, 1979; Stanley, 1984, 1992).

Letters

Letters remain a relatively rare document of life in the social sciences. Without doubt, the most thoroughgoing use of letters is still to be found in Thomas and Znaniecki's *Polish Peasant*, where on discovering that there was extensive correspondence between Poles and Polish emigrés to America, an advertisement was placed in a Chicago journal offering to pay between 10 and 20 cents for each letter received. Through this method they were able to gain many hundreds of letters, 764 of which are printed in the first volume of their study, totalling some 800 pages and arranged in fifty family sequences. Each sequence is prefaced with a commentary that introduces the family members and the main concerns. The letters, highly formal, are designated 'bowing letters' and exist primarily 'to manifest the persistence of familial solidarity in spite of separation' (1958: 303). In addition to this, Thomas and Znaniecki suggest that the letters perform five main functions corresponding to five main types of letters. These are:

2. Ceremonial letters – sent on such familial occurrences as normally require the presence of all the members of the family – weddings, christenings, funerals, Christmas, New Year, Easter. These letters are substitutes for ceremonial speeches.
4. Informing letters – providing a detailed narration of the life of the absent member of the family group.
6. Sentimental letters – which have the task of reviving the feelings in the individual, independently of any ceremonial occasion.

8. Literary letters – which have a central aesthetic function.
10. Business letters (cf. Thomas and Znaniecki, 1958).

The letters are used inductively to arrive at a more general characterization of peasant society, particularly its subjective aspects. It remains to this day the most detailed use of letters, and an example is given below. Since 'The Series' is too long to reproduce, I have selected an extract from a concluding section on 'fragments'. It deals with demoralization of a wife in the absence of her husband. The latter, in spite of his emigration, shows more familial feeling, even with regard to the children, than the wife. The letter tends to establish a relation of solidarity between the husband and the rest of the family as against the wife.

> 'Praised be Jesus Christus.' . . . And now, dear father, what does all this mean that you write me? Why does my wife not wish to come to America, and writes me such stupid things that I am [illegible word] with her? I have sent her a shipticket for all, and she writes me such silly things and is not ashamed of it. When I sent the ticket I sent for all, and not for her alone. Could I leave the children? My heart does not allow me to leave my own children. Then, dear father, if she does not wish to listen it will end badly for her. Dear father, bow to her [ironically] and take the children to yourself, and I will send you directly two hundred roubles for the children, and let her do as she pleases. And if not, then give this shipticket to [sister] Kostka. Let Kostka come with this ticket. She has only to give the name and the age of my wife. Let her come with the children, and when Kostusia [Kostka] comes we will do well together, and my wife, as she was a public woman, so may she remain a public woman. And if the children fear to go, please, father take them to your home; I will send you 200 roubles. Let her not make a fool of me in America, as if I were her servant; this is neither right nor necessary. When someone read me that letter of hers, finally I did not let him finish, because I was ashamed.

> If nobody comes with this ticket, I will get the money back and will send it directly to you, father, for the children. And if not, let Kostusia come alone if the children don't want to come. [B. Leszczyc] (Thomas and Znaniecki, 1958: 816–17)

Another vivid use of letters in social science is to be found in Gordon Allport's editing and interpreting of the *Letters from Jenny* (Allport, 1965; Simeoni and Diani, 1995b). These letters were written by an ageing woman to two friends of her son – Isabel and Glenn – between 1926 and her death in 1937. As Jenny is thwarted by everything around her (especially by her son), and totters from one deep despair to another, she takes time out to write it all down and post it to these remote friends. They rarely meet and the whole story unfolds as a dramatic first person narrative. The readers can tease their way into Jenny's obsessive relationship with her son, into her crises, into her changing reconstructions of things written earlier, to an increasingly predictable series of 'resigned' moments, even happy ones, followed by a long slump into what she calls her 'slough of despond'. The vividness of the letters derives from the way they report life as it happens – each dreadful anxiety is shared with the letter's recipient. And all the way through, too, we get glimpses of the wider social world; she works for some time in a children's home and captures in her letters the appalling conditions where she has to be 'a whipper, a common spanker of little children, a beast, a cur for fifty dollars a month' (Allport, 1965: 32); she ends up her days in an old people's home where she initially feels 'wonderfully well' (p. 97), and finally cries how she is 'hungry to death for a little human companionship' (p. 130).

The case of Frank Moore, an institutionalized alcoholic, in *Escape from Custody* (Straus, 1974) differs from both the immigrant's and Jenny's letters in so far as the recipient in this case is the sociologist. For over 25 years Frank Moore corresponded directly with Robert Straus about his experiences of drifting in and out of institutions, in and out of work and on and off alcohol dependency – 'the life of a wharf rat' as he puts it. Sometimes, as when he is treated on 'antabuse' to shake him off alcohol, the letters can carry a sense of optimism – 'this antabuse treatment, to my mind, affords the first real test with regards to any constructive treatment. I hope I shall be worthy of the opportunities this place seems to afford,' he writes on 17 June.

Such writings indicate that many insights can be gained from the study of letters, yet these materials are only rarely to be found in social science. And in good part this may simply be due to the obvious fact that such letters are increasingly hard to come by – letter-writing appears to be a dying art and even when letters are sent they are most commonly thrown away rather than stored and collected. Bundles of 300 or so letters from the same person to the same recipient (like Jenny's described above) must today be seen as relatively rare and exciting finds. And even when one recipient keeps all the letters, it is unlikely that both will so that even with the immigrants' letters only one side of the exchange was typically found (cf. Riley, 1963: 242). When letters are used these days, they tend to be letters that are written to magazines and newspapers or letters that are solicited by the researcher as in, for example, Nancy Friday's volumes on sexual fantasy (Friday, 1976). That said, there are signs of a resurgence of interest in letter writing through 'electronic mail' (although this does seem to take a quite different and more casual mode!). It could be that in the future the analysis of e-mail will take on an increasingly significant role.

Nevertheless, even when such letters are available, social scientists are likely to remain suspicious of their value on a number of scores. First, as Ponsonby remarks, 'letters may be said to have two parents, the writer and the recipient' (Ponsonby, 1923: 2). Consequently, every letter speaks not just of the writer's world, but also of the writer's perceptions of the recipient. The kind of story told shifts with the person who will read it – witness the different letters produced by Robert Burns to his mistress, his friends, his wife on the same day. The social scientist then should view a letter as an interactive product, always enquiring into the recipient's role. In all the studies described above this is largely a mystery; the recipients included unknown family members, a sociologist and two remote friends. What would the stories told look like if the letters had been sent to other recipients: if the Polish peasants wrote to the sociologist, if Frank Moore wrote to remote friends, and Jenny wrote to her family! They would surely look very different indeed.

A further problem with letters concerns what Webb et al. referred to as the 'dross rate' (1966:105). Letters are not generally focused enough to be of analytic interest – they contain far too much material that strays from the researcher's concern. Thus Allport acknowledges that he has cut Jenny's letters down by two-thirds (Allport, 1965: vi), presumably because they otherwise would have produced unmanageably boring and repetitive ramblings that would be of little value to social science. Yet, of course, in cutting out this dross rate, Allport may also be engaged in selecting Jenny's ideas to focus upon issues that interest him. A form of hidden censorship and selective screening may be taking place.

'Vox Populi' and Guerrilla Journalism

When many lives are recorded in less depth than life histories, and offered to the reader with little commentary, we can speak of 'guerrilla journalism' – a term coined by one of the leading exponents of this method, Studs Terkel, for himself. Terkel's great skill lies in simply getting people to talk into his recorder: in *Hard Times* they tell of the Depression, in *Division Street: America* they tell of city life in Chicago, in *American Dreams* they talk of aspiration and change in America, and, most celebratedly, in *Working* 130 Americans speak of their jobs, the violence it does to them and their 'search for daily meaning as well as daily bread' (Terkel, 1968, 1970, 1977, 1978, 1981). Characteristically, this style of work – with its affinity to the naturalistic novels of Zola, the voices to be found in Mayhew and the reportage of Agee and Evans in *Let Us Now Praise Famous Men* – shuns any claims to being theoretical or scientific: the search for criteria of adequacy like those given by Dollard are of no concern. Thus, Terkel comments in the opening of his oral documentation of city life in Chicago:

> Being neither sociologist nor a research man, motivational or otherwise, I followed no blueprint or book or set of statistics. I played hunches – in some instances, long shots . . . I was on the prowl for a cross section of urban thought, using no one method or technique . . . I realized quite early in this adventure that interviews, conventionally conducted, were meaningless. (Terkel, 1968: 19–21)

Terkel listens, records, transcribes and then publishes, with the minimum of comment and the maximum of content. Whether what the people say is valid is left to the reader, although Terkel's memoirs *Talking to Myself* provide personal accounts of some of the interviews (Terkel, 1978) and elsewhere he has commented on his method (Grele, 1975; Parker, 1996).

'The Literature of Fact': Faction, the New Journalism, and the New Auto/Biography

One curious breed of life document, largely neglected by the social scientist, is the writing that takes on the form of a fictional novel but which is dealing with true events fully researched by the author (Berger, 1977; Weber, 1981; Zavarzadeh, 1976). Such an approach has a long history – Defoe's *A Journal of the Plague Year*, Dickens's *Sketches by Boz*, or Orwell's *Down and Out in Paris and London* are early examples. More recently, social scientists have been know to fictionalize their fieldwork, often to make it more readable and more accessible as a novel (as in *Return to Laughter*, by Laura Bohana (pseud. Eleanor Smith Bowen), 1954). This can make the line between fact and fiction hard to draw (as in the controversies surrounding the Yacqui Indian tales of Carlos Castaneda, see Chapter 12). The whole idea gained prominence in America in the postwar period, notably with the publication of Truman Capote's *In Cold Blood* (1966). For this 'murder story' Capote researched a notorious slaying of an entire family by two young men, who were subsequently caught, tried and executed. Whilst the story unfolds, the reader is aware that this is fact not fiction. Yet it is produced with the skill of an artist, not that of a scientist.

The boundaries of this life document are 'blurred' here. It incorporates all those studies which are clearly literary and humanistic but which deal with researched fact rather than fiction. Tom Wolfe's name for it is '*The New Journalism*' (the title of a 1973/5 book), which he defines simply as 'journalism that would read like a novel'. It involves detailed research into a real life topic that is then written up in a literate, fiction format, usually jettisoning a grand style for a more down-to-earth approach. Partially such writing sets out to dethrone the novel, achieving a novelistic style but around factual matters.

Sometimes this genre can be made to embrace the tradition of oral interview, such as the works of Studs Terkel (as above) or the journalist and war correspondent John Hersey, whose *Hiroshima* provides six interviews with atomic bomb survivors (1972). Sometimes it is signposted as a highly subjective account by an observing writer – Agee's personal tale of share-croppers in the Mid-West during the Depression is a classic example (Agee and Evans, 1965). Sometimes the social scientist is actually seen to exemplify it – Oscar Lewis's work, for example, is frequently cited. There is clearly no firm boundary to this style of work except that it all manages to weave a literary (and literate!) tale around detailed research and analysis of a real life event.

Although around for some 30 years or so, this 'literature of fact' keeps sprouting new forms and rejuvenating itself: 'style journalism' (Peter York), 'rock journalism' (Tony Parsons), travel writing (Bill Bryson), 'true crime' reporting (for example, Gordon Burns's accounts of Peter Sutcliffe and Fred West, and Blake Morrison's account of the Jamie Bulger case) and 'confessionalism' of all kinds (cf. Denzin, 1997).

Possessions and 'Biographical Objects'

What a person owns, or fails to own, can serve as a useful 'memory jogger' in research. But it goes deeper than this – indicating a lifestyle and identity. Pierre Bourdieu puts this powerfully:

> Identity is found in all the properties – and property with which individuals and groups surround themselves, houses, furniture, paintings, books, cars, spirits, cigarettes, perfume, clothes, and in the practices with which they manifest their distinction, sports, games, entertainment, because it is the synthetic unity of the habitus, the unifying generative principle of all practices. Taste, the propensity and capacity to appropriate (materially or symbolically) a given class of classified, classifying objects or practices, is the generative formula of a life style. (Bourdieu, 1984: 173)

To grasp the significance of this, conduct a little experiment on yourself. Simply move around your house or room, inspecting each item in it – from clothes to furniture, from photos to books, from CDs to memorabilia. Ponder the circumstances in your life that led to you getting this 'possession' – your interests and friends, where you were at the time, what's happened to it since, your feelings towards it then and now. A bookcase or a record/CD collection is a goldmine of biographical incidents – many items may have been acquired randomly and have little history, but many others will speak hugely complex stories. Ponder too what this says about your lifestyle. Sometimes, this looking over 'the family silver' can provide telling metaphors for a life (cf. Krieger, 1996). Rummaging through attics can be particularly rewarding and, on occasions, dustbins are not without a tale to tell. Indeed, there is a whole specialist interdisciplinary field of 'garbology' studies, which spends its time rummaging through dustbins and rubbish tips to suggest that 'what people have owned – and thrown away – can speak more eloquently, informatively and truthfully about the lives they lead than they themselves ever may (Rathje and Murphy, 1992: 54; cf. Webb et al., 1966: 41).

A classic illustration of this concern is the systematic examination of the possessions of fourteen poor families living in a Mexico City slum, by Oscar Lewis (1970). As he puts it:

> The inquiry opens up a mine of interesting questions. What proportions of their income do poor people spend on furniture, on clothing, on religious objects, on luxury items, on medicines? How much of what they buy

is new? How much second hand? To what extent do they depend on gifts or hand me downs? How do families in poverty finance their purchases? Where do they do their shopping? How wide are their choices? What is the physical condition of their possessions? How long do they manage to hold on to them? I was able to obtain rather detailed information on all these matters. (Lewis, 1970: 442)

His analysis considers thirteen categories of possession and does provide a number of interesting insights. For instance, all the poor families had at least one shelf for religious ornaments, but this was the only category of possessions where the poorer families had spent more than the better off.

This interest in how possessions speak about lives has developed into a major part of 'cultural and consumption studies', a newish field of study which focuses especially on 'material cultures' and how objects come to illustrate and play key roles in lives. These studies look at the life choices and decisions that lead people to collect objects like 'clothing, vehicles, homes, foods, drinks, magazines, fragrances, pets, entertainments and alterations to our bodies – all convey information to us and others about who we are' (Belk, 1995: 64). Often such objects are part of a person's 'cultural capital' (cf. Bourdieu, 1984), helping to fashion their position in the hierarchy of the society in which they live.

Although modern western cultures may find meanings to lives in all these consumable possessions, 'biographical objects' can be found in all societies and can assume very different meanings. The anthropologist Janet Hoskins (1998), for example, has studied the Kodinese of Eastern Indonesia and shown that although they may not 'tell their stories' in particularly western modes, they do have 'objects' – drums, betel bags, special cloths with special iconography – which assume enormous significance in the telling of their tales.

My listing of adjuncts to a life story could continue. Some researchers, for example, have made use of the inscriptions on tombstones (Warner, 1963), scrutinized suicide notes (Schwartz and Jacobs, 1979), looked at CVs (Danahay, 1996; Miller and Morgan, 1993), read obituaries (Nardi, 1990), examined photographs and art in people's homes – who is displayed and how (Halle, 1993) – looked at the making of quilts and the stories behind them (including the AIDS quilt) (Lewis and Fraser, 1996), and examined monuments of all kinds. Everywhere, it seems, there are documents of life awaiting the sociological eye.

Life Stories and the 'Other Senses': The Case of the World of the Visual

Most of the western human sciences are 'verbal' and structured through narratives and the written word: it is comparatively rare to find arguments made through visual images. Words matter, images are suspect. The same is true of life stories. In the main they are organized through the conventions of writing: lives are written. Yet we also inhabit worlds of other senses – of sight and touch, of sound and smell. In some cultures, other senses may be seen to play a much larger role – the Ongee of the Adaman Islands, for example, live in worlds ordered much more by smell, whilst the Trotzil of Mexico find a world where heat and temperature underpin the cosmos (cf. Classen, 1993). By and large, 'a world of other senses' has not been featured in the human sciences. We do not generally document the smells and tastes of lives; though as the new millennium is reached, certain of these senses are playing (belatedly) an increased role. Sound and recordings are becoming more prominent and there are growing numbers of 'sound archives' (the new British Library in London, for instance, houses a wide selection of recordings in the National Sound Archive). Likewise, visual representations have moved from being highly specialist art forms to being accessible to almost everybody – photographs, films, videos and computer graphics are becoming more and more 'democratized' in evermore sophisticated forms, providing wonderful accessories to the telling of a life. In what follows, I will briefly locate some issues around the visual – but there are many excellent book-length introductions to this important and expanding area (e.g. Chaplin, 1994: see further reading at the end of the chapter).

Photographs

To start thinking about this, three quotes may be helpful:

> It is the advent of the Photograph ... which divides the history of the world. (Barthes, 1984)

> In no other form of society in history has there been such a concentration of images. Such a density of visual images. (Berger, 1972)

> You could never envisage all the camera has seen, countless images scattered at random in time and space like the fragments of a vast and ancient mosaic, the remnants of a visual holocaust, the ruins of representation . . . colossal . . . a unique map, a phantom topography, coiling the entire globe, an endless collage which in the end forms ... another world, the true surrealist universe ... you will never know a limit to all the stories, plots, parables, histories, myths and fictions spawned in this oneiric archive – assuming it can exist – the truths it could tell if only we knew how to read its languages, interpret its codes, translate its evidence ... (McQuire, 1998: Introduction)

These are startling quotes. They suggest at once the newness, the power and the pervasiveness of the photograph. They suggest that contemporary history is shifted by the photograph. And they hint strikingly at the way in which the camera has entered the modern mind. If diaries and letters became central life documents (as least in the middle classes) during the nineteenth century, then they have now been rapidly overtaken by photography. Born at approximately the same time as sociology, photography has gone on to become many things. In Susan Sontag's early essay *On Photography* (1979), she suggests inter alia that the photograph has become the democratiser of personal documents (in family albums and holidays shots for all), a major new genre of art, the embodiment of individualism (in the rise of photographic portraiture), a mode of refusing experience, a strategy for conveying immortality, and last but not least, a form of surveillance and control. Likewise, John Berger's telling account *About Looking* (1980: 52) suggests how quickly photography came to be used for matters as diverse as 'police filing, military reconnaissance, pornography, encylopedia documentation, family albums, postcards, anthropological records ... sentimental moralizing, inquisitive probing, ... aesthetic effects, news reporting, ... formal portraiture ...'. Others, more recently, have seen it as creating a radical shift in the very ways we live – as generating a new visual technology which becomes a way of life and shaping what Celia Lury has called a 'prosthetic culture' where the naturally given body is transformed into a more experimental and shifting one. A camera can 'frame, freeze and fix its objects', turning how the body and the world is seen into something different from what it once was (1998: 3). In their growing (digitalized) sophistication, photographs can now be taken inside the darkest recesses of the human body, as well as at the farthest reaches of our planet. They can be 'morphed' via computer technologies into photos that bear no resemblance to an actual reality. They can document a life, but they can also invent a life.

Yet despite the billions of photographs being produced by lay person and professional alike each year for a multitude of purposes, many branches of the human sciences, and especially sociology, remain relatively untouched by it. In the 1880s, Lewis W. Hine – trained as a sociologist at Chicago and New York – used photos to express the subjective story, of 'photo-interpretations', especially those that revealed social inequities – of young children in factories, of poor housing, of immigrants arriving at Ellis Island off New York (Hine, 1977). And in the earliest days of the *American Journal of Sociology*, photographs were a regular feature in connection with its muck-raking, reformist articles: between 1896 and 1916 thirty-one articles used 244 photographs (see Stasz, 1979a). Likewise, many of the early Chicago studies – Frederick Thrasher's The Gang, for example – included an array of photographs. Recent studies in this tradition such as Mitch Duneier's *Slim's Table* (1992) and *Sidewalk* (1999), which both include photos – in the former case there seem to have been lots to draw upon from the work of Ovie Carter (Duneier, 1992: 164–8). Still, in the main sociologists have not taken much interest in what should now be viewed both as a major artefact of twentieth-century life and a (potentially) major tool for investigation.

The lead has primarily come from journalistic photographers (such as Jacob A. Riis's visual depiction of impoverished styles in New York City's slums (Riis, 1971), and photojournalists (such as the National Press Photographers Association, 1978). The breakthrough in social science is usually seen to be in the work of anthropologists: particularly the pioneering work of Gregory Bateson and Margaret Mead on *Balinese Character: A Photographic Analysis* (1942). Married, and both working on Balinese culture for nearly a decade prior to this classic study, they sought to capture the *ethos of the culture*; words seemed lacking, and they struck upon the idea of using photographs. Indeed, with Bateson photographing and Mead directing, they took some 25,000 photos over two years. They did not select or get people to pose for photos but took them rapidly and randomly and then used them subsequently (or at least 759 of them!) to inform and illustrate the text which described aspects of the culture of the Balinese. Overall the book's photos are organized into cultural categories: spatial orientation and levels; learning; integration and disintegration of the body; orifices of the body; auto-cosmic play; parents and children; siblings; stages of child development; and rites of passage. In a chapter on rites of passage, for instance, photos of marriages and funerals are placed opposite a text which describes them. Recently, some of Malinowski's earlier photographic work has been published for the first time (Young, 1999).

Sociology turned its attention to the photograph more seriously during the 1970s: a small group of American sociologists became concerned about its use, organized exhibitions of their photographic work, and coined the term 'visual sociology'. Howard Becker (1974), for instance, wrote a major review of the state of the field in general (looking at its history, uses, theoretical issues and general problems) for the journal *Studies in the Anthropology of Visual Communication* and a new 'International Visual Sociology Association' came to be established with its own journal and newsletter (Harper, 1994).

There are many ways in which photography can be put to work for sociology. Curry and Clarke (1977) suggest it may serve as an illustration, as visual information or as source material for analysis, whilst Wagner (1979: 16–19) suggests fives modes of photographic research: as interview stimuli, for systematic recordings of social phenomena, for sustained content analysis, for 'native' image-making and for 'narrative visual theory'. Photographic theory – by contrast – tends to champion a more critical approach. Using semiology and psychoanalysis, it has developed a critical analysis of the process of 'signification' – how signs and meanings are produced – and the relation between the photographic image and reality (cf. Barthes, 1984; Burgin, 1982; Sontag, 1979). In what follows, I will chart just four strands of use in social science, which hint at this increasing complexity: how photos may be used as *documentation*, as *visual theory*, as *resource* and as *critical representation*.

Perhaps the most obvious use to date is that of the photograph *as documentation* – an essentially descriptive task where the photo is designed simply to illustrate text. Thus, Don Kulick's study of Brazilian *Travesti* (1999) includes a number of photographs of transvestites and transsexuals which bring a richer life to the text: you can see what injecting silicon into the buttocks does to them! Jerry Jacobs's photographs of a retirement community, *Sun City* (1974), captures the cleanliness and desolation revealed in the ethnographic text. On the surface, these are unextraordinary, unremarkable yet surprisingly uncommon ways in which photographs could be used to enhance life stories. This 'documentary tradition' can also be extended to book-length studies. Michael Lesy's *Wisconsin Death Trip* (1973) illustrates the approach. Fortuitously, he gained access to some 3,000 glass negatives taken by a small-town photographer between 1890 and 1910 which, while formally posed, nevertheless represented the ordinary 'events these people, or people like them, once experienced'. Small-town life, the Great Depression, massive incipient change, religion, disease, death: the photos capture vividly these and other themes conveying in one complex image what would take thousands of words to capture. Interspersed with the full-page photographs are direct textual quotations – newspapers, novels, madhouse records of the period – which, taken all together, 'recreate a revision of a past time so separated from the present by the cunning sleights of the fearful memories of one human lifetime, that to recall, reveal and recreate such a past is as difficult as driving a tunnel through a granite mountain to the sea' (Lesy, 1973). It is a startling work, and, like most mentioned in this study, has to be 'read' for its substance: I cannot start to do it justice. Yet it signposted a new tradition for personal documents, one that Lesy himself followed further, three years later, in his *Real Life: Louisville in the Twenties* (1976), another rich photographic essay. Lesy's books also illustrate the possibility of gaining a much closer relationship between document and theory, for the photos are fully linked in with the text; they do not merely illustrate, they integrate.

The model for this kind of work is revealed in the classic 1930s study of average – and thereby poor – white families of tenant farmers in the Southern States of America: *Let Us Now Praise Famous Men* by James Agee and Walker Evans. Here Agee, no sociologist, spent time absorbed in the lives of the tenant families whilst Evans (later to be famed for his *American Photographs*, 1938) produces the first volume of the study with photographs of places, objects and people. As Agee says, 'The photographs are not illustrative. They, and the text, are co-equal, mutually independent, and fully collaborative (1965: xiii).

A few sociologists have taken this further, through what has been called *'narrative visual theory'*, where the 'implicit elements of social theory are clearly acknowledged' (Wagner, 1979:18). Here the photos are systematically selected through a tacit theory – Jackson looks at prison life (1977, 1978), and Harper looks at tramps (1978). They come close to being ethnographies, which instead of relying upon the written word become organized through visual imagery. In some cases, photos have been taken as a basis for organizing an autobiography (e.g. Barthes, 1977; Spence, 1986). From this, the task may be to theorize lives through photography.

Photos may also be used as a *resource* for further explanations. Photos may be taken, and then discussed with the subjects in a technique known as 'photo elicitation' (cf. Collier and Collier, 1986). In Banish's work on *City Families* (1976), the technique was to combine interview with photography. This researcher first visited selected families in order to take photographs of them as they wished to see themselves and then returned both to talk about the photographs, to ask which was their favourite and to interview them about their hopes and aspirations in life. The study is composed of the preferred photographs on one page matched with the interviews and oberservations on the opposite page. Of added interest in this study is the range of families studied and the contrasts drawn between the families of two cities: London and Chicago.

From this comes one of the most apparent methods for using photographs in social science: to ask the respondent for *a look at their family albums* (cf. Musello, 1979; Spence and Holland, 1991). In a most striking way, all manner of details about childhood relationships, friendship, family rituals and family history can be highlighted. Jo Spence and Patricia Holland, for example, ponder what is allowed and what is not allowed to go into family photos, and suggest that such photos work at the borders between a personal memory, a personal unconscious, and a social history which bridges wider social conventions of public myth and 'cultural memory' (for more on this see Chapter 10). More widely, in a general study of photography Akeret coins the term 'photoanalysis' and suggests the following useful scheme of questions to be asked:

What is your immediate impression [of the photograph]? Who and what do you see? What is happening in the photo? Is the background against which the photo was taken of any significance, either real or symbolic? What feelings does it evoke in you? What do you notice about physical intimacy or distance? Are people touching physically? How are they touching? How do the people in the photo feel about their bodies? Are they using their bodies to show them off, to hide behind, to be seductive, are they proud of their bodies, ashamed? What do you notice about the emotional state of each person? Is he: shy, compliant, aloof, proud, fearful, mad, suspicious, introspective, superior, confused, happy, anxious, angry, weak, pained, suffering, bright, curious, sexy, distant ... Can you visualize how those emotions are expressed in facial dynamics and body movement? If there is more than one person in the photo what do you notice about the group mood? Is there harmony or chaos? How do people relate? Are they tense or relaxed? What are their messages towards each other? Who has the power, the grace? Do you see love present? What do you notice about the various parts of each person? Look carefully at the general body posture and then the hands, the legs, the arms, the face, the eyes, the mouth. What does each part tell you? Are the parts harmonious or are there inconsistencies? Pay particular attention to the face, always the most expressive part of the person. Learn to read any photo as you would read a book from left to right then downwards. Go over it again and again, each time trying to pick out something you have missed. Ask yourself more general questions, as many as you can think of. What is obvious and what is subtle? What is the sense of movement or is there any? What memories and experiences does the photo stir in you? How do you identify with the people in the photo? How are you alike, how different? What moves you most about the photo? What do you find distasteful about it? Is there anything that disturbs you? Try to define the social and economic class of the people photographed. What is their cultural background? If it is a family, would you want to be a member of it? Would you want your children to play with theirs? If the photos are personal – of you, your family, friends or associates – try to remember the exact circumstances of the photo session. How have you changed since then? How have you remained the same? (Akeret, 1973: 35–6)

The list, concludes Akeret, could be endless. His questions are primarily geared towards psychological interpretations rather than cultural ones; a sociologist would need to tease family albums and photographs of respondents through a series of sociological problems. In short, there is a major tool here for socio-logists but one that remains considerably underused.

Questions such as these, then, hint strongly at another way of approach-ing photographs in social science: as *critique*. Much – if not most – recent work in photography approaches the image in a highly critical mode. For example, in her very telling analysis of family albums, *Family Frames* (1997), Marianne Hirsch shows through a series of case studies that whilst our habits of seeing family albums are usually routinized, they can be violated and jolted through radical departures from the so-called family norm. She com-pares, for example, rather traditional images of families found in books like Edward Steichen's *The Family of Man* (1955), with those images found in Meatyard's *Family Album of Lucybelle Crater* (1974) (where family members are photographed with grotesque masked faces); in Sally Mann's *Immediate Family* (1992) (where her children are posed often naked with a kind of 'seductive' childhood innocence); or in the work of Christian Boltanski (where hundreds of anonymous photos, often hung in impersonal ways, radically challenge notions of family unity) (Semin et al., 1997). Photos, we learn, can be used to 'unfix the gaze' (Hirsch, 1997: 141). More and more, we need this critical photographic work to be included with life stories. We need to sense, along with Barthes, that photographs do not simply call up the past or provide routes into memory: they are themselves their own invented images that can be used to invent their stories.

Film and the 'Documentary Tradition'

Norman Denzin (1995) has called the twentieth century the 'cinematic age', a time when the cinema and its moving visual images have come to assume enormous importance as a means of communication in many people's lives across the globe. Once again, only a few social scientists have ever counten-anced the significance of film. It has been left to a whole group of others – the documentary, journalistic and ethnographic film makers – to take seriously its possibilities. Yet the medium should surely be the social scientist's dream: life as it is lived accurately recorded as it happens, and constantly available for playback and analysis! There will be problems, for sure, but it is a most remarkable resource which could have changed the face of much social science out of all recognition during the twentieth century. Somehow, it scarcely touched it.

Initially, it was the 'documentary film makers' who breathed life into an old form. Robert Coles provides a pithy history:

> The noun *document* goes back centuries in time. It is derived from the Latin *docere*, to teach, and was originally, of course, used to describe something that offered clues, or better, proof, a piece of paper with words that attested evidence. In our time, a photograph or a recording or a film have also qualified as documents. In the eighteenth century (1711), the word *document* became more active – a verb whose meaning conveyed the act of furnishing such evidence; and eventually . . . the range of such activity expanded: first one documented with words on paper; later one documented with photographs and a film crew. Interestingly the verb would get used this way, too: 'to construct or produce (as a movie or novel) with authentic situations or events', and 'to portray realistically'. Here the creative or imaginative life is tempered by words such as 'authentic' or 'realistic' . . . In the early nineteenth century (1902) the adjective documentary emerged – a description of evidence, naturally, but also as 'relating to or employing documentation in literature or art' . . . In this century . . . the noun documentary arrived, telling of a product, 'the documentary presentation of a film or novel' . . . (Coles, 1997: 19–20)

At the turn of the nineteenth century, the first motion pictures often focused on recording 'actualities' – like *Record of a Sneeze* (1894) and *Workers Emerging from a Factory* (1895) – usually shot in one take and lasting little more than a few minutes. By 1903, 'editing' was discovered and with it, the possibility of manipulating the images – shooting speeds, time, continuities, space. Soon anthropological ethnographers started to film various tribal peoples engaged in social rituals – Spencer, in 1901, filmed Australian aborigines in kangaroo dances and rain ceremonies, while in 1914 Curtis filmed the Kwakiutl Indians. But the birth of the documentary film is commonly agreed to be Robert Flaherty's (1922) *Nanook of the North*, about Eskimo life. Flaherty, a compassionate romantic appalled by the dehumanization of modern technology (cf. Calder-Marshall, 1963), lived in 'Eskimo country' for eleven years and, under the most adverse conditions, shot his film on the life of one specific individual – Nanook. In this film he reveals the constant struggle for life in a hostile environment. Sensitively, the power of the image is left behind:

> One of Flaherty's most successful visual techniques was to follow an exotic act visually, showing it step by step as it developed, not explaining

it in words. In one sequence of *Nanook* we see Nanook tugging on a line leading into a hole in the ice. We are engaged in that act, and think about it. Eventually, the suspense is broken: our questions are answered when Nanook pulls out a seal. Flaherty creates the same visual involvement when Nanook makes the igloo – especially at the end of the sequence, when Nanook cuts a slab of ice for a window, sets it in place, and fixes a snow slab reflector along one side. For a time we are puzzled and, therefore, involved. But when Nanook steps back, finished, we understand. (Heider, 1976: 24)

But even here, in its founding moment, we can see a critical problem. Just where were Flaherty and his camera to be placed inside the small igloo when Nanook was being filmed? How was it staged – the film cameras were exceedingly large in those days? Where was the author of the film? 'Critical documentary' only emerged later to pose such questions of the apparent authenticity of the materials.

In its original form, Flaherty's film and his others – *Moana, Man of Aran, The Land* and *Louisiana Story* – were silent, and most that followed until the early 1960s lacked synchronous sound. Although a founding classic, it is now seen as a highly 'romantic' text – raising further issues about the narrative organization of such films (see Chapter 9 for a wider discussion of narrative). In contrast, later documentarists offered more 'realist' accounts – especially depicting the lives of great cities – like Walter Ruttman's *Berlin: The Symphony of Great Cities* (1927). In the work of the founder of the 'British School' of documentary – John Grierson – the camera was now focused 'inward on the problems of the "average" person and analyzed the situation of individuals in occupations and the importance of national and local issues and institutions'. This is not the place even to attempt to write a history of the documentary film – there are many good books which do this (e.g. Heider, 1976; Sherman, 1998). But it is important to sense another tool in the making – one which more recently has culminated in all kinds of important developments: from *'cinema vérité'* (e.g. Frederick Wiseman's films discussed below; the controversial *Harlan County, USA* by Barbara Kopples, which looked at the strike of coal miners in Kentucky), *'docu-soaps'* (like those featured on televison which focus on such topics as airports, families, hotels, or small communities), where a 'fly-on-the wall' approach is adopted; and *critical documentaries*, such as Bonnie Klein's *Not a Love Story* (1981), which provides a radical feminist analysis of pornography.

For Karl Heider, *Dead Birds* (1961) about the Dani, marks the watershed of ethnographic film; thereafter synchronic sound enabled people to talk about their lives as well as simply living them on film. Robert Gardener's Ethiopian film *Rivers of Sand* takes a Hamar woman relaxing before the camera and speaking about her life, with shots interspersed to illustrate her commentary. Heider concludes his review by suggesting that since 1963 ethnographic film has become 'institutionalized, bureaucratized and established' (1976: 44), reviews of films being a regular feature of the *American Anthropologist* since 1965, and a special organization, the Society for the Anthropology of Visual Communication, emerging in 1973 with its own journal. Film is now accepted as an integral part of the anthropologist's armoury.

This is far from the case in sociology. There have been a few attempts, such as Morin's work with Rouch on Parisians talking about the summer of 1960 (the Algerian War dominated) in *Chronicles of a Summer*, but in the main sociologists have either ignored the medium or used documentaries created by film makers, like those of Frederick Wiseman (Atkins, 1976).

Frederick Wiseman's films perhaps come closest to embodying sociological concerns: most deal directly with the ways in which individuals throughout their hierarchies cope (or fail to) with the day-to-day pressures of social institutions. As he puts it:

> What I'm aiming at is a series on American institutions, using the word 'institutions' to cover a series of activities that take place in a limited geographical area with a more or less consistent group of people being involved. I want to use film technology to have a look at places like high schools, hospitals, prisons, and police, which seems to be very fresh material for film; I want to get away from the typical documentary where you follow one charming person or one Hollywood star around. I want to make films where the institutions will be the star but will also reflect larger issues in general society, (in Rosenthal, 1971: 69)

Hence his 'documents' treat not 'lives' but 'institutions' – the police in *Law and Order* (1969), hospitals for the criminally insane in *The Titicut Follies* (1969), army life in *Basic Training* (1971) as well as films on *Welfare, High School* and *Hospital*. For Wiseman, it is blindingly obvious that all films are 'subjective' documents – how could they be otherwise? Yet they are 'fair': honest, worked at, not driven by ideological commitment, desirous of showing that people are much the same in their daily struggles and 'very suspicious of people who can make . . . glib classifications, whatever that classification may be, and wherever it may fall politically' (Wiseman, 1971: 325).

The Rise of Video

> In today's world life does seem to be on videotape. Monitors reflect faces as shoppers walk along department store aisles. Videotaping is a common sight at children's soccer and baseball games and at weddings, bar mitz-vahs, and birthday parties. The prevalence of video in our lives has steadily expanded. We can document our own lives as we perceive them, and we can record our vision of events. At the heart of the video explosion is the desire not only to record oneself and one's family but to present that view of the self back to the self after documentation. (Sherman 1998: 257–8)

Generally 'standard cine film' is expensive, requires specialist knowledge, often requires numerous 'takes' and skilful editing, plays to cinema audiences and is almost an 'elite' form when compared to the democratized video recorder and film. For with video, we find a medium that is cheap, accessible, home based and extremely versatile – requiring relatively little skill in the first instance. It differs too from standard television by providing highly individual (or individuated) watching. First used in 1956 (for television production practices) and becoming domestically available in 1969 (with Sony and Akai), only in 1978 did the first reliable systems appear on the market (Sony's now defunct Beta, and JVC's VHS). So for the first edition of this book, video was just emerging as a popular form: but now – 20 years on – it is everywhere – a volatile, expansive, proliferating media with a seemingly inexhaustible array of functions: to probe, document, persuade, analyse, archive and play with events. Once again, I can only express surprise at how few sociologists seem to have made much use of it; and indeed a whole new generation of 'video' experts seems to have emerged outside of sociology to do sociology's work! There are now several generations of 'video workers' who have used video as radical means of transforming the orthodox visual image and of providing a whole library of 'alternative video forms'.

Video can be used for a variety of purposes, some of its more colourful roles being 'video petitions, interplanetary cameras, robotics probes, surveillance eyes . . .' (Renov and Suderburg, 1996: xv). In life story research, it has been used more mundanely – for instance, as a permanent *archival record* of key events, as for example in the mass collection of holocaust survivor stories, where the aural/oral tape is supplemented by the visual testimony (cf. Langer, 1991). It has also been used as 'a technology of memory' (a way of jogging the memory or 'thickening it'), as a 'technology of confession' (as in Wendy Clarke's 'Love Tapes' project) (see Moran, 1996).

One of its most telling roles has been in the growth of the *video diary*. Here a teller of a story records a fragment of their own life – most famously as seen in the BBC video series *Video Nation*, shown since 1994 on a regular, nightly slot of BBC. Lasting about two minutes each, the recordings constitute a major new form of 'vox populi' – with the BBC providing assistance in their production. Each tape is logged in detail, cross-referenced and archived in the British Film Institute's national Film and Television Archive. By late 1998, some 7,000 videotapes – adding up to 10,000 hours of recording – had been organized around dozens of subjects. These included such themes as 'On the Job' (work and unemployment), 'State of Play' (how we use our spare time) 'Life, Death, God and Everything' (on the nature of belief). There are also versions of the concept in Hong Kong, Israel and Africa. The series gives camcorders, videotapes and training to over 250 people in Britain and then asks them to make their film on aspects of life in the UK. (There is also an even more 'populist version' of this in various television programmes where people just send in their own video clips – like *America's Best Home Movies*.)

Box 1: Some Documentary Film Landmarks

1895   Louis and Auguste Lumière's Workers Emerging from a Factory – one of a number of early 'shorts'
        Newsreels

1890s   Charles Pathé and the Pathé Gazette (1907) 'March of Time' (in the US some 20 million watched this at 9,000 cinemas each week), 'This Modern Age' (the UK version)

1910   Herbert Ponting, *With Scott in the Antarctic*

1921/2 Robert Flaherty, *Nanook of the North* – the life of an Inuit and his family, and their hard life on the ice. Shows a strong collaboration between Nanook and Flaherty

1926   Alberto Cavalacanti, Rie*n que les heures* (a day in Paris)

1927   Robery Flaherty, *Moana* – 'a visual account of events in the daily life of a Polynesian youth' (Grierson, 1966: 13)

1927   Walter Ruttman, *Berlin: The Symphony of a Great City*

1929   John Grierson, Drifters – shows the life of herring fishermen as they cast their nets and face a storm

1929   Basil Wright and Henry Watt, *Night Mail* – poetic representation of a post train on its journey from London to Glasgow

1936   Pare Lorentz, *The Plow that Broke the Plains*

1937   Leni Riefenstahl, *Triumph of the Will* – the famous documentary that displayed Nazi Germany

1945   Carol Reed, *The True Glory*

1954   Lionel Rogosin, *On the Bowery*

1957   CBS, *The Twentieth Century*

1960   Jean Rouche initiates *cinema verité* with *Chronicle of a Summer* – follows a group of Parisians with varying experiences ('unhappy in love', a 'concentration camp survivor' etc.), and seen as a real life drama. At the end, the film is discussed by everybody

1962   Frank Capra, *Why We Fight*

1962   Wolfe Koening/Roman Kroita, *Lonely Boy*

1968   Frederick Wiseman, *High School* – one of a number of celebrated Wiseman films, this one showing a US High School

1976   Barbara Copple, *Harlan County*

1977   Peter Adair's *Word is Out* – a range of elderly gays tell their 'coming out' stories

1980   *The Life and Times of Rosie the Riveter*

1981   Bonnie Klein and Linda Lee Tracey, *Not a Love Story: A Film About Pornography* (looks at women's experiences of porn)

1989   Michael Moore, *Roger and Me*

1990   Jennie Livingstone, *Paris is Burning*

1993   Tom Joslin's *Silverlake Life: The View from Here* – a landmark auto-video of a couple infected and dying with HIV

1995   Frederick Wiseman, *High School 2*

Taking all this further is the development of what may be called 'video autoethnography'. Here people may be trained or enouraged to make a video about aspects of their life that concern them. Sometimes this may be done individually: Ruth Holliday (1999) provided her 'queer' subjects with camcorders and asked them to record the ways they dressed for different contexts – at home, work and play – and then to provide a commentary on the films as they were edited. As she says, video diaries gave 'respondents the potential for a greater degree of reflexivity than other methods, through the process of watching, re-recording, and editing their diaries before submission'. Each diarist had at least a month to make their diary (p. 476). In contrast, Salome Chasnoff, got her group of African American and West Indian teenage mothers – 'happy, relaxed young women' (1996: 111) – to make a collective video on their own motherhood. They became *The Fantastic Moms*, and they established themselves as the experts. They became the 'authorities on the subject' through 'researching, planning, storyboarding, enacting, framing and shooting, reflecting, reviewing, being viewed' (p. 129); through 'running the tape recorder, writing the script, posing the questions, expressing the opinions' (p. 115); and finally through being in and making the film. In the final video film, they established who they were in three key ways:

> (1) as speaking subjects, first person, present tense, I say what I am and what I am not; (2) as performing subjects, I speak for myself, for my own design; and (3) as subjects of speech, I am the one of whom I speak. They particularised and historicised themselves, demystifying the stereotype [of black motherhood] . . . (p. 129)

Within this video, they were able to provide a strong counter-story to the dominant story one of sad, deprived, desperate young mums.

Thus, video becomes a powerful form of critique. Orthodox media accounts of lives – ones that use familiar settings, storylines and language – start to be seriously challenged by an 'alternative video media', where often life stories are told in disturbing and unsettling ways. Women's stories, 'race' stories, stories of people with AIDS and HIV – and many others – have become the subjects of these new critical videos (cf. Juhasz, 1995, 1999; Renov and Suderburg, 1996). Reviewing a number of such videos focused around HIV and AIDS films, Alexandra Juhasz (1995) suggest that these video alternatives

> articulate a rebuttal to or a revision of the mainstream media's defin-itions and representations around AIDS, and [help] to form [a] community around a new identity forced into existence by the fact of AIDS. Producing alternative AIDS media is a political act that allows people who need to scream with pain or anger, who want to say, 'I'm here, I count', who have internalized sorrow and despair, who have vital information to share about drug protocols, coping strategies or government inaction, to make their opinions public and to join with others in this act of resistance . . . (Juhasz, 1995: 3)

Modes of video The film theorist Bill Nichols (1991, discussed by Sherman, 1998: 261) has outlined five major modes of documentary film and video. To some extent, they mirror the development of life stories, autobiography and research in general, and this suggests the ways in which life stories come to be seen. First, there is the *expository* – following on from Flaherty, where the authority speaks from on high. The author of the documentary tells the tale. Second, there is the *observational* – here, real time is followed, and there is a focus on individuals: the camera tries to empathize with them, tries to 'be in their shoes'. It is the classic ethnographic mode. Third, there is the *interactive* – here, the camera itself becomes a self-conscious presence: the viewer can no longer imagine the film is just there or the story is just being told, because the camera – often shaking or being seen – reminds us that this is humanly produced film through a camera. It is *cinema verité*. But, fourthly, this can be taken further: and a *reflexive* mode suggests a much more critical approach to the problems of representation. Finally, in the *performative*, self-consciousness and reflexivity mixes with multiple narratives (as in *Common Threads, Tongues Untied*).

Critique and the Camera: The Camera Always Lies

What should have become very clear during this brief trip to the visual image in life story work is the ways in which the medium is increasingly used as a radical, critical tool. If anybody ever thought that 'the camera never lies' or the 'photo represents reality' this has become firmly challenged. In just the same way as life stories are seen as 'constructions', so too are visual images: the camera always lies and the question becomes: how much does it lie and in what ways? In Woody Allen's film *Zelig*, for example, the hero played by Woody Allen is able to appear as a parade of significant twentieth-century characters against an imported film montage of 'world significant' newsreel clips – making it appear that he is present. Likewise, in Oliver Stone's hugely controversial film *J.F.K.* (based on the assassination of John F. Kennedy) he is able to splice actual news footage with the fictional, conspiratorial narrative that he presents. Actual documentary merges with fiction. And with the arrival of computer photo technology these tricks of playing with the camera have become available to everyone. Through the skills of computer programs, photographs can be completely reorganized: splicing old characters with new, deleting friends and lovers who are no longer friends and lovers; and placing known people against new and unknown backdrops. Photos from the past may be updated; and photos from the present may be rendered old and sepia.

This is just the playful iceberg tip. What is now possible is for subjects themselves to take hold of the (web) camcorder and present the ways in which they view the world, the stories of their lives in ways that may challenge dominant story modes. 'The visual' can be used as a means of social change.

Conclusion

In this chapter I have been deliberately wide ranging: from photography and film through diaries and letters. But I have not aimed to be comprehensive or detailed, merely to suggest a whole battery of research tools, widely ignored and neglected in both research texts and courses. They cry out for more and more use in the social sciences. They have enormous potential for exploring concrete social experience in a humanistic fashion. They are powerful yet still relatively neglected tools. And they harbour potentials for radically transforming the human sciences in the twenty-first century.

References

Agee, J. and Evans, W. (1965) *Let Us Now Praise Famous Men: Three Tenant Families.* London: Peter Owen.

Akeret, R.V. (1973) *Photoanalysis: How to Interpret the Hidden Psychological Meaning of Personal and Public Photographs.* New York: Wyden.

Allport, G.W. (1942) *The Use of Personal Documents in Psychological Science.* New York: Social Science Research Council.

Allport, G.W. (ed.) (1965) *Letters from Jenny.* London: Harcourt Brace Jovanovich.

Atkins, T.R. (1976) *Frederick Wiseman.* New York: Simon and Schuster.

Banish, R. (1976) *City Families: Chicago and London.* New York: Pantheon.

Barker, R. and Wright, H. (1951) *One Boy's Day.* New York: Harper and Row.

Barthes, R. (1977) 'The death of the author', in *Image–Music–Text.* Glasgow: Fontana/Collins. (Originally published in French, 1968.)

Barthes, R. (1984) *Camera Lucida.* London: Fontana.

Bateson, G. and Mead, M. (1942) *Balinese Character*, Vol. II. New York: New York Academy of Science.

Becker, H.S. (1974) 'Photography and sociology', *Studies in the Anthropology of Visual Communication*, 5: 2–26.

Belk, R. (1995) 'Studies in the new consumer behaviour', in D. Miller (ed.), *Consumption: A Review of New Studies.* London: Routledge. pp. 58–94.

Bell, L. (1998) 'Public and private meanings in diaries: researching family and childcare', in J. Ribbens and R. Edwards (eds), *Feminist Dilemmas in Qualitative Research.* London: Sage. pp. 72–86.

Berger, J. (1972) *Ways of Seeing.* Harmondsworth: Pelican.

Berger, J. (1980) *About Looking.* London: Writers and Readers Cooperative.

Berger, M. (1977) *Real and Imagined Worlds: The Novel and Social Science.* London: Harvard University Press.

Bogardus, E.S. (1926) *The New Social Research.* Los Angeles: Press of Jesse Ray Miller.

Bourdieu, P. (1984) *Distinction: A Social Critique of the Judgement of Taste.* Cambridge, MA: Harvard University Press.

Bowen, E.S. (Laura Bohanan) (1954) *Return to Laughter.* New York: Harper.

Burgin, V. (ed.) (1982) *Thinking Photography.* London: Macmillan.

Calder-Marshall, A. (1963) *The Innocent Eye: The Life of R.J. Flaherty.* London: W.H. Allen.

Capote, T. (1966) *In Cold Blood.* London: Hamish Hamilton.

Cavan, R.S. (1928) *Suicide.* New York: Russell and Russell.

Chambers, R. (1998) *Facing It: AIDS Diaries and the Death of the Author.* Michigan: University of Michigan Press.

Chaplin, E. (1994) *Sociology and Visual Representation*. London: Routledge.

Classen, Constance (1993) *Worlds of Sense. Exploring the Senses in History and Across Cultures*. London: Routledge.

Coles, R. (1997) *Doing Documentary Work*. Oxford: Oxford University Press.

Collier, J. Jr and Collier, M. (1986) *Visual Anthropology: Photography as a Research' Method*, 2nd edn. Albuquerque, NM: University of New Mexico.

Coxon, A.P.M. (1996) *Between the Sheets: Sexual Diaries and Gay Men's Sex in the Era of AIDS*. London: Cassell.

Curry, I. and Clarke, A.C. (1977) *Introducing Visual Sociology*. Dubuque, IA: Kendall/Hunt.

Danahay, M.A. (1996) 'Professional subjects: prepacking the academic CV', in S. Smith and J. Watson (eds), *Geting a Life: Everyday Uses of Autobiography*. Minneapolis, MN: University of Minnesota Press, pp. 351–67.

Davidoff, L. (1979) 'Class and gender in Victorian England: the diaries of Arthur J. Munby and Hannah Cullwick', *Feminist Studies*, 5: 87–141.

Denzin, N.K. (1978a) *The Research Act*, 2nd edn. Chicago: Aldine.

Denzin, N.K. (1995) *The Cinematic Society: The Voyeur's Gaze*. London: Sage.

Denzin, N.K. (1997) *Interpretive Ethnography: Ethnographic Practices for the 21st Century*. London: Sage.

Duneier, M. (1992) *Slini's Table: Race, Respectability and Masculinity*. Chicago: University of Chicago Press.

Fothergill, R.A. (1974) *Private Chronicles: A Study of English Diaries*. London: Oxford University Press.

Friday, N. (1976) *My Secret Garden*. New York: Pocket Books.

Gershuny, J. and Sullivan, O. (1998) 'The sociological uses of time-use diary analysis', *European Sociological Review*, 14: 69–85.

Grele, R. (ed.) (1975) *Envelopes of Sound: Six Practitioners Discuss the Method, Theory and Practice of Oral History and Oral Testimony*. Chicago: Precedent Publishing.

Halle, D. (1993) *Inside Culture: Art and Class in the American Home*. Chicago: University of Chicago Press.

Harper, D. (1994) 'On the authority of the image: visual methods at the crossroads', in N.K. Denzin and Y. Lincoln (eds), *Handbook of Qualitative Research*. London: Sage. pp. 403–12.

Heider, K.G. (1976) *Ethnographic Film*. Austin, IX: University of Texas.

Hersey, J. (1972) *Hiroshima*. Harmondsworth: Penguin.

Hine, L. (1977) *America and Lewis Hine*. New York: Aperture.

Hirsch, M. (1997) *Family Frames: Photographs, Narrative and Postmemory*. London: Routledge.

Holliday, R. (1999) 'The comfort of identity', *Sexualities*, 2 (4): 475–91.

Hoskins, J. (1998) *Biographical Objects: How Things Tell the Stories of People's Lives*. London: Routledge.

Jackson, B. (1977) *Killing Time: Life in the Arkansas Penitentiary*. New York: Cornell University Press.

Jackson, B. (1978) 'Killing time: life in the Arkansas Penitentiary', *Qualitative Sociology*, 1: 21–32.

Jacobs, J. (1974) *Sun City: An Ethnographic Study of a Retirement Community*. New York: Holt, Rinehart & Winston.

Juhasz, A. (1995) *AIDS TV: Identity, Community and Alternative Video*. Durham, NC: Duke University Press.

Juhasz, A. (1999) 'It's about autonomy, stupid: sexuality in feminist video', *Sexualities*, 2 (3): 333–42.

Krieger, S. (1996) *The Family Silver: Essays on Relationships Among Women*. Berkeley, CA: University of California Press.

Kulick, D. (1999) *Travesti: Sex, Gender and Culture among Brazilian Transgendered Prostitutes*. Chicago: University of Chicago Press.

Langer, L. (1991) *Holocaust Testimonies: The Ruins of Memory*. New Haven, CT: Yale University Press.

Lesy, M. (1973) *Wisconsin Death Trip*. New York: Pantheon.

Lesy, M. (1976) *Real Life: Louisville in the Twenties*. New York: Pantheon.

Lewis, J. and Fraser, M. (1996) 'Patches of grief and rage: visitor responses to the NAMES Project AIDS Memorial Quilt', *Qualitative Sociology*, 19 (4): 433–51.

Lewis, O. (1970) *Anthropological Essays*. New York: Random House.

Lewis, O. (1959) *Five Families*. New York: Basic Books.

Lury, C. (1998) *Prosthetic Culture: Photography, Memory and Identity*. London: Routledge.

Maas, S. and Kuypers, J.A. (1974) *From Thirty to Seventy: a 40 Year Longitudinal Study of Adult Life Styles and Personality*. London: Jossey–Bass.

McQuire, S. (1998) *Visions of Modernity*. London: Sage.

Meatyard, R.E. (1974) *The Family Album of Lucybelle Crater*. New York: The Book Organization.

Miller, N. and Morgan, D. (1993) 'Called to account: the CV as an autobiographical practice', *Sociology*, 27 (1): 133–43.

Monette, P. (1992) *Borrowed Time: An AIDS Memoir*. New York: Avon Books.

Moran, J.M. (1996) 'Wedding Video and its generation', in M. Renov and E. Suderburg (eds), *Resolutions: Contemporary Video Practice*. Minnesota, MN: University of Minnesota Press pp 360–81.

Mowrer, E.R. (1927) *Family Disorganization*. Chicago: University of Chicago Press.

Musello, C. (1979) 'Family photography', in J. Wagner (ed.), *Images of Information: Still Photography in the Social Sciences*. Beverly Hills, CA: Sage. pp. 101–18.

Nardi, P. (1990) 'AIDS and obituaries: the perpetuation of stigma in the press', in D. Feldman (ed.), *Culture and Aids*. New York: Praeger. pp. 159–68.

National Press Photographers Association (1978) *The Best of Photojournalism*. London: Orbis Publishing.

Nichols, B. (1991) *Representing Reality: Issues and Concepts in Documentary*. Bloomington, IN: Indiana University Press.

Palmer, V.M. (1928) *Field Studies in Sociology: A Student's Manual*. Chicago: University of Chicago.

Parker, T. (1996) *Studs Terkel: A Life in Words*. New York: Henry Holt and Co.

Pepys, S. (1970 edn) *The Diary of Samuel Pepys: A New and Complete Transcription* (edited by R. Latham and W. Matthews), Vols 1–9 London: Bell.

Ponsonby, A. (1923) *English Diaries: A Review of English Diaries from the Sixteenth to the Twentieth Century with an Introduction on Diary Writing*. London: Methuen.

Rathje, W. and Murphy, C. (1992) *Rubbish! The Archaeology of Garbage*. New York: HarperCollins.

Renov, M. and Suderburg, E. (1996) *Resolutions: Contemporary Video Practices*. Minnesota: University of Minnesota Press.

Riis, J.A. (1971) *How the Other Half Lives*. New York: Dover. (First published 1890.)

Riley, M.W. (1963) *Sociological Research: I: A Case Approach*. New York: Harcourt, Brace and World.

Rosenthal, A. (1971) *The New Documentary in Action: A Casebook in Film Making*. Berkeley, CA: University of California Press.

Schwartz, H. and Jacobs, J. (1979) *Qualitative Sociology: A Method to the Madness*. London: Collier–Macmillan.

Semin, A., Garb, T. and Kuspit, D. (eds) (1997) *Christian Boltanski*. London: Phaidon.

Sherman, S.R. (1998) *Documenting Ourselves: Film, Video and Culture*. Lexington, KY: University of Kentucky Press.

Simeoni, D. and Diani, M. (eds) (1995b) 'Taking Jenny at her word', *Current Sociology*, 43 (2/3): 27–40.

Sontag, S. (1979) *On Photography*. Harmondsworth: Penguin.

Sorokin, P. and Berger, C. (1938) *Time Budgets of Human Behaviour*. Cambridge, MA: Harvard University Press.

Spence, J. (1986) *Putting Myself in the Picture: A Political, Personal and Photographic Autobiography*. London: Camden Press.

Spence, J. and Holland, P. (1991) *Family Snaps: The Meaning of Domestic Photography*. London: Virago.

Stanley, L. (ed.) (1984) *The Diaries of Hannah Cullwick*. London: Virago.

Stanley, L. (1992) *The Auto/Biographical I; Theory and Practice of Feminist Auto/Biography*. Manchester: Manchester University Press.

Stasz, C. (1979a) Texts, images and display conventions in sociology', *Qualitative Sociology*, 2(1): 29–44.

Steichen, E. (1955) *The Family of Man*. New York: Museum of Modern Art.

Straus, R. (1974) *Escape from Custody*. New York: Harper and Row.

Terkel, S. (1968) *Division Street: America*. London: Allen Lane.

Terkel, S. (1970) *Hard Times: An Oral History of the Great Depression*. London: Allen Lane.

Terkel, S. (1974/1977) *Working*. Harmondsworth: Penguin.

Terkel, S. (1978) *Talking to Myself: A Memoir of My Times*. New York: Pocket Books.

Terkel, S. (1981) *American Dreams: Lost and Found*. London: Hodder and Stoughton.

Thomas, W.I. and Znaniecki, F. (1958) *The Polish Peasant in Europe and America*. New York: Dover Publications (First published 1918–21; republished in 2 vols 1927.)

Wagner, J. (ed.) (1979) *Images of Information: Still Photography in the Social Sciences*. Beverly Hills, CA: Sage.

Warner, L. (1963) *Yankee City*. New Haven: Yale University Press.

Webb, E.J., Campbell, D.I., Schwartz, R.D. and Sechrest, L. (1966) *Unobtrusive Measures: Non-reactive Research in the Social Sciences*. Chicago: Rand McNally.

Weber, R. (1981) *The Literature of Fact: Literary Non-Fiction in American Writing*. Athens, OH: Ohio University Press.

Wiseman, F. (1971) 'Interview with Wiseman', in G.R. Levin, *Documentary Explorations*. New York: Doubleday. pp. 313–28.

Wolfe, I. (1973) *The New Journalism*. New York: Harper and Row.

Young, M.W. (1999) *Malinowksi's Kiriwina: Fieldwork Photography 1915–1918*. Chicago: University of Chicago Press.

Zavarzadeh, M. (1976) *The Mythopoeic Reality: The Post War American Non Fiction Novel*. Urbana, IL: University of Illinois Press.

Zimmerman, D.H. and Wieder, D.L. (1977) 'The diary diary–interview method', Urban Life (now *Journal of Contemporary Ethnography*), 5 (4): 479–97.

60

The Virtual Objects of Ethnography

Christine Hine

The Crisis in Ethnography

thnography has changed a lot since its origins as the method anthropologists used to develop an understanding of cultures in distant places. It has been taken up within a wide range of substantive fields including urban life, the media, medicine, the classroom, science and technology. Ethnography has been used within sociology and cultural studies, although it retains a special status as the key anthropological approach. In new disciplinary settings, the emphasis on holistic description has given way to more focused and bounded studies of particular topics of interest. Rather than studying whole ways of life, ethnographers in sociology and cultural studies have interested themselves in more limited aspects: people as patients, as students, as television viewers or as professionals. The ethnography of familiar and nearby cultures has also augmented the ethnography of remote and apparently exotic ways of life. These settings have brought their own challenges as ethnographers struggle to suspend what they take for granted about their own cultures, and attempt to negotiate access to settings where they may be dealing with the culturally more powerful (Jackson, 1987). The upshot of these developments has been a wide diversity of approaches to ethnography, although these share a fundamental commitment to developing a deep understanding through participation and observation. Hammersley and Atkinson provide a basic definition, applicable to most studies, of what ethnography is:

> In its most characteristic form it involves the ethnographer participating,
> overtly or covertly in people's daily lives for an extended period of time,

Source: *Virtual Ethnography* (London: SAGE, 2000), pp. 42–66.

watching what happens, listening to what is said, asking questions – in fact, collecting whatever data are available to throw light on the issues that are the focus of the research. (1995: 1)

The practice of ethnography has continually faced challenges concerning objectivity and validity from the harder sciences. A methodology that offers little in the way of prescription to its practitioners and has no formula for judging the accuracy of its results is vulnerable to criticism from methodologies such as surveys, experiments and questionnaires that come equipped with a full armoury of evaluative techniques. In the face of these critiques the popularity of qualitative methodologies, including ethnography, is based on their strong appeal as ways of addressing the richness and complexity of social life. The emphasis on holism in ethnography gives it a persuasive attraction in dealing with complex and multi-faceted concepts like culture, as compared with the more reductive quantitative techniques. Ethnography is appealing for its depth of description and its lack of reliance on *a priori* hypotheses. It offers the promise of getting closer to understanding the ways in which people interpret the world and organize their lives. By contrast, quantitative studies are deemed thin representations of isolated concepts imposed on the study by the researcher.

One response to positivist-based, quantitative critiques of ethnography has centred on claims that ethnography produces an authentic understanding of a culture based on concepts that emerge from the study instead of being imposed *a priori* by the researcher. Cultures are studied in their natural state, rather than as disturbed by survey techniques or experimental scenarios. This argument depends upon a realist ethnography which describes cultures as they really are (it also, of course, depends on accepting realism and objectivity as the aspiration of any methodology). More recently the realist and naturalistic project has come into question from within the qualitative field, as realist notions more generally have been challenged by constructivist approaches to knowledge (Berger and Luckman, 1971). The basis for claiming any kind of knowledge as asocial and independent of particular practices of knowing has come under attack, and ethnography has not been exempt. The naturalistic project of documenting a reality external to the researcher has been brought into question. Rather than being the records of objectively observed and preexisting cultural objects, ethnographies have been reconceived as written and unavoidably constructed accounts of objects created through disciplinary practices and the ethnographer's embodied and reflexive engagement. These developments in epistemology have constituted what Denzin describes as a 'triple crisis of representation, legitimation, and praxis' (1997: 3) for qualitative research, including ethnography. The triple crisis that Denzin describes threatens ethnography on all fronts: its claims to represent culture; its claims to authentic knowledge; and the ability of its proponents to make principled interventions based on the knowledge they acquire through ethnography. Marcus relates the comprehensive nature of the challenge to ethnography:

Under the label first of 'postmodernism' and then 'cultural studies', many scholars in the social sciences and humanities subjected themselves to a bracing critical self-examination of their habits of thought and work. This involved reconsiderations of the nature of representation, description, subjectivity, objectivity, even of the notions of 'society' and 'culture' themselves, as well as how scholars materialized objects of study and data about them to constitute the 'real' to which their work had been addressed. (1997: 399)

The 'crisis', rather than suggesting the abandonment of ethnography altogether, can be seen as opening possibilities for creative and strategic applications of the methodology. The 'ethnography of ethnography' (Van Maanen, 1995) occasioned by the new epistemology entails a re-examination of features of the methodology that might have seemed self-evident. The whole methodology is thus opened up for re-examination and refashioning. This provides an opportunity for reshaping and reformulating projects in the light of current concerns. Recognizing that the objects we find and describe are of our own making entails owning up to the responsibility that recognition imposes. It offers up the opportunity of making the kind of research objects we need to enter and transform debates, and opens up the relationships between research subjects, ethnographers and readers to reconfiguration. This chapter takes the ethnographic 'crisis' as an opportunity for making a form of ethnographic enquiry suited to the Internet, involving a different kind of interaction and ethnographic object from those with which ethnography has traditionally been concerned. This approach involves embracing ethnography as a textual practice and as a lived craft, and destabilizes the ethnographic reliance on sustained presence in a found field site.

The aim of this examination of ethnography is to find a different way of dealing with some problems with an ethnographic approach to the Internet as described in Chapter 2. These problems include the authenticity of mediated interactions as material for an ethnographic understanding and the choice of appropriate sites to study the Internet as both a culture and a cultural object. The problems with an ethnographic approach to the Internet encompass both how it is to be constituted as an ethnographic object and how that object is to be authentically known. Within a naturalistic or realist version of the ethnographic project these issues seem to render the ethnography of the Internet highly problematic. The aim of this chapter is to examine some recent developments in ethnographic thinking that are particularly useful in developing an alternative approach to the study of the Internet. The account will focus on three crucial areas for looking at the Internet ethnographically. These areas are:

- the role of travel and face-to-face interaction in ethnography
- text, technology and reflexivity
- the making of ethnographic objects.

The examination of these areas is used to formulate the principles of a virtual ethnography that draws on current ethnographic thinking and applies it to the mediated and spatially dispersed interactions that the Internet facilitates.

Ethnography and the Face-to-Face

A major issue to be confronted in designing an ethnographic study of the Internet is the appropriate way of interacting with the subjects of the research. Ethnography has traditionally entailed physical travel to a place, which implies that face-to-face interaction is the most appropriate. Before the widespread availability of CMC, mediated forms of communication simply did not seem sufficiently interactive to allow the ethnographer to test ideas through immersion. If mediated interaction is to be incorporated into an ethnographic project, the basis for focusing ethnographic engagement or immersion on face-to-face interaction needs to be considered. The availability of mediated interaction provides the opportunity to question the role of face-to-face interaction in the construction of an ethnography. We can then examine what it is about their reliance on face-to-face interaction that makes ethnographers' accounts of their research convincing, and explore the possibilities for a reconceptualization of ethnographic authenticity that incorporates mediated interaction on its own terms.

The way of considering face-to-face interaction discussed here owes its basis to the 'representational crisis' (Denzin, 1997). The publication of *Writing Culture* (Clifford and Marcus, 1986) marked a growing recognition that ethnographic writing was not a transparent representation of a culture. The written products of ethnography were narratives or accounts that relied heavily on the experience of particular ethnographers and on the conventions used to make the telling of those accounts authoritative and engaging (Van Maanen, 1988). Ethnography was a 'story-telling institution' (Van Maanen, 1995), and the stories told could be more or less convincing, but were not necessarily to be evaluated on a basis of their truth to a preexisting 'real' culture. Whatever the sincerity with which they were told, ethnographic stories were necessarily selective. Ethnographies were 'textual constructions of reality' (Atkinson, 1990). This perspective provides an opportunity to analyse the importance of face-to-face interaction by looking at the role that is played in accounts by the fact of the ethnographer having been to a field site for a sustained period. The primacy of the face-to-face in ethnography can be understood by reflecting upon the way in which ethnography's production as an authoritative textual account has traditionally relied upon travel, experience and interaction. This is particularly useful as a way of avoiding making *a priori* judgements of the richness (and ethnographic adequacy) or otherwise of communications media: an assumption that has proved problematic in relation to CMC (Chapter 2).

Travel has played an important part in the construction of an ethnographic authority. The days of reliance on second-hand accounts and the tales of travellers are cast as the 'bad old days', in which the ethnographer was insufficiently embroiled with what was going on to be able to provide an authoritative analysis, and, worse, could be misled by relying on the re-representations of others. Kuper (1983) equates the 'Malinowskian revolution' in ethnography as comprising the uniting of fieldworker and theorist in a single body, such that the one who went, saw and reported was also the one who analysed. The concept of travel still plays an important part in distinguishing ethnography from other analytic approaches. As Van Maanen states:

> Whether or not the field worker ever really does 'get away' in a conceptual sense is becoming increasingly problematic, but physical displacement is a requirement. (1988: 3)

Van Maanen seems here to be casting the problem as ethnographers taking their own analytic frameworks with them, and therefore failing to address the field site they visit on its own terms, as they have claimed. While for him physical travel is not enough to ensure conceptual distance, travel to a field site is a prerequisite for the ethnographic analysis. It is still not clear, however, what it is that makes travel so fundamental. Some clues are provided by analyses of the ways in which ethnographers write about their experience of travelling and arriving. The role played by travel in constructing ethnographic authority is pointed to by Pratt in her analysis of the role of 'arrival stories' in ethnographers' accounts:

> They [arrival stories] play the crucial role of anchoring that description in the intense and authority-giving personal experience of fieldwork . . . Always they are responsible for setting up the initial positionings of the subjects of the ethnographic text: the ethnographer, the native, and the reader. (1986: 32)

Travel in this analysis becomes a signifier of the relationship between the writer and readers of the ethnographic text and the subjects of the research. The details that the ethnographer gives of the way they got into the field encourage us as readers to accept the account that follows as authentically grounded in real experience. Along with travel comes the notion of translation (Turner, 1980). It is not sufficient merely to travel, but necessary also to come back, and to bring back an account. That account gains much of its authoritative effect with the contrast that it constructs between author and reader: the ethnographer has been where the reader cannot or did not go. It is instructive to note that the critique of Margaret Mead's *Coming of Age in Samoa* (1943) was based on another ethnographer having been there too, and having experienced a different cultural reality to the one Mead described (Freeman, 1996). The authority of the critique depends on Freeman's travel. A critic who had not been there might have found Mead's account implausible, but probably could not mount such a detailed and persuasive refutation.

The ethnography of the Internet does not necessarily involve physical travel. Visiting the Internet focuses on experiential rather than physical displacement. As Burnett suggests, 'you travel by looking, by reading, by imaging and imagining' (1996: 68). It is possible for an ethnographer sitting at a desk in an office (their own office, what's more) to explore the social spaces of the Internet. Far from getting the seats of their pants dirty, Internet ethnographers keep their seats firmly on the university's upholstery. The lack of physical travel does not mean, however, that the relationship between ethnographer and readers is collapsed. Baym (1995c) has her own version of an arrival story, as does Correll (1995). Both focus not on the ways in which they physically reached a field site, but on the ways in which they negotiated access, observed interactions and communicated with participants. These descriptions set up a relationship in which the ethnographer has an extensive and sustained experience of the field site that the reader is unlikely to share (besides an analytic distance which mere participants are unable to share). Methodological preambles are far from innocent in the construction of ethnographic authority. The ethnography described in this book is no different. Chapter 4 is there not just to tell you what I did, but to convince you that I did something that authorizes me to speak. Devices such as the technical glossary at the end of this book display the ethnographer's competence with the local language, just as do the glossaries included with ethnographies conducted in distant places and other languages. Whether physical travel is involved or not, the relationship between ethnographer, reader and research subjects is still inscribed in the ethnographic text. The ethnographer is still uniquely placed to give an account of the field site, based on their experience of it and their interaction with it.

The contrast between ethnographer and reader that forms a large part of the authority claim of the ethnographic text depends not just on travel, but also on experience. Again, we have a contrast with the bad old days when ethnographers remained on the verandah (conveniently close to informants but not too close) and failed to engage fully in the field. As Van Maanen says of the genre of realist tales, 'the convention is to allow the field-worker's unexplicated experience in the culture to stand as the basis for textual authority' (1988: 47). In some renditions, this experience of the culture informs the written ethnography by allowing the ethnographer to sense the culture, in ways that extend beyond sight:

> The experience of fieldwork does not produce a mysterious empowerment, but without it, the ethnographer would not encounter the context – the smells, sounds, sights, emotional tensions, feel – of the culture she will attempt to evoke in a written text. (Wolf, 1992: 128)

From these observations a sense of ethnographic presence begins to emerge in which 'being there' is unique to the ethnographer. The ethnographer who really went there is set up as the one with the authority to interpret, over and above the reader who might wish to interpret, but does not have access to a claim of having been there. Readers are thus always dependent on the second-hand account of the ethnographer. The ethnographic authority is not a transferable one: it resides always and only with the ethnographer who was there. The authority of the ethnographer is also not transferable, within this model, to the subjects of the study whom we might naively assume were also there. The research subject lacks the analytic vision of the ethnographer, and thus cannot coexist in the analytic space of the ethnography. Ethnography acts to construct an analytic space in which only the ethnographer is really there. Ethnographers exist alone in an analytic space which preserves their authority claim. According to Turner, '"the field" can be conceived of as a space – better an attitude – which far from being neutral or inert, is itself the product of "disciplinary technologies"' (1989: 13). Attempts may be made to cede this space, as in the exercise in coauthorship described by McBeth (1993), but it is the ethnographer's right to grant or withhold access.

Rosaldo (1989) evokes another sense in which experience is vital to the ethnographer. He describes his inability to comprehend the headhunter's conflation of grief with rage, until he himself suffers intense grief and finds himself angry. This foregrounds the necessity of lived experience and participation for full understanding. The ethnographer is not simply a voyeur or a disengaged observer, but is also to some extent a participant, sharing some of the concerns, emotions and commitments of the research subjects. This extended form of experience depends also on interaction, on a constant questioning of what it is to have an ethnographic understanding of a phenomenon. The authority of interaction, of juxtaposing ethnographic interpretations with those of the native, and opening them up to being altered, is another aspect of the authority that ethnography gains from the face-to-face.

The definition of ethnography as participation given by Hammersley and Atkinson (1995: 2) highlights the interactive aspect of ethnographic research. The researcher does not just observe at close quarters, but interacts with the researched to ask questions and gain the insights into life that come from doing as well as seeing. As Pratt points out, ethnography distinguishes itself from other kinds of travel, and from the accounts offered by other kinds of travellers:

> In almost any ethnography dull-looking figures called 'mere travellers' or 'casual observers' show up from time to time, only to have their superficial perceptions either corrected or corroborated by the serious scientist. (1986: 27)

At least part of this distinction stems from an assumption that ethnography is an active attempt at analysis, involving more than just soaking up the local atmosphere. As Wolf says:

> We do research. It is more than something that simply happens to us as a result of being in an exotic place. (1992: 127)

This interaction also involves the ethnographer in leaving herself open to being taken by surprise by what occurs in the fieldwork setting. By being there, participating and experiencing, the ethnographer opens herself up to learning:

> Fieldwork of the ethnographic kind is authentic to the degree that it approximates the stranger stepping into a culturally alien community to become, for a time and in an unpredictable way, an active part of the face-to-face relationships in that community. (Van Maanen, 1988: 9)

Again we are back to face-to-face interaction as an intrinsic part of ethnography. The importance of the face-to-face in Van Maanen's account is that being physically present forces the ethnographer to be a participant in events and interactions. An ethnographer who managed to be an invisible observer (a cultural lurker?) would leave the setting undisturbed, but would also leave their interpretations of it undisturbed by trial in practice. The suggestion is that the ethnographer, by opening herself up to the unpredictability of the field, allows at least part of the agenda to be set by the setting. This claim to act as a neutral voice for the field has been used to enhance the ethnographer's authority. As Pratt points out, this does create a paradox for the ethnographic account:

> Personal narrative mediates this contradiction between the involvement called for in fieldwork and the self-effacement called for in formal ethnographic description, or at least mitigates some of its anguish, by inserting into the ethnographic text the authority of the personal experience out of which the ethnography is made. It thus recuperates at least a few shreds of what was exorcised in the conversion from the face-to-face field encounter to objectified science. (1986: 33)

Ethnographers in cyberspace can, of course, lurk in a way that face-to-face ethnographers cannot readily achieve. An observer who might be physically visible and marked as different in a face-to-face setting even when silent, can simply merge invisibly with all the other lurkers in an online setting. To do this, however, is to relinquish claims to the kind of ethnographic authority that comes from exposing the emergent analysis to challenge through interaction. Both Baym (1995c) and Correll (1995) make clear that their findings are the result of observation and interaction.

Correll (1995) stresses that besides her online work she also met some of her informants face-to-face, and thus could verify some things that they said online about their offline lives. While this is presented as a way of triangulating findings and adding authenticity to them, it could also be seen as a result of the pursuit of ethnographic holism. In this case, the group did hold periodic meetings, and Correll took advantage of this convention. Many inhabitants of cyberspace, however, have never met face-to-face and have no intention of doing so. To instigate face-to-face meetings in this situation would place the ethnographer in an asymmetric position, using more varied and different means of communication to understand informants than are used by informants themselves. In a conventional ethnography involving travel, the ethnographer is in a symmetrical position to that of informants. Informants too can look around them, ask questions, and try out their interpretations, although of course they are unlikely to analyse the results in the same way or publish them as a book! The ethnographer simply exploits the role of the stranger, new to the culture, who has deliberately to learn what others take for granted. The symmetry here is that of the ethnographer using the same resources and the same means of communication as available to the subjects of the research. This leaves us with a paradox: while pursuing face-to-face meetings with online informants might be intended to enhance authenticity via triangulation (Silverman, 1993; Hammersley and Atkinson, 1995), it might also threaten the experiential authenticity that comes from aiming to understand the world the way it is for informants. Rather than accepting face-to-face communication as inherently better in ethnography, a more sceptical and symmetrical approach suggests that it should be used with caution, and with a sensitivity to the ways in which informants use it.

The question remains then whether interactions in electronic space should be viewed as authentic, since the ethnographer cannot readily confirm details that informants tell them about their offline selves. Posing the problem in this way, however, assumes a particular idea of what a person is (and what authenticity is). Authenticity, in this formulation, means correspondence between the identity performed in interactions with the ethnographer and that performed elsewhere both online and offline. This presupposes a singular notion of an identity, linked to a similarly singular physical body. As Wynn and Katz (1997) point out, critiques of this singular notion of identity are well established and in no way rely upon the new technologies. The person might be better thought of as a convenient shorthand for a more or less coherent set of identity performances with reference to a singular body and biography. We might usefully turn our attention, rather than seeking correspondence and coherence ourselves, to looking at the ways in which new media might alter the conditions of identity performance (Meyrowitz, 1985). Standards of authenticity should not be seen as absolute, but are situationally negotiated and sustained. Authenticity, then, is another manifestation of the 'phenomenon always escapes' rule (Silverman, 1993: 201). A search for truly authentic knowledge about people or phenomena is doomed to be ultimately irresolvable. The point for the ethnographer is not to bring some external criterion for judging whether it is safe to believe what informants say, but rather to come to understand how it is that informants judge authenticity. This also entails accepting that 'the informant' is a partial performance rather than a whole identity.

Rather than treating authenticity as a particular problem posed by cyberspace that the ethnographer has to solve before moving on to the analysis, it would be more fruitful to place authenticity in cyberspace as a topic at the heart of the analysis. Assuming *a priori* that authenticity is a problem for inhabitants of cyberspace is the same kind of ethnographic mistake as assuming that the Azande have a problem in dealing with the contradictions inherent in their beliefs about witchcraft. It should be addressed as an issue for the ethnography as and when it arises during interaction. The issues of authenticity and identity are addressed again in Chapter 6 in the light of an ethnographic exploration of an Internet event. Despite this transformation of the authenticity issue from a problem for the ethnographer to a topic for the ethnography, it is fair to say that the ethnography will always have to meet a different standard of authenticity to that prevailing in interactions in the field: the ethnography is ultimately produced and evaluated in an academic setting (Stanley, 1990). What faces the ethnographer is a translation task between the authenticity standards of two different discourses.

Text, Technology and Reflexivity

In the previous section, the Internet was described as a site for interaction, which, although it might not entail face-to-face communication, was still in some sense ethnographically available. This argument is based on the assumption that what goes on within the Internet is social interaction. Another way of looking, however, would see cyberspace as composed of texts, rather than being interactive. There is no definite fixed line between the two concepts. The distinction is useful in so far as it plays out different ideas about what constitutes and characterizes the two phenomena. Interaction tends to be thought of as entailing a copresence of the parties involved, and a rapid exchange of perspectives which leads to a shared achievement of understanding between those involved (although not, of course, a completely transparent understanding). What we call a text could be thought of as a temporally shifted and packaged form of interaction. While spoken interaction is ephemeral (unless transcribed by social scientists) and local, texts are mobile, and so available outside the immediate circumstances in which they are produced. Texts possess the potential for availability outside their site of production, and hence make possible the separation of production and consumption. Newspapers, television programmes, memoranda, correspondence, audio and video tapes, and compact discs all have a taken-for-granted mobility: they are packaged in a form which means they can be transferred from one person to another. Where clarification is needed, the readers of a text cannot readily ask the authors what they meant. The focus in consuming texts is therefore placed far more on the interpretive work done by readers and less on a shared understanding between authors and readers. We tend (now) not to see texts as transparent carriers of the meanings intended by their authors. It could be said, then, that what we see on the Internet is a collection of texts. Using the Internet then becomes a process of reading and writing texts, and the ethnographer's job is to develop an understanding of the meanings which underlie and are enacted through these textual practices.

There is probably little to be gained from itemizing which aspects of the Internet should be seen as interactive sites or texts. Rather, it is important to keep in mind that they can be both. There is no doubt, however, that some parts seem more interactive than others. IRC, MUDs and newsgroups can seem quite interactive, even approaching the informality of spoken conversation. Although not all contributions are visibly acknowledged, enough receive responses for the impression of an ongoing conversation to develop. The early ethnographers of the Internet have had no problems in rendering these settings as appropriate sites for ethnographic interaction. The WWW, as discussed in Chapter 2, seems to pose more of a challenge to those looking for interactive sites. In contrast to newsgroups, the WWW seems to be a collection of largely static texts (although some of these contain interactive settings or discussion lists). The texts of static web pages might be interlinked, and might change over time, but viewed individually they make available no obvious way in which the ethnographer might interact. The ethnographer could visit other web pages and then develop their own web page as a response, but this hardly meets the standards for knowledge exposed to test through interaction and experience described above. This might seem to mean that the WWW is not available for ethnographic enquiry. The ethnographic approach seems to come to a full stop at the point at which the technology no longer promotes inter-actions in which the ethnographer can play a part. It is worth looking at the ways in which texts have been used by other ethnographers, in order to find some ways forward.

Traditionally, oral interactions have been foremost for ethnographers, and texts have taken a somewhat secondary role as cultural products, worthy of study only as far as they reveal something about the oral settings in which culture resides. Hammersley and Atkinson (1995) interpret this reliance on oral interaction as part of the 'romantic legacy' of ethnography, which tends to treat speech as more authentic than writing. They suggest that texts deserve a more detailed appraisal, and that judgement about the authenticity of written accounts should be suspended. Rather than being seen as more or less accurate portrayals of reality, texts should be seen as ethnographic material which tells us about the understanding which authors have of the reality which they inhabit. Texts are an important part of life in many of the settings which ethnographers now address, and to ignore them would be to produce a highly partial account of cultural practices. Rule books, manuals, biographies, scientific papers, official statistics and codes of practice can all be seen as ethnographic material in the ways in which they present and shape reality and are embedded in practice. Ethnographers should neither dismiss texts as distorted accounts nor accept them as straightforward truths, but should draw on their own 'socialized competence' in reading and writing to interpret them as culturally situated cultural artefacts (1995: 174).

Thompson (1995) also stresses the importance of combining a view of texts (here, media texts) with understandings of the situationality of those texts. What Thompson calls 'mediated quasi-interaction' (1995: 84) is facilitated by the texts of the mass media. The mobility of texts enabled by mediated quasi-interaction, resulting in a separation in space and time of producers and consumers, is one of the key features in analysing the social effects of the mass media. Thompson stresses that while symbolic or semiotic interpretations of the content of texts may be useful, it is important also to address the situated writing and reading practices which make those texts meaningful. Hammersley and Atkinson (1995) and Thompson (1995) therefore converge on a view that the analysis of texts needs to take into account their context. Only then can we make sensible, culturally informed judgements of their significance, and indeed only then can we determine their status as accounts of reality. This does not necessarily entail judging them as true or false accounts, but it does enable a view of the text as an account which has a situated author producing text within a cultural context and a situated audience interpreting text within other cultural contexts. Viewing texts ethnographically, then, entails tying those texts to particular circumstances of production and consumption. The text becomes ethnographically (and socially) meaningful once we have cultural context(s) in which to situate it.

Swales (1998) develops a model he calls textography for his attempt to combine an analysis of texts with an understanding of their relationship to other texts and the working lives of their authors. He explicitly states that this work is a partial one and he is unable to do justice to the 'complex situationalities' of 'personal, curatorial, institutional and disciplinary' influences (1998: 142). The strategic focus on textual production leaves many other aspects unexamined. For this partial approach Swales chooses a spatially defined sample: a university building occupied by three very different departments. The spatial proximity highlights the distinctive disciplinary practices of textual production that are uncovered. Through interviews with the authors of texts and observations of them in their working context, accounts of textual practices which the authors recognize but would not have given themselves are built up. Distinct disciplinary practices are sustained by the textual links between distant sites. These textual links are made manifest in the documents which are found in the offices of those studied and which are used in their work as reference and as models for their own writing. In addition to the working context of the authors, Swales therefore implies a second context, the intertextual context provided by the texts themselves. The discipline to which Swales's authors orient exists for him in and through the texts which constitute it: a feature which is emphasized by his reliance on study within the bounded space of the departmental building. In the same way, we might think of the intertextual context of the Internet as being the space into which the work of web authors is inserted and a context to which authors orient themselves.

In the case of the Internet, tying texts to social contexts of writing is relatively straightforward. Individual web authors can be approached for their interpretations of their practices. Given an accessible field site, an ethnographer could follow the progress of development of a web site and explore the interpretations of those involved as to the capacities of the technology and the identity of the audience being addressed. This analysis could be combined with an analysis of the content of the resulting web site. In this portrayal, the ethnography is a physically located one which renders the Internet as a repository of texts rather than a site for social interaction. A webography could become a strategically oriented and partial form of ethnography, like a textography. To take this kind of detailed approach to the influences and assumptions antecedent to the appearance of a page on the WWW would be a step forwards from analysing the web pages themselves as isolated phenomena, but would still be a relatively conservative approach. We would still be tied to a bounded physical location, and the influences which we were able to take into account would be largely those which occurred in that setting. This approach would not, therefore, be taking on board the spatial implications of mediated interaction. The more complex issue is how to incorporate the availability of texts (or interactions) across physical locations which the Internet enables. This issue is considered in the next section of this chapter, on the making of ethnographic objects.

While saying that contexts like newsgroups are interactive makes them ethnographically available, viewing newsgroup contributions as textual can also provide some valuable insights. A textual focus places emphasis on the ways in which contributions are justified and rendered authoritative, and on the identities which authors construct and perform through their postings. This approach to ethnography suggests a discourse analytic stance, which remains ambivalent about the nature of the discourse which is under analysis. The reality which texts construct can be evaluated on its own terms, without recourse to an external, pretextual reality (Potter and Wetherell, 1987; Potter, 1996). Here, again, the distinction between text and interaction blurs, since the material of discourse analysis encompasses textualized records of interaction as well as solely written texts. Discourse analysis is primarily concerned with the reality which texts construct. It has been criticized for the lack of ways of verifying the interpretations which it produces, although Potter counters this with a claim that at least if the analysis is at fault, the original text is made available for readers to develop their own interpretations:

> Nevertheless there is an important sense in which this approach democratizes academic interaction. For example, the reader does not have to take on trust the sensitivity or acuity of the ethnographer. (1996: 106)

For individual textual fragments this may be appropriate, but for more complex corpora of material the democratic approach may be rather taxing to readers asked to duplicate the analytic effort of the original analyst. We do not always read academic texts in order to discover the author wrong and substitute our own analysis, however much this might sometimes seem to be the case. Availability of data does not imply democracy either, since texts are generally constructed to produce an authoritative position for their authors and discourse analysts are rarely exempt. Rather than replacing ethnography, discourse analytic approaches to Internet texts could usefully coexist with ethnographic approaches to Internet interaction. This combination could help to maintain analytic ambivalence about what the phenomena being studied *really* are. Both approaches, however, share a problem of observability: potential interactants who choose to remain silent, and potential authors who fail to write, are lost to the analysis.

Hammersley and Atkinson (1995) pay considerably more attention to the authors of texts than to the readers. This is no doubt in part due to the problems in making the interpretation of texts ethnographically visible. It is far easier to study the work of producers than consumers: producers embody their concerns in the technologies they produce, and the work of constructing a technology is highly visible and observable. By contrast, users leave no visible marks on technologies, and interpreting the technology is often something they simply get on and do. Ethnographers can, of course, as they routinely do, attempt to make the invisible visible by asking questions or exploring scenarios with willing informants. To make these practices visible the ethnographer has to work harder at producing interpretations from informants, and is opened up to criticisms of having produced a partial or biased account. Another response to this kind of ethnographic invisibility of interpretive and embodied work is to incorporate a reflexive understanding (Cooper et al., 1995). The ethnographer can use an active engagement with the Internet as a reflexive tool to a deeper understanding of the medium. Reflexivity can therefore be a strategic response to the silence of web surfers and newsgroup lurkers. It can also be a way of acquiring and examining the 'socialized competences' which Hammersley and Atkinson (1995: 174) suggest that ethnographers aim for. In learning how to use the Internet and in using it to reach their field site and collect their data, ethnographers of the Internet can use their own data collection practices as data in their own right. As discussed in Chapter 2, an ethnographer of the Internet cannot hope to understand the practices of *all* users, but through their own practices can develop an understanding of what it is to be a user.

Ethnographers are traditionally warned about the dangers of 'going native' or losing their sceptical approach to things which their informants take for granted. If the ethnographer too comes to take these things for granted, their ethnographic edge as a cultural commentator will have been lost. These kinds of insecurities, still firmly grounded in a realist notion of ethnography, may help to explain some of the reluctance of ethnographers to engage fully in the work which their informants do, and move further along the spectrum from observer to participant. This may explain why ethnographers often develop only limited competences in the technical work which their informants do, as if incompetence was in some way strategic in maintaining strangeness. Often, admittedly, periods of training and required background knowledge simply pose too great a hurdle for the ethnographer to achieve any kind of competence without thoroughly disrupting (and entertaining) the informants they set out to study. In the case of the Internet, however, the obstacles to competence are not so great: the sheer mass of web pages and newsgroup contributions out there testify that it cannot be so hard, surely, if all these people can do it. The process of becoming competent in use of the Internet is a way for the ethnographer to find out just how hard it is, and in what specific ways it is made either hard or easy. Rather than forming a barrier to ethnographic strangeness to be guarded against, competence in using the Internet acquires a multiple significance: as a ground for reflexive exploration of what it is to use the Internet; as a means to deeper engagement and conversations with other users of the Internet; as a way to developing an enriched reading of the practices which lead to the production and consumption of Internet artefacts. With due (sceptical) caution, it appears that there are good grounds for an ethnographer of the Internet to become competent in its use. The processes through which field sites are found and materials collected become ethnographic materials in themselves.

The reflexivity discussed above is a strategic use of reflexivity as a method for interrogating the field. This kind of reflexivity could be incorporated relatively comfortably into a realist account, as a way of giving more authentic and deeper portrayals of what it is to be a cultural member. Reflexivity, however, is a much-contested term, which has precise but quite different meanings in different disciplinary settings (Woolgar, 1991b). In some incarnations reflexivity has a less comfortable relationship with realism. When juxtaposed with ideas about the social construction of knowledge, the claims of ethnography to provide an objective, factual portrayal of culture become suspect. Here reflexivity is applied not just to the work of individual ethnographers, but to the methodology as a whole. Folding back ideas about the constructed nature of knowledge on to ethnography itself poses an interesting paradox: ethnographic knowledge too might be a cultural construct. This paradox becomes particularly apparent for ethnographers of knowledge production, who might claim to be producing objective descriptions of the ways in which what scientists think of as objective fact turns out to be the upshot of social processes. If knowledge is seen to be a social construct, then ethnography has very weak claims to be held exempt, and the case for validating ethnographies on the basis of their truthful representation of underlying reality becomes suspect. Three distinct strategies for dealing with this paradox have become notable.

One approach is to rehabilitate member understandings of culture alongside the ethnographer's account, thus addressing and to some extent redressing the previous imbalance which claimed a privilege for ethnography. This can imply the ethnographer's sensitivity to the ways in which the subjects of the research understand their own culture:

> By including and focusing upon the ways people perceive and define the cultural space within which they exist and their own place in it, these studies therefore view distinctions between external and internal points of view as processes of life that are contingent upon the particular contexts in which they are made. (Hastrup and Olwig, 1997: 11)

This approach to reflexivity denies the privileging of the ethnographic account and blurs the boundaries between ethnographic and member understandings. The two are different, but neither is necessarily privileged. The second distinct approach is to place the focus on the ethnographer, reflecting on the particular perspective, history and standpoint which led this ethnographer to be giving their particular account of this setting. This can imply a focus on the ways in which the presuppositions and cultural positioning of the ethnographer shape the study. In this sense, reflexivity is a sensitizing device to counteract the tendency to present ethnographic reports as portrayals of an objective reality. Some view this kind of reflexivity as indulgence, a 'self-reflexive cul-de-sac' (Moores, 1993: 4) in which the ethnographer ends up telling readers more about herself than about the culture purportedly being described. It can also be a strategic device when used sensitively to explore differences of interpretation and understanding between ethnographers and subjects. Moores recognizes the strategic significance of Walkerdine's (1986; 1990) references to her own biography in shaping her reaction and those of the family she observed to a film both parties watched together. Ethnography can be a process of self-discovery and reflexivity can be a strategic element in developing insight.

A final approach attempts to incorporate a destabilization of ethnographic authority within the text itself. In contrast to 'politically correct' acceptances of the significance of member reflexivity and ethnographer standpoint, some ethnographers have taken a more 'epistemologically correct' approach to their ethnography. In the context of claims about the socially constructed nature of knowledge, which owe large parts of their force to ethnographies in scientific laboratories (Potter, 1996), some ethnographers have embraced the challenge this poses for their own knowledge-making practices. Epistemological correctness entails making clear the constructed nature of accounts, and has given rise to a range of approaches to presentation of ethnographic accounts which aim to make clear to readers their constructed and contingent nature (Woolgar, 1991b). Denzin (1997) reports on a variety of new ways of writing ethnography, based on recognition that writing is a constructive act rather than a straightforward reflection of reality.

The three approaches described above are not mutually exclusive, and are associated with differing political commitments and disciplinary histories. No doubt these approaches do not exhaust the possibilities for creative transformation of the ethnographic project in the light of the abandonment of a commitment to realism. Recently ethnographers have begun to explore the possibilities of hypertext and multimedia for expanding access to ethnographic materials and providing opportunities for readers to form their own narratives based on the material (Dicks and Mason, 1998; Slack, 1998). The ethnography which is presented in this book is told in a largely conventional style. I simply say the things which my experiences lead me to want to say, without claiming that these represent a single true reality, but also without strictly censoring those parts which might come across in a realist way. In part, this is because I am sceptical that there is an adequately configured readership for the new representational forms in ethnography (Traweek, 1992), and it is not clear that those who do exist overlap with the readership intended for this book. Marcus and Cushman (1982) identify six readerships of ethnography: the area specialist, the general anthropologist, social scientists other than anthropologists, students, action-oriented readers and popular readership. My readership could be any one of these, if we replace the anthropological area specialist with the new category of the cyberspace specialist. Modes of representation can be strategic choices which depend on the assumed readership (not forgetting that the ethnographic text is constructed by its readers). In this I adopt Hammersley's perspective, that:

> How we describe an object depends not just on decisions about what we believe to be true but also on judgements about relevance. The latter rely, in turn, on the purposes which the description is to serve. (1990: 609)

Ways of writing and strategies of familiarization and making strange depend on assumptions about what the audience will find familiar or strange already, and hence are inherently selective (Rosaldo, 1989). This suggests an approach which explicitly embraces the necessary selectivity and constructedness of accounts and which makes clear that this is the account I chose to give in the context of the questions which seem to me to be important. The ethnography which is presented in the next three chapters is neither a truth nor a fiction, but an account of an ethnographically constructed field of social interactions. Just because an ethnography is not a straightforward representation of the real does not mean that it cannot be sincere, unfashionable though sincerity is in playful postmodern times. What seems to be important is that we examine the circumstances which lead us to be telling this story about this object at this time and in this way. As Woolgar says:

> In short, we need continually to interrogate and find strange the process of representation as we engage in it. This kind of reflexivity is the ethnographer of the text. (1991b: 28)

One way in which I have addressed this issue is to compare my own interpretive and representational practices with those of my informants. Another part of examining how we come to be telling a particular ethnographic story is looking at the ways in which the object of the ethnography is constituted. While ethnographers in the past or in other settings may have been able to look at bounded physical settings, when studying the Internet the concept of the field site is no longer so straightforward. In the next section I consider the opportunities which this disruption offers.

The Making of Ethnographic Objects

The traditional emphasis in ethnography on field sites which map on to physically bounded places has some important implications for the constitution of ethnographic objects. The objects produced and studied through ethnography, its communities and societies, have been largely understood in spatial terms (Clifford, 1992). While ethnographers have often been sensitive to the influences of external contacts and influences, fieldwork places an emphasis on culture as something which is local. A 'manageable unit', carved out on grounds of self-evident boundaries, often came to stand in for what culture was (1992: 98). A similar observation could be made about the more substantively based ethnographic projects with which sociology has often been concerned. Silverman (1993) uses Gubrium and Holstein's (1987) work to show that while we might think of the household as the place to go in order to study the family, there are multiple other sites in which the 'family' is performed, such as television programmes, courtrooms and policy forums. The sites which we choose to study are often based on common sense understandings of what the phenomenon being explored is, intrinsically linked with an idea about where that activity goes on, whether the activity be the technical work of software engineering or the experimental work of science (Low and Woolgar, 1993; Knorr-Cetina, 1992).

The tendency to treat the field site as a place which one goes to and dwells within reinforces an idea of culture as something which exists in and is bounded by physical space. This tendency is exacerbated by the historical roots of anthropology in the study of relatively isolated communities, and by the continuing practice of concentrating on a particular region. The very idea of the field as a place which the ethnographer goes to, and comes back from, implies that the ethnographer is the only link between the two and bolsters the impression of separate cultural sites, 'ours' and 'theirs' (Ferguson, 1997). In this way, the world as seen through ethnographic eyes becomes a 'mosaic of unique and distinct cultures' (Hastrup and Olwig, 1997: 12). In sociological approaches the ethnographic object may be carved out through a substantive focus: the school, the street corner, the doctor's surgery, the laboratory. This object, however, is still a bounded physical location, and the aim becomes to describe the life which occurs within that space. The strategic applications of ethnography within sociology carve out particular facets of life for substantive investigation and tend to treat a physical or institutional boundary as the limit for their ethnographic interest (Hammersley, 1990).

In the face of increasing media saturation in all parts of the world and the prevalence of migration, a concern has been growing within anthropology that the implied notion of bounded cultures requires re-examination (Clifford, 1992). More and more, cultures appear to be interlinked, aware of one another, and connected through physical mobility of people and things (Appadurai, 1996; Gupta and Ferguson, 1992; Marcus, 1995). Whole areas of anthropology, cultural studies, sociology and geography have become 'saturated with the vocabulary of mobility' (Thrift, 1996a: 297). This new emphasis provides opportunities for ethnographers to study the reflexive awareness which comes from the inter-visibility of different cultural locations. The balance of authority in ethnographic accounts subtly shifts, as it becomes harder to render the ethnographer/traveller as uniquely privileged in their ability to see across cultures:

> In the present postcolonial world, the notion of an authentic culture as an autonomous internally coherent universe no longer seems tenable, except perhaps as a 'useful fiction' or a revealing distortion. In retrospect, it appears that only a concerted disciplinary effort could maintain the tenuous fiction of a self-contained cultural whole. Rapidly increasing global interdependence has made it more and more clear that neither 'we' nor 'they' are as neatly bounded and homogeneous as once seemed to be the case. (Rosaldo, 1989: 217)

Theoretical developments have not necessarily been mirrored by changes in methodological orientation (Hastrup and Olwig, 1997). Recently, however, there has been a considerable effort to struggle with the implications of connectivity and interrelations for the conduct of ethnography. The concern with translocal phenomena in ethnography has been particularly apparent in science and technology studies (Franklin, 1995) and media and cultural studies (Radway, 1988). Two distinct but related responses to the issue of cultural interconnectedness have arisen. One way to deal with this is to aim for a richer, deeper and more holistic notion of the articulation of diverse cultural fragments within particular locations (Radway, 1988; Abu-Lughod, 1997; Hirsch, 1998). Situating their argument within media reception and consumption studies, these authors question the particular notions of audiences which emerge from studies based on the reception of a specific media text or technology. They argue that these studies fail to consider the multiple discourses, identities and locations in which the 'audience' or 'consumers' are implicated. Aiming for holism does bring some problems, and is somewhat at odds with Ang's (1996) suggestion that the way forwards for reception studies is to embrace partiality (in its several senses). The idea of a holistic study of a given context is a disciplinary fiction which fails to acknowledge the partiality and selectivity of any ethnographic description (Hammersley, 1990; Stanley, 1990). It also fails to take on board the full implications of interconnectedness: how can there be a holistic study of a site if its boundaries are unstable and only occasionally enacted? Where does the local stop and the global begin?

As a strategy, and leaving aside aspirations to holistic description, a multi-dimensional approach does have an appeal. This strategy would no doubt be a useful one for a study of the Internet. A useful complement to online studies which treat the Internet as a separate cultural sphere would be to conduct sustained contextual studies of the ways in which the Internet is articulated into and transforms offline relationships. This would enable a much richer sense of the uses of the Internet and the ways in which local relationships shape its use as a technology and as a cultural context. We could consider the ways in which domestic or working settings were transformed by the interpolation of the new context provided by the Internet, and the ways in which that context was transformed by local concerns. We could, to some extent, study the interplay between the different notions of context which local settings and Internet provide. Moving the study of the Internet to offline settings rather than online ones would be a strategic choice with some obvious benefits. It is difficult to see, however, how this approach would give more than a fleeting impression of the spatiality of the Internet itself and the ways in which the relations within it are organized by the interaction with and construction of separated sites. Concentration on a single geographic location could end up focusing on Internet as technology at the expense of Internet as cultural context. For my purposes, I am drawn away from holism and towards connectivity as an organizing principle. This focus is an attempt to remain agnostic about the most suitable site for exploring the Internet.

Efforts to struggle with ethnography's reliance on bounded locations by focusing on connectivity rather than holism have been made notably in the collection edited by Olwig and Hastrup (1997) and in Marcus (1995). Hastrup and Olwig suggest that a new sensitivity to the ways in which place is performed and practised is required. This might involve viewing the field, rather than a site, as being a 'field of relations' (1997: 8). Ethnographers might still start from a particular place, but would be encouraged to follow connections which were made meaningful from that setting. The ethnographic sensitivity would focus on the ways in which particular places were made meaningful and visible. Ethnography in this strategy becomes as much a process of following connections as it is a period of inhabitance. In similar vein, Marcus suggests that ethnography could (should?) be adapted to 'examine the circulation of cultural meanings, objects and identities in diffuse time-space' (1995: 96). He suggests a range of strategies for ethnographers to construct fields in the absence of bounded sites, including the following of people, things, metaphors, narratives, biographies and conflicts. The heterogeneity of this collection of organizing concepts suggests that this will not be easy, and that ethnographers who follow Marcus's advice will need to embrace the insecurity of never quite knowing when one is in the field. Among the problems which Marcus acknowledges that multi-sited ethnography will bring is an anxiety about diluting the fieldwork engagement that ethnography depends upon. The engagement from sustained immersion in a particular place is replaced, in part, by the sensitivity of the ethnographer to mobility across a heterogeneous landscape and the differential engagements which this enables and requires. This sensitivity is exemplified in the work of Martin (1994) on the concept of the immune system, and Heath (1998) in her ethnographic tracing of the transformations of Marfan syndrome between multiple locations and articulations. Both studies are explicitly multi-sited, in a straightforward 'more than one place' sense, but are also thoroughly concerned with connection and transformation. Both are able to show how knowledges and places have complex and often unpredictable relationships, and how knowledges are transformed in the processes of recombination and rearticulation which mobility entails.

Sites have a tendency to focus our attention on the ways in which things are kept together as part of a cultural unit. We are focused on the local, the contextual, the interrelated and the coherent. The ethnographic description itself has a tendency to make the field seem homogeneous (Friedman, 1997). By focusing on sites, locales and places, we may be missing out on other ways of understanding culture, based on connection, difference, heterogeneity and incoherence. We miss out on the opportunity to consider the role of space in structuring social relations (Thrift, 1996a). Castells (1996a; 1996b; 1997) introduces the idea that a new form of space is increasingly important in structuring social relations. This space is the space of flows, which, in contrast to the space of place, is organized around connection rather than location. Flows of people, information, money, circulate between nodes which form a network of associations increasingly independent of specific local contexts. The concept of the space of flows will be examined in greater depth in Chapter 5. Here, it serves as a reminder that the organization of social relations is not necessarily linked to local context in a straightforward way. By analogy, the field site of ethnography could become a field flow, which is organized around tracing connections rather than about location in a singular bounded site.

The emergence of multi-sited ethnography, conceived of as an experiential, interactive and engaged exploration of connectivity, is encouraging news for ethnography of the Internet. It offers up possibilities for designing a study which is based on the connections within and around the Internet and enabled by it but not reliant on any one understanding of it. Chapter 2 discussed the reliance of accounts of Internet culture on bounded social settings such as newsgroups and MUDs. In focusing thus narrowly on boundaries which seemed self-evident, it was suggested that these ethnographies missed out on some of the potential offered by ethnography as a way of investigating the making of bounded social space and the importance of interaction between differently connected spaces. Online ethnographies despatialize notions of community, and focus on cultural process rather than physical place. This can, however, be at the expense of minimizing connections with offline life. Despatializing notions of community, in itself, does not guarantee that justice will be done to the complexity of connections which the new technology makes possible. To do this, we need to turn from (static, located) boundaries to networks and connections (Strathern, 1996). Following Strathern's advice, the ethnographer could usefully follow connections and also pay attention to the ways in which connections available in principle are cut in practice to limit the infinite extension of networks. Whether the online is separate from the offline, and in what ways, becomes an intrinsic part of the ethnography rather than a prior assumption. Connective ethnography turns the attention from 'being there' to 'getting there' (Clifford, 1992). We can ask what people are doing in their web pages and newsgroup postings: what does their traversal of space mean to them, and what does it achieve? Abandoning the offline/online boundary as a principled barrier to the analysis allows for it to be traversed (or created and sustained) through the ways in which connections are assembled.

To take a connective approach is not to suggest that no bounded locations exist on the Internet, or that the 'being there' is never important on the Internet. As Clifford (1992) and Featherstone (1995) suggest, diverting attention to travel does not mean assuming that everyone is a traveller and nobody dwells any more. This kind of connective ethnography remains agnostic about the 'real' existence of places and categories. Rather than cataloguing the characteristics of Internet communication, the virtual ethnographer asks, not what is the Internet, but when, where and how is the Internet (Moerman, 1974)? A connective ethnography could be a useful adjunct to space-based approaches. The World Wide Web, as a mixture of varyingly interlinked cultural sites and cultural connections, could form a model for a new way of orienting an ethnography to the field. This is not to say that web surfing is going to be used to stand in for ethnographic engagement. Following hypertextual links may be part of the strategy, but connectivity is also performed in the borrowing of material and images from other sites and other media, by the authorship and readership of sites, by the portrayals of the Internet in other media, and in myriad other ways. Connection could as well be the juxtaposition of elements in a narrative, the array of pages thrown up by a search engine, or a set of hyperlinks on a web page as an instance of communication between two people. The goal of the ethnography becomes to explore what those links are, how they are performed and what transformations occur *en route* in a snowballing approach (Bijker, 1995) that is sensitive to heterogeneity. Each performance of a connection becomes an invitation to the ethnographer to move on. This suggests an active engagement through exploration and interaction rather than a disengaged textual analysis.

Accepting a multi-sited or connective notion of ethnography opens up many different ways of designing and conducting an ethnographic project. Choices and movements are made on the basis of strategic and often arbitrary decisions, which dictate the shape and boundaries of the resulting ethnographic object. We end up with a multitude of different sites and sources for studying the Internet, even if we rely only on those most obviously and intuitively relevant. A first attempt at cataloguing sites in which the Internet is enacted and interpreted produces the following non-exhaustive list:

- web pages
- accounts of making web pages
- instructions on how to make web pages
- programs to help in making web pages
- reviews of web pages
- media reports on Internet events
- magazines and newspaper supplements devoted to the Internet
- fictionalized accounts of Internet-like technologies
- computer equipment retailers
- software developers
- stock markets
- newsgroups
- MUDs
- IRC
- video conferences
- accounts of the purpose of newsgroups
- Internet service providers' advertising and introductory materials
- Internet gateways and search engines
- homes and workplaces where the Internet is used, and the practices we find there
- training courses
- conversations between friends, families and work colleagues
- academic Internet studies like this one.

A holistic understanding of the Internet seems a futile undertaking in the face of this list. However hard the ethnographer works, she or he will only ever partially experience the Internet (Thornton, 1988). The challenge addressed in Chapter 4 is to incorporate as many of these sites and sources as practicable while retaining a coherent but explicitly partial ethnographic project. What follows is the story of one journey through which an Internet was made, by following connections motivated by the foreshadowed problems in Chapter 1.

The Principles of Virtual Ethnography

This chapter and the preceding one have reviewed literature on ethnographic methodology to develop an approach to the Internet which embraces the complexity offered by this form of mediated interaction. In the next three chapters

I attempt to flesh out the conclusions reached in this literature review by discussing a project designed to put this approach into action. First, however, it is worth reiterating the principles for virtual ethnography which form the foundations for the experiment in ethnography described here.

1. The sustained presence of an ethnographer in the field setting, combined with intensive engagement with the everyday life of the inhabitants of the field site, make for the special kind of knowledge we call ethnographic. The ethnographer is able to use this sustained interaction to 'reduce the puzzlement' (Geertz, 1993: 16) which other people's ways of life can evoke. At the same time, ethnography can be a device for inducing that same puzzlement by 'displacing the dulling sense of familiarity with which the mysteriousness of our own ability to relate perceptively to one another is concealed from us' (1993: 14). Virtual ethnography is used as a device to render the use of the Internet as problematic: rather than being inherently sensible, the Internet acquires its sensibility in use. The status of the Internet as a way of communicating, as an object within people's lives and as a site for community-like formations is achieved and sustained in the ways in which it is used, interpreted and reinterpreted.

3. Interactive media provide a challenge and an opportunity for ethnography, by bringing into question the notion of a site of interaction. Cyberspace is not to be thought of as a space detached from any connections to 'real life' and face-to-face interaction. It has rich and complex connections with the contexts in which it is used. It also depends on technologies which are used and understood differently in different contexts, and which have to be acquired, learnt, interpreted and incorporated into context. These technologies show a high degree of interpretive flexibility. Interactive media such as the Internet can be understood as both culture and cultural artefact. To concentrate on either aspect to the exclusion of the other leads to an impoverished view.

5. The growth of mediated interaction renders it unnecessary for ethnography to be thought of as located in particular places, or even as multi-sited. The investigation of the making and remaking of space through mediated interactions is a major opportunity for the ethnographic approach. We can usefully think of the ethnography of mediated interaction as mobile rather than multi-sited.

7. As a consequence, the concept of the field site is brought into question. If culture and community are not self-evidently located in place, then neither is ethnography. The object of ethnographic enquiry can usefully be reshaped by concentrating on flow and connectivity rather than location and boundary as the organizing principle.

9. Boundaries are not assumed *a priori* but explored through the course of the ethnography. The challenge of virtual ethnography is to explore the making of boundaries and the making of connections, especially between

the 'virtual' and the 'real'. Along with this goes the problem of knowing when to stop. If the concept of ethnography (and/or culture) as having natural boundaries is abandoned for analytic purposes, we can also abandon the idea of a whole ethnography of a given object. Stopping the ethnography becomes a pragmatic decision. The ethnographic object itself can be reformulated with each decision to either follow yet another connection or retrace steps to a previous point. Practically it is limited by the embodied ethnographer's constraints in time, space and ingenuity.

11. Along with spatial dislocation comes temporal dislocation. Engagement with mediated contexts is interspersed with interactions in other spheres and with other media. Virtual ethnography is interstitial, in that it fits into the other activities of both ethnographer and subjects. Immersion in the setting is only intermittently achieved.

13. Virtual ethnography is necessarily partial. A holistic description of any informant, location or culture is impossible to achieve. The notion of pre-existing, isolable and describable informants, locales and cultures is set aside. Our accounts can be based on ideas of strategic relevance rather than faithful representations of objective realities.

15. Virtual ethnography involves intensive engagement with mediated interaction. This kind of engagement adds a new dimension to the exploration of the use of the medium in context. The ethnographer's engagement with the medium is a valuable source of insight. Virtual ethnography can usefully draw on ethnographer as informant and embrace the reflexive dimension. The shaping of interactions with informants by the technology is part of the ethnography, as are the ethnographer's interactions with the technology.

17. New technologies of interaction make it possible both for informants to be absent and to render them present within the ethnography. In the same way, the ethnographer is both absent from and present with informants. The technology enables these relationships to be fleeting or sustained and to be carried out across temporal and spatial divides. All forms of interaction are ethnographically valid, not just the face-to-face. The shaping of the ethnographic object as it is made possible by the available technologies is the ethnography. This is ethnography *in*, *of* and *through* the virtual.

19. Virtual ethnography is not only virtual in the sense of being disembodied. Virtuality also carries a connotation of 'not quite', adequate for practical purposes even if not strictly the real thing (although this definition of virtuality is often suppressed in favour of its trendier alternative). Virtual ethnography is adequate for the practical purpose of exploring the relations of mediated interaction, even if not quite the real thing in methodologically purist terms. It is an adaptive ethnography which sets out to suit itself to the conditions in which it finds itself.

Principles 1 to 9 should follow fairly self-evidently from the discussions of this chapter and the previous one, and follow on from some of the main currents in ethnographic thinking discussed in those chapters. Principle 10, however, probably needs further explanation. Ethnography always has been adaptive to the conditions in which it finds itself. This may help to explain the traditional reluctance of ethnographers to give advice to those about to start fieldwork. There are no sets of rules to follow in order to conduct the perfect ethnography, and defining the fundamental components of the ethnographic approach is unhelpful. The focus of ethnography on dwelling within a culture demands adaptation and the possibility of overturning prior assumptions. In virtual ethnography the adaptation of methodology to circumstance raises the issues which principles 1 to 9 address.

There seems to be a contradiction here. If we adhere to principle 10 then it would seem that we undermine the other nine principles, since to be adaptive and adequate to the purpose would seem to make adherence to principles in itself problematic. There is a temporal shift here. Most readers of ethnography will recognize the written product of an ethnography as being an after-the-event construction, the product of an overlapping but largely linear process of planning, data collection, analysis and writing. The written product rarely reflects this sequence of events, and methodological considerations which arose during the data collection phase may be presented as preceding and even justifying the decisions which gave rise to them. This text is no different in the liberties it takes with the temporal sequence. The methodological principles detailed here arose through the conduct of the ethnography itself, as it became clear what an adaptive ethnography might look like in the context of the Internet. In this sense principle 10, although it is presented last, is the fundamental principle which underlies the rest and makes them possible. Adapting and interrogating ethnography keeps it alive, contextual and relevant. After all, if we are happy enough that technologies are appropriated and interpreted differently in different contexts, why should we not be happy for ethnography to be similarly sensitive to its contexts of use? It is no more a sacred and unchanging text than the technologies which it is used to study. In the following chapter I describe the ethnographic project which forms the basis for this book. In describing the case, I will also attempt to retrieve some of the decisions which gave rise to the methodological principles listed above.

References

Abu-Lughod, L. 1997 The interpretation of culture(s) after television. *Representations* 59: 109–134.

Ang, I. 1996 *Living Room Wars: Rethinking Media Audiences for a Postmodern World.* London: Routledge.

Appadurai, A. 1996 *Modernity at Large: Cultural Dimensions of Globalization.* Minneapolis: University of Minnesota Press.

Atkinson, P. 1990 *The Ethnographic Imagination: Textual Constructions of Reality.* London: Routledge.

Baym, N.K. 1995c The performance of humour in computer-mediated communication. *Journal of Computer Mediated Communication* 1(2). http://shum.huji.ac.il/jcmc/vol1/issue2/baym.html.

Berger, P.L. and Luckman, T. 1971 *The Social Construction of Reality: a Treatise in the Sociology of Knowledge*. London: Allen Lane.

Bijker, W.E. 1995 *Of Bicycles, Bakelite and Bulbs: Towards a Theory of Socio-technical Change.* Cambridge, MA: MIT Press.

Burnett, R. 1996 A torn page, ghosts on the computer screen, words, images, labyrinths: exploring the frontiers of cyberspace. In G.E. Marcus (ed.) *Connected: Engagements with Media*. Chicago: University of Chicago Press. pp. 67–98.

Castells, M. 1996a *The Rise of the Network Society*. Cambridge, MA: Blackwell.

Castells, M. 1996b The net and the self: working notes for a critical theory of the informational society. *Critique of Anthropology* 16(1): 9–38.

Castells, M. 1997 *The Power of Identity*. Cambridge, MA: Blackwell.

Clifford, J. 1992 Travelling cultures. In L. Grossberg, C. Nelson and P.A. Treichler (eds) *Cultural Studies*. London: Routledge. pp. 96–116.

Clifford, J. and Marcus, G.E. 1986 *Writing Culture: the Poetics and Politics of Ethnography.* Berkeley, CA: University of California.

Cooper, G., Hine, C., Rachel, J. and Woolgar, S. 1995 Ethnography and human–computer interaction. In P. Thomas (ed.) *Social and Interactional Dimensions of Human–Computer Interfaces*. Cambridge: Cambridge University Press. pp. 11–36.

Correll, S. 1995 The ethnography of an electronic bar: the Lesbian Cafe. *Journal of Contemporary Ethnography* 24(3): 270–298.

Denzin, N.K. 1997 *Interpretive Ethnography: Ethnographic Practices for the 21st Century.* Thousand Oaks, CA: Sage.

Dicks, B. and Mason, B. 1998 Hypermedia and ethnography: reflections on the construction of a research approach. *Sociological Research Online* 3(3). http://www.socresonline.org.uk/socresonline/3/3/3.html.

Featherstone, M. 1995 *Undoing Culture: Globalization, Postmodernism and Identity.* London: Sage.

Ferguson, J. 1997 Paradoxes of sovereignty and independence: 'real' and 'pseudo' nation-states and the depoliticization of poverty. In K.F. Olwig and K. Hastrup (eds) *Siting Culture: the Shifting Anthropological Object.* London: Routledge. pp. 123–141.

Franklin, S. 1995 Science as culture, cultures of science. *Annual Review of Anthropology* 24: 163–184.

Freeman, D. 1996 *Margaret Mead and the Heretic.* Ringwood, Victoria, Australia: Penguin.

Friedman, J. 1997 Simplifying complexity: assimilating the global in a small paradise. In K.F. Olwig and K. Hastrup (eds) *Siting Culture: the Shifting Anthropological Object.* London: Routledge. pp. 268–291.

Geertz, C. 1993 *The Interpretation of Cultures* (1973). London: Fontana.

Gubrium, J. and Holstein, J. 1987 The private image: experiential location and method in family studies. *Journal of Marriage and the Family* 49: 773–786.

Gupta, A. and Ferguson, J. 1992 Beyond 'culture': space, identity and the politics of difference. *Cultural Anthropology* 7(1): 6–23.

Hammersley, M. 1990 What's wrong with ethnography? The myth of theoretical description. *Sociology* 24(4): 597–615.

Hammersley, M. and Atkinson, P. 1995 *Ethnography: Principles in Practice.* 2nd edition. London: Routledge.

Hastrup, K. and Olwig, K.F. 1997 Introduction. In K.F. Olwig and K. Hastrup (eds) *Siting Culture: the Shifting Anthropological Object.* London: Routledge. pp. 1–14.

Heath, D. 1998 Locating genetic knowledge: picturing Marfan Syndrome and its travelling constituencies. *Science, Technology and Human Values* 23(1): 71–97.

Hirsch, E. 1998 Bound and unbound entities: reflections on the ethnographic perspectives of anthropology *vis-à-vis* media and cultural studies. In F. Hughes-Freeland (ed.) *Ritual, Performance, Media.* London: Routledge. pp. 208–228.

Jackson, A. (ed.) 1987 *Anthropology at Home.* London: Tavistock.

Knorr-Cetina, K.D. 1992 The couch, the cathedral and the laboratory: on the relationship between experiment and laboratory in science. In A. Pickering (ed.) *Science as Practice and Culture.* Chicago: University of Chicago Press. pp. 113–138.

Kuper, A. 1983 *Anthropology and Anthropologists: the Modern British School.* London: Routledge and Kegan Paul.

Low, J. and Woolgar, S. 1993 Managing the social–technical divide: some aspects of the discursive structure of information systems development. In P. Quintas (ed.) *Social Dimensions of Systems Engineering: People, Processes, Policies and Software Development.* New York: Ellis Horwood. pp. 34–59.

McBeth, S. 1993. Myths of objectivity and the collaborative process in life history research. In C. Brettell (ed.) *When They Read What We Write: the Politics of Ethnography.* Westport, CT: Bergin and Garvey. pp. 145–162.

Marcus, G.E. 1995 Ethnography in/of the world system: the emergence of multi-sited ethnography. *Annual Review of Anthropology* 24: 95–117.

Marcus, G.E. and Cushman, D. 1982. Ethnographies as texts. *Annual Review of Anthropology* 11: 25–69.

Martin, E. 1994 *Flexible Bodies: the Role of Immunity in American Culture from the Days of Polio to the Age of AIDS.* Boston: Beacon.

Mead, M. 1943 *Coming of Age in Samoa: a Study of Adolescence and Sex in Primitive Societies.* Harmondsworth: Penguin.

Meyrowitz, J. 1985 *No Sense of Place: the Impact of Electronic Media on Social Behavior.* New York: Oxford University Press.

Moerman, M. 1974 Accomplishing ethnicity. In R. Turner (ed.) *Ethnomethodology: Selected Readings.* Harmondsworth: Penguin. pp. 54–68.

Moores, S. 1993 *Interpreting Audiences: the Ethnography of Media Consumption.* London: Sage.

Olwig, K.F. and Hastrup, K. (eds) 1997 *Siting Culture: the Shifting Anthropological Object.* London: Routledge.

Potter, J. 1996 *Representing Reality: Discourse, Rhetoric and Social Construction.* London: Sage.

Potter, J. and Wetherell, M. 1987 *Discourse and Social Psychology: Beyond Attitudes and Behaviour.* London: Sage.

Pratt, M.L. 1986 Fieldwork in common places. In J. Clifford and G.E. Marcus (eds) *Writing Culture: the Poetics and Politics of Ethnography.* Berkeley, CA: University of California Press. pp. 27–50.

Radway, J. 1988 Reception study: ethnography and the problems of dispersed audiences and nomadic subjects. *Cultural Studies* 2(3): 359–376.

Rosaldo, R. 1989 *Culture and Truth: the Remaking of Social Analysis.* Boston: Beacon.

Silverman, D. 1993 *Interpreting Text and Data: Methods for Analysing Talk, Text and Interaction.* London: Sage.

Slack, R.S. 1998 On the potentialities and problems of a WWW based naturalistic sociology. *Sociological Research Online* 3(2). http://www.socresonline.org.uk/socresonline/3/2/3.html.

Stanley, L. 1990 Doing ethnography, writing ethnography: a comment on Hammersley. *Sociology* 24(4): 617–627.

Strathern, M. 1996 Cutting the Network. *Journal of the Royal Anthropological Institute* 2: 517–535.

Swales, J.M. 1998 *Other Floors, Other Voices: a Textography of a Small University Building.* Mahwah, NJ: Lawrence Erlbaum.

Thompson, J.B. 1995 *The Media and Modernity: a Social Theory of the Media*. Cambridge: Polity.

Thornton, R.J. 1988 The rhetoric of ethnographic holism. *Cultural Anthropology* 3(3): 285–303.

Thrift, N. 1996a *Spatial Formations*. London: Sage.

Traweek, S. 1992 Border crossings: narrative strategies in science studies and among physicists in Tsukuba Science City, Japan. In A. Pickering (ed.) *Science as Practice and Culture*. Chicago: University of Chicago Press. pp. 429–465.

Turner, R. 1989 Deconstructing 'the field'. In J. Gubrium and D. Silverman (eds) *The Politics of Field Research: Sociology beyond Enlightenment*. London: Sage. pp. 13–29.

Turner, S. 1980 *Sociological Explanation as Translation*. Cambridge: Cambridge University Press.

Van Maanen, J. 1988 *Tales of the Field: on Writing Ethnography*. Chicago: University of Chicago Press.

Van Maanen, J. 1995 An end to innocence: the ethnography of ethnography. In J. Van Maanen (ed.) *Representation in Ethnography*. Thousand Oaks, CA: Sage. pp. 1–35.

Walkerdine, V. 1986 Video replay: families, films and fantasy. In V. Burgin, J. Donald and C. Kaplan (eds) *Formations of Fantasy*. London: Methuen.

Walkerdine, V. 1990 *Schoolgirl Fictions*. London: Verso.

Wolf, M. 1992 *A Thrice-Told Tale: Feminism, Postmodernism and Ethnographic Responsibility*. Stanford, CA: Stanford University Press.

Woolgar, S. 1991b Reflexivity is the ethnographer of the text. In S. Woolgar (ed.) *Knowledge and Reflexivity: New Frontiers in the Sociology of Knowledge*. London: Sage.

61

Kin-to-Be: Betrothal, Legal Documents, and Reconfiguring Relational Obligations in Egypt
Christine Hegel-Cantarella

In 2005, a nurse in Port Said, Egypt filed a police report claiming that the father of her daughter's fiancé had stolen 10,000 Egyptian Pounds from her. In the police report it was noted that she had entrusted him this sum of money to deliver to a third party; it was also noted that the claimant had in her possession a signed receipt verifying that he had received the money from her. After getting her claim on record at the police station, the nurse hired a lawyer to represent her as a plaintiff in a criminal breach of trust case against the man. However, several months after the police report was filed the defendant's son married the complainant's daughter, the criminal breach of trust case was eventually dropped and the father of the groom was never prosecuted.

Although the nurse's complaint apparently revolved around a sum of money that went missing, in fact her complaint was meant to pressure the son of the accused to fulfill his promise to marry her daughter, to whom he was engaged. Among Egyptian Muslims, engagement is a necessary preliminary step toward a valid marriage and may be broken with few if any legal consequences. But as my work shows, Egyptians sometimes bolster the tenuous social commitment and liminality of betrothal by creating legal consequences for breaking off the engagement through a collateral obligation.

Source: *Law, Culture and the Humanities*, 7(3) (2011): 377–393.

This article considers circumstances that can undercut doctrinally stipulated mutual legitimate consent in contracting a marriage. Unlike some analyses of marriage and gender in the Middle East, it does not debate issues of arranged or companionate marriage, pre-marital negotiations related to *mahr* (dower) and reciprocal rights and duties in marriage, or the age or conditions of women's consent to marry per se.[1] Rather, it shifts the focus to male consent and considers the practice of requiring men to guarantee a proposal of marriage. In contemporary Port Said and across Egypt it is sometimes the case, typically among the poor or lower-middle class, that families of young women who receive an offer of marriage will insist that her fiancé sign a commercial document like a post-dated check or, as I will discuss, a trust receipt. This document is intended to ensure that he will attend to the wedding preparations in good faith by purchasing the domestic items he has pledged and saving money to cover associated expenses, and that he will not rescind his marriage proposal without cause.

I take as a starting point a recent legal case from Port Said, Egypt that originated in a young woman's accusation of rape against her fiancé. Besides the issues of coping and recovering from an incident of violence against the young woman, the family was preoccupied by the concern that the fiancé would not follow through on his marriage proposal. The rape allegation and the interfamilial crisis it generated bring the complex interplay between legal documents and social relations into sharper relief. In particular, the case points to some of the specific social and legal tensions inherent in betrothal in Egypt. On the one hand, betrothal brings unmarried men and women into a more intimate proximity to one another, sometimes for many years, without guaranteeing that they will marry. This poses particular social hazards for women, who, scholars have noted bear a greater responsibility for upholding family honor and a thus are more vulnerable to accusations of immoral or illicit behavior.[2] On the other hand, betrothal is legally a liminal state that does not afford couples new rights vis-à-vis one another. Betrothals are broken with regularity in Egypt as one or both parties decide not to go forward with the marriage for any number of reasons. In rare cases, damages may be awarded in a civil suit if adjudicants can prove harm resulting from a broken betrothal.

The specific risks betrothal poses for women and the steps they take to protect themselves can be further contextualized through a consideration of women's citizenship rights in Egypt and in the Middle East and North Africa more generally. Although the Egyptian constitution recognizes full equality between men and women and legal personhood independent of family units, in practice, women's rights are embedded in family and community networks rather than independently derived. Despite twentieth-century legal reforms aimed at expanding women's political and personal status rights, the patriarchal construction of family life was not recast. As such, women's citizenship is constrained through both formal and informal channels, in the way that state policies assess and serve the needs of women and in the ways that officials and members of the family and the community, including women themselves, narrow the scope of women's rights.

One important modality through which women concede or claim rights is through legal action. Annelies Moors, in writing about Islamic Family Law in the Arab world, cogently observes that the examination of both legal texts and litigation practices is critical because the two often do not correspond. Further, ". . . women's legal claims may not coincide with what they expect to gain when they turn to court."[3] Legal documents may aid in achieving aims that seem to run counter to their apparent purpose; for instance, a petition for unpaid maintenance may actually be used to pressure a husband into a desired divorce, or an action to retain custody of minors may be used to induce a spouse to give up rights to or increase custodial support payments. These indirect legal strategies put unwelcome pressure on another party in order to bring about a desired outcome.

I argue that legal documents can be used to initiate alternate and parallel legal processes that allow litigants to redirect law's gaze. Ethnographic data on the legal and informal strategies Port Saidians use to guarantee marriage proposals, considered in relation to both legal and social contexts, offers insight into how locals draw on the force of law to increase the likelihood of achieving social outcomes. Port Saidians describe this redirection of law's force as a way of putting pressure (*daght*) on another party; it can also be seen as a way of leveraging outcomes that are traditionally non-enforceable according to the law. The ubiquitous use of commercial documents like trust receipts as surety contradicts the spirit of the law designating betrothal as mutually and freely revocable. For women in particular, trust receipts serve an important function by virtue of their status as commercial documents for which Egyptian commercial law provides criminal misdemeanor charges for breach. They shift the game of marriage negotiations out of the realm of civil and family law and into the realm of criminal law, and in so doing counter the individualizing effect of law that can promote male autonomy.

Through an examination of surety practices and betrothal in Port Said, my broader aim is to respond to Moors' challenge to investigate how specific genres of legal writing interact with social relations.[4] At the center of my discussion are three documents – a police report, a trust receipt, and a marriage contract. As documents, they each belong to particular bureaucratic regimes and are associated with different branches of Egyptian law: criminal, commercial, and family law. A Weberian analysis might emphasize the ways in which these documentary technologies structure knowledge, organize behavior, and routinize interactions. However, recent ethnographic work on documents and documentation practices complicates this type of analysis by calling into question assumptions about how documents constitute forms of subjectivity and knowledge.[5] While institutional artifacts like forms, charts, and reports structure knowledge and practice according to a bureaucratic logic, these artifacts are not entirely depersonalized. The meanings of such documents are shaped by practices and understandings outside the institution, and legal documents are integral to the constitution of the self both legally and personally.[6] They are also integral to forging new forms of legal relationality (plaintiff and defendant, agent and intermediary, husband and wife) that, as I show, can transmogrify interpersonal relationships and upend existing power dynamics.

The understanding that documents produce categories of persons and activities has been enhanced by Foucauldian analyses of constitutive power regimes. For sociolegal scholars Baudouin Dupret and Jean Noel Ferrie it is in specific moments of collaborative production that new meanings and new forms of subjectivity take shape.[7] Through interactive inscription practices such as the filing of police reports claimants ascribe moral and legal categories to their own and others' actions. An ethnomethodological approach reminds us that documents are not merely repositories that organize information according to pre-existing bureaucratic norms but are artifacts wrought through practices that constitute norms. The documents I discuss in this article had already come into being at the time I learned of their existence. Thus, I am concerned with their role in transactions related to the allegation of rape, betrothal and marriage and the way they beget one another rather than with their production as specific interactions. Attention to these documents as technologies that evoke law and redirect law's gaze, rather than analyzing their content per se, reflects the way documents can generate outcomes not contingent upon the information they contain. Moreover, analysis of how litigants, and female litigants in particular, deploy documentary technologies provides insight into how legal subjects both protect their interests and reproduce gendered inequalities.

Ethnographic material from Port Said, Egypt forms the core of this analysis and I draw upon data gathered from interviews and observations of lawyers, clients, court clerks, traders and others throughout 2005 and during two return visits to Port Said in 2007. Port Said (approx. pop. 520,000) borders the Suez Canal and the Mediterranean Sea and as is typical of port cities the local economy was historically reliant on trade and ship provisioning. In 1974, following the end of the war with Israel and the re-opening of the canal, Port Said was granted Duty Free status as one of the first initiatives of President Sadat's Open Door (*infitah*) policies. Its role in the importation and sale of quality foreign goods swelled, the economy thrived and the population expanded. Old local networks and ways of doing business were altered by the presence of new immigrants from the delta region and Upper Egypt who had come to stake their fortunes in trade. Despite recent significant reductions in free zone privileges in the commercial sector and a declining local economy, the majority of Port Saidians continue to stake their future in retail trading and the service industry.[8]

The influx of large numbers of Egyptians from across the country into Port Said throughout the last quarter of the 20th century not only reshaped local trade and business practices but may also have affected the marriage market. Locals pointed out that because so many inhabitants have shallow roots in Port Said families do not necessarily share expectations when it came to marriage. The use of surety technologies between kin-to-be are interpreted as a mechanism by which people alleviate the tenuousness and lack of trust between the families of the betrothed related to new migration flows into the city since the mid-1970s. Despite local perceptions that anxiety surrounding betrothal has intensified due to increased heterogeneity in Port Said, anecdotal and scholarly accounts of betrothal and marriage contract negotiations in Cairo and elsewhere in Egypt (c.f. Hoodfar 1997; Rugh 1984; Sherif 1999) strongly suggest that the tension and conflict associated with the engagement period are a more generalized phenomenon.

I. Broken Betrothal: Noha's Case[9]

The following case, which began in 2004, was recounted to me by a divorced nurse of modest means named Noha in her lawyer's office in Port Said one evening.[10] Noha's then 16-year-old daughter, Randa, became engaged to a young man named Amr and according to Noha the engagement was good. Amr was a school friend of her son's and would often visit them at home and share meals with them. Some months into the engagement, Noha had to travel to Mansoura to stay with a terminally ill family member and while she was away Noha learned from Randa that her fiancé Amr had raped her. Moreover, Amr had taken her to a doctor who performed an illegal abortion. When Noha returned to Port Said she attempted to track down Amr with the intention of convincing him to marry and then divorce Randa. Amr, however, had gone into hiding and could not be found so mother and daughter went to the police station. There Noha filed a report stating that her daughter had been raped, naming Amr as the perpetrator, after which Amr was quickly arrested and brought down to the station. As Noha describes it, the police initially sought to resolve the situation *bishakl wadī* (in a friendly way): "As is usual, they tried to make a friendly solution. They told him he should make the marriage contract now, and the wedding party, and be done with it. He refused to do this. So they put him in jail."[11]

Amr stayed in jail for four days, at which point his father came to Noha and pleaded with her to drop the case against his son. She agreed to do so only on condition that he sign a trust receipt (*iysāl amāna*) for 10,000 Egyptian Pounds (about 1,800 U.S. dollars) to guarantee that Amr would marry her daughter. Her daughter, she argued, was "no longer a girl but a woman," and Noha wanted to have absolute certainty that Amr would follow through on the marriage. Amr's father agreed, a trust receipt was drawn up, signed and notarized at the court.[12]

After Amr's father signed the trust receipt, Noha had the rape charges against Amr dropped. Following his release Amr again refused to marry Randa. In a response, Noha reported Amr's father to the police for defrauding her of 10,000 pounds and hired Noor, a well-respected female lawyer, to raise a suit against him. The lawsuit was a breach of trust case using the trust receipt and charging that he failed to deliver 10,000 pounds as stipulated in the document. Noha pointed out that "because of this pressure (*daght*), his son finally agreed to sign the marriage contract with my daughter and they were married."

Scholars have addressed the evolution of rape in Egypt from a crime that could be rectified through *diya* payment to the woman's family and absolved through marriage of the rapist to the victim to its criminal penalization.[13] As of 1993 rape could result in a lengthy prison sentence and even the death penalty for the perpetrator, although Sonbol points out that "In Egypt, in most cases involving the rape of a virgin, the police automatically offer her the option of marrying her rapist, and if she agrees, they make sure that he complies with his obligations, that he pays her the dowry of her equal, and that he treats her as a 'good husband' should."[14] Although it is impossible to know what actually occurred between Amr and Randa, Noha and Randa's willingness to file a police report against Amr rather than keep the matter private reflects the statistical increase in reporting rape and sexual violence against women to the police in Egypt.[15] Moreover, the police took the women's allegation seriously and put Amr under investigation. This initiated the documenting of the alleged crime in a police report, and this report later served as an important artifact in altering the power structure between the parties and indirectly pressured Amr into fulfilling his promise of marriage to Randa. In addition to the police report and the marriage contract a third document was in play: the trust receipt that Noha procured from Amr's father. In order to better understand the interplay between these various legal documents some points must be made regarding trust receipts.

The Egyptian Trade Law (1999) outlines the provisions for commercial papers, including promissory notes, checks, trust receipts, and others. A trust receipt is similar to a bill of exchange and is designed to provide surety for a transfer of assets between three parties in which money or goods moves from person A (the agent) to person C (the recipient) via person B (the agent's intermediary). Such transfers are relatively common in Egypt where the majority of quotidian transactions are conducted with cash rather than through checks, credit cards, or bank transfers. There are many varieties of these receipts sold in stationery stores in Port Said and throughout Egypt, each with a slight variation in the wording of the document and the information requested. In addition, some booklets include a receipt stub that can be filled out to record the names and addresses of each of the three parties to the receipt. The following is a translation of the text of one version:

Trust Receipt

I (space for B's name), residence (space for address), ID card number (space for number), governorate (space for governorate) have received from Mr. (space for A's name and residence) the amount (space for sum) and no more. And therefore with all trust I will convey it and surrender the amount to Mr. (space for C's name and residence). If I do not surrender this amount it will be considered squandered and to be a breach of trust and carries a misdemeanor with it. The one who admits to what is in the receipt (space for B's signature). And this receipt from me is notification of surrender.[16]

Failure to deliver means that the intermediary (B) can be accused of breach of trust (*khiyānah al-amāna*), charged with, and found guilty of a criminal misdemeanor. It is therefore a commercial document that carries the potential of a prison sentence of up to three years for non-delivery, at the discretion of the three-judge panel that presides over such cases in the primary courts. In addition to the criminal misdemeanor case the plaintiff can also raise a civil case for compensation. As such, the potential of criminal prosecution upon failure to deliver monies as stipulated in a trust receipt means that there are similarities to prosecution for "bouncing" a check. One important difference between using post-dated checks and trust receipts is that the former pose a risk to the debtor's assets, which can be procured upon presentation of the check unless the funds have been withdrawn. Trust receipts don't transform personal assets or private property into collateral. Rather, they transform the body into collateral; the body is staked as surety through the threat of incarceration.

Noha's case is typical in the use of trust receipts for purposes unrelated to guaranteeing delivery of monies through an intermediary. Instead, they are used as leverage for a variety of promises by introducing the threat of prosecution in the context of contested claims. Technically this is achieved by having the claimant (i.e. the father, or in Noha's case, the mother, of the bride) sign the receipt as party A (the agent) and the one upon whom an obligation rests (the fiancé) sign as party B (the intermediary); party C is typically inconsequential as a resulting legal case will involve only the agent and the intermediary. Importantly, their use as leverage is largely constituted rhetorically; in most cases the document is never used to file a misdemeanor charge but merely represents the potential to do so.

Trust receipts are used "out of context" to secure store credit and myriad other transactional forms in Egypt, although we shall focus here on their use in the contexts of betrothal and marriage. For instance, Zulficar observes that trust receipts are used to guarantee the list (*qayma*) of a wife's furnishings and belongings.[17] Since the standardization of the Egyptian marriage contract it has played a reduced role in restoring gender balance and the protection of a wife's rights. As a result, it has become very common among lower- and middle-class Egyptian families to document the items that a wife (and her family) brings to the marriage so that they can be restored to her in case of divorce. When the list is written, the husband signs a trust receipt (or post-dated check) that is kept by the wife's family. If he fails to fulfill his obligations or divorces her with no cause he must deliver all the items on the list to her, or their monetary value, or will be taken to court for breach of trust using the trust receipt.[18]

Nathan Brown provides an example of this practice from his research on popular uses of the courts in Egypt:

> She [the prospective bride] therefore insisted that he [the prospective groom] write her a check for the value of the household furnishings he had pledged to provide. (In Egypt checks are often used not to exchange money but as guarantees of good faith, or they are postdated and used as promissory notes). He agreed, but when the engagement finally collapsed he withdrew the money from the bank account. She then took the matter to the police, because writing a check without sufficient funds is a criminal offense punishable by a jail sentence. Her family then used the criminal case to increase their bargaining power.[19]

Brown's data illustrates how the post-dated check is used to achieve multiple purposes simultaneously: to guarantee that the marriage will take place, and if it does, to guarantee fulfillment of the terms of the marriage contract, and to guarantee the list (of household furnishings) in anticipation of a potential divorce.

According to lawyers in Port Said, and based on my interviews with locals, trust receipts and post-dated checks may also be composed later in the course of a marriage in order to resolve ongoing disputes over issues like a husband's failure to pay contractually obligated maintenance. Rather than take the dispute to court, or as a measure to drop a case previously raised in the family courts, couples may opt to informally negotiate a solution and the responsible party (usually the husband) will sign a trust receipt as surety. Although women and men take their problems to the family courts in great numbers, informal dispute resolution along these lines often resolves issues more expediently as the courts are notoriously backlogged and inefficient. Salma, a local lawyer who primarily handles family law cases, noted:

> Such cases happen a lot. What happens is when there are many problems between the two people in court we try to finish the whole thing in a friendly way (*bishakl wadī*). In order for the wife to let go of the cases she's raised against him, he must do something to guarantee her rights. This guarantee could be a blank trust receipt or a check so that if he does not fulfill his duties she can sue him again. Despite the fact that the

woman could take her rights through the court, they prefer to solve it in a friendly way for the sake of the children. However, there must be this kind of guarantee just to ensure her rights.

The trust receipt can thus be used to guarantee the terms of the marriage contract in lieu of other ways of guaranteeing its terms.[20]

Husbands may also obtain trust receipts under false pretenses to stymie a wife's claims to various types of contractually stipulated marital and post-marital maintenance. Tarek, a social worker in the Port Said family court mediation offices, noted that he witnesses this phenomenon with some frequency. He has seen a number of cases where young women and new brides in particular are deceived into signing trust receipts, mislead by their husbands into believing that they are for some other purpose or insignificant. This is, in fact, what happened following Randa's marriage to Amr. Soon after the wedding Amr and his father convinced Randa to sign a number of blank trust receipts and checks by suggesting they were for some other purpose. In Noha's view, they "charmed her into doing it," and "she was too naïve" to understand their potential uses against her. Amr divorced Randa, who soon thereafter gave birth to a child, and he subsequently raised a number of actions in court against her using the trust receipts. Again, according to Noha, this was done in order to pressure her into giving up her right to child support (*nafaqa HaDāna*) for their son. As the social worker Tarek pointed out, husbands use the receipts as leverage to prevent a woman from filing a case against them later.

Trust receipts are increasingly used instead of, or alongside, post-dated checks in Port Said, but both of these devices serve the same purpose: to put pressure on the fiancé to fulfill verbal agreements and contracts. What might surety practices indicate about betrothal in Egypt and its particular social and legal perils?

II. Betrothal, Sexual Intimacy, and Women's Citizenship

Among Egyptian Muslims, marriage is a contractual relationship. The marriage contract is based on Islamic principles and legal doctrine and connotes permanence, requires mutual legitimate consent and acceptance, and allows for the stipulation of special conditions by either party. As of 1931, Islamic marriage contracts in Egypt have been standardized and state-issued. The marriage contract has gone through a number of revisions, primarily due to the efforts of advocates for women's rights, and now includes a section for "special conditions" in which the parties may list any stipulations that do not contradict Islamic principles. However, as Zulficar observes, the marriage contract has become more like a registration certificate and lost its contractual features as the terms under negotiation are largely the dower.[21]

The protracted discussions between the families that characterize the nego-tiation of marriage contracts are therefore focused on financial concerns with varying degrees of attention to the necessary conditions for a companionate and stable marriage. Marriage negotiations are the process by which the par-ties reach a mutual agreement about the terms of the contract in order for the bride and groom to contract willingly and of their own accord. Offer and acceptance in contracting, including the contracting of marriages, generally requires that parties are of sound mind and legal majority, and contract willingly and of their own accord. At the same time, these negotiations and their outcomes reflect changing ideas in Egyptian society about the qualities of a modern family.[22]

Egyptian family law specifically addresses the importance of an engage-ment period prior to marriage as necessary in order to ensure that the mar-riage is contracted faithfully and with good knowledge of the other party. Unlike betrothal for many non-Muslims in Europe and the U.S., betrothal in Egypt typically marks the beginning of a relationship rather than the culmin-ation of months or years of dating, and couples become acquainted under the watchful eyes of family members. This is less so for kin marriages between cousins and even non-kin couples may have spent time together at work or school. Among Egyptian Muslims, betrothal (*khutba*) is the first step in a series of publicly observed stages of marriage. It is formalized by the read-ing of the first *sura* of the Quran (*al-fatiha*) and by the giving of gifts of gold to the female (*shabka*). Following this, sometimes years later, is the signing of the marriage contract (*katb al-kitāb*), the wedding celebration (*al-farah*), and "the entry," or the first night of cohabitation and presumed consumma-tion of the marriage (*al-dukhla*). It is only upon the conclusion of all of these stages in this order that a marriage is both legally and socially sanctioned.

Engagement is an approved social space for couples to get to know one another prior to marriage, yet it is also a confession of desired intimacy not yet licit. Anxiety about what engagement allows and prohibits is exacerbated by the long term of many engagements. Within the last two decades it has become typical for couples to remain engaged for a year or more, and some-times for many years, while the groom, the bride, and their families earn and save money to procure an apartment, renovate and furnish it, purchase the trousseau, and prepare for the wedding festivities. According to statistical data from 1999, the average cost of marriage equals eleven times the annual house-hold expenditure per capita. This suggests that families must save for years to afford a marriage (particularly if they have a son, as males are responsible for the majority of these expenses), and thus that marriage preparations are protracted in direct relation to the economic burden they represent.[23]

Although the economics of marriage typically necessitate a long engage-ment period, some Muslim couples in Egypt subvert this pattern by privately conducting common-law or customary (*'urfi*) marriages. The 1990s saw a rise in *'urfi* marriages among young college students who sought to have a (legal) sexual relationship with one another while simultaneously avoiding the inter-family negotiations and protracted formal engagement period of a formally registered marriage.[24] The presence of 'urfi marriages alongside registered marriages points to the importance for Muslim Egyptians of limiting sexuality to the domain of marriage.[25]

Female sexuality outside of marriage is perceived as having greater con-sequences for the family (MacLeod, 1991; Rugh, 1984) and in Islamic thought women bear the primary responsibility for maintaining the sanctity of male-female relations.[26] Muslim jurists argue for gender segregation, pointing out that "interactions between women and men who are unrelated by immediate kin ties (ghair maharim) are a potential source of unvirtuous conduct and illicit relationships."[27] Mahmood notes that modesty practices, including veiling and averting eyes, are practical strategies to deter the danger of women's sex-uality to the sanctity of the Muslim community.[28] Even though men and women now have more opportunities to mix publicly than in the past, unsupervised interaction between unmarried men and women is normatively conceived as sexual and sends a message that a woman doesn't have (good morals akhlaq), threatening her chances of finding a suitable husband.[29] Ethnographic data from a 1984 study of family in Egypt emphasizes the particular consequences for females: "As one (Egyptian) mother noted: 'If this young man doesn't marry her nobody else will if they think he has even so much as kissed her.'"[30] As such, guardianship of female sexuality is intimately related to the consideration of marriage prospects. Marriage prospects diminish more quickly for women as they age so families want to ensure that years of marriage preparations don't result in a broken betrothal.[31] The breaking of an engagement means starting anew to identify a suitable mate for one's daughter and another long and poten-tially morally hazardous engagement period, further delaying marriage and motherhood.

The particular perils of betrothal for women are inextricable from the broader context of women's citizenship rights in the Middle East. As Slymovics and Joseph argue, women in the Middle East and North Africa are expected to view their interests as linked to those of male kin.[32] The mythology of the "kin contract" is that women can rely upon their male family members, and especially upon their brothers, to support and care for them. In contrast to conceptions of Western individual autonomy, the connectivity of family in the Arab world is perceived as highly functional and as enabling people to thrive.[33] At the same time, there is no associational arena not permeated by the idiom of kin and family relations, and rights and entitlements are mediated via membership in these networks. Moreover, kin networks are animated by a hierarchical patriarchal logic.[34] One manifestation of this can be seen in how women claim or give up rights to property. Although legally women retain control over their dower and over any income they bring in to the household through paid labor and inherited property, kin networks may impel them to concede property rights to male family members. As Moors observed in Palestine, women rarely turned to the courts to claim their prompt dower or to claim inherited property.[35] By giving up these rights, they sought to strengthen moral and affective ties with their husbands and with brothers, who would retain control of their sisters' property shares, and so reinforced their kin's obligations toward them. Although filial connectivity is perceived as important for women's support and protection, the imperative to marry is strong. Legal reform in the 20th century has strengthened conjugal ties and husbands have replaced other kin relations as the primary source of economic and political security for women.[36]

The patriarchal structure of families is both reflected in and supported by the state, and women's citizenship is shaped by gendered state policies and their implementation. Sociologist Iman Bibars points out that although the Egyptian constitution articulates equal citizenship regardless of gender, race, age, or religion, aspects of the personal status laws, the Penal Code, and the nationality law reduce women's citizenship rights.[37] Moreover, social welfare policies impact women's status and autonomy by making needs assessments that undervalue women and female-headed households and using marital status as a measure in determining access to state resources. Bibars demonstrates this in her analysis of divorced and abandoned women who seek access to social welfare services. State employees charged with delivering services routinely refuse aid to clients based on moral valuations such as the perception that such women are destitute because they failed in their duties as wives. As such, Egyptian state institutions sometimes fall short in providing a safety net for women who fall outside of the family ideal or whose husband or other male kin don't fulfill legal or social obligations to maintain them. Women's citizenship is further constrained through policies that allow women to be listed on the identity cards of male kin rather than mandate separate cards, a policy that particularly impacts poor and illiterate women who are often not aware of their right to obtain a separate card; their access to critical state resources is inhibited due to a lack of formal autonomy.[38] As such, women's citizenship is often constricted in the space between policies and their implementation.

Limitations on Egyptian women's citizenship rights and subordinate status have persisted despite twentieth-century legal reforms that aimed to improve gender equality because family relations were not recast.[39] During the reform era of the 1960s under Gamal Abdul Nasir, women's access to education and political power expanded while laws governing marriage, divorce and personal status remained untouched. As Salma Botman argues, "[w]omen's rights to full citizenship were restricted because of the patriarchal construction of family life, which determined that women had no independent status once they married and were subordinated to the personal power of the husbands."[40] Despite subsequent legal reform that has expanded women's rights of divorce and custody, the patriarchal family form underwrites women's citizenship.

In cases of alleged sexual violence against a woman in Egypt, the woman is likely to face accusations of impropriety if the allegations are made public, with implications for her future marital prospects and access to citizenship rights. The legal protections the law affords victims of rape are counterbalanced by gendered state practices. In the case from Port Said the complainant uses a combination of legal strategies that acknowledge legal protections for victims of rape yet ultimately reproduce the hypermoralization of sexual violence and the policing of the intimate sphere. As such, Noha's legal subjectivity is not only constituted by gender, religion, and socio-economic status but also by her daughter's liminal status as one betrothed.

III. Autonomy, Connectivity, and Documentary Interventions

Betrothal is perilous precisely because the expectations for propriety for the affianced, and especially for women, are strict whereas their legal rights vis-à-vis one another are weak. Rugh articulates the coexistence of fears of impropriety and weak legal rights, noting that "The [affianced] couple is considered particularly vulnerable to moral indiscretion at this time [while they are engaged], and their legal attachment is not so great that the relationship cannot be dissolved."[41] The extreme effort invested in ensuring that the affianced avoid impropriety is inextricable from the fact that the affianced have few legal rights or duties in relation to one another, and their status is primarily socially, rather than legally, constituted. As Nasir notes, betrothal is merely the prelude to the marriage contract; for the marriage contract to be valid, the betrothal period is necessary to ascertain the potential spouse's character and behavior through enquiries, investigations, consultations and the meeting of the couple in the presence of a chaperone.[42]

Therefore, in theory betrothal is entered into as a first step toward a valid marriage and may be broken with few if any legal consequences. To illustrate this, we can consider the Egyptian Court of Cassation hearing 14/12/1939, Appeal number 13, which notes that:

> Betrothal is only a preliminary step towards a marriage contract, a mere promise that is not binding on either party who are lawfully free to end it at anytime, especially as in the marriage contract the two parties must enjoy absolute liberty to enter into it, in view of its paramount importance to society, which freedom of action shall be hindered if either party is under the threat of being liable to damages.[43]

Betrothal is not a new legal status or a contractual relationship. Rather, it is legally liminal in order to ensure the liberty and free will of the parties considering entering into a marriage contract. Men and women alike must have the ability to break an engagement for any reason in order to avoid entering into a marriage that they may anticipate will be unsuitable and thus unsustainable. Betrothal is a promise, and there are limited circumstances under which there may be legal consequences for its withdrawal. The conclusion of Egyptian Court of Cassation hearing 14/12/1939, Appeal number 13, Year 9J states:

> However, if the promise to marry and the subsequent withdrawal therefrom are accompanied by other acts entirely independent thereof, of such a nature as to cause material or moral injury to one of the parties, such acts shall give rise to a lawful suit for damages against the party from whom they emanate on the ground that such acts, apart from the mere breach of the promise, shall constitute tort that requires redress.

Despite its liminal status, betrothal may provide, in part, the necessary grounds for civil redress under certain conditions. Moral or material injury in conjunction with withdrawal from the promise to wed (by either party) may constitute tort; breach of promise alone does not constitute tort.

Betrothal affords negligible legal rights to the affianced vis-à-vis one another; at the same time the marriage contract requires mutual consent of both parties. This suggests that in situations where a fiancé reneges on a proposal against the will of his betrothed, she and her family must work strategically to produce consent if they consider his actions detrimental to her reputation or marital prospects. In many instances this aim may be achieved through negotiation or mediation involving a respected member of the community. But in cases where social connections between the families are tenuous or there is a significant power imbalance that curtails the parties' willingness and incentive to negotiate, pressure must be produced in other ways.

In Noha's case, Amr went into hiding following the alleged rape, indicating his unwillingness to follow through with the marriage. Noha instigated negotiations regarding the broken betrothal by filing a police report alleging that her daughter was raped by her fiancé. To probe this further: a police report filed by a victim (or on his or her behalf) accomplishes many tasks: it makes a crime visible to the state, articulates and constrains a characterization of events to "legally relevant statements," and demands a juridical response.[44] Perhaps most importantly, a police report is officially a "procedural action" that becomes part of a textual chain that may eventually include a record of the public prosecutor's findings, memoranda and briefs produced by the defense lawyer, notes on or summaries of court sessions, the judgment and so forth. To file a police report might, in another circumstance, move the dispute irrevocably into the juridical field, whereby its resolution would henceforth be framed by legal procedure. In contrast, Noha's case illustrates a way in which the police report reinvigorates external negotiations and effectively returns the dispute, at least temporarily, to a non-juridical milieu. To consider this in terms of a document's "career," those administrative processes through which it moves, as Harper proposes, the career of this police report is cut short.[45] Yet its momentary existence is productive, giving Noha leverage by marshalling state power. She subsequently exchanges prosecutorial remedy for a surety device, the trust receipt.

In contrast to the police report, the trust receipt does not constrain indeterminacy by articulating the "facts" cohesively. Although described by interlocutors as a document that puts pressure (*daght*) on someone, the trust receipt, like a post-dated check, does something more specific. First, the trust receipt creates a legal fiction. The promise to marry is transformed into a commercial transaction, masking the real subject of the transaction or agreement, by which the trust receipt performs an "as-if" act. Annelise Riles, in her analysis of legal fictions, collateral expertise and financial markets in Japan (2009), draws our attention to Lon Fuller's discussion of "as-if" acts in law.[46] Lawyers and judges perform "as-if" acts with regularity, as do individuals who construct legal fictions such as asset-protection trusts. In the example from Port Said, the agent (Noha), the intermediary (Amr's father) and the undocumented party responsible for fulfilling the undocumented (but verbally agreed upon) obligation (Amr) are linked in a fictional transactional relationship. The trust receipt transforms a non-binding promise to marry into a fictional transfer of funds secured by a commercial paper that stakes the body as collateral in an "as-if" performance.

Secondly, by way of the legal fiction that creates a new (non-fictional) legal obligation, a fiancé's autonomy or freedom to act according to his self-interest is curtailed. In Amr's case, the trust receipt puts his father at risk, either financially or for criminal prosecution. From another perspective, Amr's father stakes his own freedom to secure Amr's, which makes Amr directly responsible for his father's well-being. The receipt thus shifts the focus of Amr's obligation, and in so doing increases the likelihood of fulfillment; his obligation to kin is strong, whereas his obligation to potential-kin is weak. In instances where the fiancé is the designated intermediary on the trust receipt and therefore personally liable he stakes his own potential incarceration or assets as a form of guarantee. Although a fiancé might still refuse to marry his betrothed, his autonomy is curbed by legal consequences for failure to fulfill. This stands in contrast to his autonomy as one simply affianced because the legal consequences for failure to fulfill a promise to marry are weak. The transactional relationship inscribed in a trust receipt binds the parties together, requiring the intermediary to perform an obligation that is not technically articulated in the document.[47]

This brings us back to Annelies Moors' suggestion that when women litigate or participate in the making of legal documents, their aims are not always revealed in their practices but may be indirect or circuitous; clearly this is also true for men although their aims are often somewhat different. When parties give up a right (such as the right to criminally prosecute a person who stands accused of a crime) they may do so in order to gain something they perceive as more valuable. Noha and Randa use the rape allegation not to claim state protection from sexual violence or to see punishment meted out but rather to strengthen their hand in the game of honor politics. Their circuitous legal strategies reproduce rather than revert the hypermoralization of female sexuality. But their strategies also grant them more control over the outcome of this particular crisis.

Laws related to contracting and betrothal are individuating, making specific reference to free will and mutual consent. Yet as Kandiyoti argues, ". . . an associational life premised on an autonomous self bearing rights in his or her own person does not have much resonance in a social context where connectivity rather than contractuality structures notions of selfhood. This applies equally to men and women, but it is women and the young who bear the brunt of the inequalities inherent in patriarchy."[48] Although Egyptian law identifies equality between citizens regardless of gender, which applies to a woman's right to contract or to refuse to contract, women in the Arab-Islamic families maneuver within a patriarchal framework; they "bargain with patriarchy."[49]

Trust receipts and other commercial documents are technologies that can be used to instantiate relational rights and responsibilities. They draw multiple actors, including the state and family members, into the betrothal, contrasting the individuating contractual documents with the web of legal obligations they create. The use of trust receipts to guarantee marriage proposals and even the terms of marriage contracts can be interpreted as a way women and their families strive to counter male autonomy and the relative lack of peril associated with betrothal for men.

Notes

1. See for example Nayra Atiya, *Khul-khaal, Five Egyptian Women Tell Their Stories* (Syracuse: Syracuse University Press, 1982); Beth Baron, "The Making and Breaking of Marital Bonds in Modern Egypt," In N. Keddie and B. Baron, eds., *Women and Middle Eastern History* (New Haven: Yale University Press, 1991); Homa Hoodfar, *Between Marriage and the Market: Intimate Politics and Survival in Cairo* (Berkeley: University of California Press, 1997); Hania Sholkamy, "Why Kin Marriages? Rationales in Rural Upper Egypt," In K.M. Yount and H. Rashad, eds., *Family in the Middle East: Ideational Change in Egypt, Iran, and Tunisia* (London: Routledge, 2008).
2. See for example Arlene Elowe MacLeod, *Accommodating Protest: Working Women, the New Veiling, and Change in Cairo* (New York: Columbia University Press, 1991); Andrea B. Rugh, *Family in Contemporary Egypt* (Syracuse: Syracuse University Press, 1984); Bahira Sherif, "The Prayer of a Married Man is Equal to Seventy Prayers of a Single Man: the Central Role of Marriage Among Upper-Middle-Class Muslim Egyptians," *Journal of Family Issues*, 20 (617), 1999.
3. Annelies Moors, "Debating Islamic Family Law: Legal Texts and Social Practices," In M.L. Meriwether and J.E. Tucker, eds., *Social History of Women and Gender in the Modern Middle East* (Boulder: Westview Press, 1999, p. 160).

4. Moors, "Debating Islamic Family Law," p. 167.

5. Annelise Riles, "Introduction: In Response," In A. Riles, ed., *Documents: Artifacts of Modern Knowledge* (Ann Arbor: University of Michigan Press, 2006); Adam Reed, "Documents Unfolding," In A. Riles, ed., *Documents: Artifacts of Modern Knowledge* (Ann Arbor: University of Michigan Press, 2006).

6. See for example Carol A. Heimer, "Conceiving Children: How Documents Support Case versus Biographical Analyses," In A. Riles, ed., *Documents: Artifacts of Modern Knowledge* (Ann Arbor: University of Michigan, 2006); Barbara Yngvesson and Susan Bibler Coutin, "Materiality and Documentation – Backed by Papers: Undoing Persons, Histories, and Return," *American Ethnologist*, 33 (2), 2006, p. 177.

7. Baudouin Dupret and Jean-Noel Ferrie, "Public/Private and References to Islam: a Praxiological Perspective," In M. Levine and A. Salvatore, eds., *Religion, Social Practice, and Contested Hegemonies: Reconstructing the Public Sphere in Muslim Majority Societies* (New York: Palgrave Macmillan, 2005).

8. Gamal Aly Zahraan, "Political Scenarios for the Future of Port Said," In *The Future of the City of Port Said in Light of Local, Regional, and International Variables* (Suez Canal University, 2000) (*in Arabic*).

9. All names have been changed to protect informants' identities.

10. Noha related the details of her case in the presence of one of her lawyers, who occasionally confirmed or clarified points. As such, Noha's re-telling of the "facts" bore a strong resemblance to what one of her legal representatives knew to have occurred.

11. Noha's use of the phrase *bishakl wadī* to describe this restorative process imbues it with positive value. My interlocutors in Port Said commonly used this multivalent phase to describe informal mediation and other strategies for conflict resolution by which legal action could be avoided.

12. In many cases, trust receipts are not notarized and are considered "informal." Having it notarized strengthens its evidentiary value as it becomes less likely for a defendant to argue at some later point that it was forged, a common legal strategy to create delay.

13. Laila Labidi, "Islamic Law, Feminism, and Family: The Reformulation of Hudud in Egypt and Tunisia," In V.M. Moghadam, ed., *From Patriarchy to Empowerment: Women's Participation, Movements, and Rights in the Middle East, North Africa, and South Asia* (Syracuse: Syracuse University Press, 2007); Amira Sonbol, "Rape and Law in Ottoman and Modern Egypt," In M.C. Zilfi, ed., *Women in the Ottoman Empire: Middle Eastern Women in the Early Modern Era* (Leiden: Brill, 1997).

14. Sonbol, "Rape and Law," p. 229.

15. According to Laila (2007), approximately 20,000 rapes are reported each year in Egypt, in most cases the rapist is known to the victim. Women's rights and human rights organizations have suggested that such statistics are low because many victims don't report attacks. Reem Laila, "Sex Crimes Rise," In *Al-Ahram Weekly*, Cairo, 19–25 July, 2007.

16. Translated by C. Hegel-Cantarella.

17. Mona Zulficar, "The Islamic Marriage Contract in Egypt," In A. Quraishi and F.E. Vogel, eds., *The Islamic Marriage Contract: Case Studies in Islamic Family Law* (Cambridge, MA: Harvard University Press, 2008).

18. Zulficar, "The Islamic Marriage Contract," p. 235.

19. Nathan Brown, *The Rule of Law in the Arab World* (Cambridge and New York: Cambridge University Press, 1997).

 The use of the post-dated check as a surety device is found in other contexts as well. Jane Kaufman-Winn, for instance, points out that post-dated checks predominate in Taiwan's informal financial sector as a form of security in part because Chinese law provides criminal charges for checks issued in bad faith without sufficient funds; Jane Kaufman-Winn, "Relational Practices and the Marginalization of Law: Informal Financial Practices of Small Businesses in Taiwan," *Law & Society Review*, 28 (2), 1994.

20. For example, Ron Shaham discusses marriage contractual practices in the first half of the 20th century in Egypt, noting that it was common in this period for a man's father to register in the official marriage contract his surety (*kafala*) for the wife's dower (*mahr*) and trousseau (*jihaz*). A wife could thus sue her father-in-law to claim unpaid maintenance, as well as her "*shar'* and other rights;" Ron Shaham, *Family and the Courts in Modern Egypt: A Study Based on Decisions by the Shari'a Courts, 1900–1955* (Leiden and New York: E. J. Brill, 1997, p. 30).

21. Zulficar, "The Islamic Marriage Contract," p. 235.

22. Kenneth M. Cuno, "Divorce and the Fate of the Family in Modern Egypt" In K.M. Yount and H. Rashad, eds., *Family in the Middle East: Ideational Change in Egypt, Iran, and Tunisia* (London: Routledge, 2008, pp. 207–8).

23. Diane Singerman and Barbara Ibrahim, "The Costs of Marriage in Egypt: A Hidden Dimension in the New Arab Demography," *Cairo Papers in Social Science*, 24(1/2), 2003, pp. 80–116. Moreover, The high costs of marriage fall primarily on the groom's family; in urban areas the groom and his family provide an average of 72% of the wedding costs.

24. See for example Abeer Allam, "'Urfi Delivers the Goods, at Half Price," *Middle East Times*, February 18, 2000; Gihan Shahine, "The Double Bind," *Al-Ahram Weekly*, Vol. 397, 1998.

25. Prior to 1929, when the Egyptian state incorporated Muslim marriage, all Muslim marriages were technically 'urfi as they were unregistered yet met the requirements of shari'a (mutual consent, presence of a guardian for females who had not previously married, a dowry, and two male, or two female and one male witnesses). But in contemporary Egypt 'urfi marriages are commenced under a variety of circumstances, for instance as a way for a man to secretly take a second wife. On the other end of the spectrum, Rashad and Osman note that "[i]ndeed, the emerging common-law ('urfi) marriage among young couples in Egypt, as well as other non-conventional forms of marriage, may represent a coping strategy among youth as a compromise to the economic constraints to marriage and the cultural denial of extra-marital sexual relations." Hoda Rashad and Magued I. Osman, "Nuptuality in Arab Countries: Changes and Implications," *Cairo Papers in Social Science*, 24(1/2), 2001, p. 39.

26. As Walter Armbrust shows, sexuality outside of marriage is depicted frequently in Egyptian films, yet has often been made palatable through plots in which some terrible misfortune (death or otherwise) befalls the character. Films also illustrate the sexual double standard in Egyptian society, with male characters having greater ability to experiment sexually outside of and before marriage without consequence. Walter Armbrust, "Sexuality and Film: Transgressing Patriarchy: Sex and Marriage in Egyptian Film," *Middle East Report*, Spring, (206), 1998.

27. Saba Mahmood, *Politics of Piety: the Islamic Revival and the Feminist Subject* (Princeton: Princeton University Press, 2005, p. 110).

28. Mahmood, *Politics of Piety*, p. 111.

29. Sherif, "The Prayer of a Married Man," p. 620.

30. Rugh, *Family in Contemporary Egypt*, p. 157.

31. Homa Hoodfar, *Between Marriage and the Market*, p. 69.

32. Susan Slymovics and Suad Joseph, "Introduction," In S. Joseph and S. Slymovics, eds., *Women and Power in the Middle East* (Philadelphia: University of Pennsylvania Press, 2001).

33. Suad Joseph, "Familism and Critical Arab Family Studies," In K. M. Yount and H. Rashad, eds., *Family in the Middle East: Ideational Change in Egypt, Iran, and Tunisia* (London: Routledge, 2008).

34. Deniz Kandiyoti, "The Politics of Gender and the Conundrums of Citizenship," In S. Joseph and S. Slymovics, eds., *Women and Power in the Middle East*. (Philadelphia: University of Pennsylvania Press, 2001, p. 57).

35. Annelies Moors, *Women, Property and Islam: Palestinian Experiences, 1920–1990* (Cambridge: Cambridge University Press, 1995).
36. Moors, "Debating Islamic Family Law," p. 153.
37. Iman Bibars, *Victims and Heroines: Women, Welfare and the Egyptian State* (London and New York: Zed, 2001, p. 20).
38. Bibars, *Victims and Heroines* pp. 90–95.
39. Selma Botman, *Engendering Citizenship in Egypt* (New York: Columbia University Press, 1999).
40. Botman, *Engendering Citizenship*, p. 52.
41. Rugh, *Family in Contemporary Egypt*, p. 157.
42. Jamal J. Nasir, *The Islamic Law of Personal Status* (The Hague/London/New York: Kluwer Law International, 2002); see also Nathalie Bernard-Maugiron and Baudouin Dupret, *Egypt and Its Laws* (The Hague: Kluwer Law International, 2002) on family law as regards betrothal and marriage.
43. As quoted in Nasir, *The Islamic Law of Personal Status*, p. 47.
44. Dupret and Ferrie, "Public/Private and References to Islam," p. 10.
45. Richard Harper, *Inside the IMF: An Ethnography of Documents, Technology, and Organizational Action* (San Diego: Academic Press, 1998).
46. Lon L. Fuller, *Legal Fictions* (Stanford: Stanford University Press, 1967). Fuller in turn owes a debt to Vaihinger (1924/1952) and his philosophy of "as-if." Legal fictions are merely one manifestation of fictionalization as an elemental feature of human thought and life, and Fuller points out that legal fictionalization occurs when new cases are fitted into existing categories.
47. The suggestion that the pressure of trust receipts is related to their ability to constitute new forms of legal relationality that reduce autonomy can also be evidenced in the use of trust receipts (and post-dated checks) in other contexts. Elsewhere, I discuss their use to secure credit transactions between retailers and wholesalers and between retailers and customers in the post-free zone era in Port Said (Hegel, 2009).
48. Kandiyoti, "The Politics of Gender," p. 57.
49. Deniz Kandiyoti, "Bargaining with Patriarchy," *Gender and Society*, September, 2(3), 1988.

62

'Freshly Generated for You, and Barack Obama': How Social Media Represent Your Life

Jill Walker Rettberg

A Personal Annual Report

In January 2009, the social network site[1] Dopplr.com sent each of its users a customized one-page visualization of their travels during 2008. Dopplr.com is a fairly simple site where you can enter details of your trips, connect with friends or acquaintances, and receive alerts when you're going to be in the same town as somebody you know.

When I received my report I was surprised: I had entered trips somewhat inconsistently, but my report lined everything up along a coloured timeline complete with photographs of the cities I'd visited. Looking at the report, I realized that I hadn't logged all my trips, and that there were some errors in the trips I had entered. The portrait of my travelling year was incorrect, and it upset me! I swiftly logged into Dopplr and made the corrections. And sure enough, I later received an updated report (Figure 1).

In the email containing the customized pdf, Dopplr also included a link to a blog post titled 'Dopplr presents the Personal Annual Report 2008: freshly generated for you, and Barack Obama . . .' (Jones, 2009). In the blog post they explained these personal reports, showcasing a report they'd created for Barack Obama. Obama's report was far more information-rich than mine, with dozens of lines in different vivid colours along the timeline as well as notes about how far he'd travelled and which of his colleagues had spent the most

Source: *European Journal of Communication*, 24(4) (2009): 451–466.

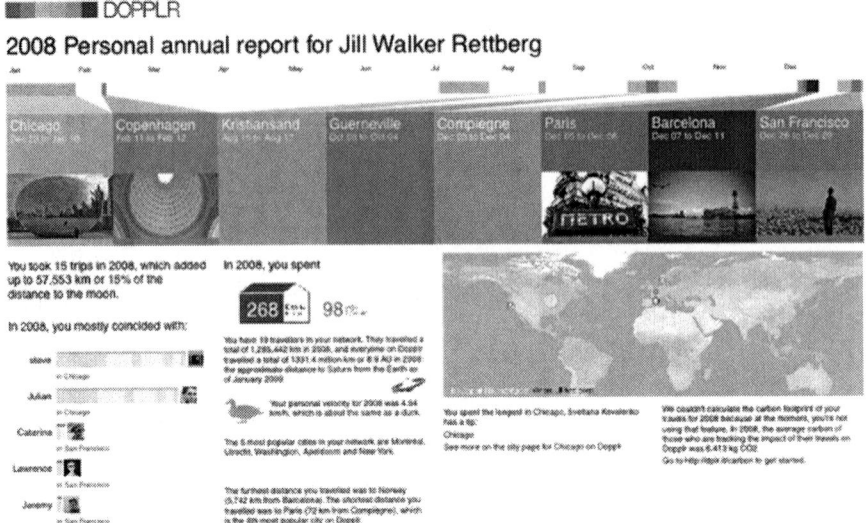

Figure 1: A visualization of the trips I told dopplr.com I was taking in 2008. This is the updated version they generated after I'd made corrections to the data I'd originally entered.

time in the same place as him. My report also included the timeline and the notes but, because I had travelled so much less than Obama, there was less content in the report.

The report fascinated me because no social network site had sent me such a portrait of my life before – and as a researcher of social media I've signed up to dozens of social network sites. By organizing my data in this way, Dopplr created a story[2] for me, a representation of an aspect of my life. They put my little story alongside one of the most well-known stories of 2008: that of Barack Obama and his successful campaign for the presidency of the United States. Obama's story, so familiar, became a cultural template or a filter for my own story.

One of the ways we find our place in our culture and among our friends and families is by creating and consuming stories and images. These representations of ourselves and of others connect to larger cultural templates, which we adopt, adapt or reject. The sequence: 'fall in love, get married, have a baby' is one such cultural template. So is the idea of the hard worker who starts out small, works diligently and finally succeeds. Others are more negative. All are in some sense stereotypes that most of us, on the individual level, will not match. But we still consume and spread these cultural templates in fairy tales, nursery rhymes, fables, sayings, popular songs, movies and narratives, as well as in visual images. We create our own stories about and representations of ourselves – in conversation with friends, in diaries, scrapbooks, Facebook profiles and YouTube videos – and when we do so we cannot help but respond in some way to these cultural stereotypes, whether we adopt them unthinkingly, adapt them to suit ourselves, or reject them explicitly.

I have previously discussed how we purposefully create various kinds of self-representations online and how important these are to us, arguing that they express our newfound subjectivity as individuals able to represent ourselves rather than simply succumb to the generalizations of mass media (Walker, 2005). In this article, I look instead at the representations that are created *of* us by social media. I discuss representations of user data that have been gathered over time and that have been compiled by the social network site into a report, narrative, visualization or other representation intended to provide the user with an overview or image of his or her own activity. I argue that such representations provide us with new ways of connecting to larger cultural templates.

Patterns

How, then, are these representations organized? Dopplr's visualization plots my data along three different axes: temporal (there's a timeline of the year), social (there's a list of which of my friends were in the same cities as me) and geographical (the map is marked with cities I've visited).

Temporal or chronological organization is the most common in narratives and in social media. The standard way of telling a story is with a beginning, middle and an end, as Aristotle stated in his *Poetics*, although there are many exceptions to this. Social media are also heavily time-based, but the standard chronological organization is reversed: on Facebook, YouTube or a blog, the most recent item is usually presented at the top of the page, privileging the instant and the now rather than the whole story.

Even in traditional narratives such as we find in novels or movies, there are ways of organizing events other than their temporal succession. Gerard Genette, one of the most well-known narratologists, writes about how events in a plot can be connected in the narration by different kinds of kinship, such as space or time. He calls all such 'anachronic groupings' syllepses:

> Geographical syllepsis, for example, is the principle of narrative grouping in voyage narratives that are embellished by anecdotes. . . . Thematic syllepsis governs in the classical episodic novel with its numerous insertions of 'stories,' justified by relations of analogy or contrast. (Genette, 1980: 85)

Organizing plot events by anachronic syllepses is not very common in traditional narratives. In fact, Genette's note is literally a footnote in his treatise on narratology. However, these sorts of anachronic syllepsis are often used in hypertext fictions (Walker, 1999), which were among the first narratives to be created specifically to be read on computers (Hayles, 2008). They are also common in non-time-based and non-narrative representations, such as visualizations, graphs and diagrams.

The kinds of grouping – or, to use Genette's word, syllepsis – that were apparent in Dopplr's report of my travels are typical of the ways in which social media sites organize our personal data for us. As noted, Dopplr uses temporal, social and geographic organization. A fourth common form of organization in social media is close to that which Genette calls thematic syllepsis in narrative. Perhaps it would be more accurate when speaking of social media to call it semantic organization, as it has to do with meaning and semantic connections.

Often the live feed of a social media site allows users to choose between different ways of viewing data that correspond to these four kinds of organization. From the front page of Flickr.com, a popular photo-sharing site, I can choose to look at the most recent photographs uploaded to Flickr in general (temporal organization), at photos taken by my friends and family (social organization), at photographs taken in a particular location (geographic organization) or at photographs about a particular topic that are specifically tagged (semantic organization). However, the reports and summaries generated by social media sites – like the report sent by Dopplr – tend to emphasize just one or a few kinds of syllepsis.

Let me give you some examples of representations that emphasize each of the four kinds of organization.

Temporal Organization

Organizing our data by when they were created or when they were uploaded is probably the most obvious and often the most effective form of structure, just as it is the most common form of organization in narrative. Temporal syllepsis tends to narrativize information. When we see a list of events or a set of images one after the other we tend to assume that they are organized chronologically, and we also tend to fill in the gaps to create a causally coherent narrative (Iser, 1988).

Two of the best known temporally organized sets of digital photographs are Miles Hochstein's 'Documented Life' (2009) and Noah Kalina's popular time-lapse video 'Noah Takes a Photo of Himself Every Day for 6 Years' (2006). Hochstein has gathered photos of himself from each year of his life, leaving space for the remaining years he hopes to live. Headshot after headshot is presented in a grid on the first page of the site, and if you click one of the images, you are presented with a page showing more images and some verbal narrative about the photographs and about his life that year – thus the photos function as both a summary of his life and as a table of contents providing easy and organized access to more details. This kind of organization is automatically generated by Flickr, where you can view your archives shown as a monthly calendar with a photograph displayed on each day. While Flickr, unlike Dopplr, does not send these calendars out as 'Personal Annual Reports', they do function in a similar way, providing the user with an automated diary of his or her life.

Noah Kalina took a photo of his own face every day for six years, and put them all together into a 5:45 minute video showing him slowly grow older.

The video, which Kalina posted on YouTube, became immensely popular and started a craze of similar videos. Today sites such as dailybooth.com and dailymugshot.com prompt users to take daily photos of themselves with their webcam. The sites provide a social infrastructure where users can follow other users and watch their photo streams; but the main goal of the sites seems to be the ways in which they will organize the photos for you, for instance in a video form very similar to Noah Kalina's original.

Another kind of temporal organization of data is provided by Trixietracker. com, a site where parents can enter data about their babies: when they eat, sleep and have their nappies changed. The system generates graphs showing patterns from day to day, allowing parents to see trends in their babies' activities and to compare their babies' sleep patterns to other babies of the same age.

You enter data into Trixietracker.com much as you do at Dopplr.com, though far more frequently. You click a button when you put your baby down to sleep, when she actually falls asleep and when she wakes up – or when you give up on trying to get her to sleep. Over time, the system will not only show you graphs of each day, as seen in Figure 2, but will also generate graphs showing

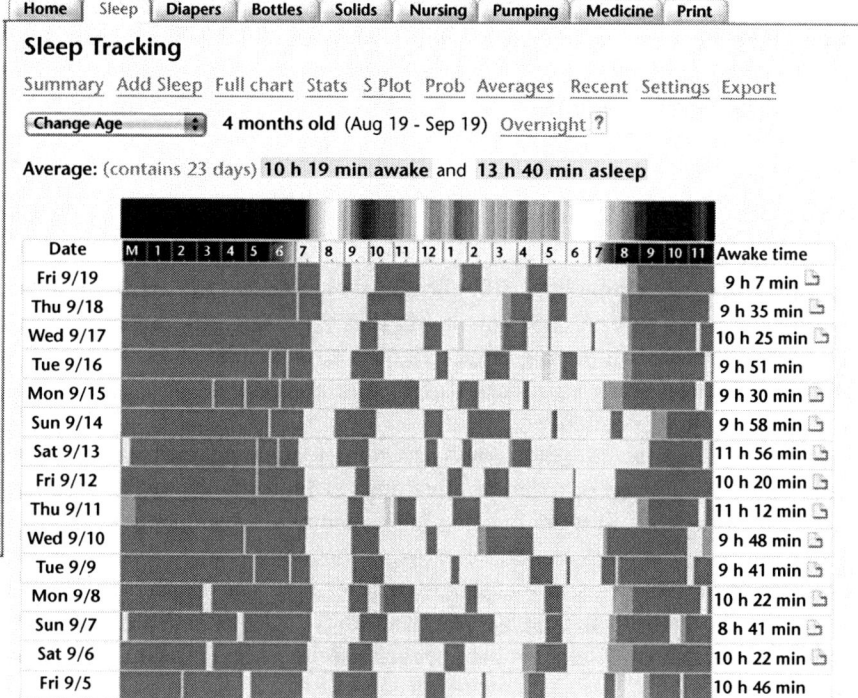

Figure 2: A graph of my baby Jessica's sleep patterns at four months based on data I entered at Trixietracker.com. The grey and white bar at the top shows probabilities of her being asleep or awake at any time of the day.

the probability of your baby being asleep at any particular time or day and allowing you to compare your baby's sleep patterns to other babies that age.

There are many other sites that allow you to track anything from your moods (moodlog.org) to how often you have sex (www.bedposted.com: 'For your eyes only, Bedpost offers zero social networking features other than partner logins'). These sites generate overviews for you, displaying your data based on time – allowing you perhaps to discover that you're more likely to be grumpy at 4 p.m. than in the morning as you had thought.

Social Organization

There are dozens of social network analysis tools for visualizing explicitly articulated social networks online. One of the more well-known examples is the Facebook Friend Visualizer, which is an application you can add to your Facebook profile that will generate visualizations of your network of friends on Facebook, showing connections between groups of your friends. There are a number of other tools that will perform similar tasks for other social network sites, such as Twitter Friends. Maps of blog networks are often drawn with lines between blogs representing the frequency of the links between them. Likewise, Flickr will allow you to view your photos according to how popular they are – how often they have been viewed, commented on and made a favourite.

Reports emphasizing social organization tend to be in diagrammatic rather than narrative form, although they may include images and other content.

Semantic Organization

I mentioned the calendar view of a user's photos on Flickr as an example of temporal organization. Flickr also allows users to access the archives of their photos on Flickr through the key words they have used to 'tag' each photo. So you might click on the tag 'Mum' and see all your photos of your mother, in a sense generating a visual diary of your relationship to your mother over the time you have used Flickr.

Semantic organization filters data according to meaning rather than according to time, geography or social connections. So photographs can be organized according to who is in them or what is happening – 'sleeping' or 'smiling' or 'eating' are common tags. Semantic organization may become more common as search engines become more sophisticated: for now, the most common kinds of semantic organization are based on meta-data explicitly entered by the user: tags on photos as on Flickr, for instance, or happiness levels as on the knitting site Ravelry.com.

Ravelry.com is a site where knitters and crocheters document their projects and discuss projects, yarns, patterns and supply shops. Each user has a 'notebook' (rather than a profile) where all his or her projects are displayed.

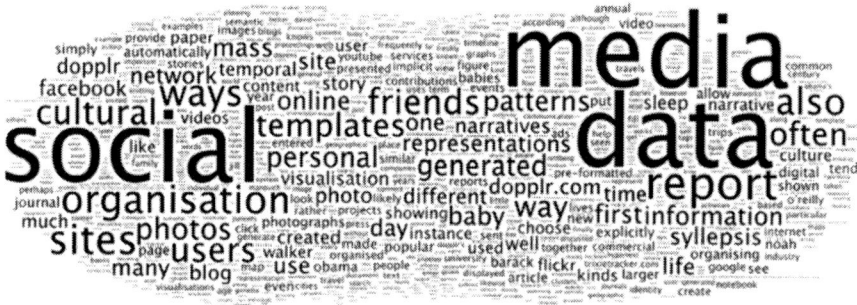

Figure 3: A tag cloud or 'wordle' generated from the text of this essay at wordle. com. Font size shows which words are used most frequently.

This notebook is organized very much as a scrapbook or, literally, a notebook, where the user stores information for her or his own future use, such as whether she or he liked the yarn, what the gauge was knitting that yarn on those needles and any modifications made to the pattern. Ravelry doesn't generate automated reports, but the notebook becomes an important documentation for the user. It can be viewed in chronological order, but also using semantic organization, for instance showing the projects in order of 'happiness' and using each project's happiness ranking according to how much the crafter enjoyed making it. On Ravelry, a user is thus represented by the knitting and crocheting she or he makes, as well as by blog posts, contributions to forums and patterns that the user has designed and shared.

Tag clouds or text clouds are another way in semantic relationships can be shown. These so-called clouds measure how frequently a word is used in a text, on a blog or by a user and displays the most frequently used words in a cloud where the most used are shown in larger, bolder type than the others. Sometimes words that tend to be used together are shown more closely to each other. Figure 3 shows a cloud of the text of this essay. While the semantic organization in such a cloud is currently limited to font size representing the frequency of word use, when a user generates a cloud from a blog he or she has kept for years, it can be a powerful representation of issues that are important to the user – and that the user has perhaps not been conscious of prioritizing as clearly as shown by the cloud.

Geographic Organization

As GPS is becoming built in to more and more of our cameras and phones, geography is one of the simplest and most effective ways of organizing user content. GPS-enabled devices allow photos, text and other content to be automatically placed on a map, but sites often also allow users to place themselves on a map manually, as with Google maps. Dopplr's report uses geographical organization heavily. I can choose to see my photos in Flickr displayed on a map, and sites like Brightkite.com and Plazes.com allow users to 'check in' and log where they are, displaying this information as a timeline or organized on a map. On a larger scale, there are visualizations of blog posts or Facebook activity shown on maps of the world, generating representations of our activities similar to pictures of lit-up cities taken from space.

Cultural Templates

Although I never thought of doing so, I could have created a visualization of my travel like the one Dopplr generated on my own.[3] There are many ways in which people do regularly document their lives, from compiling photo albums, creating elaborate scrapbooks and writing diaries for personal or family use to the annual Christmas 'round robin' letters written as a summary of the year, photocopied and sent to a hundred friends. These forms of media creation have been little studied by media and communications scholars, who have largely focused on the dominant mass media of the 20th century. Recently, Marika Lüders coined the term 'personal media' in opposition to mass media (Lüders, 2008). This term includes not only analogue media as mentioned earlier, but also online media, including much social media.

Personal media can be created freely, for instance on blank paper or a blank journal, or it can use predetermined templates. For instance, many parents buy preformatted baby journals and simply fill in the blanks: baby's first smiled on this date, first walked on that, here's a photo of baby on the day she was born and here's a lock of her hair obediently placed in a thoughtfully provided little plastic envelope. Social media sites similarly provide templates for users to fill in, structures in which users can upload their photos, videos, texts, data or simply type a quick response to Facebook's prompt: 'What's on your mind?'[4]

While preformatted baby journals are already normative, the automatically generated digital 'reports' of our lives – or of our babies' sleep patterns – are even more controlled. If you don't like the prompts given on a page in your baby journal, you can tear the page out or glue a large photograph over the text. I can't change anything about the layout of my Dopplr.com or Trixietracker report (although I can download the data from Trixietracker.com and format them myself in Excel). I can choose not to fill out all the information they ask for, but the generated report will simply report the gaps as well, and the lack of information is itself showcased: Doesn't she have more friends than that? Why did she choose not to allow Dopplr to calculate the carbon footprint of her flights?

In her book *Mediated Memories*, José van Dijck (2007: 7) calls preformatted baby journals an example of 'normative discursive strategies' that 'either implicitly or explicitly structure our agencies'. In an article on art and user-generated content, Lev Manovich (2009) compares the corporate structures of social media and user-generated content to Adorno and Horkheimer's critique of the cultural industry:

> Given that a significant percentage of user-generated content either follows the templates and conventions set up by the professional entertainment industry or directly reuses professionally produced content, does this mean that people's identities and imaginations are now even more firmly colonized by commercial media than they were in the twentieth century? In other words, is the replacement of mass consumption of commercial culture in the twentieth century by mass production of cultural objects by users in the early twenty-first century a progressive development? or does it constitute a further stage in the development of the culture industry as analyzed by Adorno and Horkheimer in *The Culture Industry: Enlightenment as Mass Deception* (1944)? (Manovich, 2009: 321)

These are clearly important perspectives to be aware of, but perhaps they are too generalized and abstract. Later in his article Manovich admits that, for all the mediocre copies, there are also works of great artistic quality created by amateurs online. And, of course, most people who use social media or who create personal media are not trying to create great art. Indeed, José van Dijck goes on to note 'it is quite remarkable how many people gain creative energy out of shaping their own histories and subjectivities in response to existing cultural frameworks' (van Dijk, 2007: 8).

In this article, I am not so much interested in the quality of what we create as in the ways we connect our contributions (baby sleep patterns, travel data or knitting projects) to larger cultural templates, templates that are certainly often exploited by commercial media but that are not the sole product of them. Even without a preformatted baby journal there are cultural templates we will tend to follow. In western culture, we all see a baby's first smile, first teeth and first steps as important milestones, and we are likely to document them in some way. Parents who don't own a preformatted journal or a mass-produced memory box with instructions are still likely to save a lock of hair from a child's first haircut and to keep the first milk tooth a child loses. Documenting these events helps us structure our lives and our memories. They also help ground us in our cultures.[5] The relationship between these cultural templates and commercial forces is symbiotic, not one-way.

Implicit and Explicit Data

Many of the sites discussed in this article are examples of Web 2.0 services, a term Tim O'Reilly first coined in 2005, and that he later summarized in 2008 as the 'design of systems that harness network effects to get better the more people use them, or more colloquially, as "harnessing collective intelligence"'. Web 2.0 is a much-maligned term, but one that has proved to have staying power, and it broadly encompasses the sites and services that we tend to think of as social media. Thinking of social media through the lens of technologist Tim O'Reilly rather than from the point of view of media and communications studies is valuable because it emphasizes different things. One of the points O'Reilly has most frequently made about Web 2.0 is that it's about data. It's about *our* data – both the data we contribute explicitly and the data that are implicit; that we're not aware of contributing. Likewise, social media aren't just about the contributions that people make deliberately or explicitly, such as when you upload a video to YouTube, update your status on Facebook, write a new blog post or contribute to a discussion on an online newspaper. Social media are just as much about our implicit contributions. Google knows what I search for and which search results I choose to click on. Twitter knows how often I log on and how often I post. Amazon knows which books I view, which books I purchase and which I don't. Facebook logs how long I spend on their site at a time and which kinds of ads I click. Ninety-nine percent of YouTube's users may be lurkers, never posting a single video, but YouTube still knows how they rate videos, which videos are liked or at least visited by the same people, and which videos are the most popular.

Companies harvest our data because they can use it to sell better ads, but also in order to create better services for us. Previously this collection has often been somewhat hidden to users. Companies use such data internally, of course, and show us some results – Amazon tells us which books it thinks we will like based on our purchases, for instance. When I tell Dopplr.com where I'm travelling, it can use the data to customize their service to me, to tell advertisers where their users travel and to build further services.

When Dopplr.com sent me the visualization of my travels in 2008, they made the explicit and implicit data I contributed to their service visible to me in a new way. They showed me my own story. They showed me the patterns of my travels over the course of a year. Obviously I already knew the information they were showing me – I was the traveller. But I hadn't seen it all put together in that way. Google's Web History is perhaps even more striking in its display of our implicit data. When I search for something on Google I don't think about how the data will be collected by Google. But when I signed up for Google's Web History, Google started showing me monthly calendars, colour-coded to show how often I searched on each day of that particular month (see Figure 4). Before the Internet, most representations of me would have been completely made by myself or by my friends and family – home videos, diaries, photo albums and so on. Today, commercial websites generate representations of me based on my data. They are perhaps doing little more than a mirror. But they are also normalizing the idea that surveillance is constant and even to my benefit.

A common early reaction to bloggers was that they were narcissistic. In Greek myth, poor Narcissus was so infatuated with the image of his own face, reflected in a pool of water, that he finally fell into the pool and drowned. Online, an often-discussed risk of gazing at your own reflection is that the information

Web Activity
« Feb   Mar 2009   Apr »

S	M	T	W	T	F	S
1	2	3	4	5	6	7
8	9	10	11	12	13	14
15	16	17	18	19	20	21
22	23	24	25	26	27	28
29	30	31	1	2	3	4

Today, Jun 1

1 - 30   31 - 75   76 - 150   151+

Total Google searches: 13449

Figure 4: If you sign up for Google Web History you can see calendars showing how frequently you use Google search on different days. This is an example of temporal organization; you can also see what search terms you use most often (semantic organization), which sites you visit most often or simply all the sites you've visited.

you put online may be seen by and abused by stalkers, paedophiles and online bullies. In these cases, malicious individuals generally put information together manually. A more systemic concern about our increasingly prolific sharing of our own personal data is that our data is automatically aggregated by the sites we frequent, often in ways we are not aware of. Facebook's executives probably don't read our individual status updates (although they certainly could) but their systems know a great deal about us: data we've explicitly entered (name, sex, age, residence, education, friends) as well as data they gather implicitly (When are we most active on Facebook? Which friends do we communicate most with? Which ads and applications are we most likely to click on? How popular are we? How many photos do we appear in?). Likewise, Google, Yahoo and other large companies have vast quantities of data about our use of their services, and through advertising networks, often about our behaviour on external sites as well.

This data is primarily used for advertising. Facebook apparently doesn't sell the data itself, but they sell ads and promise advertisers that ads will be shown to the users who are most likely to be interested in the product. However, there are more nefarious uses of personal data. In China, Google and Yahoo have given the government access to information about dissidents that has led to their conviction for political crimes. The EU's data retention directive (Directive 2006/24/EC) requires member countries to store data about all Internet and telephone traffic for at least six and up to 24 months. This information is only supposed to be accessed in the case of suspicion of a 'major crime', but protesters have objected that this total surveillance or dataveillance (defined by Roger Clarke [1988: 500] as 'the systematic monitoring of people's actions or communications through the application of information technology') is a serious breach of privacy. Reports about our travel patterns and graphs of our babies' sleep patterns remind us that the technologies that please us and help us document and understand our lives can also be used against us, for commercial or ideological purposes. And yet we continue to feed our information into the system.

Filtered Self-Portraits

In previous research (Walker, 2005) I have argued that our fascination with creating digital self-portraits is indicative of our collective coming of age where we as a culture are discovering that we have voices online and can express ourselves rather than simply accepting the mass media's views of the world. Like an infant discovering her or his own image in a mirror or a teenager trying out different styles of clothes, handwriting or makeup, in the early 21st century we are becoming accustomed to the Internet and finding out who we are in this context.

The generated portraits of ourselves that I have discussed in this article are similar in many ways, but are to a greater extent controlled by commercial interests and limited by the strict templates applied to our data. Beyond entering my data, I have no control over the way Dopplr.com portrays me in their personal annual reports. In a sense, this is a partial return to mass media. In this mass customization, each individual is fed into the same template. Perhaps this is exactly what we want. For by seeing my data displayed in exactly the same way as Barack Obama's or a friend or celebrity, I see aspects of my own life from outside. And as I do so, my place in the larger stories and cultural templates of the world is confirmed.

Notes

1. I follow danah boyd and Nicole Ellison's definition of social network site (boyd and Ellison, 2007): 'We define social network sites as web-based services that allow individuals to (1) construct a public or semi-public profile within a bounded system, (2) articulate a list of other users with whom they share a connection, and (3) view and traverse their list of connections and those made by others within the system.' While the sites discussed in this article are social network sites, I am here more concerned with the way the individual interacts with the site than how the social network is articulated and functions.
2. This report is a story or narrative in a very minimal narratological sense: it presents events in order, but causality, which is required in some definitions of narrative, is not shown. However, as the intended reader is primarily the person who has experienced the events that are represented, one might argue that causality is implicit.

3. New York designer Nicholas Felton's annual reports on his personal activities, all beautiful examples of personal information graphics, are excellent examples of how people *can* craft such reports themselves. But Felton is an exception rather than the rule. See feltron.com for examples.
4. Prior to March 2009, Facebook asked 'What are you doing right now?'
5. Van Dijck notes that 'Western European and American practices of remembering and recording significantly diverge from Asian or African mores in this area' (van Dijck, 2007: 6). It is worth considering how this affects a more globalized online society. We often assume that simply translating the language of a web service is sufficient, but this may not be the case. An example is the meaning of the built-in way of RSVPing to events in Facebook, where users can choose between 'Yes', 'No' and 'Maybe'. These words are faithfully translated into many different languages, but work differently in different cultures. In a study conducted by Lucie Sejrup (2009), Norwegian users tend to answer 'Maybe' when they mean no, because to give an outright no would be considered rude. However, users from other countries have indicated no qualms about answering 'No'. Similarly, the ways in which social media summarize our contributions and digital memories to us may be culturally specific. Thank you to Daniel Jung and the Study Group for Social Media at the University of Bergen for these cultural comparisons.

References

Boyd, Danah M. and Nicole B. Ellison (2007) 'Social Network Sites: Definition, History, and Scholarship', *Journal of Computer-Mediated Communication* 13(1); at: jcmc.indiana. edu/vol13/issue1/boyd.ellison.html

Clarke, Roger (1988) 'Information Technology and Dataveillance', *Communications of the ACM* 31(5): 498–512.

Genette, Gerard (1980) *Narrative Discourse: An Essay in Method.* New York: Cornell University Press.

Hayles, N. Katherine (2008) *Electronic Literature: New Horizons for the Literary.* Notre Dame, IN: University of Notre Dame Press.

Hochstein, Miles (2009) 'Documented Life: An Autodocumentary'; at: www.documentedlife. com/autodocumentary.htm

Iser, Wolfgang (1988) 'The Reading Process: A Phenomenological Approach', in David Lodge (ed.) *Modern Criticism and Theory: A Reader.* London: Longman.

Jones, Matt (2009) 'Dopplr Presents The Personal Annual Report 2008: Freshly Generated For You, and Barack Obama . . .', DopplrBlog, 15 January; at: blog.dopplr.com/2009/01/15/dopplr-presents-the-personal-annual-report-2008-freshly-generated-for-you-and-barack-obama

Kalina, Noah (2006) 'Noah Takes a Photo of Himself Every Day for 6 Years', YouTube, 31 July; at: www.youtube.com/watch?v=6B26asyGKDo

Lüders, Marika (2008) 'Conceptualizing Personal Media', *New Media and Society* 10(6): 683–702.

Manovich, Lev (2009) 'The Practice of Everyday (Media) Life: From Mass Consumption to Mass Cultural Production?', *Critical Inquiry* 35(2): 319–31.

O'Reilly, Tim (2005) 'What is Web 2.0: Design Patterns and Business Models for the Next Generation of Software', O'Reilly Radar, 30 September; at: oreilly.com/pub/a/oreilly/tim/news/2005/09/30/what-is-web-20.html

Sejrup, Lucie (2009) 'Facebook Uses: How and Why? Uses and Gratifications Keeping up with the Technology', Master's Thesis, University of Bergen.

Van Dijck, Jose (2007) *Mediated Memories in the Digital Age.* Stanford, CA: Stanford University Press.

Walker, Jill (1999) 'Piecing Together and Tearing Apart: Finding the Story in *Afternoon*', paper presented at the proceedings of the 10th ACM Conference on Hypertext and Hypermedia, Darmstadt, Germany, 21–25 February; at: bora.uib.no/handle/1956/1073

Walker, Jill (2005) 'Mirrors and Shadows: The Digital Aestheticisation of Oneself', paper presented at the proceedings of the conference Digital Arts and Culture, Copenhagen; at: bora.uib.no/handle/1956/1136

63

History, Living Biography, and Self-Narrative

Shay Sayre

> *History is not what was but what is.*
> – William Faulkner

We approach the past in a variety of ways. This chapter offers three ways of understanding products and consumers from a historical vantagepoint. The notion that a problem is only understood within its historical context is illustrated here in a personal anecdote concerning demarketing. While developing a campaign for saving natural resources, I chastised a friend for taking long showers and leaving the lights on during his visit to my home. He replied that he'd been raised by the state [orphanage] where there were no controls on or concerns about water and electricity usage. Reflections of his experiences brought to light some relevant consumption issues.

First, my campaign had assumed that everyone was raised to respect energy sources, and that conservation would come naturally when people were reminded of its scarcity during hot summer months. After listening to my friend, I realized that education about energy usage was necessary for marketing targeted to a general audience. By considering the history of one consumer, I identified the context for grounding the campaign.

Understanding who consumers are means knowing "where they were when" – in other words, knowing the historical influences on their lives. The same principle applies to products. My grandmother's dislike of homogenized

---

Source: *Qualitative Methods for Marketplace Research* (Thousand Oaks: SAGE, 2001), pp. 66–79.

peanut butter stems from the fact that she made her own and enjoyed stirring the oil into the peanut meat before eating it. History provides a glimpse of her temporal relationship to peanut butter, and her biography brings depth and details to an understanding of that relationship. If I were marketing peanut butter to granny and her peers, I should bring a "homemade" quality into copy and visual advertising elements.

This chapter highlights the importance of history and life stories for understanding consumers and their relationships to products over time. The role of these methods in marketplace research is important as audiences diversify and mature. Historical methods play a vital role for understanding consumer life stories and self-narratives.

The Historical View

History is inherently political. There is no single standard by which we can identify 'true' historical knowledgeRather there are contests about the substance, uses and meanings of the knowledge that we call history.[1]
– Joan Scott, 1989

Historical research demands a point of view that includes an interpretive framework to deliver the author's notion of "meaning."[2] This notion is explained by an advertising analogy. From a feminist perspective, male art directors creating early advertising characterized women as objects to be gazed on. In a historical context, we see that portrayals of women reflected the times, not because of men's notions of meaning but because women assumed role-based duties of homemaker and mother. Feminists considered such duties to be subordinating and demeaning; thus, 1970s advertising was accused of subordinating women.

Today, women are once again embracing their more domestic roles and are less offended by advertising portrayals of them as mothers and wives. By bringing a historical context to the problem of how to present women in television commercials, we approach today's consumers with sensitivity and insight. History is more than a passing of time with dates to memorize; it has continuing relevance for the present.

Some interesting histories are product centered. Coke, for instance, has a fascinating history of television commercials. Beginning in 1956, Coke was carried into cowboy drama where actors talked to the audience about the product. "Things go better with Coke," sang the Andrews Sisters in their poodle skirts from the 1950s. An international chorus characterized Coke as "The Real Thing" during a 1970s commercial filmed in a meadow with panoramic views. Why do we care about the history of Coke? Because Coke's story dramatizes the role of products in our lives and the role of advertising in reflecting our lives.

The goal of historical research is to *illuminate.* Historical demographies study family life to illuminate product usage in the home. Case studies look at companies to illuminate an organizational culture's meanings. History characterizes the past and provides richness to unique or particular events.

Writing a Product History

If you're going to produce a product history, you begin by *reading secondary sources* of the period under study, using Homer, the most common computerized library index to a library. Books and magazines and newspaper articles describing your era of interest are a good beginning. Pay attention to footnotes and reference citations for clues to other materials. Next, locate *primary sources*, which are documents from the period you are trying to explain. Here's where detective work comes in. Coke's history appears in video archives that contain original versions of the commercials.

The Directory of Archives and Manuscript Repositories in the U.S. is a good place to learn what is available and where it's located. Many universities provide grants or funding for "travel to collections," where you may study original documents first hand. For her history of perfume advertising, one researcher spent a year at the Smithsonian Institute combing advertising archives, her main source of primary data.

In a study of women's underwear and the rise of women's sports,[3] two researchers took a historical approach to understand the relationship between garments and athletic performance over time. They began in 1988, when sprinter Florence Griffith-Joyner's record time in the 100-meter race proved she could outrun any man in the world. The incident makes the most sense when placed in a historical context. Had anyone suggested the possibility of this happening a century before, they would have been laughed out of town. One hundred years ago, all men and women were convinced that active sport was not for women, who were thought to be physically and biologically unsuited for it.

The study traces women's competition over the years with respect to dress, particularly underwear. Relegated to wearing dresses instead of knickers for hygienic reasons, women could not compete in active sports until electricity allowed the heating of wash water, and detergent was invented to remove fungus-causing microbes from woolen undergarments. Elastic changed underwear by replacing tapes or strings in drawers. Golf matches were won in ankle-length dresses until tennis permitted a shorter costume in 1926. Cotton replaced wool, corsets were discarded, and bras allowed women to compete more comfortably. History documents the changes in underwear and technology that significantly assisted the rise of women's sports.

The client, an elastic manufacturer, hailed these discoveries. The product hero – elastic – was neatly woven into the company's history. The company portrayed itself as a true advocate of women's sports, embracing sponsor-ships to improve its image and capitalize on the discovery of this relationship by marketplace researchers.

Evaluating Documentary Evidence

Historical research is essentially a document search. But locating documents is only the beginning. The primary role of historian as detective is evaluating the evidence of a document's authenticity. Journals, letters, and diaries are com-mon sources of evidence for marketplace and communications researchers. If the writing is from the period from which it claims to originate, it will reflect a writing style and vocabulary indicative of the times. Forgeries of documents are not uncommon; artwork and wartime journals are especially vulnerable targets for forgers.

A good researcher will distinguish between "genuine" and "authentic." *Genuineness* is whether or not the document is *forged* or an action is false. A consumer reporter who reviews a Mercedes Benz without test driving it pro-vides a genuine review because it is not forged, but it is not authentic because he or she did not drive the car. *Authenticity* is offering an ostensibly *truthful* document. An authentic recording may be copied and sold in another country as an original; the recording is authentic because the star did the original, but it is not genuine because it is a copy of the original.

Internal and external techniques, called criticisms, are useful for verifying document authenticity. *External criticisms* are comparisons made between two texts and author verification. *Internal criticisms* verify (a) the historical accu-racy of an account, (b) the linguistic and stylistic accuracy of the writing, and (c) the bias of the author. *Author credibility* appraises the writer's proximity to the event and how important the event was to the writer (by determining or eliminating the presence of bias).

Consumer Journal Evidence

Some researchers collect consumer product usage journals as evidence when writing product histories. Once in possession of journals, researchers must ask what the journal reveals about its author. What is the level of revelation – is this the person's private or public voice? Is the author conscious of a potential reader? Other questions to answer are the following:

2. What does the journal tell you about the social-cultural context of the consumer's life?
    - What does the journal tell you about the author's age, sex, ethnic or racial heritage?
    - Is the author a native citizen or an immigrant?

4. What is the consumer's personal or relational world like?
   - Who are the consumer's significant others?
6. What social values are important to the consumer?
8. How does the consumer's reality and values relate to the social context in which he or she lives?
   - Is the journal revealing or concealing?
10. Where would you go to answer the questions left from reading the consumer journal?
    - What other sources and evidence exist?

Here are a few examples of how historical research fits within a marketplace framework. Pin-up advertising calendars are the documents of evidence for a historical study conducted for Snap-On tool company.[4] The study surveys the history of the pin-up calendar, discusses its promotional role, and presents an interpretive analysis of images of women featured on calendars from 19th-century origins to the present. Calendars from company archives were content analyzed for suggestive poses and scanty attire. The results were compared with legal cases of workplace harassment of women at corresponding intervals. Results found that the pin-up advertising calendar's century-long status as a sanctioned promotional medium is being challenged by recent court rulings and general social climate relating to sexual harassment. Based on this research, the company has pulled its promotional calendars featuring women.

In another historical study, two researchers argued that the mania-depression continuum (highs and lows) describes relationships that can be found among several consumption phenomena previously thought to be unrelated. Such phenomena include risk taking, sensation seeking, product involvement, innovativeness, and hedonic consumption.[5] They examined a specific population through historical sources to access the tradition of association between manic depression and consumption behavior. Their sources were clinical and genetic literature and biographical studies of prominent persons now considered to have been manic-depressive (e.g., Beethoven and Van Gogh) as well as current autobiographical texts by persons diagnosed as manic-depressive. The study identified manic and depressive consumption practices among this population. The results allowed marketers to comprehend and predict consumption phenomena for consumers whose lives are marked by cycling into and out of mania and depression.

Last, a historical method having applications for marketing was used in a study to understand alien residents and offspring of immigrants who live in ethnic communities.[6] Researchers presented the historical contexts that have shaped immigration and assimilation in America and society's understanding of those phenomena. They suggest that history, which may not give a clear answer to formulating appropriate marketing strategies for the second generation of immigrants, does indicate important issues for future investigation.

Product and company histories, which borrow from anthropology to investigate what people thought as well as what they did in the past, are useful for addressing questions of policy, ethics, and appropriate business practices. They play a significant role in developing marketing strategy to reflect changing consumer needs and wants.

Using the Consumer as Researcher

The symbolizing self centers on its own narrative, a life story that is itself created and constantly recreated.

– Robert Jay Lifton

Stories describe turning points in people's lives and help us understand how products figure into their social and personal lives. They feature one person and his or her experiences as told to a researcher. Stories are given many different names, most falling under the rubric of *biographical studies*, which includes individual biography, autobiography, life history, and oral history.

Marketplace researchers select a type of biographical study according to the purpose of the research. *Individual biographies* are written about another person, living or dead, using archival documents and records. Bell's biography of author Virginia Woolf is one example. With *autobiographies*, people write about themselves; *Ogilvy on Advertising* is the autobiography of a famous creative director.

Life histories are reports of an individual's life gathered during interviews and conversations with the person. They are conducted to determine how a life reflects society's cultural themes. Life histories of travelers, filmgoers, amusement park junkies, and so forth are gathered so we might better understand how these forms of consumption fit into the lives of our target audience. Collected over time, these projects are often ongoing and involve several different researchers. In a collaborative approach to life histories, multiple researchers gather information about a person and come together to compare notes. The result is timely and beneficial for understanding the consumption experience of a single target audience member.

Oral histories are collections of historical materials that bring to light a variety of people's lives, from common folks talking about their jobs, such as Studs Terkel's *Working*, to historical recollections of famous people. Ballads and folksongs, archived in libraries and private collections, give marketers incredible insight about the role of products in the lives of consumers.

An author may tell the stories of others by incorporating much of his or her own perspective in the written document; this method is called *interpretive biography*.[7]

Interpretive biographies are recommended for marketplace research because they "blur the lines between fact and fiction,"[8] providing readable accounts of consumer lives that are more easily assimilated by clients and corporations than the more classical approach to biographical writing. Writers' lives are most reflected in interpretive biographies that present a chronology in life-course stages and experiences. The focus is on gathering consumption stories and organizing them around themes in the person's life. The researcher searches for meaning in these stories, looking also for larger structures to explain these meanings within a historical context.

Stories as Purchase Experiences

The basis for all consumer histories is the *stories* they tell as fictional accounts of real consumption events. People tell stories about their personal marketplace experiences to researchers as narrative discourse. Self-stories are often told to focus groups. Stories of addictive consumption are told to members of 12-step programs or shared during motivational seminars. Stories, sometimes motivated by group reactions and response, are often entertaining. Consumer research on compulsive consumption appears as a self-narrative or a story written for a specific audience.[9] During a study of antisocial behavior conducted for a video surveillance company, two men recall stories from their pasts:

> I think appearance makes a lot of difference to how people react to you. Like, one time I went in a 7–11 store to rob it. . . . I was smiling and looked pretty good. When I asked the guy for the money, he shook his head no. So I pulled up my collar, messed my hair, frowned, and robbed a store down the way. No problem this time . . . when I yelled and acted crazy, he gave up the cash.

This girl and me, we went into a music store 'cause I needed some guitar strings. She pretended to slip on the floor, and like, yelled loud so the guy came over and tried to help. That's when I grabbed the pack of strings and we walk out. Then I see a rerun of this movie, "Alice Doesn't Live Here" or something, and they do the same trick, and I think, did I copy them . . . or what?

Personal experience narratives are also useful for marketplace research. They differ from stories in that personal narratives are more likely to be based on commonplace anecdotes or mundane experiences told to an individual, whereas stories involve pivotal life experiences. Here is an example of a woman talking about her recent personal experience of shopping at Home Depot:

> When I got there . . . it was a huge store . . . I started looking around for some tile. Big banners hung down, so I read where it said "tile" and headed in that direction. I found lots of tile . . . all kinds . . . and I was confused about what kind I needed for my bathroom. The contractor just said to pick out some tile . . . he didn't say what kind. So I stood there for a while, and finally a young man came up to me. . . . He asked if I needed help. So I told him my problem, and he spent a half hour with me. He seemed to know what

he was talking about . . . certainly more than I knew . . . so I took some samples to show the contractor. It was a nice experience. I will go back there again.

Group storytelling sessions are useful for investigators who can work with participants over time using specific writing assignments. Topics such as shopping for a friend, watching a soap opera, taking a trip to Disneyland, and so forth are assigned, and participants return with their stories written for sharing with the other group members. Such story sharing is different than a focus group because topics are preassigned, and members are free to include whatever information they deem pertinent to the topic. Stories and discussions of those stories give researchers an inside glimpse of a phenomenon under study.

During a group discussion of Disneyland, consumers nodded in agreement about the dismal task of waiting in line for each ride or attraction. The waiting process was mentioned in all of their stories and anecdotes. Some waiting experiences were comical, others tragic. Disney used the information collected during this group storytelling session to reevaluate their queuing procedures. A policy to limit park entrance minimized the time visitors spent waiting in line. Group sessions conducted after the new policy went into effect revealed fewer "waiting" stories, indicating the policy's success.

Marketplace Biographies

Biographies produce narrative texts to be interpreted as documentary evidence of real experiences. To be useful for marketing, biographical texts must be organized and analyzed using an *interpretive* framework of analysis. This framework – a process of reading lives – has several steps, which are discussed briefly here.

During interviewing, researchers gather contextual biographical materials. Interviewers then prompt consumers to expand on various sections of their stories. The researcher or research team interprets the narratives, isolates segments, and identifies patterns of meaning. Researchers compare the texts of several respondents for similarities and differences, to form theoretical generalizations that produce a model of their consumption world. The research is triangulated for multiple perspectives on the same consumption experience.

Two interpretive formats are used for marketplace research using biographical text: The first is written from the subject's perspective for interpretation, and the other occurs when the subjects help the researcher interpret their point of view. Researchers using the first format can collect the data, excuse consumers, and proceed with interpretation on their own. In the second instance, consumers must remain in the study throughout the entire analytical stage.

Consequences of consumer stories about their shoplifting or robbing experiences provide a pattern useful to a video surveillance company for positioning cameras and briefing clients on offender behavior. Self-narratives collected about shopping experiences in large home supply outlets reveal that consumers who were helped with their purchase decisions are more apt to return to that particular outlet than to a competitor.

Product and company histories are collected to situate them within a *historical* framework. Consumer story anecdotes and lived experiences provide primary data of consumption narratives within a *cultural and materialistic* framework. In both cases, the researcher plays an active, not passive, interpretive role in data analysis. Immersion in research data is a necessary condition for successful marketplace researchers.

Researcher as Consumer

Occasionally, marketers use their own personal experiences as a research method. The process can occur individually or as a group and is another way of telling a consumption story. Each story has a plot that begins with past experience, describes a current experience, and ends with how the experience will affect future experiences. To act as aresearch instrument, you focus experiences in four directions simultaneously: inward, outward, backward, and forward. Inward focus captures your internal feelings, hopes, reactions, and so forth; the outward focus is your environment, your reality. Backward and forward are the past-present-future aspects of the experience. The data for your research are collected in journal entries, field notes, photographs, letters, artifacts, and so on, and should be thought of as field texts. Collected artifacts are used to trigger your memory so that you can recall the story to write up at a later time.

Using all the collected data, you then organize your materials so they make sense and construct a story. The story is written from your point of view and should combine all the elements of the experience, including conversations with others and your personal thoughts. While writing, imagine you are in conversation with an audience. Think of all the questions they might ask you about your experience and answer them. Include photographs and depth descriptions in your story so readers can feel what you felt.

Biographical research groups doing research can share their experiences from the story narratives to identify patterns and themes. A final report summarizes the collective approach to the phenomenon, including what things you had in common and what things were different.

The advantage of using yourself as collection instrument is that you are able to bringmore insight to a consumption experience than you can achieve by interviewing others. Asa traveler, your trip becomes a journey of discovery that, when recalled, provides valuable clues for understanding the difficulties and joys associated with tourism and travel. Once scoffed at by traditionalists, the self-narrative is now considered a legitimate method for conducting consumer and marketplace research.

Whether gathered from historical, biographical, or personal narratives, the past informs consumption experiences better than surveys or scaling techniques can inform them. The personalized perspective brings dimension and depth to consumer research and is readily available to students of all marketplace phenomena.

Case in Point: Biographical Life History as Consumer Research[10]

Client: Newport Beach Surgery Center

Problem: How to market cosmetic surgery to women over 40

RQ: *What is the consumption experience of aesthetic cosmetic surgery?*

Data Collection:

2. Self-disclosure through a variety of elicitation devices, such as
   - # High school yearbooks
   - # Family and personal photo albums Personal diaries
   - # Media from the 1950s and 1960s, including audio recordings, magazines, comic books, and films
   - # Collection of 40 pairs of eyeglasses worn during the consumer-researcher's life
4. Documents of information on face lift procedures
6. Interviews with plastic surgeons
8. Informal discussions with women who had successfully completed the operation and with family and friends about these decisions
10. Postoperative photographs
12. Audio tapes of preoperative and postoperative narrative The researcher, once deciding on plastic surgery, agreed to compile thoughts and feelings before and during the operation by the funding center. Following surgery, the researcher decided on a retrospective examination as to her motives for the surgery. Memorabilia, momentos, media, and visual records (listed earlier) were collected for analysis to help the author recall her life as it related to making a decision to undergo surgery. Elicitation devices were used to initiate the writing process, which began several months after the operation during an overseas assignment in Brussels and continued for 4 months.

Data Analysis: The author immersed herself in a process of analysis to understand what past and present elements led to the decision to elect surgery. Emotional and physical changes occurred during the analysis period.

Notes were sorted, edited, and arranged in chronological order. Four areas of influence emerged from the notes: Presurgery account of significant events, categories of influencers in the decision process, details of the surgery and recovery period, and reflections on the purchase.

Results: The author identified six factors that were primary contributors to the decision to have cosmetic surgery:

2. Place of residence and its accompanying lifestyle and expectations of residents
4. Peer group and their social values
6. Popular media during childhood and current Hollywood influence
8. Family, including two grown children, sister, mother, and grandmother
10. Timing of operation coinciding with personal and professional milestones
12. Adequate financial resources

Several factors were incorporated into a report for the surgery center, such as physician selection, satisfaction with the care and medical service received, and an analysis of print advertising for plastic surgery services in the immediate area.

A 40-page article was accepted for publication in a consumer research journal.

Discussion: This project is a unique approach to exploring cosmetic surgery. Other research reported on respondent testimony about why they had surgery, how they felt after, and reactions from their friends and family. Valuable information was gleaned from a series of in-depth interviews, and the researcher analyzed testimonies for similarities and differences.

What was not contained in past research was the perspective of a consumer before, during, and after the consumption of a face-lift. The resulting narrative provides a window of understanding for women considering surgery and for the medical professionals who market such services.

The client was able to use the narrative as a launching point for developing informational tools and a sensitive marketing campaign. Rather than featuring bathing-suit-clad, large-breasted coeds, ads contained the faces of mature women discussing their options for continuing and vibrant lives. Hotlines and Web pages were developed to link potential users with women who had undergone surgery. The surgery center provided these links and a physician referral service free of charge, using criteria provided from the research to match consumer needs with provider services.

Conclusion: Life history method enabled the author to elaborate on a consumption experience more completely than previously achieved with other research methods and techniques. The study revealed that, for one woman, consumption choices were made for reasons that revolved around her place in the physical and psychological universe that defined her. By understanding that place, marketers can more appropriately target their audience.

Notes

1. From Scotte, J. W. (1989). History in crisis? The other's side of the story. *American Historical Review, 94,* 680–692.
2. For a complete treatment of the subject, see Tuchman, G. (1994). Historical social science: Methodologies, methods and meanings. In N. Denzin & Y. Lincoln (Eds.), *Handbook of qualitative research* (pp. 306–323). Thousand Oaks, CA: Sage.
3. From Phillips, J. (1993). History from below: Women's underwear and the rise of women's sports. *Journal of Popular Culture,* 27(2), 129–146.
4. Based on a study by Frederick-Collins, J. (1993, April). *The working man's constant companion: The pin-up advertising calendar and sexual harassment in the workplace.* A paper presented to the annual conference of the American Academy of Advertising, Montreal, Canada.
5. See Hirschman, E., & Stern, B. (1998). Consumer behavior and the wayward mind: The influence of mania and depression on consumption. *Advances in Consumer Research, 25,* 421–427.
6. See Lavin, M., & Archdeacon, T. (1989). The relevance of historical method for marketing research. In E. Hirschman (Ed.), *Interpretive consumer research.* Provo, UT: Association for Consumer Research.
7. See Denzin, N. (1989). *Interpretive biography.* Newbury Park, CA: Sage.
8. From Creswell, J. (1998). *Qualitative inquiry and research design: Choosing among five traditions* (pp. 50–51). Thousand Oaks, CA: Sage.
9. See Hirschman, E. (1992). The consciousness of addiction: Toward a general theory of compulsive consumption. *Journal of Consumer Research, 19,* 155–79.
10. From Sayre, S. (1999). Using introspective self-narrative to analyze consumption: Experiencing plastic surgery. *Consumption Markets & Culture,* 3(2), 99–128.

64

Moving Stories: Using Mobile Methods to Explore the Everyday Lives of Young People in Public Care

*Nicola J. Ross, Emma Renold, Sally Holland
and Alexandra Hillman*

Introduction: Using Mobile Methods to Research Everyday Lives

The article focuses on the use of mobile methods in an ethnographic and participatory research project that explored the everyday lives of a group of young people in care, the (Extra)ordinary Lives project.[1] The article critically examines the productiveness of two different mobile methods employed in our research, 'guided' walks and car journey interactions. These are discussed in relation to the generation of meaningful understandings of everyday lives through the creation of enabling research environments, encounters and exchanges. 'Guided' walks involved a young person walking with a researcher, leading the researcher through locales of significance to them that formed part of their local geographies. The car journey interactions were generated as researchers and participants travelled together to and from designated fieldwork sites, journeys that formed part of the regular routines set up to facilitate young people's access to fortnightly project sessions.

Source: *Qualitative Research,* 9(5) (2009): 605–622.

In exploring the productiveness of these methods this article draws upon an emergent field within the social sciences, mobilities research, that focuses attention on journeys themselves as important in place-making practices (see, Binnie et al., 2007; Sheller and Urry, 2006). The new mobilities paradigm in the social sciences has turned attention to the ways in which mobile research methods can be utilised to understand everyday experiences through embodied, multi-sensory research experiences. Journeys themselves are focused upon as dynamic, place-making practices foregrounding movement, interactivity and the multi-sensory, focusing attention on research relationships, contexts and engagements (see Anderson, 2004; Hall et al., 2008; Kusenbach, 2003; Lee and Ingold, 2006; Moles, 2008; Pink, 2008).

No Place without Self and No Self without Place

Many of the recent studies that utilise mobile methods are informed by phenomenological approaches to place, and the writing of Casey in particular, that:

> The relationship between self and place is not just one of reciprocal influence . . . but also, more radically, of constitutive coingredience: each is essential to the being of the other. In effect, there is *no place without self and no self without place.* (Casey, 2001: 684, original emphasis)

Casey conflates his term 'place-world' with Soja's (1996) term 'thirdspace' to emphasize the importance of 'a world that is not only perceived or conceived but also actively *lived* and receptively *experienced*', enacted through the body by processes of 'outgoing' (bodily encountering places) and 'incoming' (traces of place being inscribed on the body) over time shaping the meaning of places and significances of them for people (Casey, 2001: 687–8, original emphasis). This is a performative process, through the practice of our fieldwork we (researchers and participants) mutually construct the field, not a fixed field but rather 'the field as event', transformed over time through our continued practice, always in a state of becoming (Coleman and Collins, 2006: 12). Many of the recent studies that utilise mobile research methods are also informed by de Certeau's (1984) work emphasizing the immediacy and nowness of walking, and as Thrift (2004) discusses, of driving and 'passengering', as multi-sensory, place-making practices. Mundane practices and everyday experiences are subject to scrutiny, turning attention to the embodied experiences of different travel modes, constructing journeys as 'dwelling-in-motion' and focusing on the multitudes of activities they comprise (Sheller and Urry, 2006: 214). Our research contributes to this emerging field, exploring the affordances of mobile research encounters in generating rich accounts of the, often nomadic, everyday lives of young people in care and exploring the productiveness of motion, commotion and distraction to the sharing of intimate narratives.

The (Extra)ordinary Lives Research Project

To set the context for the discussion of mobile methods it is pertinent to outline briefly the (Extra)ordinary Lives project. The research focused on the everyday lives and relationship cultures of a group of young people in public care and the possibilities and challenges of enabling their active participation in the research process, from design through to dissemination. The project was informed by participatory methodologies in childhood studies, where children and young people themselves are positioned centrally within the research process, generating accounts of their lives (see Christensen, 2004; Gallagaher and Gallagher, 2008; Holland et al., forthcoming 2009). We employed a participatory approach in response to the social location of the young people involved. Young people in care are a group subject to much scrutiny, their lives regularly monitored and assessed with aspects of their private lives discussed at review meetings and care proceedings. We sought to avoid the outcome-based, fixed portrayal of children in care as 'failed subjects' with poor educational, emotional, behavioural and health prospects (DfES, 2006; Garrett, 1999) and did not wish to intensify the scrutiny which they are subject to. We thus set out to create a research context that we hoped would enable the young people involved to set the limits on their own involvement in the research project and facilitate the co-generation of meaningful representations of their everyday lives (see Holland et al., 2008; Renold et al., 2008). We also adopted an ethnographic approach to record and explore the possibilities and challenges of enabling the active participation of young people in the research process. The 'data' generated are thus comprised of multiple, overlapping and intertwined strands.

Between October 2006 and July 2007 a team of four researchers worked with eight young people utilising a range of mobile and participatory methods to co-generate multi-media accounts and representations of the lives of this group of young people in public care. Contact with the young people was initially built around fortnightly group project sessions, held at a local family centre, where a range of activities were made available (e.g. film-making, photography, music-making, and craft based activities). The young people were aged from 10 to 20, 6 girls and 2 boys, all white and Welsh. Their care arrangements varied. At the time of fieldwork, of the six younger participants (aged 10–15), 3 were in kinship care, and 3 were in foster care. The two older participants were care leavers, though each had experience of living independently, one had returned to live with her previous foster family. Some of the young people had previous experience of living in residential settings.[2] Not all of the research encounters were based around these project group sessions and it is part of the out of session contact that this article centres on: the 'guided' walks and car journey interactions, exploring the affordances of these mobile methods in creating enabling research contexts and generating meaningful understandings of young people's everyday lives.

Marking Lines of Lives: 'Guided' Walks and Car Journey Interactions

Though different in format the 'guided' walks and car journey interactions had similarities, each lent the research encounter a degree of flexibility and openness, and yet an immediacy and connection to young people's everyday experiences. They 'rooted' research engagements in the everyday present, yet they opened avenues for memories and imagined futures to be aired and explored. They generated insights into the young peoples' everyday lives, and an assemblage of fragmented narratives on their often complex family relationships, their home(s), neighbourhoods, and peer relations, set within the wider context of everyday talk of the near and present (e.g. from their school day or places, people and things passed en route). These interactions on the move and conversations that took place within them were interspersed with interruptions, of stuttering, paused, lost, repeated exchanges, within which the intimate was interspersed with the mundane. Space for narratives to be shared was opened up, closed down, diverted, and revisited in response to the negotiation of these shared experiential journeys.

The multi-sensory experiences of mobile research encounters were foregrounded in these journeys as experienced, and as recorded in our data records of them. We have discussed in more detail elsewhere the capacities of the various recording technologies to 'capture' these experiences: the movement, sounds, smells, rhythm, emotion, feel and so forth of these encounters, and to differences in multi-sensory research encounters as experienced, as recorded, and as represented (Ross et al., 2008; see also Dicks et al., 2006; Emmison and Smith, 2000; Pink, 2008). These mobile research encounters were recorded in researchers' fieldnotes and the young people had the opportunity, if the wished, to audio and/or video record all or part of the walks they undertook, and to make audio recordings of some of the car journey interactions. The young people themselves had control of the digital technologies used, deciding on the content of their recordings, and what of this recorded material they wishes to keep and/or to share with the research team.

'Guided' Walks: Passageways to Perspectives

The 'guided' walks typically involved a young person walking with a researcher, leading them through locales of significance to them that formed part of their everyday, local geographies. This allowed the young people involved to convey their movement through, and site themselves in, their everyday environments. The term 'guided' walk' is used to give the participant led aspect of the research encounter prominence, and also to reflect the mode of movement involved. However, the inverted commas around guided are used to problematize this neat construction of one walker simply guiding another. Although the intention was that when walking together the participant, rather than researcher, should take the lead on decisions regarding the choice of route taken (over ground and in narratives) and their negotiation of this, the taking of the walk together meant of course that the walk formed part of a co-generated research encounter, with inputs from each interlacing in its construction. They formed, as Anderson (2004: 260) suggests, a 'collage of collaboration'. Those that undertook walks with a researcher ably communicated their intimate knowledge of their localities. Attention was drawn to favoured places, features, animals and things passed and to their social relations in their localities, meeting places, play spaces, friends' homes, local shops etc., illustrating the richness that walking with participants can bring to understandings of everyday lives, providing insights into young people's active, emotional and imaginative engagements in their localities.

When discussing visual anthropologists' use of walking with while filming their subjects, Pink (2007: 247) suggests that this creates a 'sense of closeness to their experience' immersing the filmmaker in the locales of their subjects, 'hearing the definitions of the places and persons that make up the route' creating a 'form of sociality between filmmaker and subject as they walk and pause, alongside or behind.' Similarly, Lee and Ingold (2006) construct walking with as a productive means to comprehend relationships between people and place, a rich way of socializing, closeness created through shared bodily engagement with the environment, sensing all that is going on around as the route is taken in step. They suggest that by focusing on the mobilities of others we can come to unravel the ways in which place itself is comprised of multiple interlacing routes. Lines of lives mapped out in the 'oft-repeated walks', the mundane, everyday journeys that through repetition 'produce a thicker association of the route with the walker' (Lee and Ingold, 2006: 77). For us, it was this immersion into the young people's everyday local geographies that was a key function of the 'guided' walks, the journeys as experienced.

Car Journey Interactions: Making Meaningful Routinized Journeys

The car journeys differed from the 'guided' walks not only in terms of the mode of movement used, but in terms of the 'guiding' of the route, and in terms of their frequency. They were not originally envisaged as being part of the data collection, but just a necessary means of enabling young people to attend the project sessions. As the project progressed, it became clear that these conversations that took place in the car were potentially interesting data in themselves, and young people were invited to record the conversations if and when they wished. Generally the shortest or most easily negotiable route was taken between pick up and drop off points (young people's homes or schools and the project session location), but while en route there were opportunities for the young people to share their knowledge of their city with the researchers. There was scope for some diversions to be made, passing by places of importance to the young person, taking a route via a local park or a former home area, with young people sometimes capitalizing on researchers' lack of knowledge of the city to choose a preferred route. While the 'guided' walks were generally undertaken only once, the car journeys were repeated fortnightly. Set routines were established over time with young people often being collected and dropped off by the same researcher for each of the sessions. The regularity of the routine meant that relations between certain young people and researchers were strengthened during this contact time, each becoming increasingly familiar with the other.

There is increasing interest in the embodied practices of driving and 'passengering', the emotional, multi-sensory experiences of car dwelling, within the mobilities literature (see Bull, 2003; Sheller, 2004; Thrift, 2004). With regards to children's experiences of carspace, the car has been constructed as 'supervised, bounded space' (Barker, 2003: 137) often symbolized as a 'protective capsule' through which the dangerous world is traversed (Sibley, 1995: 136). Other travel modes (walking, cycling, bus travel) are viewed as offering children greater opportunities to engage in and with their localities in active and imaginative ways – socializing, playing, sensing (Mitchell et al., 2006; Ross, 2007). With respect to the sharing of car space, Laurier et al. (2008) looked at the ways in which cars 'framed' interactions, 'audibly sealed' yet 'publicly visible', the motion of the car contrasted with relative immobility in the interior space, the rowed seating arrangements directing gaze forwards not toward each other, conversations punctuated by pauses and breaks, and other activities, listening to the radio, looking out of the window. They suggest this context aided interspersion of more serious or difficult conversations within the mundane of the routinized journey – conversations that 'might generate pauses, need pauses, and yet want those pauses not to become too uncomfortable.' Likewise, Ferguson (2008) pointed to the potential of routinized car journeys to create a place of communication when commenting upon the car journey as a site of social work practice. Referring to instances when social workers travel with young people in public care for access visits, to new placements, or for meetings, he constructs the car journey itself as a valuable time for talk between practitioner and young person. These insights resonated with our own findings, that the mobile experience of these research encounters lent inroads into and routes out of narratives, aiding young people in the pacing of the sharing of their accounts, and for researchers to broach potentially sensitive topics.

Directing Intimacies: Moving between the Mundane and the Meaningful

Looking at the productiveness of the mobile methods used in our research with regards to research interactions, communicated quite clearly their potential for generating free flowing conversation. Discussing firstly the car journey interactions, it was evident that talk of interest to our substantive research themes was set within the more everyday car talk of routes and directions, the mundane talk of driving and passengering, as the following extract demonstrates. This transcript from an audio extract of a car journey interaction takes place as one of the younger participants, Rosie, and Sally (researcher) travel together on one of their regular journeys home from a fieldwork session.

Sally: So you still see some of your dad's family do you even though you don't see your dad?
Rosie: They lives across the road from him, from me.
Sally: Oh really?
Rosie: Not my mum.
Sally: Yeah.
Rosie: Her house, – You just go up there and turn and there is my house, yeah.
Sally: Yeah.
Rosie: The other day my sister
Sally: Yeah
Rosie: Are you going straight up?
Sally: I have gone this way now, yeah.
Rosie: Yeah, my sister, has seen him, my dad up -
Sally: Oh 'cause it's funny because we were just talking about him last time and you were saying that you hadn't seen him for years.
Rosie: I know! I haven't, but my sister has seen him, but I don't want to see him. No way will I!
Sally: No. And how did your sister feel about it?
Rosie: Well it's not her dad is it? We're
Sally: Oh I see.
Rosie: We're like half sisters
Sally: I know you are.
Rosie: But we think we're like, we're proper sisters
Sally: Yeah
Rosie: 'Cause we've got a different dad.
Sally: Yeah
Rosie: Yeah, we, we, um, we thinks we're real sisters. Though really we are.
Sally: It is how you feel that matters. Isn't it?
Rosie: Yeah, but we got like, – Go straight up here if you want. I know the way.
Sally: Ok, show me a different way.

This extract, like many of the conversations Rosie and Sally shared as they travelled back and forth together, was interspersed with intimate talk about places passed and associations with events that took place there involving Rosie and her family. Rosie is in kinship care. She lives with her grandparents and has regular contact with her mother. Through these regular car journeys we gained insights into her everyday life at home and in her locality and issues of importance to her: the strong locally based ties to family and neighbourhood, her longing to live with her mum again, her two bedrooms, tensions in family relations between her mum and dad's side of the family, her close relationship with her half sister, fights she has with her brother, trips to the dentist, her favourite teddy, adults of significance to her (and other children) in her locality, such as the man who fixes bikes. These insights into Rosie's everyday life would not have been gleaned from more structured interviews – as with the other younger participants involved in the study direct questioning with Rosie generated scant response. In the car setting, the researcher's main focus of attention was the road, and driving safely, resulting in a certain inattentiveness to the conversation held at times. Such inattentiveness was productive in allowing the young people space and time to control the sharing of their narratives in an unpressurized manner, more able to direct conversations held with the researcher. In Rosie's case, she would usually switch on the digital recorder when she got into the car, and when she considered that enough had been said, she would spend the rest of the journey listening back to the recording. At this point she had the opportunity to delete the recording if she wished.

Likewise, the 'guided' walks encouraged free flowing conversation, offering a means through which young people could share past memories, associations, and future imaginings that the journey brought to mind. They placed the young people's everyday locales at the centre of the research encounter, evident in the following extract, a transcript created from an audio recording made of a 'guided' walk. The researcher, Nicola, journeyed with Jodie along the multitude of paths and routes that Jodie knew in her local area (a housing estate on the outskirts of a city), through natural areas and parks that she valued, stopping as Jodie filmed (using a small handheld camcorder) these places, special to her, and the birds in the trees, the pond and the mole hills. This research journey conveying the centrality of animals in Jodie's life, her strong sense of place and locally based relations that her kinship placement had maintained.

Jodie:	I like those sort of dogs.
Nicola:	Aha, they're quite cute, aren't they?
Jodie:	I like small dogs.
Nicola:	They're quite funny when they run.
Jodie:	When we first had my dog, Charlie, um he was skinny and, 'cause like the last owner he had didn't look after him.
Nicola:	Oh, did he get, not treated very well?
Jodie:	Yeah, and my nan went down the pet shop, down the place where you get the dogs from. She walked in, she seen Charlie, she goes, she was with my auntie, she goes 'Sharon, I want that dog by there.' And my auntie, the first thing she said was, 'Mum, I think you'd better go round and look, there'll be better dogs than him.'
Nicola:	Aha
Jodie:	And then my nan says, goes 'Oh yeah I know, but I want that one by there.' So then they looked round and they come back to Charlie and my mum, my nan, ehm, she was like, she asked the

> man whether she could take him home, like the day she seen him, and they said no, because they've got to keep him for like another week or so.
>
> *Nicola*: Ah, to sort of
> *Jodie*: Yeah, to see whether the owners come back.
> *Nicola*: Ah. So they get a wee while to change their mind then do they after they put them in?
> *Jodie*: Yeah. But my nan said, 'Oh if the, if the owner ain't very nice with her, like treats her like dirt, then why should she have her back, or they have her back, because they don't deserve animals.
> *Nicola*: Aha, because they weren't looking after it very well.
> *Jodie*: But my nan loved it.
> *Nicola*: But the owner didn't come back then so she got it?
> *Jodie*: Pardon?
> *Nicola*: The owners didn't come back then, so that was alright?
> *Jodie*: Yeah. So she had the dog in the end.
> *Nicola*: Aha
> *Jodie*: And then like when we first had, when we had. Shall we go in here or?
> *Nicola*: Yeah, we'll go up this way.
> *Jodie*: When we had him, he was skinny, his colour of his fur changed
> *Nicola*: Aha
> *Jodie*: It was like all light and everything. But now it's gone darker, he's put on a bit of weight.
> *Nicola*: Oh, he looks healthy now, yeah.
> *Jodie*: Yeah, he's had a haircut, because when we first had him, he, all this ears were like, because they're quite fluffy
> *Nicola*: Aha
> *Jodie*: It was all mangled and the skin was like
> *Nicola*: Wasn't getting brushed properly and everything.
> *Jodie*: My nan tried to brush it but like she couldn't get through it because of all the knots. So she had a cut, had it cut in the summer and now he's gone way better than he was.

Here, Jodie shares a story about her dog, and how he came to be part of her family. As the conversation unfolds it speaks to Jodie's, and her family's attachment to their dog, and to animals generally, and to her own and her family's thoughts on care and family. The open flow of the talk and lack of direct or probing questioning from the researcher allowed these details to emerge, yet remain only partially revealed. Jodie herself set the boundaries on what she wished to share. Jodie generally preferred not to engage in much talk of an intimate or private nature during her involvement in the research, indeed she consented to take part in the research only after it was made clear that the research would not be like a form of therapy in which she might feel forced to talk about her past experiences. Respecting young people's views and concerns, consent was negotiated with young people throughout the research process on an individual basis (see Renold et al., 2008). The 'guided' walk was one of the few occasions that Jodie engaged in intimate talk, for example recounting details of her life when she lived with her mother, making connections through her focus on animals or places in the present, to remembered events. As in her recounting in the extract above of the day that Charlie the dog was spotted by her grandmother, taken into their family, cared for and nursed back to health, many of these stories she shared had a tragic undercurrent. The neglected dog that her grandmother saved, the dog she had while living with her mum that got stuck in the pond and had to be rescued, the hamsters that fought one day, injuring each other so badly that one died. It is perhaps revealing to note that at the start of the extract about Charlie the dog Jodie refers to the previous owner as male, not looking after the male dog Charlie, yet, part way through, changes the pronoun to her for the dog and refers to the previous owner as female before utilising the plural: 'if the owner ain't very nice with her, like treats her like dirt, then why should she have her back, or they have her back, because they don't deserve animals', giving insights to her own constructs of caring, and perhaps also making connections to her own personal experiences of care and neglect here. We can only surmise, given Jodie's reluctance to discuss directly with us these more private aspects of her life, and following our ethical framework, our respect for the young people's right to share with us only the details of their lives that they wished to share, preventing further exploration.

Engagements and Disengagements: Pacing the Sharing of Narratives

The mobile methods utilised in the study situated research encounters in the everyday locales of participants. This was key to creating a context in which the young people could talk freely about their everyday lives in a spontaneous way. These shared journeys lent the research interactions an open and evolving format. Conversation gaps, which may have appeared particularly lengthy in the stillness of a more static, fixed location, more formalized interview, were less noticeable, the conversation itself only one contribution to the mass of other elements that comprised the journey – the people, places and things passed and sounds, sights, smells, feel and so forth of these encounters. In the 'guided' walks, the rhythm of the walk itself offered potential for engagements and dis-engagements, walking in unison disrupted by quickening or slowing of pace, moving towards and away from each other. Walking with young people through their everyday locales triggered the sharing of narratives from the mundane to the intimate and significant, the rhythm of the journey creating a context through which young people could pace the sharing of their narratives. Similarly with the car journey interactions, the commotion of the journey, what was passed en route mingling with in-car activities – young people turning on the radio, singing along, the researcher negotiating the route, attention focused on driving, lapsing between engaged and distracted listening and talking – provided both stimulus for, and interruptions and disruptions to, interactions.

The multitude of sensory cues that comprise embodied shared journeys, are productive in creating enabling research contexts and engagements. Such embodied and mobile research interactions, immersed in the ordinary commotion of the everyday were effective in aiding young people to manage the pacing, generation and sharing of accounts of their everyday lives and for researchers to gain meaningful understandings of these accounts. Motion and emplaced knowledge serving to mediate normative generational power relations.[3] Likewise, Hall, Lashua and Coffey (2008: 1030) when discussing their use of mobile methods, whereby young people led researchers on 'walking tours' of their local neighbourhoods, reframed these encounters as sound-walks, the 'mobile exploration of (local) space and soundscapes', after coming to recognize the productive effect of movement and noise in shaping these research encounters:

> Noise (also movement) breaks up conversation, or rather punctuates it, gives it an everyday rhythm of stops and starts . . . Interviews as, or nested within, sound-walks lose focus – to productive effect; they *range*, topically as well as topographically. This wandering returns conversation to the everyday, and noise augments this process . . . supplying an aggregate, ambient bustle and hum in the midst of which one's own voice becomes ordinary again – just one sound among many. (Hall et al., 2008: 1034, original emphasis)

To illustrate further the productiveness of distracted rather than attentive research encounters, which characterized the mobile methods, we look in detail at two episodes, firstly from a car journey interaction and secondly from a 'guided' walk. The ways in which motion and commotion have a productive effect on research interactions are detailed by examining an episode from one car journey interaction, which highlights in particular the enabling capacity of noise in relation to research engagements and disengagements. Following on from this we discuss disruptions during a 'guided' walk, that result in lost narratives, yet highlight the ways in which such interruptions are not entirely problematic, serving to divert conversations onto other topics.

Motion, Commotion and the Multi Sensory

Bull (2003: 264–367; 2008) looking at 'car habitation' (mainly from the perspective of solo drivers) suggests that listening to music in the confined, privatized space of the car, with the volume turned up high enough to drown out the other soundscapes of the journey such as the car engine or noises from the surroundings, transforms the driving experience into a more liberating one. This association of car space with freedom was also evident in our study despite the different context, the sharing of car space, by researcher and young person. The following extract, a transcript from an audio recording taking place as Cerys and Emma (researcher) make one of their regular journeys to a field-work session, demonstrates Cerys' utilisation of the car stereo, and the great degree of control she had of this during the car journeys, to allow her to create her own auditory sphere. The dynamics of the research encounter very much dictated by Cerys' desire to chat with Emma as they journeyed together to and from the project session or to listen instead to music which she liked in Emma's collection of CDs or from the radio. Here, Cerys who has just been collected directly from school by Emma spends the first 5 minutes or so of the journey detailing a fight she had with another girl. The extract shown catches the end of this conversation, with Cerys drawing this narrative to a close.

> *Cerys:* Well my old key worker Julie, who I'm really close to, works in her home, in Sadie's home, the girl who I had a fight with.
>
> *Emma:* Oh really.
>
> *Cerys:* And she was on duty that night and then Gary phoned up and said, 'Sadie's just got beat up by Cerys.' And she went, 'Cerys who?' He went, 'Little Cerys who used to live here.' And she went, 'Some things never change.' And then she got home, – Sadie and Gary said that she's gonna get home, – and she said, she has a go at Julie over me. She was like, – then Julie said, 'Well Cerys put you in your place guaranteed, 'cause Cerys' done, always been like that. And she would have battered hell out of you so that's what you get for starting on the wrong girl and saying the wrong thing.'
>
> *Emma:* Oh really.
>
> *Cerys:* She said, 'Now hopefully you've learned your lesson 'cause if you don't she'll just do it again.' Oh look they've got the same car, down there. All the way down there now. Loser. It was really funny, I was like that, yeah, OK, alright.
>
> *Emma:* Is that the home that we drove by?
>
> *Cerys:* I'm going ice-skating tomorrow.
>
> *Emma:* Are you?
>
> *Cerys:* Yeah.
>
> *Emma:* Again.
>
> *Cerys:* With my mum.
>
> *Emma:* Cool. Oh your mum!
>
> *Cerys:* Thanks for the pictures. Yeah. Mad innit.
>
> *Emma:* Yeah. That's, that's something different innit?
>
> *Cerys:* Tell you what I haven't had on
> [Cerys turns radio on, then looks for a CD to play.]
>
> *Emma:* I know it's all I've got at the moment. Oh. I meant to bring some more.
>
> *Cerys:* Shut up. [Cerys says to the radio as she puts on an Amy Winehouse CD and sings along]

Cerys uses music, first trying the radio, then a CD, as a means to bring to an end some intimate talk. She draws herself away from the intimate talk first by beginning to talk about what's going on around her, she changes subjects rapidly, ignores Emma's inputs, then turns on the radio, searches for a CD to play and finally starts to sing along. In doing so she makes clear her choice to end the conversation, a choice made easy by the ready availability of alternative sounds to fill the void created by the ending of the conversation, avoiding any potentially awkward silences. Many of the latter car journeys that Cerys and Emma made together became increasingly dominated by the music which Cerys selected to play – usually played loud, which often resulted in a turning up/turning down battle for the control of the volume with Emma, and often a replaying of tracks over and over again by Cerys if the music was talked over. Cerys's immersion in the music appeared pronounced at such times. Arkette (2004: 160) argues that sound 'is never a neutral phenomenon. Each sound is imbued with its own lexical code: sound as sign, symbol, index; as ostensibly defining a personal territory in the case of the ghettoblaster or car stereo' and that these 'sound markers' can be used to reinforce identity. The flexibility and openness of the car journey interactions facilitated young people's expression of such identity markers and exploration of these musical identity markers by the researchers in conversations held with young people at the time, or revisited later. It was clear that Cerys was capitalizing upon her freedom to be 'hyper', a term she often used to describe herself when she was being loud and animated and making her presence felt to those around. Cerys' noise generation, playing music loud or shouting out of the window, are means through which she can disengage herself from the research context, and during the journey make herself publicly audible as well as 'publicly visible' (Laurier et al., 2008).

In the confines of the car, creating distance can be achieved through various orientations of the body, looking or leaning out of the window, leaning forward to search for a CD to play or radio channel to listen to, looking down to play with a handheld game or mobile phone. We have discussed elsewhere young people's process of 'becoming participant' and the ways in which we learnt to pick up on the cues that signalled young people's disengagements from the research process (Hillman et al., 2008; Renold et al., 2008).

The multitude of occurrences that the journey threw up and activities that could be focused upon offered the young people greater opportunity to decide when to engage in conversation and to direct the subject of this. This lack of an intense focus on the talk itself, unlike the context of more structured interviews held in stillness, was key in enabling the young people to share their stories at their own pace. Distractedness, rather than attentiveness, due to the researcher's need to concentrate on the road, was a productive element of these mobile research encounters. The capacity for such disengagements demonstrates the effectiveness of the mobile methods in supporting our participatory aims, of working collaboratively with the young people to allow them to generate, in their own time, their own representations of their everyday lives. The mobile and multi-sensory journeys enabling young people to lever some control over the scope of their research engagements.

Disrupting Routes: Dead Ends, Diversions and Meanderings

As we have discussed the 'guided' walks had an unstructured, flexible format, with the aim of responding to the direction and interests of the young person as they walked with the researcher through settings familiar to them, deciding on the route, the pace and the pauses. However, the reality of the journey, shared and experienced together, meant that the journey was at all times co-generated. The following extract, a transcript created from an audio recording from a 'guided' walk, where one young person, Megan, is out in her locality with Nicola (researcher), draws attention to disruptions to the idea of the walk as participant guided (over ground and in narratives). The researcher's perceptions of immediate risks, increasingly impact on the research interactions and the researcher begins to impose constraints on the route taken as the walk continues and starts to direct talk to focus on what she perceives as immediate risks, cutting off routes into other conversations that Megan wishes to take. Nonetheless, this extract also reveals some of the ways in which the walk offered up the opportunity for such power differentials to be challenged. Megan, seeming to pick up on Nicola's anxiety, draws upon her knowledge of her local area to reassure Nicola that she knows well the route that she is taking and will get them home safely:

> Nicola: And watch for the cars. Yeah, we'll just wait here until it's passed. Okay, we can cross over now. Do you want to cross now?
>
> Megan: No, 'cause I'm walking down here.
>
> Nicola: Ah, we're walking on this side.
>
> Megan: Don't worry about that side! We'll get home alright, don't worry.
>
> Nicola: Aha.
>
> Megan: There's the river. It goes that way.
>
> Nicola: So you're on this side then?
>
> Megan: Yep. That's the, ehm, park.
>
> Nicola: And you normally take the routes that aren't the path then?
>
> Megan: Yeah. Me and my cousin, me and my cousin will either walk that way or if not we'll walk this way.
>
> Nicola: Aha.
>
> Megan: Any way. The only time my sister walks this way to her friend's house and if not to school. I told my mum that she's going out. Eh! Shoes look alright now!

The routes taken by Megan, often bypassed the laid out route of the formal path, as she walked along her own paths through her everyday locality, breaking and bending the rules that were laid out by others. In the audio recording of this extract parts of the talk are difficult to hear, almost drowned by the sounds of the passing cars, speeding by, as they walk along the grassy verge at the side of a busy road that runs around the housing estate. Listening carefully the sounds of their feet squelching in the mud can be heard as they walked along the rain soaked grassy verge. Slight anxiety and breathlessness can be heard in the researcher's voice, as they walk at quite a fast pace, uphill, along the muddy verge, following the route that Megan has chosen.

The mobile research encounters were interspersed with such disruptions, meaning that certain narratives were lost. As the extract shown pointed to, much of Megan's narratives about places being passed were lost, yet these disruptions led onto the sharing of other narratives. Talk turned to the routes Megan takes, to her awareness of risks and to safety messages she receives from her family. The plethora of encounters, diversions and disruptions that comprised the experience of the walk allowed the conversations to jump around, incorporating the intimate and the mundane, the near and present, remembered and imagined, in the free flowing movement of the walk and talk allowing young people to share their narratives in a manner which resonated with the meanderings of everyday conversations.

Conclusion: The Productivity of Shared Experiential Journeys

The new mobilities paradigm in the social sciences problematizes sedentarism, thinking that normalizes the static, bounded and rigidly 'placed' as the cornerstones of identity and experience. Attention is increasingly paid to the 'complex interrelation between travel and dwelling, home and not-home' (Sheller and Urry, 2006: 211) in mobilities research and to appropriate methods for researching such experiences through the development of mobile research methods. This article critically examined the use of two mobile methods in research that focused upon the everyday lives of a group of young people in care, where mobility (between homes, families and communities) was a defining feature of being 'in care'.

This article discussed the ways in which mobile research methods can be utilised to create enabling research environments, encounters and exchanges, generating time and space for participants and researchers to co-generate and communicate meaningful understandings of everyday lives. For us, the use of mobile methods offered much value in generating rich accounts of the everyday lives of young people in care and supported our participatory approach, connecting well with the young people's own cultures of communication. We found that the interactions that took place on the move were dynamic, characterized by a more free flowing dialogue, moving from topic to topic, returning to previous topics, allowing unstrained gaps and pauses. The pressure to converse was removed somewhat from these research encounters, the experience of the journey in motion, throwing up diversions to such attentiveness to each other revealing the productivity of distraction. In line with our thinking, Lee and Ingold (2006: 67–8) refer to 'attunement' when purporting that 'walking does not, in and of itself, yield an experience of embodiment, nor is it necessarily a technique of participation' it is the act of *walking with* that is important in these respects that 'walking affords an experience of embodiment to the extent that it is grounded in the inherently sociable engagement between self and the environment'. We would argue that such 'attunement' was also facilitated through act of sharing the journey and car space in the routinized trips that facilitated young people's access to the project sessions. These mobile methods contributed to our participatory research design, enabling young people to exert some choice over their means and level of involvement in a research project by allowing opportunities to generate data on their own terms and to interrupt the flow of data generation as they wish (see also Holland et al., forthcoming 2009).

The two mobile research methods focused upon, 'guided' walks and car journey interactions, were each successful in generating insightful understandings of these young people's everyday lives. It was evident that as each negotiated the routes taken together, young people placed themselves in their everyday locales, interweaving their narratives of the mundane ordinariness of the everyday with the intimate details of their personal histories and future imaginings. These placed and place making research engagements respond to the inter-relatedness of self and place and point to the benefits of utilising and reflecting upon such context specific research interactions in our research practice. They opened out for us the more tightly framed notions and concerns of 'placement' common in social work discourse, to give due attention to place as constitutive and integral to the making of self.

Notes

1. The (Extra)ordinary Lives project was funded by the ESRC as part of the Qualiti node of the National Centre for Research Methods.
2. A decision was taken early on in the project to limit participants to those young people who attended the initial sessions held over the first couple of months, as they had attended regularly and formed a tightly-knit social group. The intensive nature of the project meant that it was not possible to increase the number of young people attending any one session and unethical, we felt, to restrict the attendance of those already involved in the research project.
3. For further discussion of power relations embedded in participatory research as dynamic and relational see Holland et al. (forthcoming, 2009).

References

Anderson, J. (2004) 'Talking Whilst Walking: A Geographical Archaeology of Knowledge', *Area* 36(3): 254–61.
Arkette, S. (2004) 'Sounds Like City', *Theory, Culture & Society* 21(1): 159–68.
Barker, J. (2003) 'Passengers or Political Actors? Children's Participation in Transport Policy and the Micro Political Geographies of the Family', *Space and Polity* 7(2): 135–51.

Binnie, J., Edensor, T., Holloway, J. Millington, S. and Young, C. (2007) 'Mundane Mobilities, Banal Travels', *Social & Cultural Geography* 8(2): 165–74.

Bull, M. (2003) 'Soundscapes of the Car: A Critical Study of Automobile Habitation', in M. Bull and L. Back (eds) *The Auditory Culture Reader*, pp. 357–74. Oxford: Berg.

Casey, E.S. (2001) 'Between Geography and Philosophy: What Does it Mean to be in the Place-World?', *Annals of the Association of American Geographers* 91(4): 683–93.

Christensen, P. (2004) 'Children's Participation in Ethnographic Research: Issues of Power and Representation', *Children & Society* 18(2): 165–76.

Coleman, S. and Collins, P. (2006) 'Introduction: "Being . . . Where?" Performing Fields on Shifting Grounds', in S. Coleman and P. Collins (eds) *Locating the Field: Space, Place and Context in Anthropology*, pp. 1–21. Oxford: Berg.

de Certeau, M. (1984) *The Practice of Everyday Life*. Berkeley, CA: University of California Press.

DfES (2006) *Care Matters: Transforming the Lives of Children and Young People in Care*. London: HMSO. URL: http://dfes.gov.uk/consultations/downloadableDocs/6731-DfES-Care%20Matters.doc

Dicks, B., Soyinka, B. and Coffey, A. (2006) 'Multimodal Ethnography', *Qualitative Research* 6(1): 77–96.

Emmison, M. and Smith, P. (2000) *Researching the Visual: Images, Objects, Contexts and Interactions in Social and Cultural Enquiry*. London: Sage.

Ferguson, H. (2008) 'Liquid Social Work: Welfare Interventions as Mobile Practices', *British Journal of Social Work* 38(3): 561–79.

Gallagher, L. and Gallagher, M. (2008) 'Methodological Immaturity in Childhood Research? Thinking through "Participatory Methods"', *Childhood* 15(4): 499–516.

Garrett, P. (1999) 'Mapping Child-Care Social Work in the Final Years of the Twentieth Century: A Critical Response to the "Looking After Children" System', *British Journal of Social Work* 29(1): 27–47.

Hall, T., Lashua, B. and Coffey, A. (2008) 'Sound and the Everyday in Qualitative Research', *Qualitative Inquiry* 14(6): 1019–40.

Hillman, A., Holland, S., Renold, E. and Ross, N.J. (2008) 'Negotiating Me, Myself and I: Creating a Participatory Research Environment for Exploring the Everyday Lives of Children and Young People "In Care"', *Qualitative Researcher* 7: 4–7.

Holland, S., Renold, E., Ross, N.J. and Hillman, A. (2008) 'The Everyday Lives of Children in Care: Using a Sociological Perspective to Inform Social Work Practice', in B. Luckock and M. Lefevre (eds) *Direct Work: Social Work with Children and Young People in Care*. British Association for Adoption and Fostering (BAAF).

Holland, S., Renold, E., Ross, N.J. and Hillman, A. (forthcoming 2009) 'Power, Agency and Participatory Agendas: A Critical Exploration of Young People's Engagement in Participative Qualitative Research', *Childhood*.

Kusenbach, M. (2003) 'Street Phenomenology: The Go-Along as Ethnographic Research Tool', *Ethnography* 4(3): 455–85.

Laurier, E., Lorimer, H., Brown, B., Jones, O., Juhlin, O., Noble, A., Perry, M., Pica, D., Sormani, P., Strebel, I., Swan, L., Taylor, A.S., Watts, L. and Weilenmann, A. (2008) 'Driving and Passengering: Notes on the Ordinary Organisation of Car Travel', *Mobilities* 3(1): 1–23.

Lee, J. and Ingold, T. (2006) 'Fieldwork on Foot: Perceiving, Routing, Socializing', in S. Coleman and P. Collins (eds) *Locating the Field: Space, Place and Context in Anthropology*, pp. 67–85. Oxford: Berg.

Mitchell, H., Kearns, R.A. and Collins, D.C.A. (2006) 'Nuances of Neighbourhood: Children's Perceptions of the Space between Home and School in Auckland, New Zealand', *Geoforum* 38: 614–27.

Moles, K. (2008) A Walk in Thirdspace: Place, Methods and Walking', *Sociological Research Online* 13(4), URL: http://www.socresonline.org.uk/13/4/2.html

Pink, S. (2007) 'Walking with Video', *Visual Studies* 22(3): 240–52.

Pink, S. (2008) 'An Urban Tour: The Sensory Sociality of Ethnographic Place-Making', *Ethnography* 9: 175–96.

Renold, E., Holland, S., Ross, N.J. and Hillman, A. (2008) ' "Becoming Participant": Problematising "Informed Consent" in Participatory Research with Children and Young People in Care', *Qualitative Social Work* 7(4): 431–51.

Ross, N.J. (2007) ' "My Journey to School . . .": Foregrounding the Meaning of School Journeys and Children's Engagements and Interactions in their Everyday Localities', *Children's Geographies* 5(4): 373–91.

Ross, N.J., Renold, E., Holland, S. and Hillman, A. (2008) 'Moving Stories: Using Mobile Methods to Explore the Everyday Lives of Children in Public Care', Qualiti Working Paper 009, URL: http://www.cardiff.ac.uk/socsi/qualiti/WorkingPapers/Qualiti_WPS_009.pdf

Sheller, M. (2004) Automotive Emotions: Feeling the Car', *Theory, Culture & Society* 21: 221–42.

Sheller, M. and Urry, J. (2006) 'The New Mobilities Paradigm', *Environment and Planning A* 38: 207–26.

Sibley, D. (1995) *Geographies of Exclusion: Society and Difference in the West*. London: Routledge.

Skeggs, B. (2004) *Class, Self, Culture*. London: Routledge.

Soja, E.W. (1996) *Thirdspace: Journeys to Los Rosiees and Other Real-and-Imagined Places*. Oxford: Blackwell.

Thrift, N. (2004) 'Driving in the City', *Theory, Culture & Society* 21: 41–59.

65

'Entering the Blogosphere':
Some Strategies for Using Blogs
in Social Research

Nicholas Hookway

Introduction

The emergence of the Internet and other forms of computer-mediated communication has been accompanied by a substantial body of scholarly writing concerned with interpreting the types of interactions and social worlds now being built within cyberspace (Danet, 1998; Featherstone and Burrows, 1995; Jones, 1998; Porter, 1997; Rheingold, 2000; Turkle, 1995; Wellman et al., 2001). Most of this research has focused on what Silver (2000) calls the 'twin pillars of cybercultural studies': virtual communities and identities. Much of the debate on virtual communities has centred on the extent to which cyberspace offers an answer to the (post)modern problem of 'bowling alone' (Putnam, 2000) while the discussion of online identity production has addressed the question of how the virtual world's 'culture of simulation' (Baudrillard, 1983; Danet, 1998; Turkle, 1995) facilitates a type of postmodern realization of the 'decentred' and 'disembodied' self.

While social scientists have been occupied with the question of how and to what extent cyberspace shapes social life, they have also become interested in the question of how cyberspace can expand the social researcher's toolkit (Jacobson, 1999; Liamputtong and Ezzy, 2005; Mann and Stewart, 2000; O'Connor and Madge, 2001). Although the research possibilities and issues involved with online research methods are relatively unexplored

Source: *Qualitative Research*, 8(1) (2008): 91–113.

(Hewson, 2003; Mann and Stewart, 2000), it is generally recognized that cyberspace offers a new and exciting frontier for social research. Recent edited collections by Batinic et al. (2002), Hine (2005), Johns et al. (2004) and Jones (1999), together with works by Coombes (2001), Hewson et al. (2003) and Mann and Stewart (2000), have made significant practical, theoretical and methodological contributions to the development of this field. In particular they have highlighted how traditional research methods might be transferred to the online context, how the Internet sets up new research possibilities and the issues and difficulties, including ethical and legal, encountered when conducting online research.

In the social sciences, quantitative survey style applications have made the most extensive use of the Internet as a medium for data gathering (Best et al., 2001; Coomber, 1997; Dillman, 2000; Solomon, 2001). Qualitative research, while a little slower to take up Internet methods, has gained momentum in the last few years (Hessler et al., 2003; Liamputtong and Ezzy, 2005; Selwyn and Robson, 2003). This research has addressed how existing qualitative techniques of data gathering such as interviewing (Beck, 2005; Davis et al., 2004; O'Connor and Madge, 2001), focus groups (Franklin and Lowry, 2001; Gaiser, 1997; Williams and Robson, 2003), and ethnography (Hine, 2000; Paccagnella, 1997) can be adapted to Internet technologies. Other mediums of Internet communication such as email (Hessler et al., 2003; Selwyn and Robson, 2003), Internet home pages (Walker, 2000) and bulletin boards (Herzog et al., 1997) have also been drawn upon as qualitative data sources.

One area that has yet to be developed by social scientists as a rich source of qualitative data is the weblog. Rivalling web pages as the favoured medium of online self-representation, a weblog, or 'blog' as they are more commonly known, refers to a website which contains a series of frequently updated, reverse chronologically ordered posts on a common web page, usually written by a single author (Bar-Ilan, 2005; Herring et al., 2005; Serfarty, 2004). Blogs are characterized by instant text/graphic publishing, an archiving system organized by date and a feedback mechanism in which readers can 'comment' on specific posts. Blogs are typically housed by software programs that enable users of low technical competence to present attractive and regularly updated online material (Thelwall and Wouters, 2005).

Blogs offer substantial benefits for social scientific research providing similar, but far more extensive opportunities than their 'offline' parallel of qualitative diary research. First, they provide a publicly available, low-cost and instantaneous technique for collecting substantial amounts of data. Further, blogs are naturalistic data in textual form, allowing for the creation of immediate text without the resource intensiveness of tape recorders and transcription (Liamputtong and Ezzy, 2005: 232). The anonymity of the online context also means that bloggers may be relatively unselfconscious about what they write since they remain hidden from view. Like the majority of online research strategies, they also enable access to populations otherwise geographically or socially removed from the researcher (Hessler et al., 2003; Mann and Stewart, 2000). Their global nature means they are well positioned for conducting micro-comparative research, and may have empirical applications for contemporary discussions of globalization. Moreover, the archived nature of blogs makes them amenable to examining social processes over time, particularly trend and panel type longitudinal research. These qualities of practicality and capacity to shed light on social processes across space and time, together with their insight into everyday life, combine to make blogs a valid addition to the qualitative researcher's toolkit.

I aim to cover three main areas in this article. First, I introduce the 'blogosphere' and discuss how it might be treated as an online extension of diary research. I also raise some of the methodological issues involved in doing blog research, particularly in terms of impression management and trustworthiness. Second, I outline some practical techniques for researchers entering the 'blogosphere'. I look specifically at finding relevant blog sites, and sampling and recruiting participants. Finally, I canvass some of the ethical issues involved in doing blog research.

Into the Blogosphere

Over the last 20 years, cyberspace has spawned a range of text-based, digital genres – from chat rooms, to multi-user domains, to peer-to-peer file sharing networks – in which Internet users can write, communicate and interact with each other (Gurak et al., 2004: 1). The newest online genre to enter popular consciousness, being touted as the 'next evolution of web-based experience' (Kahn and Kellner, 2004: 91), are blogs.[1] The rapid growth in the popularity of blogs has been driven by the twin motors of free, user-friendly blogging applications such as Blogger and LiveJournal and the global media exposure of 'A-list' bloggers like Salam Pax (aka the 'Baghdad Blogger') and Wil Wheaton (Blood, 2002; Gurak et al., 2004; Mortensen and Walker, 2002; Serfarty, 2004: 458). Current estimates of the number of blogs online are varied: conservative estimates are in the range of 2.8 million (National Institute for Technology and Liberal Education, 2006) while more liberal ones suggest the existence of 31.6 (Henning, 2006) to 100 million blogs (Riley, 2005). Riley (2005) claims that there are over 450,000 hosted blogs in Australia, 2.5 million in the UK and anywhere up to 50 million in the USA.

There are a number of weblog genres in existence from pure filter blogs (literally filters of one's web surfing), to warblogs and celebrity blogs, through to educational, professional and pornographic ones. Typically however, blogs take the form of online diaries or what I call 'self-narratives', where private and intimate content is posted in daily, monthly and yearly snippets (Herring et al., 2004). The online diary is generally light on links with the focus being on the 'drama' (Goffman, 1959) of everyday interactions, selves and situations. The narrative structure produced is linear, rigorously defined by chronology and has no sense of an ending. The personal and candid nature of online diaries combined with their open-endedness – in many ways reminiscent of the form and content of soap operas – gives them their addictive and captivating quality (Serfarty, 2004).

The increasing popularity of blogs is reflected in their growing presence in popular and academic discourse. Like earlier forms of technological innovation blogs have been credited with a socially transformative capacity, conceptualized as a new genre of open-access, participatory journalism (MacDougall, 2005; Wall, 2005) as reinvigorating a flagging 'public sphere' (Ó Baoill, 2004), encouraging civic and political engagement (Kahn and Kellner, 2004; Kerbel and Bloom, 2005), creating new forms of community (Blanchard, 2004; Wei, 2004) and identity (Bortree, 2005; Hevern, 2004), and as a new medium for facilitating knowledge production within education (Brooks et al., 2004; Huffaker, 2005; Sade, 2005) and business sectors (Dyrud et al., 2005; Festa, 2003; Scammell, 2006). Despite the growing research on blogs and blogging – most of which has been produced by information/computer science and media/rhetoric/communication studies – the research opportunities they afford for the social sciences, particularly qualitative research practices remains unexamined.

Going Online: From the Diary to the Blog

This article stems from my decision to use blogs as a research technique for exploring the question of how contemporary urban Australians experience morality in their everyday lives, particularly how actors try to live a 'good life' and what that standard of the 'good' actually means in relation to the process of everyday moral decision making. In this section I outline the substantive and practical reasons for why and how I came to choose blogs as an empirical technique for investigating this question. I also raise some of the methodological issues involved with doing blog research.

Research that invokes 'everyday life' as its conceptual focus needs to be tailored to questions of 'what happens in reality' (Johnson and Bytheway, 2001: 183). This raises the methodological question of how to capture empirically the moral reality of everyday life. As Phillips and Harding (1985: 93) suggest, asking people directly about their moral beliefs and actions is difficult, raising issues of validity. Traditional techniques such as interviews rely on participants' willingness to talk candidly about the processes and experiences of moral decision-making. Even if trust and rapport is established, there remains the problem of bridging the gap between informants' socially situated subjectivities and their actual practice. There is also the problem of how to contextualize the topic in meaningful and morally neutral ways. A common technique in psychological research has been to present respondents with hypothetical moral situations, Kohlberg's (1981) use of vignettes being the classic example. The difficulty with this technique is first, that it denies the lived and situated experience of moral decision making and second, it leaves open the potential for impression management. Like survey research, these techniques are open to the possibility that responses are conveyed through a normative screen which minimizes the potential for feelings of moral guilt or 'sin'. This problem is compounded by methodologies that rely on memory and are therefore susceptible to memory impairment and retrospective reconstruction. While there undoubtedly is a place for such methods, techniques that capture situated action unadulterated by the scrutiny of the researcher are advantageous. One data source that overcomes these problems is the diary.

Diaries are an established research strategy in historical and anthropological research and are increasingly finding their way into social research (Plummer, 1983, 2001; Toms and Duff, 2002). As the 'classic articulation of dailiness' (Juhasz, 1980: 224), social scientists have used diaries as a technique for collecting data on daily life and as a means for understanding social actors both as observers and informants of social life (Toms and Duff, 2002: 1233). By no means exhaustive, diaries have been used qualitatively to investigate health behaviour (Elliott, 1997; Johnson and Bytheway, 2001; Verbrugge, 1980), gender and sexuality (Coxon, 1994; Hampsten, 1989), sleep (Hislop et al., 2005), daily expenditure (Silberstein and Scott, 1991) and to conduct surveys on how people spend and use their time (Avis et al., 2001; Gershuny, 2002). One of the key advantages of diary research is that it can help avoid problems associated with collecting sensitive information using traditional survey or interview methods (Corti, 1993; Elliott, 1997; Hampsten, 1989; Juhasz, 1980). Another benefit is that they capture an 'ever-changing present' (Elliott, 1997: 3) where there is a tight union between everyday experience and the record of that experience (Toms and Duff, 2002). This proximity between event and record means that diaries are less susceptible to problems of memory impairment and retrospective reconstruction than interviews and focus groups (Verbrugge, 1980).

There are a variety of diaries that can be used as raw material for research. They can be clustered into two main types: unsolicited 'documents of life' (Allport, 1943: xii), which are spontaneously maintained by respondents and solicited 'researcher-driven diaries' (Elliott, 1997: 22), which are created and maintained at the request of a researcher. Each of these has their problems in terms of meeting the goals of this research project. The unsolicited diary presents the difficulty of identifying potential participants and the problem of matching the diary content to the research aims. Second, the solicited diary, while overcoming issues of identification and relevance, poses the problem of 'participation willingness' – how many participants would be prepared to record their moral decision making over a set period of time, especially without monetary compensation? In addition, we are back to our original problem of impression management – the research diary after all is a document explicitly maintained for the purposes of the researcher (Toms and Duff, 2002: 1233).

Weblogs offer a viable alternative, giving diary researchers the best of both worlds. On the one hand, blogs help overcome issues of finding and accessing unsolicited personal diaries, while on the other hand, they are not 'contaminated' by the predating interest of a researcher. Nevertheless, while blogs are naturally occurring text they are still typically written for an implicit, if not explicit, audience. It is this potential presence of an audience and its immediacy to authors that is one of the key ways in which blogs differ from traditional forms of personal diary keeping – not to mention that blogs enable dialogue and even co-production between authors and readers.[2] I would like to consider how this affects the validity of data that one can collect from blogs, particularly in terms of impression management and trustworthiness.

Impression Management, Anonymity and Trustworthiness

Although there are varying degrees of online exposure with blogging, the practice fundamentally involves placing private content in the public domain. Researchers may therefore need to recognize the role of potential discursive display or performance in blogging. Drawing on the work of Goffman (1972), blogging might be conceptualized as a disembodied form of 'face-work', concerned with the art of self-representation, impression management and potential self-promotion. Taking this line of argument, bloggers may strategically select and write into existence convincing life-episodes that frame themselves as having desired qualities, such as 'good', 'moral' and 'virtuous'. Blogging in this scenario is just another 'stage' for what Goffman (1959: 244) refers to as the 'the very obligation and profitability of appearing always in a steady moral light'. In other words, the result of using blogs as a way of 'getting at' everyday expressions of morality may be no different to my argument about Kohlberg's use of moral hypotheticals – you end up with another form of impression management!

I would argue, however, that the anonymity of the online context disrupts this picture of blogging. Goffman's notion of 'face-work' is restricted to the interactional order of face-to-face relations overlooking the social conventions of online anonymity. If you like, the stage is there and the audience are in their seats but the social actor is masked. This online mask enables bloggers to write more honestly and candidly, mitigating potential impression management. The anonymity of the online context means that bloggers may be relatively unselfconscious about what they write since they remain hidden from view. Thus there seems to be a paradox built into blogging: bloggers are writing for an audience and are therefore potentially engaged in a type of 'face-work' but at the same time they are anonymous, or relatively unidentifiable. This tension between visibility and invisibility gives blogging a confessional quality, where a less polished and even uglier self can be verbalized. One can express one's faults, one's mishaps – whatever might be difficult to tell as we 'enter the presence of others' (Goffman, 1959: 1) in face-to-face relations.

Although the online anonymity of blogging potentially sidesteps problems of 'face-work', the flipside is that it raises issues about potential identity play and deception. This is of course not specific to blogs as an online genre with there being somewhat of a moral panic regarding the predatory potential of the Internet. Here people going online, typically conceived of as paedophiles or old men, can disguise their identities to prey on vulnerable young people. This picture of the predatory 'stranger' lurking in the dark alleys of the Internet has been fuelled by a lot of early Internet research, which focused on the social implications of online anonymity, particularly in terms of simulated identity production (Danet, 1998; Turkle, 1995). In these accounts, the Internet supposedly allows for a type of 'bunburying', where an illusory, playful and deceptive self can dominate – for example, men can pretend to be women and vice-versa.

How trustworthy then are the expressions of self that bloggers provide? How do you know what bloggers are telling you is true? They could be an elaborate fiction. In fact, this is typically the first question I am asked when I tell people I am using blogs as a data source. While I do not – and cannot believe that I can definitely answer this question – what I can do instead is animate a series of questions that are worth considering in response to *this* question.

The first question is 'does it really matter?' Even if bloggers do not tell the 'truth', these 'fabrications' still tell us something about the manner in which specific social and cultural ideas such as morality are constructed. Here issues of 'truth' are not really at stake as the emphasis is on how the constitutive elements of blogs work to produce 'particular effects' (Silverman, 2001: 122). The issue of deception might however be an important consideration for a researcher who wants to read off external realities from the textual data – for example, a researcher who wants to undertake a more systematic analysis (men vs women, older vs younger, etc.) of how the construction of certain cultural ideas in blogs are affected by sociological variables such as age and gender. The validity of the 'does it matter?' question first depends then on whether a researcher is looking at how blogs work to produce particular effects or whether they are looking at how blogs correspond with an 'offline' reality.

The second question is 'how can the truth be ensured in any research scenario?' How do you know, for instance, if someone is being honest in an interview, and for that matter, how someone ticks boxes on a survey questionnaire? The question of whether you can trust what people are saying in their blogs seems to reflect not only an exaggerated vision of online identity play but also the tendency for data unprovoked by a researcher to be treated with a degree of suspicion (Silverman, 2001: 120). This attitude is indicative of how textual data are often approached as 'background' material with the real research only beginning when the researcher starts asking questions. One cannot help thinking then, that the stubborn mistrust of naturally occurring data like blogs is reflective of living in what Silverman (2001) calls the 'interview society' – a society occupied by social scientists, media presenters and journalists who are convinced that the only path to individual 'authenticity' is through the face-to-face interview.

In the next section I put some of these methodological issues aside, focusing on the personal process of making sense of this relatively new aspect of the online world and some of the steps taken to order it for the purposes of social research. First, I look at entering the blogosphere; second, I address the practical questions of finding and sampling weblogs on the Internet, including navigating the visual and textual content of blogs; lastly I comment on the process of recruiting blog participants and some of the ethical issues involved.

Blogs and Social Research: A Path Less Travelled

Entering the blogosphere as a blog 'newbie', was like gazing into a dark and tangled labyrinth. The endless criss-crossing hyper tracks and trails of the blogopshere were overwhelming. 'It' seemed unwieldy and unmanageable – words that immediately arouse anxiety in the social researcher. The volume of blogging sites and the 'seemingly infinite multiplication of voices' (O'Neil, 2005: 7) – let alone their visual complexity – was staggering. As O'Neil (2005: 7) notes, it is 'impossible for any one reader to have experienced all, or even most, of the blogs in existence'. Establishing a road-map in what felt like the 'black hole' of the blogosphere represented a serious challenge.

The experience was a concrete example of what social theorists like Baudrillard (1988) and Jameson (1991) are getting at when describing the disorientating and anxiety-provoking effects of postmodern spaces: forms which they argue disable the individual's capacity to map oneself cognitively and perceptually in space, removing totality and a sense of the whole from one's grasp. But this was not a physical environment like the Los Angeles Bonaventure hotel or a shopping mall but a mediated world of text, graphics, video, audio and hyperlinks. Reaching the desired goal meant discovering how to navigate and interact within that world.

Finding Blogs

The first step was to establish where and how to locate blogs. The majority of weblogs are hosted by blog content management systems (BCMS), so an initial scoping exercise of such applications was undertaken. Taking prompts from my previous blog research and websites such as 'weblogs compendium', 'yahoo weblog hosting' and 'about.com', an initial pool of 13 BCMS was identified: (1) Blogster; (2) LiveJournal; (3) Xanga; (4) Typepad; (5) Diaryland; (6) Blogit; (7) Blogharbour; (8) Squarespace; (9) Blurty; (10) Blogger; (11) Opendiary; (12) Journalspace; and (13) Whitepage (an Australian BCMS).

These were assessed according to two main criteria: (1) their hosting of personal diary style weblogs and (2) the availability of a search engine that enabled identification of weblogs according to location (including country, state and city) in addition to demographic information such as age and gender. In fact all these sites hosted diary, or personal journal style weblogs.

Sampling Blogs

The majority of blog content management systems include a search feature, which allows readers to find bloggers according to demographic information such as age and location as well as interests and hobbies. This feature can also be appropriated by social researchers to sample participants. Of the thirteen BCMS trialled, nine include a blog searching device. Four of these are restricted to content based searching (Blogster, Blogharbour, Blogger, Journalspace). In this case, searches are limited to the content of blog posts with no means of selecting bloggers by social variables such as location, age, ethnicity or gender. For example, performing a query for 'Australia' with Blogster's search engine, though netting some bloggers from Australia, produces any blogger who has used the word 'Australia' in their posts. This is problematic if researchers are interested in examining a social process within a particular geographical territory.

Nonetheless, this kind of generic blog content searching can aid purposive sampling. For instance, a social researcher may use a BCMS search engine to search for key terms that bear on a particular social process or phenomenon. An example might be a researcher who is interested in investigating body governance by looking at men and women's dietary habits as revealed in blogs. This could be achieved by performing a search query based on key terms such as diet, food and weight loss/gain.

Web based services such as 'Pubsub', 'blo.gs' and 'technorati' are also good for such purposes, tracking and matching a large number of blogs held on multiple BCMS. PubSub (2006), for instance, claims to monitor over 23 million blog postings in real time, meaning that a search query is continually matched against newly updated postings. Scheidt (2005), for example, used PubSub as a technique for sampling eight 'teen' weblogs in her study on the performative metaphors used in adolescent blog names. Such services have also been employed for random sampling. For instance, Herring et al. (2004) used the Blo.g service to produce a random sample of 203 blogs for the purposes of undertaking a genre analysis of weblogs. However, because these services search by post content they still suffer from the problem of being unable to confine blogs to particular sociological co-ordinates such as location, age, gender or ethnicity.

Xanga, Diaryland, LiveJournal, Blurty and Opendiary have the most comprehensive and 'research-friendly' search features. Xanga and Diaryland both include a search feature that enables 'location' (country, state and city) and 'interest' based queries[3] while LiveJournal (upon paid membership), Blurty and Opendiary enable searches by location, interest and age. None, however, allow searches by gender and ethnicity. Since the aims of the research required a sample that approximated the general Australian population the last three websites were the obvious choice. However, in order to simplify the process of data collection, LiveJournal became the main data source. LiveJournal was deemed to be the most appropriate because it had the following features: (1) user-friendly interface; (2) systematic search engine which enabled identification of blogs by location (country, state, city) and age; (3) a sizeable share of the blog market in Australia[4] and (4) a reputation as a site purely for online diaries (O'Neil, 2005: 14).

Establishing an Online Presence

After selecting LiveJournal as the primary source for generating research-relevant bloggers, an online presence was established as a means of entering the world of potential research participants. This was achieved by the creation of a LiveJournal blog and a research website. The weblog (http://nicholas 8976.Livejournal.com) included a brief biographical sketch of the research, research interests, a photo and a link to the research website (http://www.utas. edu.au/sociology/students/hookway/). The website contained more detailed information about the project and a further chance to 'meet the researcher'. This worked not only to complement the researcher's 'offline' identity through provision of contact details such as physical address and phone number but also as a way of establishing legitimacy. As one LiveJournaler commented in an email communication with me, 'I googled you and found http://fcms.its.utas. edu.au/arts/sociology/pagedetails.asp?IpersonId=3035 so you seem legit.'

Data Collection

Data collection comprised two main phases: a passive phase of blog trawling and an active phase of blog solicitation. The first phase involved examining Sydney and Melbourne blogs, of different ages, for concrete incidents of moral decision making or more abstract discussions about the nature of the 'good life'. Specifying age groups helped ensure variation of age within the sample. This is important in light of suggestions that most bloggers are between the ages of 13 and 19 (Bortree, 2005; Henning, 2003) – a trend that is also reflected in the demographic characteristics of LiveJournal users. These criteria were met by using LiveJournal's advanced search feature. For example, a search would be performed for LiveJournalers from Melbourne between the ages of 30–40 who had updated in the last month (at 4 April 2006, such a search produces about 270 blogs).

The trawling phase of data collection proved time consuming and relatively ineffective. This was in part due to inexperience and unfamiliarity with the world of blogs but also because of the nature of the content sought. The initial approach involved reading the blogger's entire back catalogue, which on average was three to four years' worth of posts. It could take up to three or four days to read one blog – often to find that the blog was not relevant. Eventually reading was limited to the first two or three posts to determine background information. If this content contained material that indicated some reflexive moral content then the latest year of posts was perused. The search was also impeded by the absence of appropriate cultural knowledge that a substantial number of blogs are demarcated 'friends-only'. Many of the more self-representational and personal kind of blogs were out of reach; as one blogger put it: 'all the good stuff's under friend and key'.

Over a 4-month period, approximately 200 blogs were read, which translates to an incalculable number of individual posts and comments. Of these, only 11 diaries from Sydney and Melbourne were deemed relevant. This dogged pursuit of an elusive goal can perhaps be best understood through the analogy of the gambler. There is a compulsive quality to blog searching which researchers must be aware of. Careful search parameters and guidelines should be established to deal with the irrational sense that the next post or the next blog will 'strike gold'. Nonetheless, although this time was relatively unproductive in terms of participant numbers, some random exploration of the blogosphere is essential in establishing 'a feel' for both the visual design and content of blogs.

Learning How to Look at Blogs

One of most striking things about blogs is their diverse, and sometimes, complex visual designs and layouts. While blogs are textual, unlike their offline cousins, they are simultaneously visual documents (Scheidt and Wright, 2004). Blogs encourage not only textual expression but also visual expression via user icons, memes, template selection, design and colour scheme, titles, sidebars, selection of images and typeface (see Figure 1). As Badger (2004: 1) claims, 'if we think of weblogs as being homepages that we wear then it is the visual elements that tailor the garment to fit the individual'.

Since this was largely virgin territory there was no established framework for interpreting the visual layout of blogs. However, over time it became easier

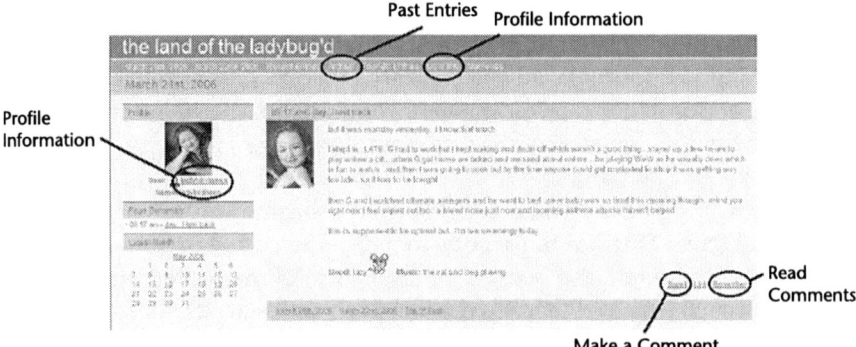

Figure 1: Visual layout of a typical LiveJournal blog

to locate profile information (userinfo or by clicking on username), past entries (archive), how to make (speak) and read existing comments (remember). Familiarity with the way in which bloggers would use graphics from external sources, like Internet quizzes ('quizilla' is particularly popular on LiveJournal), as a way of expressing themselves also helped. As this framework for understanding the visual layout of blogs was developed the easier it became to 'scan' – a style of viewing that Badger (2004) assumes we automatically adopt when 'reading' blogs – the content of blog pages. It is almost like one needs to learn not only how to read blogs but also how to view them.

Musings on the Everyday

In terms of textual content, blog posts, like diaries, were primarily a reflection of everyday happenings and events. As Gumbrecht (2004: 2) points out, the 'blogged-about universe' can be on almost anything: daily appointments, work, partying, romantic interests, dreams, friends and daily interactions. Scattered among these descriptions and analyses of the minutiae of everyday life are references to various forms of popular culture, be it the music they are listening to (sometimes playing in the background of the blog), books they are reading or movies and TV they are watching.

The online diaries of LiveJournal vary greatly in degrees of self-reflection and analysis. At one end of the 'self-reflection continuum' are purely descriptive blogs, which non-reflexively recount the events of the day, from what the blogger has eaten for breakfast to who they have seen that day. At the other end of the continuum, are highly confessional and self-analytical blogs in which bloggers make sense of their identity and relationships with others. For my purposes, I trawled for the latter style of blog as they were more likely to be of a morally reflective nature. The following quotations illustrate these two extremes:

32-year-old male: Things i've done recently: been to ikea, been to my local furniture shop, been to ikea again, been to ikea yes i know, . . . again . . . bought a rug, bought a lamp, bought a bigger lamp . . . dug my lawn up, re-sown lawn, bought some shredded bark . . . walked along the beach, moved the shelving unit from the lounge to the kitchen, paid for my flight, cut my hair . . . had a performance review at work, asked for a pay rise, got laid, filed a years worth of bill . . . thats all for now

36-year-old male: I wish i had the magic to give Janine the life i stole from her. of all the people i've hurt in my life, it's her that i feel most dreadful about. she put so much trust and faith in me . . . and i really loved her. i still do. yet i screwed her over and tore that wonderful heart in two. if only i had some way to make it so i'd never happened to her life . . . if i could just patch up my era [*sic*] with a big sander bandaid . . . so that it had been him that she'd met and not me. admittedly, i'd lose a part of my life that means a lot to me . . . but i'd really rather never to have hurt her. and no matter how sorry i am, and how deeply i feel the grief, the apologies i give her can never unhurt her.

Phase 2: Soliciting Bloggers

The second phase of blog data collection encompassed a more active form of recruitment. Frustrated with the 'trawling' approach, a new strategy of recruitment was devised. Similar to offline forms of recruitment an invite (see Figure 2) was constructed and posted on Australian LiveJournal (LJ) communities. An LJ community is an online forum where multiple bloggers can post into a shared journal page about a similar topic or interest.

Selecting and Advertising within a Blog Community

The first step was to identify the relevant communities to advertise within. Using LJ's advanced search feature, an exhaustive list of generic place based communities for Melbourne and Sydney was established. Only five were found: *Melbournians*, *Sydneysiders*, *Sydneyfemales*, *Sydneysingles* and *Melbournemaniac*. Due to the limited number of such communities, it was decided

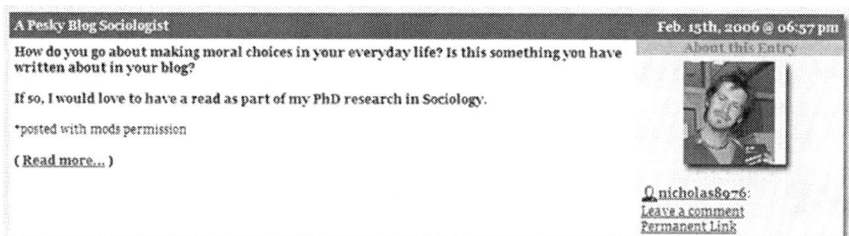

Figure 2: Blog invite

that sub-cultural and lifestyle communities like *Melbourneslash* (fan fiction community) and *Sydneygoths* should be included. Thirteen such communities were located for Melbourne and Sydney.

Once a community was selected, the moderator (who oversees the running of the community) was emailed a copy of the invite and permission to post was sought. If an email contact or one-way chat program username was not provided (e.g. MSN or ICQ), a comment was left in the moderator's blog. If permission was given, the researcher then joined the community. This was necessary as posting access is restricted to community membership. Posting required some basic skills in HTML coding, such as using an LJ cut,[5] creating a hyperlink, bolding text and uploading a user icon. Instructions for doing this are provided by the LJ help service. LJ also provides online technical support for its users.

To maximize participant response further, the decision was made to extend sampling to other major Australian metropolitan centres. I posted to place based LJ communities such as *Adelaideains, Brisneyland, Perthnuts, Canberra*; lifestyle communities like *Altadelaide* and *Perthindie*; and broader Australian communities such as *Aussieaddme, Aussielj, Asylumaustralia* and *Queeraustralia*. University based communities such as *Perthuni's, Anustudents* and *Sydneyuni* were also included in the sampling frame. At last count, invites have been posted to forty-seven communities. At this stage only two moderators have declined my offer to post the research invite.

Researcher/Respondent Interaction

Typically participant/researcher communication proceeds along the following three steps. First, the interested blogger makes contact by either leaving a comment on the post or by emailing.[6] At this time, interested participants who have a 'friendly only' account grant access to hidden posts by adding the researcher to their 'friends list' (referred to as 'flist'). Second, the researcher responds either via email, if provided, or by the comments section. In this communication, the respondent is thanked for their interest in the project and any questions regarding the project are answered. Bloggers are also asked to identify any specific posts in their blog where they have discussed or reflected upon moral issues, particularly as they relate to their own decision-making process.[7] Lastly, the respondent either fulfils the request by emailing a list of URLs to relevant posts or suggests that their blog is trawled for such instances. Sometimes the request is ignored.

Despite fears that the posting would be ignored or even incite anger in the communities, this technique was highly productive, generating forty-nine responses and a further eight recommendations for other possible blogs. The major benefit to solicitation over trawling is its obvious time efficiency. Getting the 'blogger to come to the researcher' rather than the other way around, frees the researcher from the time commitments of trawling and finding content relevant to the focus of the research. Nevertheless, relying on such an approach depends on the availability of community forums like those held on LiveJournal.

Ethics of Blog Research

With the emergence of online tools like blogs for conducting research come new and challenging ethical dilemmas and controversies (Bowker and Tuffin, 2004; King, 1996; Sixsmith and Murray, 2001; Walther, 2002; Waskul and Douglas, 1996). The discussion of the ethical problems of online research has recently occupied the content of journals (e.g. *The Information Society, Ethics and Information Technology*), institutional reports (e.g. American Association for the Advancement of Science (AAAS)) and working committees (e.g. The Association of Internet Researchers (AoIR)). At the centre of this emerging dialogue is the question of the adequacy of conventional 'offline' ethical guidelines for conducting research in online contexts.

An important aspect to this question is what the conventional notions of private and public mean in online research venues. This is pertinent to the collection and analysis of blogs. Do blog researchers need to gain authorial permission from bloggers when recording their posts? Is blog material academic fair game or is informed consent needed?

While there is no consensus among social scientists, responses to the broader question of what is private and what is public online tend to fall into one of three camps (Hutchinson, 2001). First, there are researchers who argue that archived material on the Internet is publicly available and therefore participant consent is not necessary (Sudweeks and Rafaeli, 1995; Walther, 2002). This position often rests on an analogy between online forums and public space, where the observation and recording of publicly accessible Internet content is treated like research on television content, a piece of art in a public gallery or letters to the editor. Second, some researchers claim that online postings, though publicly accessible, are written with an expectation of privacy and should be treated as such (Elgesem, 2002; King, 1996; Scharf, 1999). Lastly, there are those who argue that online interaction defies clear-cut prescription as either public or private. Waskul and Douglas (1996: 131), for example, argue that cyberpsace is simultaneously 'publicly-private and privately-public'. They warn online researchers of mistaking public accessibility of online forums for the public nature of the interactions, instead emphasizing how actors themselves construe their participation in online environments.

There is a strong case for blog researchers to adopt the 'fair game–public domain' position. Blogs are firmly located in the public domain and for this reason it can be argued that the necessity of consent should be waived. Further, blogs are public not only in the sense of being publicly accessible – and heeding Waskul and Douglas' (1996) warning – but also in how they are defined by users. Blogging is a public act of writing for an implicit audience. The exception proves the rule: blogs that are interpreted by bloggers as 'private' are made 'friends only'. Thus, accessible blogs may be personal but they are not private.

Alongside privacy issues, blog researchers need to be aware of copyright law (Jacobson, 1999: 137; Walther, 2002). In Australia, the UK and the USA, Internet content is automatically copyrighted (Australian Copyright Council, 2005a; UK Patent Office, 2006; US Copyright Office, 2000). Copyright protects a range of original literary, dramatic, musical or artistic 'works', including those posted on the Internet. This means that the moment a blog entry is uploaded onto a content management system it is protected by copyright. Bloggers therefore have exclusive rights over the reproduction of their work. While this would appear to be significantly limiting for researchers, there are special provisions built into the copyright act(s) which allow for 'fair dealing' of copyrighted material for the purposes of study or research. The Australian Copyright Act (1968), for instance, sets out five factors in determining whether use of copyrighted material can be deemed 'fair': (1) 'the purpose and character of the dealing'; (2) 'the nature of the work'; (3) 'the possibility of obtaining the work within a reasonable time at an ordinary commercial price'; (4) 'the effect of the dealing on the potential market for, or value of, the work'; and (5) 'the amount and substantiality of the part copied in relation to the whole work' (Australian Copyright Council, 2005b: 2). Considering that use of copyrighted material in this context is for a non-commercial purpose, the work is arguably of low skill, the work is not available commercially, there is no effect on the market value of the work and the extracts used are small and non-substantial, use can be deemed 'fair'. While fair use needs to be determined on a case by case basis, it would seem that blog researchers are relatively unrestricted by 'fair use' restrictions.

In addition to understanding 'fair use' provisions for scholarly activity the question of whether to preserve anonymity or credit bloggers for their work is another area of ethical consideration. In Australia, the Copyright Act (1968) stipulates that creators of 'works' have 'moral rights' which includes right to attribution of authorship (Australian Copyright Council, 2005c). There is an evident tension therefore between the norms of protecting participants' identity and acknowledging blog authorship. I adopted a position of 'moderate' disguise that privileges the protection of participants' identity over credit to the author (Bruckman, 2002: 229). This means that online pseudonyms (blog usernames) are changed and any potentially identifying information in blog quotations are disguised. This decision is also consistent with section 195AR of the Australian Copyright Act, which states that there are certain conditions in which non-attribution to an author can be deemed 'reasonable'. This is determined by the purpose, nature, manner and context in which the material is used. In this case, considering that use of blogs is for the purpose of research; the work is a blog (rather than something more substantial); authors are not disadvantaged in any way; the manner in which the work is used calls for anonymity and there is no financial gain involved, non-attribution seems 'reasonable'.

Conclusion

While 1999 may well be remembered as the year blogging exploded, it is yet to be seen how this newest addition to online life can be utilized as a qualitative social research technique. The aim of this article then was to make an important first step in building this knowledge base. Alongside indicating the research potential of weblogs, it has provided a researchers' guide to accessing the blogosphere, looked at what blogs are, where they are hosted and how to use blog search tools for sampling. It has also identified some of the methodological and ethical issues associated with blog research.

Like all methods of social research, blogs have their pitfalls and benefits. On the one hand, entering the blogosphere, with its endless maze of blogs and blog voices, can be a disorientating, time-consuming and overwhelming experience that only reluctantly yields relevant data. Further, some researchers – though I have argued against this position – may worry about impression management and the general trustworthiness of blogs. There are also issues with identifying potential participants and the problem of finding blogs relevant to research aims. However, from my experience, these issues can be addressed by using one blog content management system like LiveJournal and using community forums to solicit specific blog content.

In terms of benefits, blogs offer a low-cost, global and instantaneous tool of data collection. They also provide a very useful technique for investigating the dynamics of everyday life from an unadulterated first-person perspective and offer a research window into understanding the contemporary negotiation of the 'project of the self' in late/post modern times. With adequate research parameters in place, blogs can have an important and valuable place in the qualitative researcher's toolkit.

Notes

1. Historical accounts of blogging typically credit software developer Dave Winer as creating the first weblog in 1996 while the coining of the term is attributed to Jorn Barger, who described his online journal *Robot Wisdom* in 1997 as a 'weblog' – literally a 'log of his web surfing' (Gurak et al., 2004: 1). The abbreviation 'blog' was subsequently applied by Peter Merholz in 1999 (Herring et al., 2004: 1).
2. It is important not to treat 'public' as a blanket concept when approaching blogs. For instance, most blogging applications allow bloggers to control their level of exposure on a post-to-post basis from 'private' to 'friends-only' to 'public'.
3. Xanga achieves location searches by 'Metros' and interests/themes by 'Blogrings' (blogs that are connected by a shared theme or interest such as 'arts and humanities', 'health and medicine' and 'entertainment') whereas Diaryland allows keyword, taste in music, authors and music based searches.

4. According to LiveJournal's own statistics (31 March 2006) they host over 10 million accounts, of which, about 2 million are active in some way. There are over 92,000 accounts in Australia alone.
5. An LJ cut is a link that conceals part or all of a post. Most of the moderators I have contacted have requested that a majority of the invite be put behind a cut in order to minimize space used in the forum.
6. In both cases, I receive an email. LJ includes a function where bloggers can be notified of comments to posts by email. This is helpful as it saves having to check each community posting individually for comments.
7. It is worth mentioning that being so accessible means that a researcher is susceptible to both research specific and unspecific questions. For example, respondents would ask general questions about the research such as the type of morality I was referring to, why I chose blogs and how I was protecting confidentiality and anonymity while others wanted me, with no particular intention of participating in the project, to explain questions like what sociology is and how you fill out an ethics application. The latter raises questions about 'netiquette' and the expectations around behaviour for researchers going into online settings: should they ignore such queries or are they in some way obliged to help out?

References

Allport, G. (1943) *The Use of Personal Documents in Psychological Society.* New York: Social Science Research Council.

Australian Copyright Act (1968) SECT 195AR. URL (consulted May 2006): http://www.austlii.edu.au/au/legis/cth/consol_act/ca1968133/s195ar.html

Australian Copyright Council (2005a) *Information Sheet: An Introduction to Copyright in Australia.* URL (consulted May 2006): http://www.copyright.org.au/pdf/acc/infosheets/G010.pdf

Australian Copyright Council (2005b) *Information Sheet: Copying for Research or Study.* URL (consulted May 2006): http://www.copyright.org.au/pdf/acc/infosheets/G053.pdf

Australian Copyright Council (2005c) *Information Sheet: Moral Rights.* URL (consulted May 2006): http://www.copyright.org.au/pdf/acc/infosheets/G043.pdf

Avis, J., Bathmaker, A.-M. and Parsons, J. (2001) 'Reflecting on Method: The Use of a Time-Log Diary to Examine the Labour Process of Further Education Lecturers', *Research in Post-Compulsory Education* 6(1): 5–18. URL (consulted 20 September 2005): http://www.triangle.co.uk/rpe/

Badger, M. (2004) 'Visual Blogs', in L.J. Gurak, S. Antonijevic, L. Johnson, C. Ratliff and J. Reyman (eds) *Into the Blogosphere: Rhetoric, Community, and Culture of Weblogs.* URL (consulted March 2006): http://blog.lib.umn.edu/blogosphere/visual_blogs.html

Bar-Ilan, J. (2005) 'Information Hub Blogs', *Journal of Information Science* 31(4): 297–307.

Batinic, B., Reips, U.-D. and Bosnjak, M. (eds) (2002) *Online Social Sciences.* Seattle, WA: Hogrefe & Huber.

Baudrillard, J. (1983) *Simulations.* New York: Semiotext(e).

Baudrillard, J. (1988) *America.* London: Verso.

Beck, C. (2005) 'Benefits of Participating in Internet Interviews: Women Helping Women', *Qualitative Health Research* 15(3): 411–22.

Best, S.J., Krueger, B., Hubbard, C. and Smith, A. (2001) 'An Assessment of the Generalizability of Internet Surveys', *Social Science Computer Review* 19(2): 131–45.

Blanchard, A.L. (2004) 'Blogs as Virtual communities: Identifying a Sense of Community in the Julie/Julia Project', in L.J. Gurak, S. Antonijevic, L. Johnson, C. Ratliff and J. Reyman (eds) *Into the Blogosphere: Rhetoric, Community, and Culture of Weblogs.* URL (consulted March 2006): http://blog.lib.umn.edu/blogosphere/blogs_as_virtual.html

Blood, R. (2002) 'Weblogs: A History and Perspective', in J. Rodzvilla (ed.) *We've Got Blog: How Weblogs are Changing our Culture.* Cambridge, MA: Perseus.

Bortree, D. (2005) 'Presentation of Self on the Web: An Ethnographic Study of Teenage Girls' Weblogs', *Education, Communication and Information* 5(1): 25–39.

Bowker, N. and Tuffin, K. (2004) 'Using the Online Medium for Discursive Research about People with Disabilities', *Social Science Computer Review* 22(2): 228–41.

Brooks, K., Nichols, C. and Priebe, S. (2004) 'Remediation, Genre, and Motivation: Key Concepts for Teaching with Weblogs', in L.J. Gurak, S. Antonijevic, L. Johnson, C. Ratliff and J. Reyman (eds) *Into the Blogosphere: Rhetoric, Community, and Culture of Weblogs.* URL (consulted March 2006): http://blog.lib.umn.edu/blogosphere/remediation_genre.html

Bruckman, A. (2002) 'Studying the Amateur Artist: A Perspective on Disguising Data Collected in Human Subjects Research on the Internet', *Ethics and Information Technology* 4: 217–31.

Coomber, R. (1997) 'Using the Internet for Survey Research', *Sociological Research Online* 2(2). URL (consulted March 2006): http://www.socresonline.org.uk/socresonline/2/2/2.html

Coombes, H. (2001) *Research Using IT.* Hampshire: Palgrave.

Corti, L. (1993) 'Using Diaries in Sociological Research', *Social Research Update* 2. URL (consulted October 2005): http://www.soc.surrey.ac.uk/sru/SRU2.html

Coxon, A. (1994) 'Diaries and Sexual Behaviour: The Use of Sexual Diaries as Method and Substance in Researching Gay Men's Response to HIV/AIDS', in M. Boulton (ed.) *Challenge and Innovation: Methodological Advances in Social Research on HIV/AIDS.* London: Taylor & Francis.

Danet, B. (1998) 'Text as a Mask: Gender, Play and Performance in the Internet', in S. Jones (ed.) *Cybersociety 2.0: Revisiting Computer Mediated Communication and Community.* Thousand Oaks, CA: Sage Publications.

Davis, M., Bolding, G., Hart, G., Sherr, L. and Elford, J. (2004) 'Reflecting on the Experience of Interviewing Online: Perspectives from the Internet and HIV Study in London', *AIDS Care* 16(8): 944–52.

Dillman, D. (2000) *Mail and Internet Surveys: The Tailored Design Method.* New York: John Wiley & Sons.

Dyrud, M., Worley, R. and Quible, Z. (2005) 'Blogs: A Natural in Business Communication Courses', *Business Communication Quarterly* 68(1): 73–6.

Elgesem, D. (2002) 'What is Special about the Ethical Issues in Online Research?', *Ethics and Information Technology* 4: 195–203.

Elliott, H. (1997) 'The Use of Diaries in Sociological Research on Health Experience', *Sociological Research Online* 2(2). URL (consulted February 2005): http://www.socresonline.org.uk/socresonline/2/2/7.html

Featherstone, M. and Burrows, R. (eds) (1995) *Cyberspace, Cyberbodies, Cyberpunk: Cultures of Technological Embodiment.* London: Sage Publications.

Festa, P. (2003) 'Blogging Comes to Harvard', *CNET News.com.* URL (consulted April 2006): http://news.com.com/2008–1082–985714.html

Franklin, K. and Lowry, C. (2001) 'Computer-Mediated Focus Group Sessions: Naturalistic Inquiry in a Networked Environment', *Qualitative Research* 1(2): 169–84.

Gaiser, T. (1997) 'Conducting On-Line Focus Groups: A Methodological Discussion', *Social Science Computer Review* 15(2): 135–44.

Gershuny, J. (2002) 'Mass Media, Leisure and Home IT: A Panel Time Diary Approach', *IT and Society* 1(2): 53–66.

Goffman, E. (1959) *The Presentation of Self in Everyday Life.* Harmondsworth: Penguin.

Goffman, E. (1972) *Interaction Ritual: Essays on Face-to-Face Behaviour.* Harmondsworth: Penguin.

Gumbrecht, M. (2004) 'Blogs Are "Protected Space"', paper presented at *The Workshop on the Weblogging Ecosystem: Aggregation, Analysis, and Dynamics.* URL (consulted May 2005): http://www.blogpulse.com/papers/www2004gumbrecht.pdf

Gurak, L.J., Antonijevic, S., Ratliff, C. and Reyman, J. (2004) 'Introduction: Weblogs, Rhetoric, Community, and Culture', in L.J. Gurak, S. Antonijevic, L. Johnson, C. Ratliff and J. Reyman (eds) *Into the Blogosphere: Rhetoric, Community, and Culture of Weblogs.* URL (consulted March 2006): http://blog.lib.umn.edu/blogosphere/women_and_children.html

Hampsten, E. (1989) 'Considering More Than a Single Reader', in Personal Narratives Group (ed.) *Interpreting Women's Lives: Feminist Theory and Personal Narratives.* Bloomington, IN: Indiana University Press.

Henning, J. (2003) 'The Blogging Iceberg: Of 4.12 Million Hosted Weblogs, Most Little Seen, Quickly Abandoned', *Perseus Development Corp.* URL (consulted October 2005): http://www.perseus.com/blogsurvey/iceberg.html

Henning, J. (2006) 'The Blogging Geyser: 31.6 Million Hosted Blogs, Growing to 53.4 Million by Year End', *Perseus Development Corp.* URL (consulted May 2006): http://www.perseus.com/blogsurvey/geyser.html

Herring, S.C., Scheidt, L.A., Bonus, S. and Wright, E. (2004) 'Bridging the Gap: A Genre Analysis of Weblogs', in *Proceedings of the Thirty-Seventh Hawaii International Conference on System Sciences* (HICSS-37). URL (consulted March 2006): http://www.blogninja.com/DDGDD04.doc

Herring, S.C., Scheidt, L.A., Bonus, S. and Wright, E. (2005) 'Weblogs as a Bridging Genre', *Information, Technology & People* 18(2): 142–71.

Herzog, H.A., Dinoff, B. and Page, J.R. (1997) 'Animal Rights Talk: Moral Debate over the Internet', *Qualitative Sociology* 20(3): 399–418.

Hessler, R., Downing, L., Beltz, C., Pelliccio, A., Powell, M. and Vale, W. (2003) 'Qualitative Research on Adolescent Risk Using E-mail: A Methodological Assessment', *Qualitative Sociology* 26(1): 111–24.

Hevern, V. (2004) 'Threaded Identity in Cyberspace: Weblogs and Positioning in the Dialogical Self', *Identity: An International Journal of Theory and Research* 4(4): 321–35.

Hewson, C. (2003) 'Conducting Research on the Internet', *Psychologist* 16(6): 290–3.

Hewson, C., Yule, P., Laurent, D. and Vogel, C. (2003) *Internet Research Methods.* London: Sage Publications.

Hine, C. (2000) *Virtual Ethnography.* London: Sage Publications.

Hine, C. (ed.) (2005) *Virtual Methods: Issues in Social Research on the Internet.* Oxford: Berg.

Hislop, J., Arber, S., Meadows, R. and Venn, S. (2005) 'Narratives of the Night: The Use of Audio Diaries in Researching Sleep', *Sociological Research Online* 10(4). URL (consulted March 2006): http://www.socresonline.org.uk/10/4/hislop.html

Huffaker, D. (2005) 'The Educated Blogger: Using Weblogs to Promote Literacy in the Classroom', *AACE Journal* 13(2): 91–8. URL (consulted March 2006): http://firstmonday.dk/issues/issue9_6/huffaker/index.html

Hutchinson, R. (2001) 'Dangerous Liaisons? Ethical Considerations in Conducting Online Sociological Research', in *TASA 2001 Conference Proceedings*, the Australian Sociological Association. URL (consulted October 2007): http://64.233.179.104/scholar?hl=en&lr=&client=safari&q=cache:8D2rQxywgk8J:www.tasa.org.au/members/docs/2001_12/Hutchinson.pdf+related:8D2rQxywgk8J:scholar.google.com/

Jacobson, D. (1999) 'Doing Research in Cyberspace', *Field Methods* 11(2): 127–45.

Jameson, F. (1991) *Postmodernism, or, The Cultural Logic of Late Capitalism.* Durham, NC: Duke University Press.

Johns, M., Chen, S.S and Hall, G. (eds) (2004) *Online Social Research: Methods, Issues and Ethics.* New York: Peter Lang.

Johnson, J. and Bytheway, B. (2001) 'An Evaluation of the Use of Diaries in a Study of Medication in Later Life', *International Journal of Social Research Methodology* 4(3): 183–204.

Jones, S. (ed.) (1998) *Cybersociety 2.0: Revisiting Computer-Mediated Communication and Community*. Thousand Oaks, CA: Sage Publications.

Jones, S. (ed.) (1999) *Doing Internet Research: Critical Issues and Methods for Examining the Net*. London: Sage Publications.

Juhasz, S. (1980) 'Towards a Theory of Form in Feminist Autobiography: Kate Millett's Flying and Sita, Maxine Hong Kingston's The Woman Warrior', in E. Jelinek (ed.) *Women's Autobiography: Essays in Criticism*. Bloomington, IN: Indiana University Press.

Kahn, R. and Kellner, D. (2004) 'New Media and Internet Activism: From the "Battle of Seattle" to Blogging', *New Media and Society* 6(1): 87–95.

Kerbel, M. and Bloom, J. (2005) 'Blog for America and Civic Involvement', *Harvard International Journal of Press/Politics* 10(4): 3–27.

King, S. (1996) 'Researching Internet Communities: Proposed Ethical Guidelines for the Reporting of Results', *The Information Society* 12(2): 119–27.

Kohlberg, L. (1981) *The Philosophy of Moral Development*. San Francisco, CA: Harper & Row.

Liamputtong, P. and Ezzy, D. (2005) *Qualitative Research Methods*. Melbourne: Oxford University Press.

LiveJournal (2006) Statistics. URL (consulted March 2006): http://www.livejournal.com/stats.bml

MacDougall, R. (2005) 'Identity, Electronic Ethos, and Blogs: A Technologic Analysis of Symbolic Exchange on the New News Medium', *American Behavioral Scientist* 49(4): 575–99.

Mann, C. and Stewart, F. (2000) *Internet Communication and Qualitative Research: A Handbook for Researching Online*. London: Sage Publications.

Mortensen, T. and Walker, J. (2002) 'Blogging Thoughts: Personal Publication as an Online Research Tool', in A. Morrison (ed.) *Research ICTs in Context*. Oslo: InterMedia/UniPub.

National Institute for Technology and Liberal Education (2006) *NITLE Blog Census*. URL (consulted May 2006): http://www.blogcensus.net/?page=Home

Ó Baoill, A. (2004) 'Weblogs and the Public Sphere', in L.J. Gurak, S. Antonijevic, L. Johnson, C. Ratliff and J. Reyman (eds) *Into the Blogosphere: Rhetoric, Community, and Culture of Weblogs*. URL (consulted March 2006): http://blog.lib.umn.edu/blogosphere/weblogs_and_the_public_sphere.html

O'Connor, H. and Madge, C. (2001) 'Cyber-Mothers: Online Synchronous Interviewing Using Conferencing Software', *Sociological Research Online* 5(4). URL (consulted March 2006): http://www.socresonline.org.uk/5/4/oconnor.html

O'Neil, M. (2005) 'Weblogs and Authority', paper presented at *Blogtalk Downunder*. URL (consulted January 2006): http://incsub.org/blogtalk/?page_id=107

Paccagnella, L. (1997) 'Getting the Seats of Your Pants Dirty: Strategies for Ethnographic Research on Virtual Communities', *Journal of Computer-Mediated Communication* 3(1). URL (consulted March 2006): http://jcmc.indiana.edu/vol3/issue1/paccagnella.html

Phillips, D. and Harding, S. (1985) 'The Structure of Moral Values', in M. Abrams, D. Gerard and N. Timms (eds) *Values and Social Change in Britain*. London: Macmillan.

Plummer, K. (1983) *Documents of Life*. London: Allen & Unwin.

Plummer, K. (2001) *Documents of Life 2: An Invitation to Critical Humanism*. London: Sage Publications.

Porter, D. (1997) *Internet Culture*. London: Routledge.

PubSub (2006) URL (consulted February 2006): http://www.pubsub.com/

Putnam, R. (2000) *Bowling Alone: The Collapse and Revival of American Community*. New York: Simon & Schuster.

Rheingold, H. (2000) *The Virtual Community: Homesteading on the Electronic Frontier* (Revised Edition). Cambridge, MA: MIT Press.

Riley, D. (2005) 'The Blog Herald Blog Count October 2005: Over 100 Million Blogs Created', *The Blog Herald*. URL (consulted April 2006): http://www.blogherald.com/2005/10/10/the-blog-herald-blog-count-october-2005/

Sade, G. (2005) 'Weblogs as Open Constructive Learning Environments', paper presented at *Blogtalk Downunder.* URL (consulted March 2006): http://incsub.org/blogtalk/?page_id=56

Scammell, A. (2006) 'Business Writing for Strategic Communications: The Marketing and Communications Mix', *Business Information Review* 23(1): 43–9.

Scharf, B. (1999) 'Beyond Netiquette: The Ethics of Doing Naturalistic Discourse Research on the Internet', in S. Jones (ed.) *Doing Internet Research.* London: Sage Publications.

Scheidt, L. (2005) 'The Performativity of Naming: Adolescent Weblog Names as Metaphor', paper presented at *The Health of the Discipline*, National Communication Association (NCA), Boston MA. URL (consulted March 2006): http://www.loiss-cheidt.com/working_papers_archive/The_Performativity_of_Naming.pdf

Scheidt, L. and Wright, E. (2004) 'Common Visual Design Elements of Weblogs', in L.J. Gurak, S. Antonijevic, L. Johnson, C. Ratliff and J. Reyman (eds) *Into the Blogosphere: Rhetoric, Community, and Culture of Weblogs.* URL (consulted March 2006): http://blog.lib.umn.edu/blogosphere/common_visual.html

Selwyn, N. and Robson, K. (2003) 'E-mail as a Research Tool', in R. Miller and J. Brewer (eds) *The A to Z of Social Research.* London: Sage Publications.

Serfarty, V. (2004) 'Online Diaries: Towards a Structural Approach', *Journal of American Studies* 38(3): 457–71.

Silberstein, A.R. and Scott, S. (1991) 'Expenditure Diary Surveys and Their Associated Errors', in P. Biemer, R.M. Groves, L.E. Lyberg, N.A. Mathiowetz and S. Sudman (eds) *Measurement Errors in Surveys.* New York: John Wiley & Son.

Silver, D. (2000) 'Looking Backwards, Looking Forward: Cyberculture Studies 1990–2000', in D. Gauntlett (ed.) *Web.Studies: Rewiring Media Studies for the Digital Age.* London: Oxford University Press.

Silverman, D. (2001) *Interpreting Qualitative Data: Methods for Analysing Talk, Text, and Interaction.* London: Sage Publications.

Sixsmith, J. and Murray, C.D. (2001) 'Ethical Issues in the Documentary Data Analysis of Internet Posts and Archives', *Qualitative Health Research* 11(3): 423–32.

Solomon, D. (2001) 'Conducting Web-Based Surveys', *Practical Assessment, Research & Evaluation* 7(19). URL (consulted 15 March 2006): http://PAREonline.net/getvn.asp?v=7&n=19

Sudweeks, F. and Rafaeli, S. (1995) 'How Do You Get a Hundred Strangers to Agree? Computer-Mediated Communication and Collaboration', in T.M. Harrison and T.D. Stephen (eds) *Computer Networking and Scholarship in the 21st Century University.* New York: SUNY Press.

Thelwall, M. and Wouters, P. (2005) 'What's the Deal with the Web/Blogs/the Next Big Technology: A Key Role for Information Science in e-Social Science Research?', *CoLIS Lecture Notes in Computer Science* 3507: 187–99.

Toms, E.G. and Duff, W. (2002) 'I Spent 1½ hours Sifting through One Large Box . . .': Diaries as Information Behaviour of the Archives User: Lessons Learned', *Journal of the American Society for Information Science and Technology* 53(4): 1232–8.

Turkle, S. (1995) *Life on the Screen: Identity in the Age of the Internet.* New York: Simon & Schuster.

US Copyright Office (2000) *Copyright Basics.* URL (consulted May 2006): http://www.copyright.gov/circs/circ1.html#wci

UK Patent Office (2006) *What Is Copyright?* URL (consulted May 2006): http://www.patent.gov.uk/copy/definition.htm

Verbrugge, L. (1980) 'Health Diaries', *Medical Care* 18(1): 73–95.

Walker, K. (2000) '"It's Difficult to Hide It": The Presentation of Self on Internet Home Pages', *Qualitative Sociology* 23(1): 99–120.

Wall, M. (2005) '"Blogs of War": Weblogs as News Journalism', *Journalism* 6(2): 153–72.

Walther, J.B. (2002) 'Research Ethics in Internet-Enabled Research: Human Subjects Issues and Methodological Myopia', *Ethics and Information Technology* 4: 205–16.

Waskul, D. and Douglas, M. (1996) 'Considering the Electronic Participant: Some Polemical Observations on the Ethics of On-line Research', *The Information Society* 12(2): 129–39.

Wei, C. (2004) 'Formation of Norms in a Blog Community', in L.J. Gurak, S. Antonijevic, L. Johnson, C. Ratliff and J. Reyman (eds) *Into the Blogosphere: Rhetoric, Community, and Culture of Weblogs*. URL (consulted March 2006): http://blog.lib.umn.edu/blogosphere/formation_of_norms.html

Wellman, B., Quan-Haase, A., Witte, J. and Hampton, K. (2001) 'Does the Internet Increase, Decrease, or Supplement Social Capital? Social Networks, Participation, and Community Commitment', *American Behavioural Scientist* 45(3): 437–56.

Williams, M. and Robson, K. (2003) 'Re-engineering Focus Group Methodology for the Online Environment', in S.-L. Chen and J. Hall (eds) *Online Social Research: Methods, Issues and Ethics*. New York: Peter Lang.

66

Fieldnotes in Public: Using Blogs for Research

Nina Wakeford and Kris Cohen

Introduction

U nlike other social research methods that have been adapted from established forms for online use, such as the interview or the focus group, the weblog or 'blog' is a format that emerged from within Internet culture, outside any formal research context. Blogs offer a straightforward interface for publishing multimedia content on the Internet, and have acquired the reputation for being more interactive than the average web page, and for being able to generate a community of interlocutors. Their potential for social research lies in the ease of publishing multimedia content, combined with their potential for linking and open response by readers. However, the conventions which have grown up around blogging pose challenges for its use in social research, and in this chapter we set out the key issues which need to be borne in mind when considering the use of blogging as part of a research project. In describing the workings of recent research blogs, our focus is on the methodological potential of the format, rather than on blogs merely as a vehicle for the dissemination of research. Whereas other online research methods now have an ample literature, with significant debates and emerging conventions, blogs lack any substantive commentary in terms of their use methodologically. Although this chapter summarises what little writing exists on blogs as research tools, it is inevitably forward-looking, bearing in mind that many graduate students in particular are using blogs for their work, although as yet few have written explicitly about them.

Source: Nigel Fielding, Raymond M. Lee and Grant Blank (eds), *The SAGE Handbook of Online Research Methods* (London: SAGE, 2008), pp. 307–326.

Simply put, a blog consists of a set of postings on the web with embedded hypertext links and often comments from readers. The dominant culture of blogging dictates that these postings are sequenced and timed according to a set of emerging conventions. They are also structured by the capacities of the particular blogging tool used, such as the popular service 'Blogger'. Most blogging software permits the full range of multimedia files to be uploaded – written text, photos, sound files, video clips – and often has templates for the arrangement of such content. Blogs have received widespread media attention and, in their proliferating forms, currently represent a significant format of popular culture, often involving links to other services such as YouTube.

Social scientists are only just beginning to explore blogs as an online tool, and many researchers use them merely as a means of publication. Some researchers are adapting the blog to fit their disciplinary approaches, which draw largely on qualitative research and ethnographic traditions of writing. In fact one of the most interesting potentials of blogging is how the activity can emphasise and expose the process of doing research, both to ourselves as researchers and to participants. Even though blogs are sometimes dismissed as purely personal chronicles, they do have the potential to change the ways in which data collection, data analysis, and writing up are carried out.

The utility of blogging for online research depends primarily on what kind of multimedia content can be uploaded to the blog, and how feedback and links can be organised. However, as well as these issues of technical infrastructure, which are central to any online research method, and are ever-changing as new versions of software appear, using blogs also requires that we have some understanding of the specific social conventions of blogging. The fundamental issues concern the particular expectations around temporality, interactivity and orientation to adding content. Conventions of mainstream blogging include regular and frequent updating, whether writing, photos or other content; the expectation of linking to other bloggers and online sources; a month-by-month archive; the capacity for feedback through comments to the blog; a particular style of writing which is often characterised as spontaneous and revelatory. However blogs have also played a much larger role in debates about the capabilities of the Internet itself, and the ways in which blogs are presented and read can only be fully understood by identifying these discourses.

Web 2.0 and the Growth of Blogging

Blogging is part of a wider set of activities that has been associated by the technology industry with the 'next generation' of the Internet, and in considering how they might be used in a research project it is crucial to understand the ways in which blogs have been positioned as launching a new kind of digital era. O'Reilly Media, a major technology industry publisher and conference organiser, launched the concept of Web 2.0 in 2004, stressing that what it claimed was a new age of the Internet would be marked by user participation, openness and the consequent effects of large-scale social networks (O'Reilly, 2005). For example, Wikipedia, with its millions of reader contributions, epitomises a Web 2.0 service, in contrast to the Encyclopedia Britannica Online, which is an example of a Web 1.0 model of knowledge management (O'Reilly, 2005). Social networking tools such as Facebook, Myspace and LinkedIn are examples of Web 2.0 services, as are social bookmarking systems such as de.icio.us, and environments that rely on user-submitted and edited content such as YouTube. What these all have in common is an orientation towards collaborative content creation, using the networking and linking features of the Internet itself. The development of Web 2.0 also relies on another collaborative aspect of Internet culture: the idea of Open Source software and associated resistance to software which cannot be further developed by its users. Indeed, it has been suggested that in the era of Web 2.0 the quality of a software package should be evaluated in terms of the number of participants who can participate in its development (Raymond, cited in Bruns, 2007). This has also been called 'peer production' (O'Reilly, 2005).

Compared to environments such as Wikipedia, with its centralised website www.wikipedia.org, blogs are a highly distributed and ad hoc network of such collaboration. There is a range of remotely hosted blogging software sites, including Blogger, Typepad and Xanga, as well as software which allows hosting of your own blog, and community blog software which is Open Source. Yet they share another key aspect of what might be called Web 2.0 culture. Web 2.0 users have been described as sharing an orientation towards the continuous evolution of the artefact under construction (Bruns, 2007). By convention, blogs are not static, but ongoing and dynamic environments driven by links to other blogs as much as by the continual addition of content. Just like web home pages, blogs rely on basic web functions, but most also make use of changes in technological architectures which allow not only a hyperlink to another page, but a subscription to it, and notification every time the designated page changes. One author, cited by O'Reilly in a recent report, has explained that constant notification allows an 'incremental web' with a 'feed-centric protocol' rather than the delivery mechanism of HTML (Skrenta, 2005). Typical Web 2.0 features, such as 'Really Simple Syndication' (RSS) feeds and 'permalinks', alongside the chronological organisation, mark out blogs from a standard website from a technical point of view.

So when using blogs for social research, one does so against a backdrop of heightened expectations about their fundamentally networked nature. Adrian Miles points out that this is constitutive of their 'blogness':

> Blogs are about these relationships between parts: while, say, printed books may exist in isolation, independently of one another, it is absurd to think of there being a single, isolated blog, precisely because a blog is determined by its relationship with other products of blogging, whether

individual posts or entire blogs. If a blog were published in print (that is, published as a book), then it is no longer a blog; its 'blogness' is broken. (Miles, 2006: 218)

It is not only the interrelationship between blogs that is emphasised by such authors, but also the way in which they have accentuated the potential impact of user-led content creation on traditional media and forms of publication. Axel Bruns has proposed the concept of 'produsage' to characterise this change. Produsage is offered as a corrective to a traditional model, in which information is thought to flow from producer to distributor to consumer. Rather,

> ... the production of ideas takes place in a collaborative, participatory environment which breaks down the boundaries between producers and consumers and instead enables all participants to be users as well as producers of information and knowledge – frequently in an inherently and inextricably hybrid role where usage is necessarily also productive: participants are *produsers*. (Bruns, 2007: 101)

Bruns has described four key characteristics of this new model:

- a shift from dedicated individuals and teams as producers to a broader-based, distributed generation of content by a wide community of participants;
- fluid movement of produsers between roles as leaders, participants and users of content – such produsers may have backgrounds ranging from professional to amateur;
- artefacts generated are no longer products in a traditional sense; they are always unfinished, and continually under development – such development is evolutionary, iterative and palimpsestic;
- produsage is based on permissive regimes of engagement which are based on merit more than ownership and they frequently employ copyright systems which acknowledge authorship and prohibit unauthorised commercial uses, yet enable continuing collaboration on further content improvement. (Bruns, 2007: 101)

On a larger scale, blogs have been heralded as part of 'a new mode of innovation' in which the process of creative collaboration that they represent is key to technological progress in general (Quiggin, 2006). In this new 'creative commons' it is claimed that motives for innovation are creative rather than monetary or organisational. The 'openness' of blogs is crucial to this perspective, and the academic blog 'Crooked Timber' has been offered as one example of how collaborative academic discussion might proceed in this environment (Quiggin, 2006). In 'Crooked Timber' book reviews, contributors and original authors open up their reviews and responses to comments on the blog and subsequently all content is archived.

Whether or not blogs are helping to constitute a new era of Internet culture, or are evidence of a new model of content creation, it is clear that they have proliferated at a rapid rate in the last ten years, and that their growth has received coverage in mainstream media. Jorn Barger, credited as editor of one of the first weblogs, 'Robot Wisdom', coined the term 'weblog' in 1997 and defined it as 'a Web page where a Web logger 'logs' all the other Web pages she finds interesting' (cited in Blood, 2004). Although blogs are often presented in terms of a radical break with other forms of online communication, they are also commonly reported as having emerged out of online forums, web journals and e-mail lists (Blood, 2004). Just as other parts of Internet culture are formed of a combination of online and offline elements, so blogs can also be described as having multiple genealogies:

> ... a media genealogy (through zines, broadsides, etc.), a social genealogy (through Internet forums, book clubs, tea rooms), and a technological genealogy (through homepages, ham radio, letters ... (Cohen, 2006: 162)

Herring et al. (2005) have suggested that blogs are a particular digital *genre*, and exist on a continuum between standard HTML documents and asynchronous, computer-mediated communication such as newsgroups – the former being asymmetrical broadcast multimedia and the latter being constantly updated symmetrical exchange. Herring characterised the blogs that she studied as sitting in the middle; interactive, but largely asymmetrical, and frequently updated.

Often blogs are compared to diaries and journals, yet this comparison is not without its problems, as Cohen (2006) points out. Diaries and journals are generally private forms of expression. Blogs by contrast are largely public in so far as they appear on the Internet, unless the author has shut off open-access privileges. What follows is a problematic relationship to the notion of the 'public' in terms of blogs. However the analogy of a diary is useful in so far as it reflects the temporal structuring of a blog; entries are usually identified by time and date. They also are organised chronologically, although in reverse, with the last entry appearing at the top of the front page of the blog. Therefore the audience of a blog is likely to first see the most recent contribution by the author.

Blood's description of the early (pre-1999) blogs indicates that the key features were short entries, links to the wider web and, most importantly, updates throughout the day – unlike web journals that had a convention of an entry per day per page (Blood, 2004). One of the creators of Blogger stated that the 'blog concept' was about three things – 'Frequency', 'Brevity' and 'Personality' (cited in Mortensen and Walker, 2002: 249). Adam Reed's research confirmed this frequent rhythm of posting amongst journal bloggers who were members of one of the main directories of UK weblogs (Reed, 2005). Reed (2005: 227) reports that at the heart of journal blogging is an 'ethos of immediacy'. One individual in his study posted three to eight times during the working day, keeping a window on his browser open so he could update his weblog between other tasks. Reed (ibid.) comments that, for such people, 'Weblog entries are meant to be 'of the moment', a record of how the individual felt or thought at that particular point in time.'

This ethos of immediacy is made possible in part by the ease of using blog software. Thanks to the rapid development of simple user interfaces and the widespread availability of free blogging services, setting up and maintaining a blog is much more straightforward than anything but the most basic web page. As Blood points out, the early slogan of software package Blogger was 'Push-button publishing for the people' (2004: 54). From late 1999, uploading content to the site was as easy as typing into a single form box field, and clicking a button labelled 'blog this'. Currently Blogger enables the creation of a blog in three easy steps: 'create an account', 'name your blog', and 'choose your template' (Blogger homepage, 2007).

Blogging is constantly evolving. The first blogs were mainly written text, but now they often include photos or video streams, such as links to YouTube. Although hyperlinks embedded in the text as jumping-off places to sources or cross-references were central to the original weblog definition, as interfaces evolved many users of Blogger posted linkless entries, prompting controversy in the original weblog community, who insisted 'Weblogs are about links' (Blood, 2004: 54). The authors of a 2005 study of 203 randomly selected blogs confirm the tendency to abandon linking, revealing less evidence than might have been expected from media reports of interlinks and orientation towards external events:

> . . . most of the blogs in our corpus are individualistic, even intimate, forms
> of self-expression, and a surprising number of them contain few or no links.
> (Herring et al., 2005: 24)

The rise of a linkless blogging culture challenges some of the claims of blogs as epitomising Web 2.0. Yet the explanation probably lies rather in the sheer proliferation of blogs and the fact that different types of blogs have now emerged, a fact that Herring's study acknowledges. As software has evolved, and the number of blogs worldwide has reached 70 million, according to the industry blog counters Technorati (Technorati, 2007), blogs have become highly differentiated. The two best-known forms are blogs that aim to replace or supplement traditional media – news or pundit blogs; and those that are highly personal accounts of daily life – diary or journal blogs. Corporate blogging and community blogs have also been documented as emergent forms (Bruns 2007: 3).

Developing Blogs for Research

Although a straightforward way to use a blog in a research project would be to upload research results for dissemination, this does not use the features for which blogs have become known. A report or other digital file, for example, might be downloaded from any website. Many academics have set up blogs, but often their purpose is to report on daily academic life, or to offer commentary on recent events in their research domain, rather than using their blog as a methodological strategy for research. Of course the day-today narration of the life of a researcher might be of interest as part of the research process. Yet amongst such blogs there is little explicit discussion of this new format as a research technology. Most academic disciplines show this kind of blogging presence, although the distribution and style vary widely. The list at academicblogs.org shows that in the social sciences, economics and politics are well represented, anthropology and sociology far less so.

Two long-running blogs by social scientists are esztersblog.com (sociologist Eszter Hargittai) and photoethnography.com/blog (anthropologist Karen Nakamura). Hargittai's and Nakamura's blogs both serve as a personal noticeboard for recent news in their field of study and for more general newsworthy events, and in addition they contain updates on work in progress. In Nakamura's case this is a resource for those interested in visual ethnography, including recommended equipment. Both of these blogs also follow mainstream blogging convention, for example containing an index of entries, allowing access to a month-by-month archive, and also providing links to related topics elsewhere on the Internet. Blogs about entering academic life have also been created by graduate social science students. 'PurseLipSquareJaw' is the long running blog of Anne Galloway, a PhD candidate in sociology, and contains a wide range of personal reflections about doctoral study, as well as a record of day-to-day graduate student experiences, including conferences and commentary on other research. In such sites blogging is presented as a quotidian activity, rather than being related to a time-limited project. Although some individuals do stop blogging, in the cases of Hargittai, Nakamura and Galloway the blog appears as a continual and unfolding work, without a clear end point.

A small number of pioneers have purposefully integrated blogging into their research projects, and their published accounts of the impact of blogs on their research show how blogging paralleled their whole project, rather than being used as a dissemination method. The first social researchers to experiment with blogs in this way were those studying digital technologies and online environments, many of them graduate students who tended to stress the personal benefits of blogging. Torill Mortensen and Jill Walker wrote the first account of research blogging in 2002. In their essay these authors discuss the way in which they first experienced blogging as part of their doctoral research:

> The weblogs were originally used as a way to keep our focus while online, serving as constant little reminders of the real topics we were supposed to write about. They soon developed beyond digital ethnographers' journals and into a hybrid between journal, academic publishing, storage space for links and site for academic discourse. (Mortensen and Walker, 2002: 250)

This hybrid nature of the blog, reflected in the layout of the page where new writing, links and archives may all be visible on one screen, is one reason why researchers have found them useful for organising ongoing projects. In this first generation of blogs, writing was the main input. For Walker they permitted a different form of writing. She has characterised her online writing as a hybrid genre that incorporated the content of the research, her core ideas, and discussions of the process and experience of researching (2002: 131).

For Mortensen and Walker, it was not just the experience of writing in this way which was liberating, but also the fact that it created a public window into the process of doing their PhDs, compensating for the relative isolation of graduate work, as well as offering a sense of having a greater voice than they would have expected as less well-established researchers.

> Blogging allowed us to circumvent the power structures of academia and geography. We found our voices. We heard ourselves, we heard each other, and we were heard by others. It was exhilarating. (2002: 127)

The significance of blogging as part of graduate student work has also been noted by Melissa Gregg, who points out that blogs create the conditions for collegiality, frank brainstorming and response (Gregg, 2006). Mortensen and Walker speak of how the temporal expectations of blogging (frequent, logged by time and date), and also the convention that thoughts would be relatively undigested, helped them not only to keep writing on the blog, but also to maintain progress in their research. In Walker's recent reassessment of her graduate student blogging, she judges that the benefits were also due to connections made with other researchers in her field and joint conversations about work in progress.

Although Mortensen and Walker's account of their blogging experience is largely positive, the feedback mechanisms that allow comments on materials posted online have permitted harsh critique of researchers who blog, because of their chosen style or topic of work. Gregg tells of the consequences of opening up your work in progress to a general audience:

> To be confronted by the opinions of others who share little concern for, or understanding of, your work is a discomforting and chastening experience. It is the quickest way to have any pretensions about academic work deflated. (Gregg, 2006: 155)

It was not just that these readers criticised the author for being 'too academic, too theoretical or too jargon-laden'. They also accused her of not entering into the 'spirit of blogging' (Gregg, 2006). The widespread expectation is that blogs are aimed at a broad readership, a convention that may clash with the needs of a research project blog. Yet Gregg makes a positive claim for blogs as 'conversational scholarship', challenging both critics of theory and jargon, and those in academia who dismiss blogs as trivial. Gregg asks if blogs are treated with such caution in academic circles because debates are archived as they happen, revealing the 'vicissitudes and vulnerability of intellectual practice'. If so, Gregg argues, perhaps we should be questioning the nature of intellectual practice as much as the utility of blogs.

Although some of the contemporary concerns of academic social science – that it be timely, interactive and widely distributed – find parallels in blogging, the few accounts of blogging about research emphasise the difficulties of adapting a format with a well-entrenched set of conventions. As doctoral students studying computer games or online narratives, Walker and Mortensen admit that they were using a format that was wholly in keeping with their topics of study and also their mode of data collection. In the course of their research they were already online many hours per day, and the distance between their contributions to online debates for their doctoral work and their blog entries was minimal. Yet they explain that one of the key challenges was dealing with the style of blogs (Mortensen and Walker, 2002: 253). They point to the variation in blogging styles encouraged by different software. In Walker's case, she changed from a service that encouraged instant publication (Blogger) to an application that existed on her personal computer rather than the web (Tinderbox). She welcomed the capacity of Tinderbox to keep some of her writing private and unpublished. This facility changed the way she wrote and published in her public blog.

Amongst the first generation of research blogs and their emphasis on the written form, Mortensen attempted to create a blog with research participants in mind. She wrote a blog that would introduce her research to the game players whom she was studying. In the same way as the creation of web pages about research projects has helped earlier generations of Internet scholars gain consent from, and interact with, potential informants (O'Connor and Madge, 2001), for Mortensen, setting up a blog established a credible online identity. Furthermore the convention of frequent updating resulted in the game players being able to follow the development of the thesis itself (Mortensen and Walker, 2002: 250). However it is difficult to know if Mortensen's use of her blog in this way is a widespread way of working. Early research blogs, such as the ones created by Walker and Gregg, followed the diary format of many individual blogs, and the way in which they write about the experience suggests that they followed many of the conventions of journal bloggers studied by Reed. Reed claims that his interviewees treated blogs as 'indexes of the self' (2005: 230). As noted earlier, the typical attitude is that weblog entries should be 'of the moment', a record of how the individual feels or thinks at the time (Reed, 2005: 227). Blogs were not primarily created with a particular set of readers in mind. Rather, 'journal bloggers regard themselves as the text's most significant visitor' (Reed, 2005: 231).

Blogging as Fieldnotes-in-Public

Despite the lack of published accounts of research blogs in action, what is clear from the available material is that the activity of uploading material to the blog becomes a key part of a researcher's day-to-day life, and that this often results in writing having more day-to-day significance while also being potentially de-dramatised. Published writing is no longer an activity to be deferred to the end of the project, but instead it becomes part of a daily routine, offered to readers as the project progresses. The best way to describe this aspect of research blogging is that it creates a form of 'fieldnotes-in-public'.

Notes and jottings resulting from observations, interviews and personal experiences have a vital place in the toolkit of the qualitative researcher and ethnographers in particular, in traditional and online fieldsites, both have discussed the role of the fieldnote (Sanjek, 1990; Emerson et al., 1995; Hine, 1998; Wolfinger, 2002). The focus on the writing of ethnographic accounts, and in particular the position of the author in these accounts, has become an ongoing issue in fields of enquiry which use the translation of *in situ* observations and conversations as the core of data gathering or ways of knowing (Clifford and Marcus, 1986; Atkinson, 1992). Some of the defining characteristics of mainstream blogging seem to fit in very well with advice given on the writing of fieldnotes. The instruction that fieldnotes should be written as soon as possible after the observation has its translation in the norm of the blog as 'brain dump' (Reed, 2005). Reed describes the attitude as 'an attempt to transplant the contents of the individual's mind directly into text' (2005: 228).

The guidance on writing fieldnotes frequently during fieldwork has its corollary in the convention of writing daily blog entries. The crucial difference is the public posting of entries online in contrast to the traditional private fieldnote, a background resource to be drawn upon for subsequent analysis and publication.

If blogs are to be explored more fully as 'fieldnotes-in-public', the most useful literature is that which focuses on fieldnotes as a writing practice within social science (Richardson, 1994; Wolfinger, 2002). In order to explore the connections more fully we now introduce a research blog set up by one of the authors (Cohen) for a study of personal photography and the Internet.

This blog demonstrates how entries can be mapped to a typology of fieldnotes adapted from Glaser and Strauss (1967) by Laurel Richardson, who has pioneered experimental writing as a method of enquiry (1990, 1992, 1994). Cohen's blog, entitled 'PhotosLeaveHome' and hosted by Blogger, was set up as part of a year-long study. Primarily an investigation of bloggers who used photography within their blogs, or 'photobloggers', Cohen conducted the research using face-to-face interviews, as well as interviews through e-mail and instant messaging. He uploaded both writing and photos to the blog, and the format followed the conventions of a standard blog page.

In Richardson's typology of fieldnotes, four categories of notes are delineated: observational, methodological, theoretical, and personal (1994: 525–26). *Observational notes*, which are concrete and detailed, offer the sense of staying close to the situation. In Cohen's blog, observational notes comment on the place or context of the interview, giving the reader an image of the encounter.

Blog Entry 4th February (Hyperlinks in Brackets)

'Thank you [interviewee] for distracting me from my project with talk about punk rock, an excellent sandwich from the world's smallest deli, and a most picturesque bench for sitting.'

More detailed entries are written just after interviews, and often go beyond mere description of the data collection to more open-ended thoughts about how the topic is being redefined by each encounter.

Blog Entry 2nd February

'In talking with [interviewee] just now, he said something which struck me as really important, and not just because it had never occurred to me before, but a little bit because it dislodges a bit of my thinking that had gotten stuck. He emphasised how his photoblog is just that, a photoblog, and important to him as such. My problem was this: because his (and many other photobloggers') photographs are so accomplished, and because in his comment box conversations, he seems to put so much emphasis on photography as such, on the technical and aesthetic aspects of a shot, I had been starting to think about *that* kind of photoblog as more of a gallery or portfolio than a blog. Which is wrong. Plain wrong, but also categorically confused. Simple classifications are just not going to work; I seem to have to learn that 10 times a day. The thing he said which really struck me was that, even or especially on a technically/aesthetically focused site, 'there's a journey of sorts that's told by the photographs themselves (which includes changes of style, focus, equipment, and so on) . . .'. By which he refers to a narrative spun out over time, a kind of continuity in the photoblog (over and above the bare fact that photographs go there) which is akin to that found in the archetypical or historical form of blogging, where, in many cases, it's the personality or some abiding interest of the blogger, related through text, which provides the continuity. And in photoblogs, [interviewee] points out, it might be the same thing, but the photographs themselves carry and form the narrative.'

Second, Richardson describes other fieldnotes as *methodological notes*, which relate to the collection of data. Reading through the entries in PhotosLeaveHome, it becomes apparent how each interview was conducted, whether online or face to face, and whether in a group or individually. Each meeting is recorded on the blog, with some sense of what kind of encounter ensued.

PHOTOS LEAVE HOME

RESEARCH NOTES FROM AN ESRC STUDY ABOUT PERSONAL PHOTOGRAPHY AND THE WEB
(OCT '04 – OCT '-05 . . . AND AFTER).

MONDAY, JUNE 27, 2005

Making Publics

[I've been writing almost as much about publics as I have about photography, for reasons that I hope to make clear in present and future writings.] This is a public sculpture that nicely tests and voices some key ideas about how publics work (and, no doubt, fail to work).

Thanks to Jean for the link.

POSTED BY KC AT 2:51 PM   ✉

SATURDAY, JUNE 11, 2005

Some Generalisations, Part 1

Here is the moment you've all been waiting for. Maybe. What is it? Generalisations! Isn't that what everyone_really_wants from a sociological study?*

Possibly this will be useful to a few people, maybe most of all to (myself and) the people I've interviewed, many of whom have asked me for a list like this. Because I'm writing this primarily with you all in mind, probably I should use "you" instead of the more impersonal "they" in the list below, but that doesn't seem quite right either. Please forgive, if you can, how impersonal and social scientific it sounds.

So, here it is: a long, largely un-substantiated, highly generalised list of characteristics or behaviours that the people I've interviewed (you all) have in common. They're not all going to sound revelatory; in fact, by their very nature as commonalities, they should be familar to most people. Then again, my impression from talking to people is that they are not at all sure how "typical" they are, or where their practices converge and diverge from others' practices. I guess that's the first commonality in my list. So, I present them in all their underwhelming glory.

I've interviewed about 80 people in all, over 2.5 years, with about 95% living in the UK and far more than half living in London. Pretty nearly equal numbers of men and women. Approx. 55/80 people upload their photos primarily to blogs (although many have more than one site); approx. 25/80 people upload their photos primarily to flickr.com. These 80 people are the grammatical subject of all the following clauses. Important note: I really have no idea how generalisable the following are to the population outside the 80 people I've met. Others will be better judges of that than I am. Ok, here goes, in no very significant order.

Imagine that each of the following begins with: "Out of 80 people, some relatively large number . . ."

-migrate over time from being interested in what photography can show to being interested in photography as an activity in and of itself

-feel as though they steadily become better (more skilled) photographers through the period of taking photos and uploading them to the internet

-start to carry their camera(s) with them all the time, wherever they go

-take a lot more photos as a (direct or indirect) consequence of posting photographs to the internet

ABOUT ME

KC

LONDON, UNITED KINGDOM

I am a research fellow at the University of Surrey, working in the INCITE research group within the Department of Sociology, and now a PhD student in the Art History department at the University of Chicago. My interests tend to nest around the social life of images and image-making, with a particular interest (of late) in technological image-making. This blog is a document of my current research.

VIEW MY COMPLETE PROFILE

PREVIOUS POSTS

The Intimate Public Sphere

Ubiquity Again

Media, Culture & Society v. 26(6) 2005

Photoblogs = Art

Something for you Cult Studs

Mis-integration

Chicago Touchdown

Publics, Markets

Dogs, Cats, Mappr, Hamster

Where is the Universal, and What is its Scale?

ARCHIVES

October 2004

January 2005

February 2005

March 2005

April 2005

May 2005

June 2005

July 2005

August 2005

September 2005

October 2005

November 2005

December 2005

-tend to bristle or quail at the word "photographer," at the suggestion that this is a name that might apply to them

-shy away from portrait photography and shots of strangers

-occasionally or frequently go on journeys or walks with the sole or primary purpose of taking photographs

-begin to change their photographic practices significantly when they get their first digital camera (more photos, more interest in showing those photos, more interest in photography as such)

-like to go on long walks

-are more interested in "urban grit" than pastoral landscapes; are more interested in "gritty" landscapes than bucolic ones

-prefer to shoot alone

-have most of their conversations about photography through the internet (in comment fields and discussion forums); that is, tend not to have very many offline friends (friends who they mostly see offline or who they got to know offline) with whom they talk about photography

-have done most of their learning about photography online, by looking at other people's photos and participating in discussions – rather than learning through offline courses. This is far more of a self-taught than an institutional form of education, but it's not really quite either one

-see most of the photographs they encounter (other people's photos) on the internet – not in galleries or books

-say they are selective about the photos they put online (in other words, apply some standards; but this comment is about the fact of selectiveness and not the types of standards people apply; these are more variable)

-say that their blog or website or photographs are mostly done for themselves (for their own pleasure and not an audience's pleasure)

-(nevertheless) are conscious of having an audience comprised of some known people (friends, family) and some strangers (a group which varies in size according to one's imaginative tendencies and the amount of comments one gets from strangers)

-have comment fields enabled and actively read them

-feel obliged to respond to most of the comments they receive

-eventually become inured to the compliments they receive for their photos

-have more than one personal website

-are skeptical about making photography into a paid activity. Two reasons: 1. because most fear that being paid or trying to get paid will fundamentally change how they feel about photography if not about the photographs themselves (most like how they feel about it as an unpaid activity) and 2. because most know that the market for photographers is stingy and closed

-(nevertheless) have ideas about how to make money with their photograph

-say that taking photographs helps them to see the world differently

[this is just a start; more to come]

*The status of generalisations is something that's in question in this project. Why? Because it's generally good practice to question the process of generalising, but more importantly, because I think the topic of my research, itself, puts that process into question (i.e. in a sense, what I've been studying is the relationship of the single photographer to the mass of photographers, the single photograph to the mass of photographs – that is an issue of generalisation, or more specifically, trying to thwart the tendencies of generalisation).

POSTED BY KC AT 2:00 PM

Ochlocracy in action

POSTED BY KC AT 11:36 AM

FRIDAY, JUNE 10, 2005

"Remixing the blogosphere"

Remixing the Blogosphere, The Guardian, 09.06.05

All in all, a surprisingly wide-ranging and copyleft-friendly article. But I'm still going to quibble.

The article's narrative backbone is that "online independent media hubs" represent an advance over blogs. Specifically, the writer (Danny Bradbury), influenced by Clemencia Rodriguez (associate professor in the Department of Communications at Oklahoma University), thinks that hubs are more communal, more collective, more collaborative and therefore create a better kind of public. Rodriguez says that: "Blogs suffer from their individualistic nature. . . 'Ninety per cent of them will never find their audience, because information and communication has to do with being part of a collective.' "

It's hard to believe that notions of community, collabortion, and collectivity still need to be subtended by an enabling notion of centrality. Aren't people watching how blogs work? How Flickr works?

I don't have a problem with the hubs they discuss, many of which seem pretty interesting (and some of which are less centralised and centralising than others), but I think if we use the emergence of media hubs as evidence that blogs and flickr sites and all manner of "individualistic"

(Continued)

Figure 1: (*Continued*)

media are a primitive and already-superannuated form of public action, we are going to lose an opportunity to see how these sites of individualistic activity foster (although not causally or cumulatively) pluralistic activity. To me, this is one of the most significant and exciting aspects of blogs and their various individualistic media siblings; the article obscures this aspect in its praise for centralised hubs as the natural evolution of blogs and all independent media.

POSTED BY KC AT 7:03 AM   ✉

SATURDAY, JUNE 04, 2005

No Longer Greek to Me

ochlocracy

POSTED BY KC AT 4:04 PM   ✉

FRIDAY, JUNE 03, 2005

Anti-Determinist* before it was cool to be anti-determinist

"The discussion of the whole problem of technology, that is, of the transformation of life and world through the introduction of the machine, has been strangely led astray through an all-too-exclusive concentration upon the service or disservice the machines render to men. The assumption here is that every tool and implement is primarily designed to make human life easier and human labor less painful. Their instrumentality is understood exclusively in this anthropocentric sense. But the instrumentality of tools and implements is much more closely related to the object it is designed to produce, and their sheer 'human value' is restricted to the use the animal laborans** makes of them. In other words, homo faber***, the toolmaker, invented tools and implements in order to erect a world, not – at least, not primarily – to help the human life process. The question therefore is not so much whether we are the masters or the slaves of our machines, but whether machines still serve the world and its things, or if, on the contrary, they and the automatic motion of their processes have begun to rule and even destroy world and things." – Arendt, Hannah (1958) The Human Condition. Chicago: The University of Chicago Press, p. 151.

I like Arendt's re-direction here. To evaluate technologies on the basis of their ability to make human life better obscures the question of "better for whom." Her focus on "world-making" (in addition to being close to Warner's definition of publics as "world-making") admits of a broader, better set of conversations. We could say, then, that Arendt's concept of technology is more public (in Habermas' sense of a public discussion which opens to debate the very bases of discussion, the presuppositions, the biases, etc. – in contrast, for instance, to PR (or a techno-determinist account of technology) which stages a semblance of debate while obscuring the assumptions upon which that debate rests). Although I think her distinction between animal laborans

and homo faber now seems at best a bit arbitrary and at worst completely misleading.

*Determinist, or, Techno-determinist: a techno-centric view of the world, as embodied, for instance, in the U.S.'s infamous Star Wars initiative, a missle defense system designed to keep America safe from nuclear attack. The techno-determinist aspect of this initiative is to think that all one has to do is build this massively expensive machine and as a simple result, all Americans will be safe. But, of course, there are a set of very political and very complex reasons why America might think it needs a missle defense system in the first place (which are completely unaddressed, even elided, by the idea of the saviour machine) as well as a set of very political and very complex consequenes of building such a machine, the least of which would be that Americans are safe.

**animal laborans: the animal who labors; this is Arendt's way of talking about the part of us which has to labor to serve our most basic needs (i.e. eating and reproduction). This is an important term for her because, in the history of discussions about publics, it has often been argued that in order to be properly public (political, communal, engaged, etc.) one has to have distance from one's baser needs and the labor required to serve them. But Arendt is, at best, ambivalent about the concept because she recognises, at the most fundamental level, that we cannot ignore the body, and that (therefore) one cannot simply remove the need to labor (Marx, for instance, famously argued that the Revolution would bring about the end of the need to labor).

***homo faber: Arendt's term of that part of humans which works (as opposed to labors) to build tools which create the world, i.e. the things, the cities, the culture that is the world.

POSTED BY KC AT 3:28 PM

Source: Web link: http://photosleavehome.blogspot.com/2005_06_01_archive.html

Figure 1

Blog Entry 3rd March

'[interviewee] + [interviewee] organised via [blogging organization] = conversation which veered recklessly between highflying technical geekery, philosophic self-investigation and complex aesthetic inquiry. In a dark sub-sub basement. At a pub with 'cheese' in the name.'

Richardson (1994: 526) describes the third type of fieldnotes as writing which, as she puts it, 'keeps me from being hooked on my "take" on reality'. These are *theoretical notes* involving hunches and alternative interpretations, as well as the making of connections. Month by month on PhotosLeaveHome, Cohen introduces and provides commentaries on a range of theories, not only about photography, but the whole range of his secondary sources, including writing on image-making more widely and the cultural politics of technology. In the following entry, right at the beginning of the project, he describes how a German painter used photography in order to paint differently. Cohen offers his own comment on the contemporary reading of this stance, and then juxtaposes the whole post with comments on the blog of the participant he is about to interview.

Blog Posting 30th January

'In the 1960s, *Gerhard Richter* began a series of paintings copied from photographic snapshots (to see a few, do a search in the previous link for "ordinary life" images). Richter liked snapshots as sources because, as he says "there was no style, no composition, no judgment." I think we get more use out of Richter's sentiment if we take him to be saying that personal snapshots lacked – were free from – the modes of style, composition and judgment that painters, like himself, who had been trained in strict painterly tradition, learned to (couldn't help but) recognise and deploy. Snapshots were free from that which he felt hindered his painting, free from painterly devices and institutionalised modes of viewing. Of course, Richter's ideas about what snapshot photography lacks are condescending, as if to say artists are the only people for whom visual concepts like style and composition are legible or relevant. His comments seem especially silly now, in light of the compositional, stylistic and formal awareness to be found in the photoblog world. For instance, check out the comment-box discussions on [interviewee] (with whom I'll be IM-ing tomorrow)'.

The final category of Richardson's typology is labelled *personal notes*, which include feelings about the research itself, people the researcher is talking to, how the process itself is unfolding, and doubts and anxieties. Cohen often comments on the ways in which his framework changes in the course of the year, particularly after interviews. These entries come the closest to Richardson's definition, although they resemble reorientations rather than sustained attacks of anxiety.

Blog Posting 26th January 2005

'Lovely thing about interviews: they don't let you hold onto either assumptions or conclusions for long. Yesterday morning, I wondered aloud and in print about whether the experience of viewing photographs online fosters a kind of double vision: on the content of the photo (seeing through the photo) and, at the same time, on the photograph itself (sight at the photo's surface). When along came yesterday afternoon's interviews with [interviewee 1] and [interviewee 2], during which [interviewee 1] described one of the pleasures of blog photography as the opportunity to glimpse the personality beneath the posts (despite their formal qualities, their grammar, their compositional qualities), and [interviewee 2] distinguished blog photography from other forms of photography (not absolutely distinguished, but provisionally) by its friendliness to accident, to informality, to what, in the context of "proper" photography, can look like a mistake or simply a "bad" photo. Bad light. Bad focus. Graininess. Somehow, these qualities suit blog photography, or blog photography welcomes them. And to [interviewee 1]'s point, maybe personality shows through (is nicely refracted by) these endearing flaws, or maybe personality travels within them'.

Despite the typology proposed by Richardson, it is clear that blog entries often fit into more than one fieldnote category. The typology might function more as a checklist for a researcher wanting to explore this way of blogging about research, while also examining other conventions of fieldnote writing (Sanjek, 1990). Yet as fieldnotes-in-*public*, the researcher also must consider the way in which provisional musings are accessible to any reader if the blog has unrestricted access. This is far from the practice of researchers in the mainstream ethnographic tradition, such as Barrie Thorne, who writes of fieldnotes as having a 'private and intimate character; one can innovate, make false starts, flare up with emotions without feeling an anonymous audience at one's shoulder' (personal communication cited in Richardson, 1994). Journal bloggers tend to construct blogs as 'a space in which persons can be themselves, free of constraints and able to say what they think and feel about everyone around them' (Reed, 2005: 230). Yet the consequences of blogging as a public intellectual were described by Gregg in the previous section. Far from being a shelter from unwanted comments, the writers of open-access blogs may feel as though there is the constant presence of an anonymous audience. This fundamentally changes the nature of the fieldnote, and highlights the importance of thinking about what kind of 'public' blogs both draw upon and create.

Modes of Address and Publicness

Ambitious claims have been made for blogs in terms of creating a new audience for academic knowledge. Such assertions draw on the promised refashioning of the Internet via Web 2.0. Halavais provides one example:

> Scholars who blog are engaging in more than personal publishing; they are shaping a new "third place" for academic discourse, a space for developing the social networks that help drive the more visible institutions of research. (Halavais, 2006: 117)

Although some blogs may indeed serve this function, examining the entries on PhotosLeaveHome suggests that researchers might first think about the direct and immediate public for the blog-research participants. Mortensen aimed to address the participant as a reader, and in PhotosLeaveHome Cohen uses the blog to inform interviewees about how the research is progressing. Every interviewee is thanked within the blog entry written directly after their online or face-to-face meeting. With their permission, their names are used as links back to their own Internet sites. This results in the blog being a hyperlinked archive that can be searched by new potential participants, as well as those who have already taken part in the project.

Readers of blogs can add content themselves if a comment feature is enabled. Although Cohen allowed this function early in the blog, in later months he had to turn it off, owing to the quantity of unsolicited spam comments that were being posted. Meanwhile he learned from interviewees that even when comments were not posted, PhotosLeaveHome was read by his participants. In another research blog used as part of an ongoing ethnographic project by Katrina Jungnickel (studioincite.com/makingwifi), comments have become a significant way in which participants indicate that they are reading the blog. As part of her immersion in two DIY community groups in Australia, Jungnickel posts regularly about her activities at meetings and other gatherings. Following her entries on the blog, comments appear from three different groups: group members, fellow researchers and unknown readers. The comment section of the blog is used not only for contributions, but also for responses by Jungnickel, so that a thread of comment and response is created. For example, in response to an entry on having been to a group convention, and posting her initial thoughts on the event, she received and replied to a posting from a fellow researcher and one of the group. These entries remained linked to her original posting so that they formed a record of the interaction.

The comment feature is one way in which readers of the blog can make themselves known on the blog itself. Other bloggers, reacting to Jungnickel's entries, linked her blog postings to their own blogs, thereby encouraging readers to reach her research blog from elsewhere online. In this way the audience for a blog is further expanded, and may draw in those who have an interest in a particular posting. There are possibilities, as yet unexplored, for this to be used in participatory research that explicitly seeks to involve those who are researched as *participants*. This has been widely discussed in relation to blogging by political representatives interested in their encouragement of citizen/voter interaction (Coleman, 2005).

Generating comments or links from a research blog does not, of course, mean that new audiences have automatically been created for academic knowledge.

In fact, Michael Warner points out that the blindness of the writer to her or his public is both constitutive and defining of publics generally. The historical power of a public, as a site of resistance or critique, was to imaginatively create, and thereby take up a position in, a world of 'stranger relations' (Warner, 2002). One could not know the extent or makeup of one's audience (this is especially true of print culture), so one imagined them, and in imagining them brought them into a kind of existence. It is in this sense that publics are autotelic (self-purposing) and auto-poetic (self-writing), reflexive relations that Warner glosses, politically, as 'poetic world making' (2002: 67–118). Thus, a researcher's relation to a public is a self-relation as much as it is a concrete relation to a known or knowable audience. The writer cultivates, in Habermas' famous phrase, an 'audience-oriented subjectivity' (Habermas, 1991).

This is perhaps why reactions to the idea of *fieldnotes-in-public* are so polarised. To write for an audience of strangers is to (re-)imagine the world for which one writes, to imagine a small world into being and place oneself within that world. If Mortensen and Walker (2002) find this process exhilarating, it is perhaps a measure of how they wanted, or needed, to reconfigure the academic world in order to inhabit it, imaginatively and practically. Gregg's comments about the way stranger-relations can deflate academic pretensions register the same effect of having one's world reconfigured.

This does not mean that the public dimension of writing fieldnotes-in-public makes that activity either solipsistic or narcissistic. Rather, when researchers think about the possibility of multiple, and perhaps conflicting, readers, they are necessarily rethinking their relationship to themself and, thereby, to their fieldnotes, to their research, to the publication and dissemination of their work, and ultimately to the discipline(s) and institution(s) in which they are embedded.

Blogs, Process and Reflexivity

The conventions of academic research dictate that publication occurs towards the end of the research process. In a research blog, as we have seen, this may be altered. Researchers can use blogs in order to emphasise the unfolding of a research project over time, and the twists and turns of the research process itself.

In PhotosLeaveHome, Cohen's writing can be thought of not just as fieldnotes, but also as a narration of a research project in which the stages are written about as they occur, rather than having been reordered for publication. For example, writing about existing literature and sources occurs throughout the months of the project, and appears on the blog as it is carried out. Writing that thanks the interviewees and acknowledges the ways in which new data collection helps an argument emerge is also scattered throughout the blog. Furthermore, summaries of findings are posted as Cohen works on them, inviting response from readers. In the same way, on Jungnickel's blog, the ways in which the project is reconceptualised during the course of ethnography – in this case with the addition of a second DIY community group – are described on the site. Readers can work their way back through the posted entries and look at previous versions of the concepts under development, and earlier reviews of literature, demonstrating the shifting focus as the project evolves. Although the reader might find this narration jumbled in comparison to a traditional report of research, it does expose, for better or worse, the temporality involved in an ethnographic project.

There has been a recent resurgence of interest in the processual nature of social reality (e.g. Meyer, 2005). Blogs provide one way of enacting and representing a sense of process, particularly if a researcher draws on the conventional norms of posting unprocessed thoughts. Halavais (2007: 118) speaks of blogs as 'a relatively transparent and unedited view of thinking-in-progress'. Social scientists might balk at the idea of transparency in relation to writing, given the extensive debates about the processes of selection and representation in even the 'rawest' fieldnote data (Sanjek, 1990). However, the idea of the processual nature of creating and maintaining self-identity finds extensive support in contemporary social theory. Most famously, Anthony Giddens (1991) has written that, in late modernity, a person's identity is to be found in sustaining a narrative about the self. Giddens suggests that the self is a reflexive project. Rather than mere introspection, a person must 'continually integrate events which occur in the external world, and sort them into an ongoing "story" about the self' (Giddens 1991: 54). Blog writing could therefore be conceived not just as one way of engaging in a reflexive project of the self, but as a format which particularly encourages both engagement with our internal worlds and also interaction with others. Whereas Giddens suggested that soap operas offered a feeling of a coherent narrative *to* audiences, we might conjecture that blogs now encourage the writing of an experience into a coherent narrative *by* those audiences themselves.

When using blogs for research, it is necessary to think about the repercussions of working with a format that might overemphasise the narrative coherence of the research process. Even the earliest autobiographical accounts of doing social research, such as those collected by Colin Bell and Howard Newby (1977) in *Doing Sociological Research*, offer stories which are characterised by false starts, having to rethink initial ideas, problems with access and so on. Fiona Devine and Sue Heath (1999: 3) point out that the work of social research involves tackling sociological issues as they arise: 'The challenge is to confront the mundane *messiness* of empirical research by addressing the practical, ethical and epistemological issues which present themselves during the research process'. The blog format can suit this purpose by encouraging regular writing about practical, ethical and epistemological issues; but how far is it suited to maintaining an account of messiness? Furthermore, the authors whose accounts were collected in *Doing Sociological Research*, and others

pursuing a more reflexive consideration of methods, such as feminist methodologists (e.g., Stanley and Wise 1993), write autobiographical accounts as post
hoc reflections of the process, and presented as a supplement to the research
findings. Blogs, by contrast, encourage immediacy and the impression that the
blog constitutes the research, rather than forming a commentary on it. It is
therefore necessary to consider the use of blogs as enacting a sense of research
process in relation to debates about the usefulness of reflexivity.

Approaches from within the sociology of scientific knowledge have promoted the idea of reflexivity as a way in which to demonstrate the constructedness of texts, including those written about research (Ashmore, 1989; Mol,
2002). Experimental texts have been produced using this principle that use
conversational forms or are written as two parallel texts (Mol, 2002). Research
blogs might be attractive to this school of writing, particularly because they
offer the possibility that the text remains in construction, and that it can be
formatted in unconventional ways. Of course, blogs mobilised in the service of
generating reflexive accounts will not be immune from the criticism which
surrounds the trend towards reflexivity (Lynch, 2000; Adkins, 2002).

Another approach, which foregrounds the status of writing about the self
in the research process, is autoethnography (Ellis, 1997; Clough, 2000). This
goes beyond the writing of personal narratives, attempting to connect such
accounts to cultural and social structures:

> Usually written in first-person voice, autoethnographic texts appear in a
> variety of forms – short stories, poetry, fiction, novels, photographic essays,
> personal essays, journals, fragmented and layered writing, and social sci-
> ence prose. In these texts, concrete action, dialogue, emotion, embodiment,
> spirituality, and self-consciousness are featured, appearing as relational
> and institutional stories affected by history, social structure, and culture,
> which themselves are dialectically revealed through action, feeling, thought
> and language. (Ellis and Bochner, 2000: 739)

Writing on a blog might be one way of doing such autoethnography, and indeed
the idea of fragmented and layered writing, including the multimedia elements possible online, seem to fit well with the expectations of the journal blog
genre.

Links to the now extensive literature on experimental writing within
social science have yet to be made by the authors of research blogs, although
there seem to be similar issues at stake. In Carolyn Ellis and Arthur Bochner's
overview of autoethnography, itself written in sections that alternate writing styles, the authors point out issues of vulnerability, pain and ethics when a
researcher is both exposed themselves and writes in a way that exposes others.
This connects to the public nature of the blog, and especially to concerns about
the ethics of research blogs. The examples given in this chapter, from Walker
and Mortensen's work on digital narratives and games, to Cohen's study of
photobloggers, to Jungnickel's ethnography of DIYers, are not projects which

involve sensitive topics, and all of these studies pose relatively little risk to research respondents. Indeed, most links on these blogs use the actual names and blogs/websites of the research participants. Nevertheless Jungnickel found herself exercising extreme caution when blogging about one of her research communities, who did not want the location of their meetings revealed. She uploads extensive documentation about her own activities, while avoiding identifiers about the group with which she is involved. The risks involved in the public nature of blogs, and the implication of posting online, need to be understood by the researcher, so that respondents who give their permission to be written about, either anonymously or not, are fully aware of the possibility that a research blog might be linked to other sites, or picked up as a feed to another blog unrelated to the original research. As the research process unfolds on a blog, the researcher should also bear in mind that the emerging account will be available to later participants, including the comments of those involved earlier in the research. Undoubtedly there are risks of vulnerability of both researcher and respondent in making freely available information about the research online, paralleling the risks in other social research settings. It is unlikely that public blogs would be suitable for the most sensitive topics, where anonymity is absolutely crucial or proprietary data is being discussed.

Despite these cautions, posting to a blog does appear to permit a more spontaneous approach to writing, and often also to writing which is highly self-reflexive. From the existing accounts, blogging is also 'intoxicating', even when used in work situations (Kaiser et al., 2007). Kaiser et al.'s study of a professional work group that used a blog during a software engineering project suggests that this intoxication derives from the distinct technological features of blogs that 'unleash passion for engaging in knowledge work' (Kaiser et al., 2007: 392). The engineers who worked on the Microsoft 'Longhorn' project exhibited 'intense and focused concentration whereby action and awareness are merged so that temporal awareness is distorted' (Kaiser et al., 2007: 400). Kaiser associates the activity of blogging with the idea of 'flow states' proposed by Csikszentmihalyi (1997), a description of the immersion involved in such activities as playing music or rock climbing. In thinking about blogs in terms of process, the research by Kaiser suggests that a more careful examination of the affective registers of this process might have to be considered. How far might research blogs also unleash these passions, and how would that change the research?

Blogs for Dispersed, Interdisciplinary Teams

Although blogs tend to be created by individual authors, they also hold out the potential to be used amongst research groups. A group of ethnographers working in Brazil, who needed to feed back information on a daily basis to team members in the United States, have used a format which linked a blog and an audiovisual presentation (Lovejoy and Steele, 2004). These researchers, based at Microsoft, created narratives about their ongoing fieldwork so that the engineers and designers who were not with them in the field could have some access to the material which they were collecting before they returned. In Brazil they conducted interviews about everyday use of technology amongst families and students, as well as asking participants to do diary studies and take photos of their lives. The researchers also took handwritten fieldnotes and video footage as well as photos of their own. Their aim was not only to collect and analyse this data, but also to offer it back to a product team who were working on a very tight timescale, and who wanted to be immersed in the data collection as it was happening. A form of blogging suited this purpose, although they used an augmented blog by integrating more data via a piece of their company's own software, Microsoft PhotoStory. The ethnographers themselves state that they 'brought our colleagues as close to the field as possible short of actually taking them along with us' (2004: 71). This attempt at proximity was achieved not only by the daily addition of a series of images, but by adding voice narration yielding a form of audio-enhanced slide show.

> After each day in the field we moved our photographs from our digital cameras to our laptops, and then went through our handwritten notes and photographs to pull together a short, narrated 'slide show', sometimes adding music or quotes from participants pulled from videotapes. This was posted by a colleague on an intranet site other [Microsoft] employees could visit. For those who wanted more detail, each Photo Story had an accompanying text blog, or web log, which added depth and richness to the images and voice annotation they saw and heard. (2004: 74)

For Lovejoy and Steele, the task was not just to transmit digital files, but to use the conventions of daily blog entries and the emergence of a cumulative story in order to share information amongst a team which was more accustomed to receiving written reports or presentations at the end of fieldwork. The relatively small file size of the daily editions meant that the digital files could even be sent by dial-up connection, although Lovejoy and Steele did rely on an intermediary to post them on the company's intranet. In this case, their form of research blogging with PhotoStory allowed both the researchers and the audience to better understand that what was being created was an artefact that was provisional and revised as the fieldwork progressed.

In large projects, where research teams may be scattered in different sites, this kind of blogging could be another way in which computer-based networks would support fieldwork. Another aspect of the corporate research world, as these researchers explain, is that data can rarely be shared outside the corporation. Unlike most public blogs, they therefore had to enable a format that permitted their content to be freely accessible to both their team and a wider Microsoft public, without risking the data about their participants reaching a wider audience. This is a particular risk in commercial settings, where visual images may be recycled from the ethnographer's presentation and reused in another part of the organisation.

Hazards of Research Blogging

As with other online methods, many of the perils involved in research blogging relate to the Internet environment in which it is carried out. The account of the project by Lovejoy and Steele is a reminder that fieldwork blogs may not be as easy to maintain without an always-on connection to the Internet, which is expected by many software applications such as Blogger. Furthermore, whether using free hosting services such as Blogger or paid hosting services which offer technical support and a greater number of features, researchers should check how sites that host their blogs treat the ownership of the blog content. The content policy of the service, as well as the terms of use and policy on copyright (and copyright infringement), should be examined at the outset of the research. For example, Blogger's content policy states 'Users may not publish material that promotes hate toward groups based on race or ethnic origin, religion, disability, gender, age, veteran status and sexual orientation/ gender identity' (Blogger, 2007). Yet some social research projects examine precisely the cultural constructions of attitudes towards these categories, and might be hindered by deciding in advance that neither the researcher nor potential interlocutors had complete freedom of expression on the blog.

The ethical issues, as signalled in the sections above, for the most part relate to the nature of the publicity and audiences that blogs may attract, and the necessity to inform respondents about the potential use of their uploaded content, including its ownership and reuse. Given that one of the tacit agreements of mainstream blog writers is that their comments may be linked or fed to another blog, it is not possible to give respondents the assurance that their comments will appear only on a single research site. In addition to this, the vulnerability of the author, to spam attacks as well as closure of the service on which the blog is housed, should be taken into consideration. Some researchers are also required by their funder to provide an archive of their data, but given the relative immaturity of the blog format, for example, the multimedia and hyperlinked nature of the material, there are no examples of how this would be achieved. There is therefore a danger that some of the research blog content, or the links, would be lost. This risk could be anticipated as far as possible in the initial decisions about layout and blog posting practice.

The conventions about the temporality of blogging, which seem for some to be its most attractive feature, also imply certain risks. As well as the effect on later stages of the research project of public accounts of initial work, a research blog might give the impression that, rather than constituting a different form of scholarship or methodological practice, it supplants conventional accounts, including the different analytic and writing temporalities that they involve.

The habit of daily, or near-daily, updates will not necessarily fit with every research project, and yet blogging at longer intervals may result in the blog losing any capacity to maintain audience interest or keep discussions going.

Conclusion

Although the promises of blogging in terms of its Web 2.0 functions might seem over-hyped to a researcher interested in online methods, blogging does offer a straightforward way to publish material and create a space for interaction on the Internet. The accounts of researchers who have actually used blogs number very few so far. However, the existence of many graduate student bloggers offers the hope that an increasing number will reflect upon their experiences of research blogs, both as ways of being graduate researchers and in terms of traditional debates involving sampling, ethics, validity and multi-method work. In this chapter we have drawn links between topics such as the writing of fieldnotes, the public nature of blogs and the issue of reflexivity. Undoubtedly, if blogs become accepted amongst a wide range of social researchers, many more practical and theoretical matters will arise. The increasing use of visual materials on blogs will be an opportunity for further methodological innovation online, drawing on the literature in visual methods (Chaplin, 1994; Rose, 2001). Given the recent rise of other online services, such as photo-sharing through Flickr, researchers already have the possibility of reference archives of images via blog entries, enabling larger sets of visual materials to be distributed. The rapid development of such online sharing sites, and the kind of infrastructures which they offer for digital content, are likely to constantly outstrip the pace of development in social science methodologies. However, given the free nature of most of these services, blogs and their associated technologies offer unprecedented sites for experimentation.

References

Adkins, L. (2002) 'Reflexivity and the politics of qualitative research'. In T. May (ed.) *Qualitative Research in Action*. London: Sage. pp. 332–48.

Ashmore, M. (1989) *The Reflexive Thesis: Wrighting Sociology of Scientific Knowledge*. Chicago: University of Chicago Press.

Atkinson, P. (1992) *Understanding Ethnographic Texts*. Newbury Park: Sage.

Bell, C. and Newby, H. (eds) (1977) *Doing Sociological Research*, London: Allen and Unwin.

Blood, R. (2004) 'How blogging software reshapes the online community', *Communications of the ACM*, 47 (12): 53–5.

Bruns, A. (2007) 'Produsage: towards a broader framework for user-led content creation'. In *Proceedings of Creativity and Cognition 6*, Washington, DC. pp. 99–105.

Chaplin, E. (1994) *Sociology and Visual Representation*. London: Routledge.

Clifford, J. and Marcus, G. (1986) *Writing Culture: The Poetics and Politics of Ethnography*. Berkeley, University of California Press.

Clough, P. (2000) *Autoaffection: Unconscious Thought in the Age of Technology*. Minneapolis: University of Minnesota Press.

Cohen, K. (2006) 'A welcome for blogs', *Continuum: Journal of Media and Cultural Studies*, 20 (2): 161–73.

Coleman, S. (2005) 'Blogs and the new politics of listening', *The Political Quarterly*, 76 (2): 272–80.

Csikszentmihalyi, M. (1997) *Finding Flow: The Psychology of Engagement with Everyday Life*. New York: Basic Books.

Devine, F. and Heath, S. (1999) *Sociological Research Methods in Context*. London: Macmillan.

Ellis, C. (1997) 'Evocative autoethnography: writing emotionally about our lives'. In W.G. Tierney and Y.S. Lincoln (eds) *Representation and the Text: Reframing the Narrative Voice*. Albany: State University of New York Press. pp. 115–42.

Ellis, C. and Bochner, A.P. (2000) 'Autoethnography, personal narrative, reflexivity: researcher as subject'. In N.K. Denzin and Y.S. Lincoln (eds) *Handbook of Qualitative Research*, 2nd edn. Thousand Oaks, CA: Sage. pp. 733–68.

Emerson, R.M., Fretz, R.I. and Shaw, L.L. (1995) *Writing Ethnographic Fieldnotes*. Chicago: University of Chicago Press.

Glaser, B. and Strauss, A. (1967) *The Discovery of Grounded Theory*. Chicago: Aldine.

Giddens, A. (1991) *Modernity and Self-Identity: Self and Society in the Late Modern Age*. Cambridge, UK: Polity.

Gregg, M. (2006) 'Feeling ordinary: blogging as conversational scholarship', *Continuum: Journal of Media and Culture Studies*, 20 (2): 147–60.

Habermas, J. (1991) *The Structural Transformation of the Public Sphere: An Inquiry into a Category of Bourgeois Society*. Cambridge, MA: MIT Press.

Halavais, A. (2006) 'Scholarly blogging: moving toward the visible college'. In A. Bruns and J. Jacobs (eds) *Uses of Blogs*. NY: Peter Lang. pp. 117–26.

Herring, S.C., Scheidt, L.A., Bonus, S. and Wright, E. (2005) 'Weblogs as a bridging genre', *Information, Technology and People*, 18 (2): 142–71.

Hine, C. (1998) *Virtual Ethnography*. London: Sage.

Kaiser, S., Muller-Seitz, G., Pereira Lopes, M. and Pina e Cunha, M. (2007) 'Weblog-technology as a trigger to elicit passion for knowledge', *Organization*, 14 (3): 391–412.

Lovejoy, T. and Steele, N. (2004) 'Engaging our audience through photo stories', *Visual Anthropology Review*, 20 (1): 70–81.

Lynch, M. (2000) 'Against reflexivity as an academic virtue and source of privileged knowledge', *Theory, Culture and Society* 17 (3): 26–54.

Meyer, S. (2005) 'Introduction to special issue "Whitehead Now"', *Configurations*, 13 (1).

Miles, A. (2006) 'A vision for genuine rich media blogging'. In A. Bruns and J. Jacobs (eds) *Uses of Blogs*. NY: Peter Lang. pp. 213–22.

Mol, A. (2002) *The Body Multiple: Ontology in Medical Practice*. Durham: Duke University Press.

Mol, A. and Law, J. (1994), 'Regions, networks and fluids: anaemia and social topology', *Social Studies of Science*, 24: 641–71.

Mortensen, T. and Walker, J. (2002) 'Blogging thoughts: personal publication as an online research tool'. In A. Morrison (ed) *Researching ICTs in Context*. Oslo: Intermedia Report, 3/2002. pp. 249–79.

O'Connor, H. and Madge, C. (2001) 'Cyber-mothers: online synchronous interviewing using conferencing software', *Sociological Research Online*, 5 (4). <http://www.socresonline.org.uk/5/4/o'connor.html>

O'Reilly, T. (2005) 'What is Web 2.0?' http://www.oreillynet.com/pub/a/oreilly/tim/news/2005/09/30/what-is-web-20.html (accessed 20 July 2007).

Probyn, E. (1993) *Sexing the Self: Gendered Positions in Cultural Studies*. London: Routledge.

Quiggin, J. (2006) 'Blogs, wikis and creative innovation', *International Journal of Cultural Studies*, 9 (4): 481–96.

Reed, A. (2005) '"My blog is me": texts and persons in UK online journal culture (and anthropology)', *Ethnos*, 70 (2): 220–42.

Richardson, L. (1990) *Writing Strategies: Reaching Diverse Audiences*. Thousand Oaks, CA: Sage.

Richardson, L. (1992) 'The consequences of poetic representation: writing the other, re-writing the self'. In C. Ellis and M.G. Flaherty (eds) *Investigating Subjectivity: Research on Lived Experience*. Newbury Park, CA: Sage.

Richardson, L. (1994) 'Writing: a method of inquiry'. In N. Denzin and Y. Lincoln (eds) *Handbook of Qualitative Research*. London: Sage. pp. 516–29.

Rose, G. (2001) *Visual Methodologies: An Introduction to the Interpretation of Visual Materials*. London: Sage.

Sanjek, R. (ed.) (1990) *Fieldnotes: The Making of Anthropology*. Ithica: Cornell University Press.

Skrenta, R. (2005) 'The incremental web': entry on Topix Weblog. http://blog.topix.com/archives/000065.html (accessed 26 June 2007).

Stanley, L. and Wise, S. (1993) *Breaking Out Again: Feminist Ontology and Epistemology*. London: Routledge.

Technorati (2007) 'The state of the live web'. <http://technorati.com/weblog/2007/04/328.html> (accessed 12 August 2007).

Tsing, A. (1993) *In the Realm of the Diamond Queen*. Princeton: Princeton University Press.

Walker, J. (2007) 'Blogging from inside the ivory tower'. In A. Bruns and J. Jacobs (eds) *Uses of Blogs*. NY: Peter Lang. pp. 127–38.

Warner, M. (2002) *Publics and Counterpublics*. New York: Zone Books.

Wolfinger, N. (2002) 'On writing fieldnotes: collection strategies and background expectancies', *Qualitative Research* 2 (1): 85–95.

Further Reading

Bruns, A. and Jacobs, J. (eds) *Uses of Blogs*. NY: Peter Lang.

Gregg, M. (2006) 'Feeling ordinary: blogging as conversational scholarship', *Continuum: Journal of Media and Culture Studies*, 20 (2): 147–60.

Reed, A. (2005) '"My blog is me": Texts and persons in UK online journal culture (and anthropology)', *Ethnos*, 70 (2): 222–42.

Schmidt, J. (2007) 'Blogging practices: an analytical framework', *Journal of Computer-Mediated Communication*, 12 (4). http://jcmc.indiana.edu/vol12/issue4/schmidt.html.

67

Visual Storytelling: A Beneficial but Challenging Method for Health Research with Young People

Sarah E. Drew, Rony E. Duncan and Susan M. Sawyer

U ndertaking research with young people can be challenging, especially when investigating sensitive topics such as sexual behavior, substance use, violence, and adherence to medical treatments. The last 10 to 15 years have seen a shift in research with young people, from the use of proxy reports from parents, teachers, and physicians to asking young people more directly about their behaviors and perspectives (Santelli et al., 2003). Procedures for this are relatively straightforward in quantitative research; for example, surveys are now designed for completion by young people. However, procedures are less straightforward for qualitative research with young people.

Qualitative approaches are valuable in researching the lived experiences of young people. Scholars of the sociology of childhood and youth studies have played an important role in emphasizing the importance of young peoples' competence as social actors, and the need to be sensitive to the way relationships between adults and young people are influenced by differential power resources (Matthews, 2007; White & Wyn, 2004). In response, the social sciences have shifted to focus more on children and youth as actors in their own right, playing a significant role in both shaping and being shaped by the social world (Cosaro, 2005; Matthews; Mayall, 2002; Tisdall, Davis, & Gallager, 2009). Consistent with these youth-centered approaches is that qualitative

Source: *Qualitative Health Research,* 20(12) (2010): 1677–1688.

researchers seek detailed information from young people themselves rather than seeking information about young people (Matthews; Punch, 2002).

The fact that children and young people can be perceived as competent social actors does not necessarily mean that research should be conducted with them in the same way as it would be with adults (Baker & Weller, 2003). Shifting from a "top-down" approach to data collection can require innovation in research methods, as many established methods such as one-on-one interviews are heavily adult centered (Baker & Weller; Dresnick, 2006; Mauthner, 1997; Pole, Mizen, & Bolton, 1999). Researchers have been encouraged to carefully tailor qualitative research methods to more adequately explore young people's experiences (Matthews, 2007).

There remain, however, a number of challenges for such research. First is the challenge to make research interesting and appealing so as to foster young people's engagement within the research process, and promote young people's participation. The second challenge is to employ strategies that help to subvert traditional adult–child hierarchies, that foster communication and facilitate the sharing of opinions, perceptions, and information that might not otherwise be easy to share. Such strategies are important in promoting a comfortable research context in which young people are more likely to provide candid responses, and to feel that what they say will be valued. Third, in-depth methods must remain flexible to suit a range of development-related capacities for personal reflection and articulation of complex thoughts. This is particularly the case when study samples span a broad age group. For example, between the ages of 10 and 18 years (as in our study), young people are still developing the skills and capacities to readily consider and articulate complex understandings. This is influenced both by their degree of life experience and their maturing cognitive development. Qualitative research designs involving children and young people must take account of such considerations and employ strategies that help promote reflection and communication about issues that might otherwise be difficult to conceptualize and express.

In this article we outline the feasibility and utility of visual storytelling as a method of youth-centered data collection in a qualitative study of self-management in young people with chronic disease. Visual research has a long and diverse history, ranging from cultural studies and anthropology to marketing. Our focus here relates specifically to the use of participant-generated visual methodologies in the context of health research with young people. Visual storytelling draws on principles from the established methodologies of photovoice and photo elicitation. It also shares some aspects of the video intervention assessment (VIA) approach in terms of the focus on young people, chronic illness, and illness management, but the specifics of the video approach are quite different from our photographic approach (Patashnick & Rich, 2005). Both photovoice and photo elicitation have been used separately with young people (Bolton, Pole, & Mizen, 2001; Clark, 1999; Clark-Ibanez, 2007; Liebenberg, 2009; Moss, 1999; Rasmussen, 2004; Samuels, 2007;

Streng et al., 2004; Walker, Schratz, & Egg, 2008), but not in combination. For example, Haines, Poland, and Johnson (2009) used both in-depth interview and photovoice approaches, but the interviews were completed prior to the photographic exercise and discussion of the images took place within a more conventional photovoice group discussion.

Photovoice was originally developed as a group-based participatory health promotion strategy (Wang, Yi, Tao, & Carovano, 1998). Its original conceptualization saw participants come together on the basis of a common interest or personal characteristic to take part in a group photographic project. It is based on a community-development philosophy with emphasis on consciousness raising, empowerment, and promoting understanding of community issues. Participants are encouraged to focus on issues of greatest significance to them, and to photograph the "realities" of their everyday encounters and experiences. Once images have been created, the group comes together again to discuss the photographs and develop titles or descriptions of selected images. This is usually done with the goal of developing an exhibition for policy makers, health care providers, and other influential advocates. Within this methodology, images are seen as a powerful medium for communicating issues and promoting change (Carlson, Engebretson, & Chamberlain, 2006; Streng et al., 2004; Wang, Cash, & Powers, 2000); the emphasis is generally more on the images themselves (accompanied by a title) as research data, rather than on considering in depth what participants might say about the images. Rather than a group project, we were interested in exploring in-depth experiences separately with adolescents because we felt this would be more likely to result in candid discussion of sensitive topics. Thus, we adapted the original photovoice model for our visual storytelling approach, in which we replaced group discussions of images with individual in-depth interviews.

Because we wanted to keep the photographs integral to the in-depth interviews, we also drew on the principles of photo elicitation as an approach to in-depth interviewing (Clark-Ibanez, 2007; Collier, 1967; Fleury, Keller, & Perez, 2009; Harper, 2002; Oliffe & Bottorff, 2007; Packard, 2008; Punch, 2002; Radley & Taylor, 2003; Rasmussen, 2004; Samuels, 2007; Stuckey & Tisdell, 2010; Wang et al., 2000). This approach to interviews can involve researcher-generated or participant-generated photographs. Photographs are introduced to the research interview based on "assumptions about the role and utility of photographs in promoting reflections that words alone cannot" (Clark-Ibanez, 2007, p. 171). Samuels (p. 199) stressed the value of the technique for "bridging the culturally distinct worlds of the researcher and the researched." In our case, the bridged worlds were those of the younger participants and the older researchers, and also the worlds of adolescents who were highly familiar with the daily challenges of living with chronic health conditions and the worlds of the interviewers who had less familiarity with this. Unlike photovoice, photo-elicitation approaches tend to emphasize images as a means of accumulating rich verbal data, which then tends to be prioritized over the visual photographs themselves.

Our research design for the development of the visual storytelling approach within a study of adolescents developing practices of chronic disease self-management was guided by six methodological elements; that is, six elements that fit with our particular inquirer stance as promoters of youth-centered research. We wanted our approach to (a) focus on young people as social actors; (b) seek research information directly from young people; (c) promote depth of communication by extending the established technique of in-depth interviewing; (d) appeal to young people with an activity they would like to take part in; (e) be enabling and empowering to young people; and (f) promote young people's voices being heard throughout the research process. A visual approach to data collection had the potential to accommodate these goals. By combining elements of both photovoice and photo elicitation we were able to avoid prioritizing either visual or verbal information in the broader study, and to view both as equally valuable data.

In this article we describe the visual storytelling method and outline the benefits and challenges of the approach as manifested in our broader research project focusing on adolescents' developing practices of self-management. The old adage, "If only I had known then what I know now," is highly pertinent in relation to our experiences with this research approach. As such, we focus here on issues of feasibility, with the goal of sharing our knowledge of what it takes to successfully employ this visual approach to data collection.

The main aim of our broader research study was to hear adolescents' and parents' perspectives on issues relating to young people's developing practices of chronic disease self-management. However, we also recognized that we had an important opportunity to obtain information and feedback about how the visual approach was received and experienced by participants as part of the broader study. The overall self-management research design offered us a valuable opportunity to look at the feasibility of a new research method and consider its utility for health research with young people.

Methods

Participants and Recruitment

Ethics approval was obtained from the Royal Children's Hospital (Melbourne) Human Research Ethics Committee. Adolescents aged 10 to 18 years with asthma, diabetes, or cystic fibrosis were eligible to participate, together with a parent. To support investigation of adolescents' developing practices of self-management, selection criteria for young people included a diversity in the length of time since diagnosis, and consequently diversity in the duration of chronicity experienced by participants. For example, cystic fibrosis is a genetic condition that is now generally identified at or close to birth. The diagnosis of asthma or diabetes might occur at any point through childhood or adolescence. Adolescents ($n = 34$) and parents ($n = 34$) were recruited in clinic waiting rooms at the same time.

Patients at the hospital commonly attend review appointments with at least one parent/guardian and as such, pairs are highly likely to be sitting together in clinic waiting rooms. Additionally, research participation for people under the age of 18 years (a) usually requires parental consent, and (b) usually requires that the parent be consulted prior to researchers asking people under 18 years if they would be interested in participating in research. For these reasons it was a necessary starting point for our recruitment approaches to involve both adolescents and parents simultaneously. We were also aiming, where possible, to recruit dyadic pairs to gain different perspectives on the understanding and practices of chronic condition self-management within any one household. The limited number of research articles published about chronic disease self-management in adolescence state clearly that parental involvement continues well into the late teenage years, and even into early adulthood (Anthony et al., 2009). A central preoccupation of our broader research inquiry was therefore to increase understandings about the shared and interconnected roles of parents and adolescents in self-management. This required an emphasis on recruiting parent and adolescent pairs.

Throughout recruitment, research staff were keenly aware of the importance of giving adolescents the opportunity to opt out of participation. A separate "young person consent form" was used as a technique for increasing adolescents' understanding of what participation entailed and for increasing their options for declining involvement. Recruitment was completed by the first and second authors, who are experienced in research with minors (Duncan, Drew, & Sawyer, 2009). As such, they were attuned to the potential for parental coercion during recruitment, and would not have proceeded with recruitment if they felt that this was occurring.

Within this article, the terms *adolescent, youth,* and *young people* are used interchangeably. As the study sample consisted of 10- to 18-year-olds, we commonly use the term *adolescent* when referring to specific aspects of the study, and the term *young people* for more general aspects.

Data Collection

Young people were provided with a 36-exposure film-based disposable camera and asked to create a series of photographs to show (a) what it was like to live with an ongoing health condition and (b) the sorts of things they might do to take care of their health. We made a deliberate choice to request such a specific focus from participants because time and budget constraints meant that we had only one opportunity for participants to create images, and one opportunity to talk in depth with them about their experiences and understandings of chronic disease self-management. The first author was simultaneously involved in another chronic-illness visual research project exploring young people's experiences with social and educational connectivity (White, Drew, & Hay, 2009). That project had a longitudinal design and afforded multiple and extended opportunities for image creation and interview discussion. In that project a deliberate choice was made to ask participants to begin with a more general visual story of their lives, knowing there was time to pursue a tighter research focus at a later stage if necessary (Guillemin & Drew, 2010). Regardless of the focused nature of the instructions for our self-management-related visual tasks, adolescents highlighted both illness-related experiences and other aspects of their lives. These images readily linked to both positive and challenging elements of their experiences.

In this self-management study, cameras were usually provided to young participants at the time of recruitment following completion of some preliminary questionnaires (separately) by both parents and adolescents. There were occasions when there was not enough time for initial questionnaires to be completed during recruitment; therefore, cameras were sometimes mailed to young people at their homes after completed questionnaires had been returned to the research staff.

Although parents were not recruited to participate in the photographic component of the project, the processes of recruitment meant that they were familiar with the research task that young people had agreed to complete. Additionally, the completion of both adolescent and parent interviews was tied to the completion of the adolescent's visual task. Follow-up processes undertaken by research staff to achieve return of the camera and scheduling of the interviews meant that researchers were repeatedly in phone contact with both adolescent and parent participants. We were careful to achieve an appropriate balance between gently requesting that the young person pay attention to the task and not coercing them to do something they did not want to do. Indeed, there were times when we encouraged individual adolescents not to bother taking photos, and to send back the camera without doing anything further if we felt the young person had lost interest in the task. We also made it clear to parents that the photographic task was completely voluntary and that the young person should only do it if they wanted to. It was assumed that parents would have a role in "reminding" their respective son or daughter about what he or she had agreed to do. This would be the case automatically in many households that include 10- to 18-year-old youth, whether the reminder related to homework, household chores, getting to sporting or social events, or even attending scheduled appointments. While implicitly relying on parents' capacities to help adolescents "manage" their commitments, we also made it very clear to parents that it was not their responsibility to ensure the photographic task was completed, or to assist their children in developing ideas for photographs.

Adolescents were not told specifically how many photos to take, but they were informed that they could have an additional camera if they found they wanted to take more than 36 photographs. A written information sheet provided with each camera stressed that the adolescent would be the first to view their developed images, and that they would have an opportunity at the start of the interview to remove any images they did not want the researcher to see. This process was established to promote return of the cameras even if participants felt the cameras contained images they did not want to share. Few participants removed photographs.

Our aim was for the image making to be completed and camera returned within 2 to 4 weeks. Occasionally cameras were returned more quickly, but it commonly took longer. The images created by each adolescent formed the basis of individual interviews, which took place as soon as possible following receipt of the camera and development of the photographs. Separate but simultaneous interviews were conducted with adolescents and parents. According to family preference, most interviews took place in participants' homes; a few took place in nonclinical areas of the hospital. Parents did not view the photographs as part of their interviews.

Completion of simultaneous but separate interviews required a team of at least 2 interviewers. The challenges of coordinating the time availability of adolescents, parents, and research staff meant that we extended our interviewing team to three people to increase our flexibility with scheduling. Interviews with adolescents (34) were completed over the course of the project by the first and second authors. Interviewers had a list of topic areas and prompts to help shape the interview discussion; however, interviews were characterized by an intertwining of participant-led conversation about the photographs and associated experiences, and responses to more direct questioning from the interviewer. Through the course of the interviews, young people explained why they had made their images, how they were taken, and what they intended to convey within individual images or in their image series as a whole. At times young people said that a parent, friend, or sibling had contributed to the decision making about or taking of a particular photo. This did not detract from the overall value and validity of the young people's photographs as data, because they were always clear about which photos were important to them as individuals and why, thus articulating a vivid and personally meaningful visual story (see also Guillemin & Drew, 2010).

Interviews with parents (34) were completed over the course of the project by the second author and another research assistant. As in interviews with young people, interviewers had a list of topic areas and prompts to help shape the interview discussion with parents, but participants were free to take a lead in the discussion according to their level of comfort in doing so.

For the purposes of exploring the utility of the method, toward the end of each interview with adolescents and parents interviewers specifically sought information about whether the camera had influenced young people's decision to participate, what benefits they might have experienced as a result of creating their visual story, and what challenges or harms they might have experienced as a result of creating their visual story. Parents were included in this assessment of the approach because of their involvement in the overall recruitment process and because of their familiarity with the visual research task as outlined above. We were not necessarily looking for concordance in assessment views expressed by parents and young people, knowing that young people and parents often prioritize and interpret aspects of life experiences differently.

Analysis

All interviews were audio-recorded and transcribed verbatim. Transcripts were imported into NVivo 8 qualitative data analysis software throughout the data collection period for data management and coding. The first author had primary responsibility for computer-assisted coding and establishment of themes (Rice & Ezzy, 2000). General principles of thematic analysis were applied (Boyatzis, 1988; Braun & Clarke, 2006). Use of these principles was also informed by a constructivist perspective on grounded theory methodology (Charmaz, 2007).

Data from adolescents and parents that related to the visual storytelling approach were broken into smaller units through open coding and then put back together in new ways through memoing (Welsh, 2002) and axial coding. This process enabled prominent themes, sub-themes, and the relationships between them to be identified and elaborated upon. Two additional steps of coding also informed the emergence of key themes; data were (a) scrutinized to explore the presence of commonality or disparity between the responses of a particular young person and his or her parent, and (b) scrutinized to establish whether participants' opinions about the approach might be related to the young person's age (i.e., related to developmental issues in self-expression), gender, or type of health condition.

Consistent with grounded theory methodology (Strauss & Corbin, 1990), data analysis was also ongoing throughout data collection. Postinterview debriefing discussions, postinterview reflexive journaling, and regular project meetings provided multiple avenues for authors to participate in discussion and consolidation of analysis. Conversations during project meetings about the substantiation of each theme and subtheme provided additional avenues for team-wide contributions to analysis.

Results and Discussion

Distinct benefits were associated with the visual storytelling approach, although a range of challenges were also apparent. The results and discussion are presented in four sections to describe the key issues during (a) recruitment, (b) image making, (c) interviews with young people, and (d) dissemination of findings.

Key Issues during Recruitment

We had anticipated that interest around the disposable cameras would positively influence recruitment. This was not necessarily the case, as only a modest recruitment rate was achieved. Of 80 eligible participant pairs (young person plus parent) who were approached, 49 (61%) agreed to participate, of which 34 pairs (42.5%) completed all aspects of the study. Very few young people expressed that the camera markedly influenced their decision to participate. Indeed, 16 adolescents indicated outright that the camera component had little effect, stating that they would have become involved anyway; yet the camera acted as an enticement in recruiting others. It also commonly increased positive feelings about the project at the time of recruitment. One young participant reported feeling excited by the approach, saying, "It's definitely a different idea," and another reported that it made the study seem "better than just the normal survey." The positive influence of the camera appeared greatest with girls regardless of age, and with boys up to the age of 15 years. Figure 1 shows key themes from young people's comments about the influence of the camera on recruitment. Parents commonly stated that their son or daughter initially saw the camera as an enticement, something that was "fun" or "a bit different" from filling out surveys or trialing new medications;

Major Influence on Participation

Yeah, that was probably why I chose it, 'cause you got to do stuff with the camera. That's probably most of the reason why I chose, yes.

Yeah, I thought it would be really interesting, actually. I thought it was a good idea.

Yeah, [it influenced my decision to take part], I thought it'd be fun, the camera part.

Little Impact on Participation

I wouldn't be as much like, excited without the camera but I still would have done it.

Even if there weren't any camera I would still go for it because it's to help others.

I think I would have probably done it anyway.

Sounded Like an Interesting Activity

I was like, this is interesting, I'll try it. . . . I probably would have done it anyway. But it was appealing.

[The camera component] actually kind of intrigued me, 'cause I'd never had anything like that before, so I thought it might be, it might be something different to do. [If the camera hadn't been part of the project], I probably would've [taken part], but it was definitely an appealing kind of thing to do 'cause we've been surveyed, over 18 years we've been surveyed a lot by people, so this is something different, which is good.

I reckon it sounded pretty fun, so I thought, "Yeah, let's do that."

Figure 1: Influence of the camera on recruitment

however, many parents stated that the image-making task became more problematic later on.

Key Issues during Image Making

"I actually enjoyed doing that." The task of creating a visual story was described by 1 in 3 participants as being fun. Furthermore, about half of the participants commented that an unexpected benefit of participating in the image-making process was that it fostered personal reflection (that they viewed positively) about living with their chronic health condition. One participant said, "It taught me a little bit more about who I am." This type of feedback came from young people across the range of ages and conditions. Several young people indicated that this personal reflection had the potential to influence their self-management activities, such as in relation to adherence with medication, seeking health information, and communication strategies and skills. Figure 2 illustrates benefits of visual storytelling highlighted by the young people.

Difficulties creating enough images and knowing what to photograph. Although some participants easily completed the task of creating a visual story of what it is like to live with a chronic health condition, about 75% required some degree of "coaching" from project staff and parents to complete the task. In certain cases, the challenge was as simple as not being able to think of enough images to use the length of film in the camera:

> Yeah, it was like, got to finish the film . . . 'cause I had it for ages and I think someone rang up and like, "Oh, can we have the camera?" And I'm, "Oh God, I'll have to finish it." . . . Finishing the whole film – I could probably do ten pictures easily, but like a whole film was harder.

About half of the adolescents expressed difficulty knowing what to photograph. For several reasons it is not surprising that young people found it difficult to represent their illness experiences photographically. First, asking young people to use cameras to document anything related to personal challenges confronts our cultural habit of using cameras to generate images of celebrations and positive experiences (Chalfen, 1987). Second, as illustrated by the participant quotes in Figure 2, thinking deeply about what it is like to live with a chronic health condition is not something adolescents often do spontaneously. Third, thinking about these issues requires some degree of abstract thinking and self-reflection, which might be more difficult for younger adolescents given their level of cognitive maturation.

About 25% of the young people struggled to photograph anything. One participant, who had initially been enthusiastic about image making, ended up completing the interview without taking any photographs. In spite of

Creating the Visual Story Was Fun

Yeah, I thought it was fun. 'Cause, um, just – I like taking photos.

Well, I actually enjoyed doing that . . . everyone wants to take photos.

It was pretty fun 'cause you got to take pictures. I like taking and clicking. It's fun for me.

Fostering Reflection

Well it actually made me think about my asthma and how it affected my life . . . it's made me think about things I wouldn't normally think about, and yeah, interesting experience.

I had to take the pictures and it was about how CF [cystic fibrosis] affected me, so I was thinking about things and I found it a bit hard maybe because I don't usually think about that, and I was sort of like – it was, it was a bit like reflecting back on what affects my life with CF.

It made me realize that I have to rely on a few things like a lot of people wouldn't have to . . . I have to take a lot more stuff to school and like make sure everything's fine during the day. So it's a bit harder. It just made me realize that – how much different it really is. Like I thought it was pretty much like the same as the normal person, but it's a lot different.

Self-Management

It's reminded me that I need to have my Seretide [asthma medication] more often.

I don't know how to explain it – Yeah, it got me to think about it [cystic fibrosis] more and think of new things and ask more questions and stuff . . . I reckon it was a good thing 'cause now I know more about it and I'd like to know more about it.

Probably being more honest than what I actually have been in the past. Like I mean more open, open to talk than what I was maybe say six months ago.

Facilitating Expression and Communication

It makes it clearer in your head sort of 'cause you know it's all up there, but it's all sort of garbled you know in here, whereas looking at the pictures saying that looks into that, that represents that, sort of helps you understand what you are thinking yourself.

I think you should use it in the future 'cause it makes, makes people think about it and like it's not, "Oh yeah, all I have to do is only answer a few questions" and stuff. Like they – and you get to see what – what their life is actually like. What, what it involves and like what they have to take and it's – I reckon it's good, good that you, you've made a camera kind of thing.

It's a good idea 'cause it's really like, if you find it hard to say like, like for some students, kids, they may be more creative, more like imagery based. Like me – me personally I'm more picture – like I remember things better by pictures.

Well at first when I heard about it I'm thinking like, "Wow, I'm not going to be able to do this. It's going to be ridiculous, you know, taking photos. How's this going to be helpful?" I couldn't, off the top of my head I'm thinking, "What the hell am I going to take photos of?" But after a while, you know, reading through the sheets that came with it and, you know it was a bit of fun I guess. You know, taking photos like that. Like I said, it was a good memory kind of job, sort of think of things to talk about and so yeah, it wasn't too bad.

Figure 2: Benefits of visual storytelling

negotiating early to use his own digital camera, that participant expressed a growing reluctance to create images. His explanation is presented in Figure 3. This example highlights that for some, a film-based disposable camera might seem an out-of-date medium with technological limitations. We argue that the real value of this approach is not in the specific medium of digital- or film-based photography, but rather in the task required by participants prior to the interview. We argue that young people's engagement with the content of inquiry through photography was a critical aspect that facilitated communication during the interview. Even though the one young man did not create

During initial recruitment, a 17-year-old with diabetes negotiated to use his own digital camera to create his visual narrative because he felt that a more sophisticated medium might aid his production of satisfactory images. Nevertheless, he still struggled to illustrate the complexity of what he wanted to convey.

After viewing some artistically created, diabetes-related photographic images on the Internet, he became concerned about his capacity to produce the type of images he wanted to produce: "I just wasn't sure how to express it. Because I wanted it to be–I just didn't think . . . it wouldn't be a true sort of reflection."

The young man expressed a desire to accurately represent what he saw as the repetitive and time-related, ongoing nature of diabetes. He was not convinced he could achieve this just by using a disposable camera or producing a straight digital photo without enhancing the image and artistically manipulating the final image.

Although he struggled to resolve his concerns about adequately representing complex conceptualizations in simple snapshots, similar themes were represented by another young man with diabetes via his disposable camera. This other young man presented an image of a large pile of used syringes (Photo 1), as well as an image of a clock (Photo 2), and a celebratory altar that his mother had set up to mark the 1,000th syringe for his insulin injections (Photo 3). The altar was made spontaneously by his mother – not specifically in relation to the image-making component of the research.

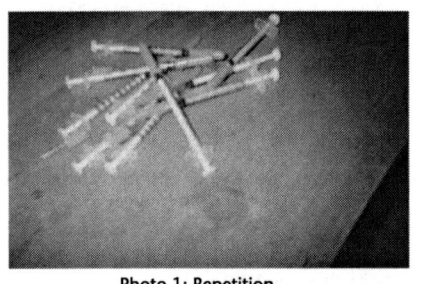

Photo 1: Repetition

Photo 2: Time related

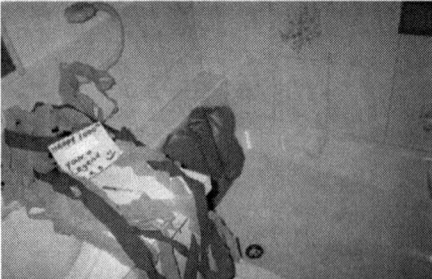

Photo 3: Ongoing nature of diabetes

Figure 3: Trials and triumphs of visual representation

any images, he nevertheless was highly engaged in thinking about how he might adequately represent his experiences and ideas, which facilitated later discussions.

Forethought and planning is required.   One of the most practical challenges around employing this research method was the amount of forethought, planning, and coordination required by adolescents. Not only did they have to remember that the task needed completing; they had to think about what to photograph, to plan ahead and coordinate aspects of location and photo content. At the most basic level they needed to ensure they had the camera with them so they could use it at opportune moments. This presented challenges for adolescents as well as for parents. Parents (primarily mothers) reported that they commonly found themselves reiterating instructions and even nagging their child to get the task completed. On rare occasions it was indicated that the image-making task "became a chore." About half of the parents discussed being partially involved in determining what would be photographed. Much less frequently, parents stated that they were fully responsible for creating certain images. These issues added to the challenge of analyzing the images as part of the broader self-management study, in terms of considering whose story was being told at a particular time. In a number of cases, parents perceived the image-making task as more difficult for their son or daughter than did the young person. For example, one mother reported that for her daughter, the image-making task was "a drag." She went on to note that she (the mother) "was probably more excited about it than what she [the daughter] was." In contrast, her daughter described making the visual story as "fun," especially "having me in the photos."

Representing a "normal kid" and a "normal life." An important challenge of self-representation and image making was highlighted by parents of young people with diabetes or cystic fibrosis, who often raised the issue of their son or daughter being reluctant to be seen as anything other than a "normal kid"; this appeared to be less of an issue for young people with asthma. Indeed, some parents and young people talked positively about increased awareness and an absence of stigma associated with asthma. This desire by adolescents to present themselves as normal is both a feature of the dominant socio-cultural discourses and storylines available for articulating illness experiences and a feature of adolescent development (Drew, 2005; Kroger, 2004). It also appears to serve as a coping strategy. Both of these aspects were interwoven within young people's attempts to provide photographic illustrations of themselves and their lives in relation to the management of ongoing health issues, and this appears to have contributed to the challenges encountered by the young people in determining and knowing what to photograph.

The quote in Figure 4 highlights the significant emotional elements that relate to the task of creating a visual story of illness experience, which might otherwise be conceived by some as a simple request for a few photographs. The quote also draws attention to the issue that many emotionally laden and difficult topics are left unspoken within families in which someone has a chronic illness – even within the context of close and supportive family relationships (Roderíguez et al., 2004).

> She didn't know what [photos] to take. She's not often – I don't think she likes to be sentimental. . . . When you emotionally challenge [my daughter] she doesn't like that because she says, "Well, it's not important." So take photos of what? She doesn't know how she feels about her CF [cystic fibrosis]. I don't think she does. . . . She didn't like it [taking the photos]. I had these great suggestions. I'd say, "Get your enzymes and make flowers out of it." She said, "Oh, Mum, that's just stupid." I had all these great ideas. She just didn't – and then she's going, "I don't know what to take." So I talked to Rony [the researcher] and I said, "Rony just wonders, 'How does CF impact on you.'" She doesn't like to share that. The physio side, she doesn't want to share that side because she still knows it's not – she's isolated. No one likes to feel they're so different, and she doesn't either. . . . I don't know why she, she doesn't open up sometimes with me. So it's very rare that we'll have a conversation. Now and then she will really tell me, but rarely because she knows it breaks my heart. . . . She knows that if she opens up emotionally to me, I'd be a mess. So that's why we have this, "Let's just keep it not too emotional," because then we'll all just break down and be a mess, and we have to survive in this world. (Mother of a girl with cystic fibrosis)

Figure 4: The challenge of self-presentation and emotion management

Key Issues during Interviews with Adolescents

Notwithstanding these challenges, the creation and presentation of photographs as a central feature of the research encounter served to empower young people. It increased their control in determining the direction of their early storytelling (visually), and provided a powerful avenue for increasing their influence over the course of the research interview (verbally). The presence of a prop during the interview also reduced the pressure of verbal interaction, as previously reported (Darlington & Scott, 2003). Overall, it appeared that the visual storytelling technique served to facilitate rapport, break down age- and status-related hierarchical dynamics, and help generate rich interview discussions between adolescents and older researchers. It seems that many of the participants found involvement in this visual storytelling research project a rewarding experience. None of the adolescents articulated their participation as harmful in any way, nor did parents.

Visual storytelling extended the scope of standard qualitative interviews with young people by making visible and drawing into the conversation elements of the young people's lives and experiences which otherwise might not have been discussed. For example, one young man provided an image of a packet of cigarettes resting on the kitchen bench of his family home. This image prompted discussion about his father's practice of sometimes smoking inside the house, which the adolescent described as exacerbating his asthma symptoms. Outlining how the behavior of a parent impacts on well-being is a difficult topic for a young person to broach. Through visual storytelling, the young man was able to easily raise and then expand on this sensitive topic. It was not otherwise mentioned in the interview.

A central motivation for developing the visual storytelling approach was to establish a method that was accessible for young people and fostered communication of sensitive and complex issues between younger participants and older researchers. Participants stated that the overall approach helped them to articulate difficult conceptualizations, aiding them in expression and communication, and helping them remember their own issues during the interview (see Figure 2). Hill (1997, p. 180) described the challenge of maximizing "children's ability to express themselves at the point of data-gathering; enhancing their willingness to communicate and the richness of the findings." Visual storytelling clearly met that challenge. Central to the success of the technique was the work done by young people prior to interview of conceptualizing expression of their experiences. We argue that this enabled them to more easily articulate, during the interview, aspects that they previously might not have thought about articulating.

Key Issues during Dissemination of Findings

We have found that visual storytelling extends the scope of communication at conferences and seminars. The emphasis within the photovoice methodology on exhibiting participants' images to capitalize on their power as a medium for communicating issues and promoting change has been borne out through our experiences of research presentations. In presenting the images, we as researchers become less of a conduit between raw data and final interpretations because audience members can quickly become engaged in viewing, assessing, and analyzing the data themselves. This illustrates success in relation to our goal of wanting the voices and perspectives of young people to be heard throughout the research process and dissemination of findings.

Conclusions

The visual storytelling approach is valuable as a youth-centered approach. It engages adolescents in reflection about their experiences prior to the research interview, which facilitates their expression and communication during the interview. Because of their degree of life experience and maturing cognitive development, young people are still developing the skills and capacities to readily consider and articulate complex understandings. Visual storytelling can help promote reflection and communication about issues that can be difficult to conceptualize and express, especially for young participants.

In providing cameras to the young people, a clear message was sent that we wanted them to be in charge of generating and shaping discussion in the research encounter. We think this approach also demonstrated that they had important perspectives to share, and that we were interested in understanding their experiences. By enabling young participants to highlight the areas of greatest importance to them, we deliberately increased their influence on the research process and reduced our reliance on researcher-generated logic about which areas were important to focus upon. As a result of utilizing visual storytelling, we obtained rich data through which young people's voices and perspectives are heard loudly and clearly.

In spite of the many benefits, there were also several challenges associated with this visual approach, especially the time required for researchers. Much time was spent on the telephone coaching young people through difficulties associated with completing the task, pursuing cameras that were not returned, and reorganizing interview times that were dependent on completion of the image-making task and return of the camera in time for the film to be processed prior to the interview. This is consistent with a project with adults, in which it was also found that participants required "encouragement from the research team to stay on task" (Baker & Wang, 2006, p. 1410).

There are two things that we are likely to do differently when using this approach in the future. First, we would be more prepared for the data collection stage to take longer than interview-only research. Second, we would build into the process a weekly phone call, mobile phone text message, or email contact with young people while they had a camera to proactively attend to the "coaching" aspects of the visual approach, and to reduce the need for parental input and monitoring in the completion process. Beyond these minor adjustments, it is our position that researchers will have to negotiate the challenges we have highlighted as inherent to the approach to get the benefits of associated rich and detailed discussions with young people.

Our exploration of the feasibility and utility of visual storytelling as a research approach has some limitations. First, the perspectives obtained were from participants who completed the project. Nothing is known of the opinions and experiences of the 7 pairs in which the young person received the disposable camera but did not complete the interview. Second, there was no comparison group in which interviews were conducted without the camera component. Although we are confident that the visual component enriched the data we collected, we lack comparative data to support this claim. Finally, the researchers who asked for feedback about the visual storytelling methodology were the same researchers who recruited participants and conducted the in-depth interviews. It is therefore possible that participants were less candid about the experience than they otherwise might have been had their feedback been anonymous.

In summary, this focus on the feasibility of our visual storytelling approach demonstrates the utility of the technique and illustrates that the method has much to offer in terms of fostering our understanding of the lived experiences of adolescents with chronic health conditions. It also has much to offer researchers who are looking for ways to engage young people in research settings more generally. In spite of the challenges encountered, we would certainly use this approach again.

References

Anthony, S. J., Kaufman, M., Drabble, A., Seifert-Hansen, M., Dipchand, A. I., & Martin, K. (2009). Perceptions of transitional care needs and experiences in pediatric heart transplant recipients. *American Journal of Transplantation*, *9*, 614–619. doi:10.1111/j.1600-6143.2008.02515.x

Baker, J., & Weller, S. (2003). "Is it fun?" Developing children centered research methods. *International Journal of Sociology and Social Policy*, *23*, 33–58. doi:10.1108/01443330310790435

Baker, T., & Wang, C. C. (2006). Photovoice: Use of a participatory action research method to explore the chronic pain experience in older adults. *Qualitative Health Research*, *16*, 1405–1141. doi:10.1177/1049732306294118

Bolton, A., Pole, C., & Mizen, P. (2001). Picture this: Researching child workers. *Sociology*, *35*, 501–518. doi:10.1017/S0038038501000244

Boyatzis, R. (1998). *Transforming qualitative information: Thematic analysis and code development*. Thousand Oaks, CA: Sage.

Braun, V., & Clarke, V. (2006). Using thematic analysis in psychology. *Qualitative Research in Psychology*, *3*, 77–101. doi:10.1191/1478088706qp063oa

Carlson, E. D., Engebretson, J., & Chamberlain, R. M. (2006). Photovoice as a social process of critical consciousness. *Qualitative Health Research*, *16*, 836–852. doi:10.1177/1049732306287525

Chalfen, R. (1987). *Snapshot: Versions of life*. Bowling Green, OH: Bowling Green State University Popular Press.

Charmaz, K. (2007). Grounded theory. In J. A. Smith (Ed.), *Qualitative psychology: A practical guide to research methods* (2nd ed., pp. 81–110). London: Sage.

Clark, C. (1999). The autodriven interview: A photographic viewfinder into children's experiences. *Visual Sociology*, *14*, 39–50. doi:10.1080/14725869908583801

Clark-Ibanez, M. (2007). Inner-city children in sharper focus: Sociology of childhood and photo-elicitation interviews. In G. C. Stanczak (Ed.), *Visual research methods: Image, society and representation* (pp. 167–195). London: Sage.

Collier, J. (1967). *Visual anthropology: Photography as a research method*. Beverly Hills, CA: Sage.

Cosaro, W. A. (2005). *The sociology of childhood* (2nd ed.). Thousand Oaks, CA: Pine Forge Press.

Darlington, Y., & Scott, D. (2003). *Qualitative research in practice: Stories from the field*. Crows Nest, NSW, Australia: Allen and Unwin.

Dresnick, M. (2006). Draw-and-tell conversations with children about fear. *Qualitative Health Research*, *16*, 1414–1435. doi:10.1177/1049732306294127

Drew, S. (2005). The delta factor: Storying survival and the disjuncture between public narratives and personal stories of life after cancer. *Storytelling, Self, Society*, *1*, 76–102.

Duncan, R. E., Drew, S. E., & Sawyer, S. M. (2009). Is my mum going to hear this? Methodological and ethical challenges in qualitative health research with young people. *Social Science and Medicine 69*, 1691–1699. doi:10.1016/j.socscimed.2009.09.001

Fleury, J., Keller, C., & Perez, A. (2009). Exploring resources for physical activity in Hispanic women using photo elicitation. *Qualitative Health Research*, *19*, 677–686. doi:10.1177/1049732309334471

Guillemin, M., & Drew, S. (2010). Questions of process in participant-generated visual methodologies. *Visual Studies*, *25*, 175–188.

Haines, R. J., Poland, B. D., & Johnson, J. L. (2009). Becoming a "real" smoker: Cultural capital in young women's accounts of smoking and other substance use. *Sociology of Health and Illness*, *31*, 66–80. doi:10.1111/j.1467-9566.2008.01119.x

Harper, D. (2002). Talking about pictures: A case for photo elicitation. *Visual Studies*, *17*, 13–26. doi:10.1080/14725860220137345

Hill, M. (1997). Participatory research with children. *Child & Family Social Work, 2,* 171–183. doi:10.1046/j.1365-2206.1997.00056.x

Kroger, J. (2004). *Identity in adolescence: The balance between self and other* (3rd ed.). New York: Routledge.

Liebenberg, L. (2009). The visual image as discussion point: Increasing validity in boundary crossing research. *Qualitative Research, 9,* 441–467. doi:10.1177/1468794109337877

Matthews, S. A. (2007). A window on the "new" sociology of childhood. *Sociological Compass, 1,* 322–334. doi:10.1111/j.1751-9020.2007.00001.x

Mauthner, M. (1997). Methodological aspects of collecting data from children: Lessons from three research projects. *Child Sociology, 11,* 16–28. doi:10.1111/j.1099-0860.1997.tb00003.x

Mayall, B. (2002). *Towards a sociology for childhood: Thinking from children's lives.* Philadelphia: Open University Press.

Moss, T. (1999). Photovoice: Youth put their world on view. *Children FIRST: A Journal on Issues Affecting Children and Their Carers, 3,* 32–35.

Oliffe, J. L., & Bottorff, J. L. (2007). Further than the eye can see? Photo elicitation and research with men. *Qualitative Health Research, 17,* 850–858. doi:10.1177/1049732306298756

Packard, J. (2008). I'm gonna show you what it's really like out here: The power and limitations of participatory visual methods. *Visual Studies, 23,* 63–77. doi:10.1080/14725860801908544

Patashnick, J. L., & Rich, M. (2005). Researching human experience: Video intervention/prevention assessment. *Australasian Journal of Information Systems, 12,* 103–111. Retrieved from http://dl.acs.org.au/index.php/ajis/article/view/96/77

Pole, C., Mizen, P., & Bolton, A. (1999). Realising children's agency in research: Partners and participants? *International Journal of Social Research Methodology, 2,* 39–54. doi:10.1080/136455799295177

Punch, S. (2002). Research with children: The same or different from research with adults? *Childhood, 9,* 321–341. doi:10.1177/0907568202009003005

Radley, A., & Taylor, D. (2003). Remembering one's stay in hospital: A study in photography, recovery and forgetting. *Health, 7,* 129–159. doi:10.1177/1363459303007002872

Rasmussen, K. (2004). Places for children – Children's places. *Childhood, 11,* 155–173. doi:10.1177/0907568204043053

Rice, P. L., & Ezzy, D. (2000). *Qualitative research methods: A health focus.* Melbourne, Australia: Oxford University Press.

Roderíguez, C. D., Rodríguez-Arias Palomo, J. L., Diz, J. C., Celis, M. V., Tuña, S. A., Larrea, M. O., . . . Varela, N. (2004). A preliminary report on multiple family discussion groups for patients with chronic medical illness and its repercussions in the management of the hemodialysis process. *Therapeutic Apheresis and Dialysis, 8,* 492–496. doi:10.1111/j.1774-9987.2004.00190.x

Samuels, J. (2007). When words are not enough: Eliciting children's experiences of Buddhist monastic life through photographs. In G. C. Stanczak (Ed.), *Visual research methods: Image, society and representation* (pp. 197–224). London: Sage.

Santelli, J. S., Rogers, A. S., Rosenfeld, W. D., DuRant, R. H., Dubler, N., Morreale, M., . . . Schissel, A. (2003). Guidelines for adolescent health research: A position paper of the Society for Adolescent Medicine. *Journal of Adolescent Health, 33,* 396–409. doi:10.1016/j.jadohealth.2003.06.009

Strauss, A., & Corbin, J. (1990). *Basics of qualitative research: Grounded theory procedures and techniques.* London: Sage.

Streng, J. M., Rhodes, S., Ayala, G., Eng, E., Arceo, R., & Phipps, S. (2004). Realidad Latina: Latino adolescents, their school, and a university use photovoice to examine and address the influence of immigration. *Journal of Interprofessional Care, 18,* 403–415. doi:10.1080/13561820400011701

Stuckey, H. L., & Tisdell, E. J. (2010). The role of creative expression in diabetes: An exploration into the meaning-making process. *Qualitative Health Research, 20*, 42–56. doi:10.1177/1049732309355286

Tisdall, E. K. M., Davis, J. M., & Gallager, M. (2009). *Researching with children and young people: Research design, methods and analysis.* London: Sage.

Walker, R., Schratz, B., & Egg, P. (2008). Seeing beyond violence: Visual research applied to policy and practice. In P. Thomson (Ed.), *Doing visual research with children and young people* (pp. 164–174). London: Routledge.

Wang, C., Cash, J., & Powers, L. (2000). Who knows the streets as well as the homeless? Promoting personal and community action through photovoice. *Health Promotion Practice, 1*, 81–89. doi:10.1177/152483990000100113

Wang, C. C., Yi, W. K., Tao, Z. X., & Carovano, K. (1998). Photovoice as participatory health promotion strategy. *Health Promotion International, 13*, 75–86.

Welsh, E. (2002). Dealing with data: Using NVivo in the qualitative data analysis process. *Forum: Qualitative Social Research, 3*, Art. 26. Retrieved from http://www.qualitative-research.net/index.php/fqs/article/view/865/1881

White, J., Drew, S., & Hay, T. (2009). Ethnography versus case study: Positioning research and researchers. *Qualitative Research Journal, 9*, 18–27. doi:10.3316/QRJ0901018

White, R., & Wyn, J. (2004). *Youth and society: Exploring the social dynamics of youth experience.* South Melbourne, Vic, Australia: Oxford University Press.

68

Beyond the Standard Interview: The Use of Graphic Elicitation and Arts-based Methods

Anna Bagnoli

Introduction

In most qualitative research interviews are a standard method of data collection. The use of interviews relies on language as the privileged medium for the creation and communication of knowledge. However, our daily experience is made of a multiplicity of dimensions, which include the visual and the sensory, and which are worthy of investigation but cannot always be easily expressed in words, since not all knowledge is reducible to language (Eisner, 2008). The inclusion of non-linguistic dimensions in research, which rely on other expressive possibilities, may allow us to access and represent different levels of experience. In my research work I have tried to go beyond the standard interview and expand the domain of investigation by adopting a variety of methods, visual and arts-based. Creatively mixing methods, as Mason suggests (2006), can encourage thinking 'outside the box', generating new ways of interrogating and understanding the social.

In this article I will be reviewing three visual methods that I have employed in the context of interviews: one arts-based projective technique, the self-portrait, and two graphic elicitation methods, the relational map, and the time-line. All these methods involve drawing, an activity that allows participants time to reflect about the issues being explored (Gauntlett, 2007). Drawing methods are most often used with children, or in cross cultural research, that

Source: *Qualitative Research*, 9(5) (2009): 547–570.

is to say when there is an assumption that participants will find it difficult to express themselves verbally. However, they can be helpful even when applied more widely, with people of all ages. The use of visual and creative methods can generally facilitate investigating layers of experience that cannot easily be put into words (Gauntlett, 2007). Images are evocative and can allow access to different parts of human consciousness (Prosser and Loxley, 2008): communicating more holistically, and through metaphors, they can enhance empathic understanding, capture the ineffable, and help us pay attention to reality in different ways, making the ordinary become extraordinary (Weber, 2008).

Graphic elicitation methods usually involve the use of diagrams, which may either be produced by the researcher or by participants (Prosser and Loxley, 2008). Interacting with diagrams provides a basis for further interviewing and communication between researcher and participants (Crilly et al., 2006). Arts-based research is an 'umbrella term' which includes a variety of different methodologies employing some art form as a method (Finley, 2008). Projective techniques include any set of procedures which, being minimally structured, allow people to impose their own forms of organization, bringing into expression their needs, motives, emotions and the like (Allen, 1958).

Projective techniques have long been used in psychology, especially in clinical settings, with a variety of media. Much research involving drawings is done with standardized tests, such as the Draw A Person (DAP); House Tree Person (HTP); Draw a Story (DAS) (Leigh Neale and Rosal, 1993). In clinical frameworks, projective drawings are analysed by testing a connection between some personality trait or variable and features such as size (Prytula et al., 1978); colour use (Marzolf and Kirchner, 1973); and formal aspects of lines (Vass, 1998). The question in such contexts concerns what is to be regarded as pathological and what is not (Vass, 1998). However, drawings and other projective techniques may be used for a variety of purposes, and not solely in contexts that presuppose the existence of any pathology. In developmental psychology, early work on drawings focused on identifying stages of development in children's abilities. Studies on drawings regained prominence in the 1970s and 1980s and attention shifted from viewing the final form as a projection of intellectual knowledge to considering the whole process of making a drawing (Thomas and Silk, 1990). In therapeutic contexts drawings are employed also within more holistic frameworks, such as in art therapy, to assess emotional needs (Silver and Ellison, 1995), and other dynamics, with attention to the meanings that participants themselves associate to them (Riley, 1999).

In more socially-based research, drawings are usually employed with children in order to make the process of interviewing more concrete: by being good memory-aids (Scott, 2000) they allow the inclusion of even very young respondents. In these contexts, it is not the drawings as such that constitute the data, but the whole process of their production (Morrow, 1998). The focus here is on children's own meanings, rather than on interpreting drawings on the basis of some pre-existing theory. Drawings may work well also as 'openers' and 'ice breakers' (Morrow, 1998) during the interview.

My use of drawings and of visual methods more generally has been led by an interest in designing participatory methods which could allow taking part in the research process according to one's own preferred modalities of expression. I was not interested in people's drawing abilities, or in evaluating the formal aspects of their drawings. My focus was on how visual methods could be used within the context of an interview in order to enhance participants' reflexivity and to gather a holistic picture of the topics under investigation that could take into account also their different needs and expressive styles.

The examples that I show in this article are drawn from two different studies. The Narratives of Identity and Migration study, my PhD project at the University of Cambridge, was an autobiographical investigation of young people and identities that I carried out in England and Italy on a case study of migration between the two countries. Forty-one young people aged 16 to 26 and coming from different but comparable backgrounds in both countries took part in this study, for which I designed a diary-based mixed-method approach that I have extensively described elsewhere (Bagnoli, 2009a) and which included the self-portrait.

The Young Lives and Times study is a qualitative longitudinal investigation of young people's lives, identities, and relationships based at the University of Leeds, which aims to run for a prospective 10 years. The young participants are drawn from different areas of metropolitan and rural Yorkshire and were 13 years old when first met. I was involved in the first two waves of this project, which were funded under the ESRC National Centre for Research Methods Real Life Methods Node. A variety of qualitative methods were applied in field-work, among which included relational maps, timelines, and self-portraits.

The Self-portrait

The self-portrait is an arts-based projective technique that I designed in the context of my PhD project on young people and identities with the aim of encouraging participants' reflexivity and getting them to think holistically about their identities and lives. I gave participants paper and felt tips, and asked them to show on the paper who they were at that moment in life, and then to add the people and things that they considered important at that time. This method successfully allowed me to gain an insight on their own visualizations about the moment in their lives they were currently living, with sensitivity for their own associations and meanings. Some of their visualizations were particularly insightful and became very important in my own process of making sense of the data I was collecting. The self-portrait drawn

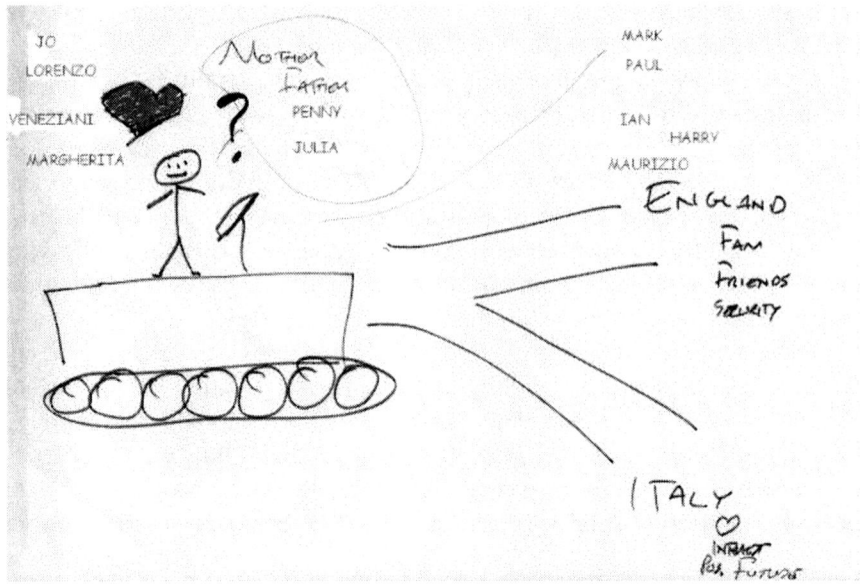

Figure 1: Johnny's self-portrait

by Johnny,[1] a 26-year-old teacher of English as a foreign language living in Florence, is one such case (Figure 1):

> *Johnny:* This is sort of me at the moment, on my track or whatever, and obviously here there's two different roads I have to choose . . . At the moment this year I have to decide really whether I'm gonna stay in Italy, and for these sorts of reasons.
>
> *AB:* What did you . . .
>
> *Johnny:* That's interest for and possible, I ought to write 'poss.' That's possible future, and here's England with family, friends and security, here is my question mark and here is my . . . on my shoulder that weighs me down, possible romantic interest there, and . . .
>
> *AB:* So is it related to Italy?
>
> *Johnny:* It could be, yes, it could probably be.

After living in Italy for more than a year Johnny is facing the dilemma as to whether to stay in Florence in his current job, which he much enjoys, or to return to Britain, where his life could offer a higher degree of security. The crossroads that he draws is a poignant and appropriate visualization for a self-perceived important turning point in his life. It is in Giddens' terms a 'fateful moment' (Giddens, 1991), that is a moment when the course of events may be altered in some major and consequential way, and an effective turn may be impressed on one's life-trajectory. With a map of the alternative possibilities in front of him, and the risks associated with both scenarios, this picture well captures the turning point status that this moment has within Johnny's overall life plan. Through pictures like this I was able to develop my analysis on the basis of participants' own images. The images in the portraits would sometimes possess a 'condensing' quality that could narrate complex stories about young people's plans, dreams, dilemmas, and emotions. Some of these metaphors could be very evocative and, as it may be the case with images (Weber, 2008), could resonate with current theorizing on research on contemporary lives. Indeed the crossroads metaphor in particular is one which I took on in my subsequent work on biographical research exploring turning points in people's lives (Bagnoli and Ketokivi, 2009).

> *Johnny*:   God! It's all too clear, isn't it? My God, look at that! Wow! *(Laughing)* Can't believe I did that!
>
> *AB*:   . . . You did this and you were saying you were on your truck deciding where to go . . .
>
> *Johnny*:   Yeah.
>
> *AB*:   Do you think you have moved in some of these directions, or are you still thinking about . . . ?
>
> *Johnny*:   Yes, I think we're a little further down this one . . . *(Indicating Italy on the self-portrait)*
>
> *AB*:   Down the Italy one.
>
> *Johnny*:   Down the Italy one, yes. Em . . . more because . . . partly . . . I thought very seriously about going back to England and taking this job. Because it was a nice job, em . . . whether it would go . . . no, it made me really think about why I was here, why I didn't want to go back to England, partly 'cos I think I'd go back thinking I've been here two years I haven't learned anything, you know, that I felt . . . and in Italy now I can . . . believe it or not, my Italian is getting a bit better, I'm now able to have relationships with my friends properly, I can talk about things . . . so I feel I can live in this world a bit easier.

When meeting Johnny for a second interview some time later I showed him his self-portrait again, his reaction was one of incredulity: The clarity with which the self-portrait captures Johnny's dilemma takes even its author by surprise. At a few weeks distance the picture already holds the fundamentals of his current situation. Johnny is able to relate to his crossroads metaphor and continue his narrative about the direction his life seems to be going. The longitudinal application of the self-portrait provided valuable results in terms of how young people accounted for change in their lives, giving an indication of the extent to which images produced at an earlier moment in time could still make sense of what one was living, or could otherwise have lost any meaning or significant associations.

Most participants seemed to enjoy this task, which provided some momentary regression to childlike expression. At times they expressed some initial resistance, and in one case one participant declined to take part, denying that she would be able to define or 'codify' herself. In most cases, however, the self-portrait helped to 'break the ice' during the interview (Morrow, 1998), making people feel more comfortable. There was, however, no such resistance when I asked a younger sample of 13-year-olds to engage in the same task, in the Young Lives and Times Study. The self-portrait was one of the visual tasks which I asked the young participants to take part in at my first meeting with them. The variety of styles in these young people's self-portraits followed the same patterns that I had found in my previous project, showing different levels of abstraction, on a continuum going from drawing to writing (Bagnoli, 2009a). The self-portraits produced by Alicia, Grace, and Billy give an idea of this range of styles.

While Johnny's earlier example is a drawing of a scene depicting a whole metaphorical situation, Alicia's drawing (Figure 2) focuses on the self. By drawing herself in a school uniform her identity as a student comes across as fundamental to her self presentation. Grace's self-portrait is what the young

People 3 things important:
- Family - all, immediate family especially
- Friends; school, camp & out of school
- Dog!
- Phone, computer, camera, music

Figure 2: Alicia's self-portrait

Figure 3: Grace's self-portrait

people themselves called a 'spider diagram', in which a number of significant dimensions are organized radially around a central element which stands for the self (Figure 3). Here the important elements appear to be family, friends, music, and sports, as well as some defining characteristics, among which the self-trait 'loud', a quality that young people seem to be very appreciative of (see next section). Finally, Billy's self-portrait (Figure 4) is more based on writing and combines an essay-like format with some drawn symbols. In this case football and family appear central to his identity.

In the same way as in my previous study, the contents of the self-portraits were the basis for further interviewing, and the longitudinal framework of the research allowed me to ask participants about the relevance of these self-portraits again in the second wave of data collection. If producing a self-portrait encountered no resistance among this younger sample, the styles of these drawings also indicated, however, a generally more limited expressive range. The boys' portraits made use of a very limited range of colours, typically black and blue, and the symbols they drew were all consistent with traditional constructions of gender identities. Including a symbol like a heart in one's self-portrait, as Johnny had done, seemed out of the question for the boys in this age cohort.

Relational Maps

A variety of studies investigating relationships have used some form of relational map as a graphic elicitation tool during interviews. A good example is provided by Josselson (1996), who has employed 'relational space maps' in her

happy

like to

Play lots of
sport

I like to go
out with my
friends

I play football with
a team
and I suport
leeds utD football
club.

my mum and Dad and
my sister because they are
my family.

my Pet cat because it can
be good coumpany.

Figure 4: Billy's self-portrait

study of human relationships, which she designed around the metaphor of the solar system. People are asked to draw themselves and the important people in their lives, taking as their model the sun and the planets revolving around. By important people, she means those people who were in the participant's mind at the time. The task is repeated several times in the interview, depending on the participant's age, for successive five-year intervals. The distance on the page should reflect the presence of the significant others within the participant's inner world. People may be indicated with a dotted circle, to show that this someone was not there physically, but just on an imaginary level, and some other people may be drawn as a group circle, when they mattered as a group, rather than on an individual level. By considering five-year intervals in the participant's life, the aim is highlighting the appearance and disappearance of others within someone's world over time, as retrospectively viewed at the time of interview. Another, more commonly used model of relational map is that employed by Roseneil (2006) in her psychosocial study of intimacy and personal life. Here participants are asked to construct a map of their relationships during the interview, placing people in order of importance within a set of concentric circles, with the closest relationships being in the inner circles and the others gradually around.

The relational map that I applied in the Young Lives and Times study is similar to these two models, but has a rather looser structure. This task came as part of the second interview that I had with each participant in the first wave of the study. After giving a blank sheet of paper and a set of felt tips I asked the young people to draw themselves in the middle of the paper, and to show the important people in their lives, indicating the different degree of their importance, by placing them closer or more distant to them. I did not specify any definite structure for the map, partly because I was interested in seeing what patterns the young people would come up with themselves. In the Real Life Methods Node our emphasis was on defining creative methods to study the social, and I thought that by relying on some wide and open instructions, we could leave more space for the participants' own interpretations and visualizations of my words. I therefore intended the instructions in much the same way Prosser and Loxley (2008) point out, as basic 'scaffolding' for participants, allowing them to construct their own representations. Relational maps were then the basis for further interviewing, which directly related to whatever the young people had drawn. Similarly to Josselson (1996), I asked participants to include people who might be important but pertaining to an imaginary level (Hermans et al., 1993), and not actually physically present in their lives. I also asked them to include any role models, people whom they admired and whose qualities they would like to have themselves, as well as anyone they might dislike for some reason, who could be regarded as a negative role model instead. In addition, I asked for 'special' objects that might be important to them as well.

Participants drew relational maps with various structures, which included what they themselves called 'spider diagrams', drawings with different horizontal layers, drawings with stick people, as well as more standard concentric circles maps, sometimes organized in complex arrangements. The different importance of the people on the map was sometimes indicated through the

Figure 5: Carlie's relational map

use of different colours, other times by adding an asterisk or circling people's names.

The relational maps by Carlie (Figure 5) and by Billy (Figure 6) are two examples of the rather common 'spider' structure. In Carlie's map the people who are drawn closest to the self are 'mum and grandma'. We also get an indication of the importance of the extended family in her life, something which is recurrent in her data. Carlie has grown up being looked after by her maternal grandmother since her mother, a single parent who had her when very young, was working. Her grandma has therefore had a central role in her life and Carlie looks up to her as a role model, because of her ability to maintain peaceful relationships within the family:

> *Carlie:*   My grandma can kind of reason with everyone without upsetting
> everyone . . . she doesn't really take sides on people's arguments
> and stuff.

In addition to family, Carlie indicates three groups of friends, coming from different environments: cadets, family, and school. Within each of these

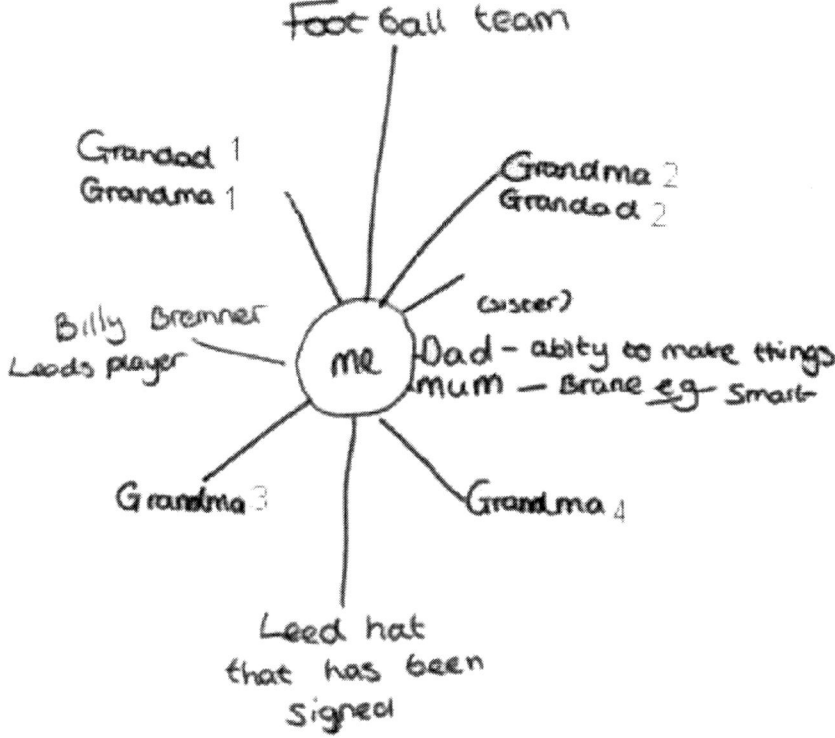

Figure 6: Billy's relational map

groups she also highlights one best friend, people she could contact in case she needed help:

> *Carlie:* If I was ever really upset or if I needed to just like ring someone up and talk to them then I can ring them and they will listen to me.

One of these friends in particular is mentioned as a role model, because she is 'crazy' and 'loud':

> *Carlie:* She's quite crazy
> *AB:* Hm mm
> *Carlie:* And erm she makes me laugh all the time but erm she kind of, she'll just say what's on her mind (. . .) she'll just speak her mind and stuff (. . .)
> *AB:* So is that what you mean when you say she's kind of crazy? Or is there any other thing she does?
> *Carlie:* Well yeah she is kind of crazy because she's just erm really loud and outspoken (*laughs*) and erm she don't really care what people think of her (. . .) she's just herself in front of everyone. She doesn't like change to fit with other people.
> *AB:* Okay. So when you say she's really loud.

Carlie: Yeah.
AB: What is it you mean exactly?
Carlie: She just, she shouts quite a lot (laughing).
AB: She shouts.
Carlie: Yeah. Not in an aggressive way just in like a fun kind of way.

Being 'loud' and 'crazy' in Carlie's and more generally in young people's jargon (see also Grace's self-portrait in Figure 3) seem to mean having the confidence to be oneself in every situation, without changing to fit in with other people. In these meanings the terms are recurrent in their words and refer to qualities that are reputed very highly in the youth culture. In this relational map we can also see one friend indicated in red (shown as 'Friend 4' in Figure 5). Carlie highlights this friend in response to my question as someone she dislikes because she cannot be trusted to keep a secret.

Billy's map (Figure 6) shows again the centrality of the family and of the extended family: in this case two great-grandmas appear in the drawing. Throughout his data Billy presents his family as a compact and harmonious unit (see also his self-portrait in Figure 4). Here he has included his mum, dad and sister as very close to him, specifying for both his parents the different ways he looks up to them: his dad is important for his 'ability to make things', his practical intelligence, and his mum because she is 'brainy', an example of academic intelligence:

Billy: Er, I put my mum's brain.
AB: Okay.
Billy: Because she's very smart. And my dad's ability to make, ability to make things.
AB: Okay. Can you tell me more about these things I mean, about your mum being so smart in, in what things for instance?
Billy: She's er – she works – well, she's work – works at a supermarket head offices and she does, she keeps everything organized because she's a manager and if any, like if we get some'at stuck with computer she knows how to come and sort it out and . . .
AB: Okay.
Billy: So she just keeps everything organized.
AB: Yes, yes. So that's quite important. And what about your dad er, ability to make things. What sort of things?
Billy: He can er, he's – he makes settees and can upholster them and if something breaks in house, like say if a table broke he could take it in garage and just notch it up and fix it a bit.

Billy in turn supports his younger sister:

Billy: If she's ever got problems at school and everybody – somebody's picking on her I'll go up and speak to the school or some'at or just – just look after her because I don't want anything to happen to her sort of.

Figure 7: Rebekah's relational map

This map also shows the importance that football has in Billy's life, something that was clear also from his self-portrait (Figure 4). The passion for football is shared with his dad, who is a manager in his local team and who is 'a big part of the football'. The football entries, in Billy's map, which include Billy's team, a Leeds player of the past that is a sports role model, and a treasured possession, a hat that has been signed by the Leeds football team, have been added in response to my own input. Billy had been extensively talking about football, and I encouraged him to add anything about football that he thought might be relevant in the map. The maps are drawn within a social interaction, the interview, and the researcher's own questions and probes contribute to the context of their production.

The third map, by Rebekah, follows the concentric circles structure, a pattern which we have seen to be rather common in research on personal relationships, and which young people may also be familiar with from their own studies (Figure 7). In this case, it was only through drawing the map, in the context of our second interview, that Rebekah started talking about her dad and the two brothers she has in London:

Rebekah: Oh, sorry I forgot. Sorry, I forgot to write that before.
AB: Who are they?
Rebekah: They're my two other brothers who live in London. Like they're my dad's children. And it's the same thing with my dad really. I'm close to them but not as close as I could be.
AB: Yes.

> *Rebekah*: They live in London as well so (. . .)
> *AB*: So you're not so close to them you're saying? You don't see them so often?
> *Rebekah*: No, not really.

Rebekah attributes the fact that she does not see her family in London so much to the geographical distance. However, as it appears from the same interview, her best friend is also based in London and she is in touch with her everyday with MSN.[2] The best friend is in fact placed in the innermost circle in the map, together with the immediate family Rebekah lives with. The relational map highlights well how this side of her family Rebekah had 'forgotten' has not an emotional centrality to her life. Here it also helps overcoming silence about some aspects of their lives that young people may not find easy or immediate to talk about. By providing a task that engages participants on another level from verbally answering questions, the map helps thinking differently about issues and may elicit information which would possibly have remained unknown otherwise.

Timelines

Time is a crucial dimension within the longitudinal research framework of the Young Lives and Times study and one aim in data collection was allowing the young people to reflect on the different temporal dimensions of past, present, and future in their lives. In the first wave, the focus was on young people's narratives about their present and their past. The second wave focused instead on young people's projections and expectations about their future lives. In both waves I employed timelines in order to elicit biographical data about time during the interviews. In the first wave, I asked the young people to draw a timeline starting from zero and going up to their current age indicating the most important events and changes that had happened in their lives. I also asked them to include any events that had happened in the wider world that might have been significant to them, and which they might remember in connection with their own biographical events. This was an attempt to link the individual dimension of lives with the macro level of collective biographies and histories. Most young people represented their timeline through a horizontal line (Figure 8). However, there were also different representations of time: Alicia's wavy line (Figure 9), and Melodie's vertical line (Figure 10). This method aimed to collect the most important turning points and biographical

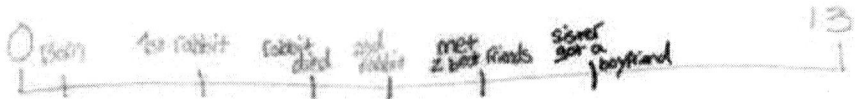

Figure 8: Roxanne's timeline

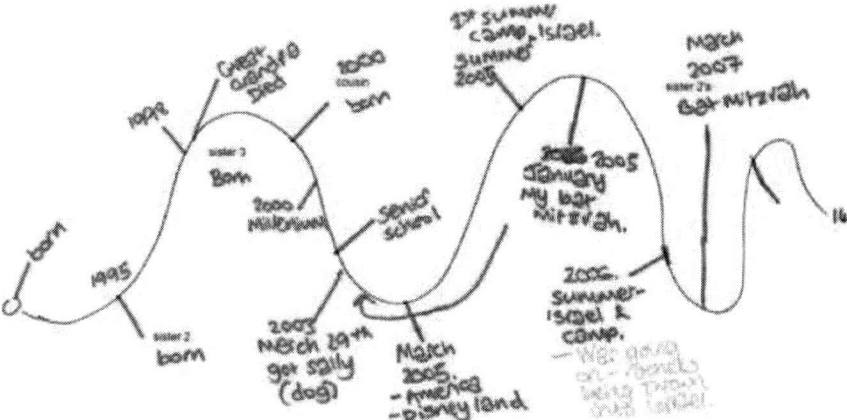

Figure 9: Alicia's timeline

events as seen from the young people's own perspectives. In Roxanne's time-line (Figure 8), the events have clearly been chosen from the young person's point of view. Roxanne loves animals and would like to be a vet in the future, and this does come across in her timeline, which emphasizes the importance of her pet rabbits in her life. Alicia's timeline (Figure 9) shows that her family culture and Jewish background frame the temporal organization of events in her life. The war in Israel is a world event she has directly witnessed. In Melodie's timeline school life and music learning dominate the selection of events structuring her life. The two world events that have been significant to her, 9/11 and the tsunami, were the most frequently mentioned by this sample of young people.

In the second wave of data collection the young people were asked to update this original timeline, by adding the events that had been significant during the year, year and a half which had passed since the first interview. They were then asked to draw a timeline for their future lives, indicating their expectations and dreams about their future. The future timelines drawn by girls show something interesting about their expectations of forming a fam-ily of their own in the future. Unfortunately a high number of boys dropped out of the study in the second wave, and the timelines of those who stayed do not show much that can be of relevance here. The most common time-line pattern among girls, and particularly middle-class girls, is exemplified by Carlie's timeline (Figure 11). Here the expectation is to go to university, then travelling, getting married at 30, and having children in one's 30s. This sort of projection reflects what has become a standard life expectation among middle-class girls, which sees motherhood delayed to one's 30s, when one has already had the chance to do other things, or, to say it in Carlie's terms, has 'finished finding who they are':

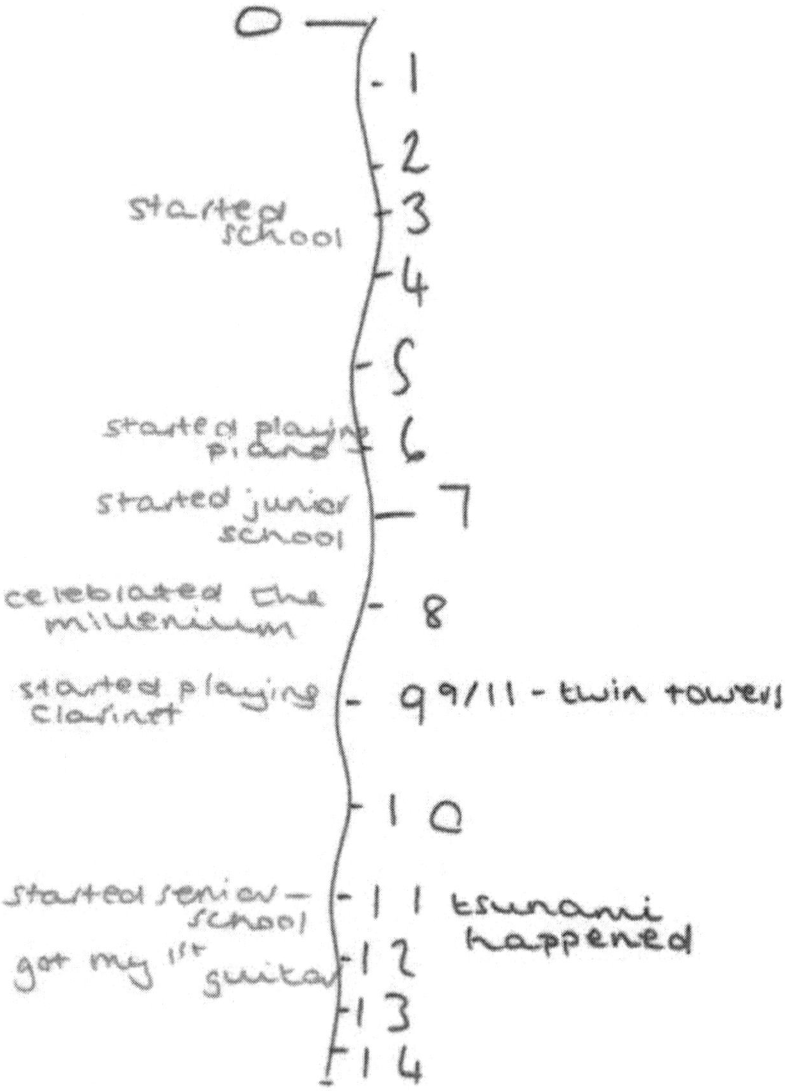

0
1
2
started school
3
4
5
started playing piano
6
started junior school
7
celebrated the millenium
8
started playing clarinet
9 9/11 - twin towers
10
started senior school
11 tsunami happened
got my 1st guitar
12
13
14

Figure 10: Melodie's timeline

19
Go to university
24
Go traveling
30
Get married
32
have children

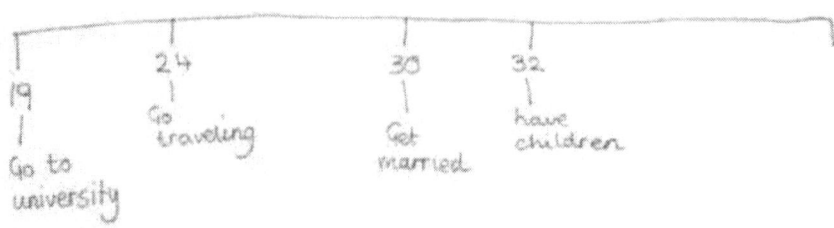

Figure 11: Carlie's future timeline

> *AB:*   So you want to have children also, and you put it after, at 32. Can you tell me a bit more about that?
>
> *Carlie:* Erm, well I think I'll be like settled down and I'll have done like all the stuff that I want to do, and like, erm, I think it's just like a nice age, 'cos you're like finished, you've like finished like being like, like finding like who you are like properly and everything like that. So, and you're like settled down and stuff so . . .

As it appears also from my previous research (Bagnoli, 2001), young people often seem to imagine a 30 threshold in their future which would somehow correspond to entrance into adulthood and settling down. The experience of travelling, which in these timelines is a standard expectation about the future, is indeed an important rite of passage and turning point for young people, whose travel, such as taking a year out, is often defined in institutional ways (Bagnoli, 2009b). Carlie's aspirations are shared also by Sophie and Naomi, two working-class girls living in a rural area of Yorkshire. However, the imagined timings of these events are different. Sophie (Figure 12) hopes to be married and with at least one child by the time she is 25. She wants 3 or 4 children, aiming to replicate her mother's family reproduction patterns:

> *Sophie:* I don't think she's a role model for me now but I think she's a role model for me for when I get to her age. I would like to be like her (. . .) Just a, a good mum really if I do have, if I do have children, just to support them and, and I'm really, erm, like, I'm quite proud of her as well cos she's, she's been through a lot, erm, with my dad when I were younger, erm, and she's, she's, she's just, just managed with three kids before she met M. (current partner) and then she met M. and she had my younger brother and I, I admire her for that.

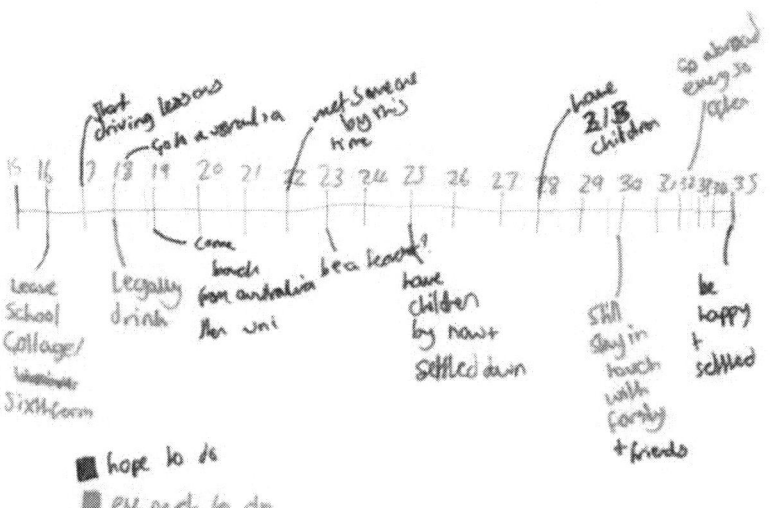

Figure 12: Sophie's future timeline

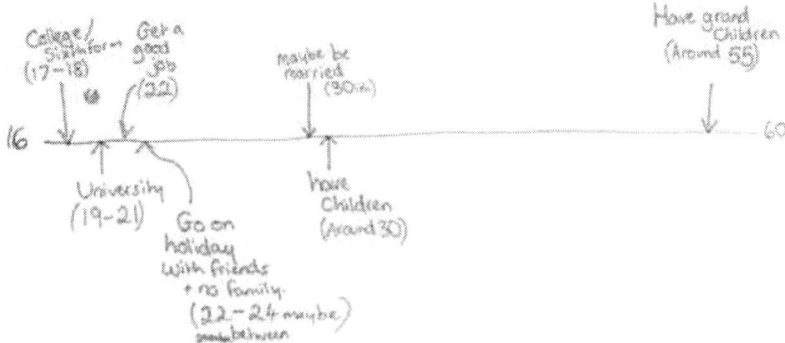

Figure 13: Naomi's future timeline

Sophie's mother is a role model providing an example of strength in the face of adversity in life: 'she's been through a lot'. The same sort of example is set by Naomi's mother, who has been able to cope with two children as a single parent, despite her illness and the difficult relationships with her partner and his own family. The timeline by Naomi, Sophie's friend, has the same pattern as Carlie's (Figure 13).

> AB: And also you'd like, er, to have children around 30?
> Naomi: Yeah. So I can have a life before that. You know (. . .) Not at 25. I, I'd, I'm, I'm not sure. I, I don't think I'd like to at 25. I might, I'd, I'd like, erm, early 30s, or really, you know, like late 20s.
> AB: Why do you think you'd want that later?
> Naomi: Because, erm, I'd, I want to have a life before I, I give it up to kids.

Naomi wishes 'to have a life before giving it up to kids': she looks up to her mother, but wishes a different life for herself, a life which may allow her to do other things before having children. She thus imagines having children in her 30s. Yet, she also imagines having grandchildren when she is 55. It would seem that she is not going to allow her own children the same 'moratorium' time she is aspiring to herself. The fact that her timeline extends up to 55 is also unusual, since most of these timelines do not go that far into the future beyond 30 or 35. The only thing that is included as meaningful in the more distant future, however, is an event related to family reproduction. Family reproduction thus emerges as central in this timeline, and in the expectations Naomi has about life, and this is interesting beyond what it makes explicit regarding young people's assumptions on appropriate ages for reproduction.

Past timelines helped collecting information regarding the events that according to the young people had been particularly significant in their biographies, and future timelines provided a projection of the events that were expected as structuring their lives in the future. The events highlighted in the timelines reflected young people's own interests, and the wider social contexts, such as family background, school, and also some world-scale events that had had a personal relevance to them. This method was helpful in engaging young people in a reflection about their past and future lives. However, it was not always successful. Discussing the issue of time with young people with mental disabilities was generally problematic, as these participants could not relate to the way of understanding time that was required for completing this task. In contrast with the self-portrait and the relational map, which showed no problem of inclusivity, the timeline had thus a more limited range of effectiveness.

Conclusions

This article has described three visual methods that I have employed in my research with the aim of allowing people to reflect creatively on the dimensions of interest to the investigation. With the self-portrait that I designed and first applied within the Narratives of Identity and Migration study my aim was to encourage the narration of a holistic picture of identities. With the relational map and the timelines that I applied in the context of the Young Lives and Times study the aim was eliciting information about the relational worlds and the events that participants considered to be turning points in their lives.

As we have seen in the examples from these two studies, the introduction of a simple visual task within the context of an interview may be very helpful for elicitation purposes. Focusing on the visual level allows people to go beyond a verbal mode of thinking, and this may help include wider dimensions of experience, which one would perhaps neglect otherwise. A creative task may encourage thinking in non-standard ways, avoiding the clichés and 'ready-made' answers which could be easily replied. In this way, an arts-based method or graphic elicitation tool may encourage a holistic narration of self, and also help overcoming silences, including those aspects of one's life that might for some reason be sensitive and difficult to be related in words.

Indeed, even visual data may be clichéd and produced in a standardized way. Yet, just as with words, even this may be informative, for example about the visual culture of some social group. Especially when participants are drawn from the same communities and know each other, as was the case with the young people taking part in the Young Lives and Times study, many of whom enrolled in the study together with their friends, one could occasionally get the impression that they had somehow discussed their responses with those of their friends. Again, this too may be treated as part of the data, informative as it may be about the worlds of their relationships and their reference points, as well as about what is considered to be appropriate self-presentation in some youth subculture.

One constant in my application of these methods has been the openness that I have tried to maintain when introducing these tasks. I kept the instructions as broad as possible, with the intent of enabling participants to structure the tasks in their own ways. This allowed me to collect a variety of patterns in the ways in which people made sense of the same instructions. However, not everyone may be comfortable working with such openness, and using a more standardized framework may just be more appropriate sometimes. Having an interest in how different people will make sense of the same task does mean that your analysis will then start being focused on the individual, and going beyond the individual case and making comparisons across larger units may sometimes be difficult.

In being attentive to people's different responses to these tasks my aim was also emphasizing their participation, allowing them to guide me in the interview by highlighting the important dimensions of experience from their own perspective. There are, however, limits to the extent to which these methods may be said to be participatory. The self-portrait is of the three the most unstructured and open method, since it does not presuppose anything about what the participant would have to do with the paper they are given. This open format does not always favour participation though: some people may feel uncomfortable with it, as it happened with one young woman, who asserted the modality of her participation by actually denying her involvement with this method. As it emerged, younger participants happily got involved with the self-portrait, whereas some degree of resistance, such as defensively pointing out one's poor drawing abilities, was sometimes present with the older sample. It must be said, however, that it was in fact with this relatively older sample that the self-portrait could collect data that were particularly evocative and insightful.

Although I gave a rather flexible context for their production, relational maps were relying on some assumptions about people: the assumption that they would see themselves at the centre of a relational world. Without the input of placing oneself in the middle of the paper, perhaps not everyone would have attributed this centrality to the self. The importance of relationships in people's lives was another assumption implied in this task: what about someone who would want to stress that they were in fact alone in the world, and for whom relationships' importance was defined through their absence? This method does lead participants to consider their lives in ways that might make sense within the context of the study, but which may not actually be the most significant to them on a subjective level.

In a similar way, timelines might have been really useful to collect the range of biographical events that young people saw as important in their lives, yet the concept of 'timeline' inherently suggests a linear interpretation of time, which as we have seen was not actually that participatory, since it made it difficult to take part for the young people with mental disabilities, who could not relate to it. Time may be subjectively experienced in ways that are not linear and that do not easily rest within the parameters of a mathematical progression. People may experience time in a circular way, with repetition being more important than progression. Perceiving life through repetition of events may link one's own experiences to past generations and even to mythical stories that are meaningful to the self. The very idea of defining one's life through a forward facing trajectory can be highly problematic. Indeed, even within this study two participants chose different ways of representing their lifetime, drawing a wavy line with ups and downs in one case, and a vertical line going downwards in another.

It must also be noted that these were solicited data, which were specifically made for research purposes. Their production was contextual to the interview, and arose out of interaction with the researcher. Some elements might not have been present in the data had it not been for my own input, which might occasionally have been stronger and more evident than other times. When producing their drawings, not dissimilarly from when answering interview questions, young people might consciously have tried to project some self-presentation that could match what in their view the researcher was looking for. The quality of the rapport established with each participant will also have contributed to the extent to which they may have felt comfortable in these visual tasks.

In this article I have shown examples of data collected through these three visual methods in relation to each other and in context with interview extracts. The analysis I carried out of these data was contextual with the rest of the materials, visual and text-based, that I collected within the projects. I do not consider visual data simply as an add-on to text-based analyses, but as significantly contributing to making sense at all different stages in the analytical process. With the aid of the Atlas.ti software I coded all data using the same multi-media coding system, which enabled me to link text with visual-based quotations and to interrogate data on multiple levels. Both images and texts were analysed in terms of the stories that were being told, according to the parameters of narrative analysis (Lieblich et al., 1998). Attention was paid both to what was present in the stories and to what was not there, and comparisons across cases were particularly useful in this respect.

Mixing methods allows one to see things from different perspectives and to look at data in creative ways. Throughout the analysis, I made an effort to establish links between documents of different type, so as to test and to validate any emerging interpretation through recurrence across multiple sources. The insights gathered from the reading of visual documents were sometimes extremely helpful thanks to the evocative quality of images, which can represent concepts in a particularly condensed manner. This made it possible to construct interpretations that were sometimes visually led. Visual data can thus centrally guide the process of analysis, allowing even participants' own metaphors to lead in constructing interpretations.

In this article, the contextual reading of images and text from these two projects provided important information on the substantive level with relation to the moments in their lives young people regarded as significant and fateful, as well as their projected life-plans, and the expectations they had about the events that might provide meaning to their lives in the future. Information was gathered also about some of the qualities and rituals that seem to be central to the youth culture, including the expectation to travel, and about the importance of different relationships, the relevance of family in their lives, including the modalities with which different people might be reference points for their identities.

The longitudinal application of these methods has shown how the clarity and 'condensing' effect that may be associated with images and which can have such strong analytical potential can sometimes come as a surprise for the authors themselves even after a relatively short time since the moment of their production. Within a prospective qualitative longitudinal research, such as the Young Lives and Times study, the researchers who will be involved in future waves of data collection will have plenty of materials in the archive that could be applied as prompts for elicitation. Seeing how the young people will respond to the drawings they produced years earlier, at 13 and 15 years old, should allow an interesting investigation of their own understandings of the changes that time will have brought to their lives. The longitudinal aspect could also potentially provide an opportunity for involving the young people in the analytical process, and for scrutinizing interpretations in the light of participants' views.

Notes

1. All names have been changed to pseudonyms that were chosen by participants themselves. Drawings have been edited, with names and other identifiers either removed or changed.
2. Instant messaging software.

References

Allen, R. (1958) *Personality Assessment Procedures*. New York: Harper & Brothers.
Bagnoli, A. (2001) 'Narratives of Identity and Migration: An Autobiographical Study on Young People in England and Italy', PhD Thesis, July 2001, University of Cambridge.
Bagnoli, A. (2009a) 'Researching Identities with Multi-method Autobiographies', in B. Harrison (ed.) (2008) *Life Story Research*, Sage Benchmarks in Social Research Methods, vol.3, pp. 376–97. London: Sage. Originally published in *Sociological Research Online* 9(2), (2004): http://www.socresonline.org.uk/9/2/bagnoli.html
Bagnoli, A. (2009b) ' "On an Introspective Journey": Identities and Travel in Young People's Lives', in A. Bagnoli and K. Ketokivi (eds) 'At a Crossroads: Contemporary Lives between Fate and Choice', *European Societies*, special issue, 11(3): 325–45.

Bagnoli, A. and Ketokivi, K. (2009) 'At a Crossroads: Contemporary Lives between Fate and Choice', *European Societies*, special issue, 11(3): 315–24.

Crilly, N., Blackwell, A.F. and Clarkson, P.J. (2006) 'Graphic Elicitation: Using Research Diagrams as Interview Stimuli', *Qualitative Research* 6(3): 341–66.

Eisner, E. (2008) 'Art and Knowledge', in J.G. Knowles and A.L. Cole (eds) *Handbook of the Arts in Qualitative Research: Perspectives, Methodologies, Examples, and Issues*, pp. 3–12, London: Sage.

Finley, S. (2008) 'Arts Based Research', in J.G. Knowles and A.L. Cole (eds) *Handbook of the Arts in Qualitative Research: Perspectives, Methodologies, Examples, and Issues*, pp. 71–81, London: Sage.

Gauntlett, D. (2007) *Creative Explorations. New Approaches to Identities and Audiences*. London: Routledge.

Giddens, A. (1991) *Modernity and Self-Identity*. Cambridge: Polity.

Hermans, H.J.M., Rijks, T.I. and Kempen, H.J.G. (1993) 'Imaginal Dialogues in the Self: Theory and Method', *Journal of Personality* 61(2): 207–36.

Josselson, R. (1996) *The Space between Us. Exploring the Dimensions of Human Relationships*. London: Sage.

Leigh Neale, E. and Rosal, M.L. (1993) 'What Can Art Therapists Learn from the Research on Projective Drawing Techniques for Children? A Review of the Literature', *The Arts in Psychotherapy* 20: 37–49.

Lieblich, A., Tuval-Masiach, R. and Zilber, T. (1998) *Narrative Research: Reading, Analysis and Interpretation* (Volume 47). London: Sage.

Marzolf, S.S. and Kirchner, J.H. (1973) 'Personality Traits and Colour Choices for House-Tree-Person Drawings', *Journal of Clinical Psychology* 29: 240–45.

Mason, J. (2006) 'Mixing Methods in a Qualitatively Driven Way', *Qualitative Research* 6(9): 9–25.

Morrow, V. (1998) 'If You Were a Teacher, It Would Be Harder to Talk to You: Reflections on Qualitative Research with Children in School', *International Journal of Social Research Methodology. Theory & Practice* 1(4): 297–313.

Prosser, J. and Loxley, A. (2008) 'Introducing Visual Methods', ESRC National Centre for Research Methods Review Paper, NCRM/010 October.

Prytula, R.E., Phelps, M.R. and Morrissey, E.F. (1978) 'Figure Drawing Size as a Reflection of Self-Concept or Self-Esteem', *Journal of Clinical Psychology* 34(1): 207–14.

Riley, S. (1999) *Contemporary Art Therapy with Adolescents*. London: Jessica Kingsley Publishers.

Roseneil, S. (2006) 'The Ambivalences of Angel's "Arrangement": A Psychosocial Lens on the Contemporary Condition of Personal Life', *The Sociological Review* 54(4): 847–69.

Scott, J. (2000) 'Children as Respondents. The Challenge for Qualitative Methods', in P. Christensen and A. James (eds) *Research with Children. Perspectives and Practices*, pp. 98–119. London: The Falmer Press.

Silver, R. and Ellison, J. (1995) 'Identifying and Assessing Self-Images in Drawings by Delinquent Adolescents', *The Arts in Psychotherapy* 22(4): 339–52.

Thomas, G.V. and Silk, A.M.J. (1990) *An Introduction to the Psychology of Children's Drawings*. London: Harvester Wheatsheaf.

Vass, Z. (1998) 'The Inner Formal Structure of the H-T-P Drawings: An Exploratory Study', *Journal of Clinical Psychology* 54(5): 611–19.

Weber, S. (2008) 'Visual Images in Research', in J.G. Knowles and A.L. Cole (eds) *Handbook of the Arts in Qualitative Research: Perspectives, Methodologies, Examples, and Issues*, pp. 41–53, London: Sage.

69

Prison Tattoos as a Reflection
of the Criminal Lifestyle

*Alicia T. Rozycki Lozano, Robert D. Morgan,
Danielle D. Murray and Femina Varghese*

The process of tattooing is a worldwide phenomenon that has been practiced for thousands of years (Butler, Trice, & Calhoun, 1963; Koch, Roberts, Cannon, Armstrong, & Owen, 2005; Post, 1968; Sanders, 1989) across cultures and social classes (Levy, Sewell, & Goldstein, 1979; Steward, 1990). Findings indicated that 3% to 24% of the general public in the United States have tattoos (Anderson, 1992; Armstrong, Owen, Roberts, & Koch, 2002a, 2002b; Frederick & Bradley, 2000; Laumann & Derick, 2006), whereas the prevalence of tattoos in the prison population is projected to be higher, ranging from 15% to 32% (Manuel & Retzlaff, 2002; Palermo, 2004).

Both people in the general public and prisons alike choose to obtain tattoos for various reasons. Images can be chosen idiosyncratically based on personal reasons or tattoos can be making a statement of identity that can be directed to others, to oneself, or both (Newman, 1982). It is possible that tattoos can serve to define each inmate's psyche and identity (DeMello, 1993). Solidifying one's identity is particularly crucial in prisons where individual identity is limited for inmates (DeMello, 1993). However, the identity that is often solidified is one of being a convict (DeMello, 1993). Should the individual decide to move away from the criminal lifestyle at a later time, the individual may wish to have tattoos removed (Bazan, Harris, & Lorentzen, 2002; DeMello, 1993). This is especially pertinent among inmates as they may select images

Source: *International Journal of Offender Therapy and Comparative Criminology*, 55(4) (2011): 509–529.

or locations on the body that identify them as criminals. For instance, images may reflect prison life, such as clock faces, spider webs, or prison bars (Baden & Roach, 2001; Buentello, 1992; Taylor, 1970) or suggest greater commitment to criminal gang life when individuals acquired tattoos on the face, head, neck, or hands (Etter, 1999; Phelan & Hunt, 1998). In addition, visible tattoos on inmates have even been linked to thought disorders, self-harming behavior, and a history of violent behavior, substance abuse, psychological treatment, and childhood problems (Birmingham, Mason, & Grubin, 1996; Harry, 1987). In general, various studies link tattoos with deviance, personality disorders, substance abuse, risk-taking behavior, and criminality (Armstrong, 1991; Braithwaite, Robillar, Woodring, Stephens, & Arriola, 2001; Drews, Allison, & Probst, 2000; Manuel & Retzlaff, 2002; Raspa & Cusak, 1990).

Tattooing behavior of criminals has been associated with the theory of the criminal lifestyle (Walters, 1990). The criminal lifestyle theory postulated that deviance is characterized by four behaviors: irresponsibility, self-indulgence, interpersonal intrusiveness, and social rule breaking (Walters, 1990). There are also four validation processes: anger/rebellion, power/control, excitement/pleasure, and greed/laziness. These processes drive behavior and can explain the motives behind criminal acts (e.g., greed, power) in addition to explaining the obvious reasons for committing an act (e.g., need for money). Perhaps the main thrust of the theory is criminal thinking styles. The idea is that career criminals have flawed ways of thinking and perceiving, which contribute to poor decision making and generally lead to illicit behaviors. The eight criminal thinking styles include mollification (blaming society for problems), cutoff (impulsive justifications for bad behaviors), entitlement (believing oneself to be so special and different from others that societal rules do not apply), power orientation (judging if others are easy targets for manipulation), sentimentality (doing good deeds to prove to themselves that they are not entirely bad people), superoptimism (thinking the odds of getting caught doing bad deeds will be in their favor), cognitive indolence (laziness), and discontinuity, or a disconnect between thoughts and behaviors that allows criminals to compartmentalize their bad behaviors and still view themselves as good (Walters, 1990).

Underlying the concept of the criminal lifestyle (Walters, 1990) is the concept of a criminal personality that is coupled with criminal thinking errors, which then drive behavior. Rationalizations and thinking distortions serve the purpose of reducing guilt and allowing criminals to see themselves as good people despite this "bad" behavior (Walters, 1990). The concept of a "career criminal" stems from empirical research showing that the majority of crimes are committed by a minority of criminals, regardless of socioeconomic status, ethnicity or race, country, age, and gender (Walters, 1990) – thus there is a need to identify offenders who potentially identify with the criminal lifestyle and who are possibly at increased risk for recidivism.

A study from the late 1960s indicated there is a greater percentage of repeat offenders who have tattoos as compared to those in the general public, although the type of tattoos was unspecified (Post, 1968). This idea that career criminals may be tattooed was more recently discussed by Walters (1990); a link between one of the four key behaviors in the criminal lifestyle theory, self-indulgence, and tattooing was noted. Self-indulgence includes ignoring consequences and also includes obtaining gratification through attention. For example, criminals may enjoy receiving the attention from others through showy physical appearances. Thus, tattoos are a way to obtain attention. Furthermore, there can be a sense of control over the environment by attracting attention to oneself by altering physical appearance. Ultimately tattoos are not, in and of themselves, criminogenic; however, some literature indicates correlations between tattoos and delinquency, adult criminality, assaultive felony, and self-indulgence (Walters, 1990).

In addition, self-indulgence revolves around obtaining immediate pleasure and postponing pain (Walters, 1990). Considering Walters's (1990) theory more broadly, the lifestyle criminal is someone who has chosen criminality as a profession. Thus, when an individual tattoos images related to his profession permanently on his body, it seems to indicate a deep commitment to that way of life, and perhaps indicates little hope for alternate lifestyles.

Although a number of studies have examined the relation between tattooing behavior and inmates, the relationship between prison tattoos, the criminal lifestyle, and recidivism has yet to be explored. The purpose in conducting this study is to better understand tattooing behavior among inmates. The tattoo literature indicates that society influences tattooing behavior and people's perceptions of tattoos. There is a difference in image and style when comparing prison tattoos to nonprison tattoos (Baden & Roach, 2001; Jankowski, 2004). There is also a difference between the thinking styles and behaviors when comparing inmates to people in the general public, that is, non-criminals (Walters, 1990). It may be prison tattoos are a manifestation of this difference, and obtaining prison tattoos is one way for inmates to identify with the criminal lifestyle and criminal culture.

Specifically, this study sought to explore whether inmates with prison tattoos endorse a criminal lifestyle, as measured by elevated scales on the Psychological Inventory of Criminal Thinking Styles, Version 4.0 (PICTS), and have higher risk of recidivism, as measured by the Self-Appraisal Questionnaire (SAQ), as compared to inmates with nonprison tattoos, inmates with no tattoos, and college students with tattoos.[1] In addition, whether inmates with prison tattoos have a greater number of convictions and greater institutional behavior problems (i.e., self-reported total number of disciplinary infractions) than inmates with nonprison tattoos and inmates with no tattoos was explored. Also, inmates with greater skin surface covered with tattoos were compared to inmates with less skin surface covered with regard to commitment to the criminal lifestyle, risk for recidivism, and institutional behavior problems (i.e., self-reported total number of disciplinary infractions). Similar comparisons were made between inmates with visible tattoos (i.e., tattoos on the head, face neck, and hands) and inmates without visible tattoos as well as inmates with antisocial-themed tattoos and inmates without antisocial-themed tattoos.

Method

Participants

Participants in this study consisted of 274 adult male inmates and college students, with inmates comprising 208 of the participants and college students comprising 66 of the participants. The average age for the entire sample was 30.1 years ($SD = 11.3$), with a range from 18 to 71 years. Racial and ethnic identity was examined for the entire sample and yielded the following results: 36.2% ($n = 98$) were Caucasian; 30.3% ($n = 82$) were Hispanic/Latino; 23.2% ($n = 63$) were African American/Black; 5.5% ($n = 15$) were Biracial; 2.2% ($n = 6$) were American Indian/Native American; 1.5% ($n = 4$) were Asian/Asian American; and 1.1% ($n = 3$) identified themselves as "Other." Regarding relationship status, 60.5% ($n = 164$) were single; 12.9% ($n = 35$) were divorced; 11.4% ($n = 31$) were partnered (currently in a relationship); 10.3% ($n = 28$) were married; 2.2% ($n = 6$) were separated; 1.8% ($n = 5$) were common law married; and 0.7% ($n = 2$) were widowed. The average number of years of education for the entire sample was 11.7 years ($SD = 2.3$), with a range from 2 to 18 years of education. Examination of educational history indicated 43.2% ($n = 116$) earned a high school diploma; 29.4% ($n = 79$) of the sample earned a General Equivalency Diploma (GED); 17.5% ($n = 47$) had no diploma; 7.0% ($n = 19$) earned an associate's degree; 1.8% ($n = 5$) earned a bachelor's degree; and 0.7% ($n = 2$) earned a graduate degree.[2]

Inmates with prison tattoos included inmates who had tattoos with prison images (e.g., clock faces, gang symbols, prison bars) as per self-report (participants were asked if they had tattoos related to prison life and to explain how the image was related to prison life), or tattoos made in prison regardless of the content. Nonprison tattoos were defined as tattoos that individuals in the general public, that is, nonprison population, might acquire; examples include tattoos depicting national origin, love, and animals. The college student sample, which served as a comparison group, consisted of college students with tattoos. This sample included students of various academic levels (i.e., first year through senior year). This sample served as a baseline comparison group for the prison samples.

Materials

A demographic form was utilized in this study. This form requested participants to provide basic information, including age, race and ethnicity, relationship status, highest educational level attained, custody level, crimes committed on current incarceration, length of current prison sentence, time served on current prison sentence, and number of disciplinary infractions during their current incarceration.

A tattoo history questionnaire was developed and requested information about the participant's most significant tattoo and information about additional tattoos when applicable. More specifically, participants were asked about their tattoos, including total number of tattoos; age acquired; location on body (hand, arm, wrist, hip, leg, ankle, foot, chest, stomach, neck, back, shoulder, buttocks, genitals, face, head, eyebrow, eyelid, other); the image; if the image was related to prison life and if so, how; the size of the tattoo; setting where acquired; circumstances (alone or with others, sober or intoxicated, professional or nonprofessional); reasons for acquiring the tattoo; the significance of the tattoo; and the time frame during which the first tattoo was considered (whether to acquire a tattoo and what type of design) before acquiring it. Furthermore, participants were asked if they wanted any of their tattoos removed, and if so, why. They were asked to describe how they felt about their tattoos and if they planned to obtain more tattoos.

The PICTS (Walters, 1995, 2006) was designed to assess the cognitions that contribute to a criminal lifestyle. The PICTS is an 80-item, self-report instrument with a 4-point response scale (where 1 = *disagree*, 2 = *uncertain*, 3 = *agree*, and 4 = *strongly agree*) that assesses eight thinking styles: mollification, cutoff, entitlement, power orientation, sentimentality, superoptimism, cognitive indolence, and discontinuity (Walters, 1995, 2006). Internal consistency reliability coefficients for the PICTS scales ranged from moderate to high: .55 to .88 for male offenders (Walters, 2006), and with the mean interitem correlations ranged between .13 and .39 (Walters, 2006). Internal consistency was measured for this study, and the Cronbach's alpha coefficients ranged from .69 to .88. Test–retest stability was also sound as analyses indicated moderately high (ranging from .73 to .85) test–retest stability after 2 weeks (with the exception of the Df-r scale) and moderate (ranging from .47 to .77) test–retest stability after 12 weeks (Walters, 2006). In terms of validity, the PICTS scales were found to correlate modestly to moderately with other measures of criminality, such as the number of prior arrests, the number of prior commitments, the age at first arrest, the age at first commitment, the Hare Psychopathy Checklist–Revised, and the Lifestyle Criminality Screening Form (see Walters, 2006, for a review).

Recidivism risk was predicted by the SAQ (Loza, 2005). The SAQ is a 72-item, true/false, self-report questionnaire that assesses criminal tendencies, antisocial personality problems, conduct problems, criminal history, alcohol and drug abuse, antisocial associates, and anger (Loza, 2005; Loza, Conley, & Warren, 2004; Mills, Loza, & Kroner, 2003). Reliability was assessed by examining internal consistency and test–retest reliability. Acceptable internal consistency reliability was demonstrated with alphas ranging from .69 to .77 (Loza et al., 2004). Internal consistency was measured for this study, and the Cronbach's alpha coefficients ranged from .36 to .84. Strong test–retest reliability was demonstrated after 1 week with a reliability coefficient for the total scale of .95 (Loza, Dhaliwal, Kroner, & Loza-Fanous, 2000). Concurrent validity was examined, and offenders with high scores on the SAQ had a higher frequency of past criminal behavior and institutional infractions and a more violent history than those with low scores (Loza et al., 2004).

Procedure

The inmate sample was obtained from general population correctional facilities housing male inmates within the Texas Department of Criminal Justice (TDCJ). The college student sample was obtained from the General Psychology research participant pool of Texas Tech University. Only males were recruited for the student group to facilitate comparisons with the inmate groups. The response rate for inmates was 57%, and the rate for the college students was 100%.

Depending on warden preferences at each institution, either posted fliers requesting inmate volunteers or a priori random selection by TDCJ staff was utilized. Thus, recruitment did not include a random assignment procedure. Students were recruited from the General Psychology course (for which there is a research requirement) at Texas Tech University. Students met the same selection criteria as inmate participants (i.e., minimum of 18 years of age; ability to read and write in English), with the exception that they were not required to have been convicted of a felony and only students with tattoos were included in this study whereas inmates both with and without tattoos were included.

All participants were tested in a group format. Testing materials were organized using manila envelopes so that each envelope contained an informed consent form, a demographic form, a tattoo history questionnaire, the PICTS and PICTS answer sheet, and the SAQ. The envelopes were distributed to participants during the data collection sessions.

The principal investigator and research assistants used a structured script for all data collection sessions. A brief overview of the forms to be completed (the demographic form, the tattoo history questionnaire, the PICTS, and the SAQ) was provided. Instructions for the PICTS and the SAQ were reviewed. Participants were then asked to complete the forms and encouraged to ask questions that arose while completing the forms. On completion of all forms, participants returned the survey packets to investigators, were thanked for their time, and dismissed.

Prison records were examined to obtain inmates' index offense, number of times in prison, and institutional behavior (e.g., disciplinary infractions, security level). Records were obtained from the inmates' travel cards, which are temporary files maintained by the TDCJ. Staff members noted that in some instances travel cards were unavailable because a particular inmate was in transition, while being relocated from one institution to another. Also, staff noted that some travel cards lacked information about the inmates' criminal history and/or institutional behavior.

Data Preparation

Prior to conducting data analyses, data were first assessed for data entry errors. Double data entry was used to eliminate data entry errors. Data were then examined for erroneous data and corrections made. For example, responses where both *true* and *false* were endorsed were treated as missing data. Next, data were examined for missing data, resulting in the removal of 2 SAQ questionnaires (1 college student and 1 inmate) and 14 PICTS questionnaires (8 college students and 6 inmates) as a result of excessive missing data. Guidelines from the SAQ Technical Manual (Loza, 2005) specify that if there are more than three items missing from any one subscale, that subscale may be invalid. Furthermore, four or more missing items on the entire SAQ may negatively impact the affected subscales; however, the remainder of the questionnaire may be interpretable. Following these guidelines, 2 SAQ questionnaires were excluded completely (1 college student and 1 inmate) because of excessive missing data. Guidelines from the PICTS manual (Walters, 2006) specify that greater than five omitted responses on the entire questionnaire makes the questionnaire invalid because many of the subscales are composed of a limited number of items. Following this rule, eight college students and six inmate PICTS questionnaires were omitted from further analyses.

The final data preparation step included examining the PICTS and SAQ for validity according to the steps outlined by the assessment manuals. No data were changed or omitted from the SAQ. Using PICTS cutoffs of a *t* score of greater than 70 on the Confusion–revised scale (Cf-r) and a *t* score greater than 65 on the Defensiveness scale (Df-r), 37 PICTS profiles were omitted from further analyses. In scoring data for the PICTS, missing data were prorated, as suggested in the scoring manual (Walters, 2006).

To address research questions regarding differences between inmates with more or less skin surface covered, inmates were split into two groups based on how much skin surface was covered with tattoos. Inmates self-reported percentage of skin surface covered with tattoos, and a median split procedure was performed to develop approximately equivalent groups (less skin surface covered, $n = 62$; more skin surface covered, $n = 67$).

To address comparisons related to visible or nonvisible tattoos, inmates were collapsed into two groups based on their responses to questions about the visibility of their tattoos. Inmates who reported the presence of a tattoo on their hands, neck, head, or face were included in the visible tattoo group ($n = 83$). All other inmates were included in the nonvisible tattoo group ($n = 125$).

Lastly, to address comparisons about antisocial verses non-antisocial tattoo content, inmates were collapsed into two groups: antisocial ($n = 89$) and non-antisocial-themed tattoos ($n = 119$). Three trained research assistants examined all tattoos reported by all participants and independently rated each tattoo as antisocial or non-antisocial (as noted, antisocial-themed tattoos were defined as tattoo images or themes that conveyed hostile messages against individuals, groups within society, or society in general; depicted aggressive, vulgar, morbid, or demonic images; indicated dire circumstances [e.g., images related to addiction]; or depicted images or themes of violations of societal rules). A two-thirds majority agreement classification scheme was used, such that tattoos were classified as either antisocial or non-antisocial if two (or all three) research assistants rated a particular tattoo similarly. A minimum of one antisocial-themed tattoo was needed for inclusion in the antisocial tattoo group.

Results

Demographic Equivalence of the Groups

Statistical analyses were conducted on demographic variables to assess the equivalence of the three inmate groups. Given expected sample differences between the college student sample and the inmate sample in this study, the college student group was excluded from the between-groups comparisons for demographic equivalence. Inmate participants in the three tattoo groups (i.e., prison tattoos, nonprison tattoos, and no tattoos) differed with regard to age, racial and ethnic identity, years of education, highest degree obtained, and time served, but not for relationship status or length of prison sentence. Inmates with greater or lesser skin surface covered by tattoos were not statistically different with regard to age, racial and ethnic makeup, relationship status, highest degree earned, years of education, length of current prison sentence, and time served on current sentence. Inmates with visible or nonvisible tattoos differed with regard to age, racial and ethnic identity, years of education, length of prison sentence, highest degree obtained, and time served but not for relationship status. Finally, inmates with antisocial versus non-antisocial tattoos differed with regard to age, years of education, but not for length of prison sentence, time served on the current sentence, relationship status, racial and identity makeup, or highest educational degree earned.

After evaluating all sets of groups with all demographic variables of interest, six of the seven demographic variables were found to be statistically different between the various inmate groupings: age, race and ethnic identity, years of formal education, highest diploma acquired, length of prison sentence, and time served on current sentence. These six demographic variables were correlated with the 18 dependent variables consisting of 15 PICTS scales, the SAQ Total Scale, number of convictions, and total number of disciplinary infractions (see Table 1). Based on correlations of these variables with the dependent variables, as well as theoretical considerations, age and time served on current sentence were held as covariates for most of the data analyses, as indicated below.

Statistical Preparation

Normality was examined by visually scanning histograms for resemblance to a normal curve. Dependent variables were examined for the four groups (i.e., inmates with prison tattoos, inmates with nonprison tattoos, inmates with no tattoos, and college students with tattoos) as well as the three additional sets of groups (i.e., visible/nonvisible tattoos, greater/lesser skin surface covered, antisocial/non-antisocial groups). Generally, the distributions resembled a normal curve except in cases where the distributions were positively skewed; however, where skewness was observed, the skewness was interpreted as appropriate for the respective variables. For example, skewness for a PICTS subscale indicated that inmates had lower t scores on that particular subscale and were therefore less pathological on that particular measure of criminal thinking. In addition, skewness and kurtosis values were examined for the four groups on the dependent variables. Values were also scanned for extreme scores; extreme values were absent in the majority of cases. Some extreme values were noted for the nonprison tattoo group with regard to total number of convictions and for the no tattoo group with regard to the PICTS Mollification and Interpersonal Hostility subscales. These values were not deleted; however, these values were noted for consideration when interpreting the results of the analyses. The assumption of normality is expected to be of minimal concern given sample sizes are sufficient to protect against problems with normality (Tabachnick & Fidell, 2007).

In addition, data were analyzed for possible violations of t test, ANOVA, and multivariate analysis of variance (MANOVA) assumptions. First, data were assessed for any possible outliers by utilizing stem and leaf plots and comparing means to 5% trimmed means (Pallant, 2005). Stem and leaf plots provided a means by which to visually scan for potential outliers, which were generally minimal in number if present. The means and 5% trimmed means for dependent variables by the four main groups were scanned, and results generally indicated little difference between these mean scores (from a fraction to three or four points), which indicated that removing the most extreme 5% of scores (both low and high scores) would do little to impact the mean for that variable (Pallant, 2005). Thus, in these cases, removing outliers would do little to affect analyses (Pallant, 2005). However, one PICTS subscale, Interpersonal Hostility, had a modest difference between the mean and 5% trimmed mean for the three inmate groups (6 to 7 points difference), and therefore, this supplemental scale was interpreted with caution.

Table 1: Correlations between race, age, years of education, time served, length of sentence, and level of education and all dependent variables

Dependent variable	Race	Age	Years of education	Time served	Length of sentence	Level of education
Total convictions						
Pearson correlation	.024	.012	−.235**	.043	.002	−.235**
p (two-tailed)	.735	.871	.002	.556	.978	.002
Disciplinary infractions						
Pearson correlation	−.029	−.138	−.183	.210**	.082	−.094
p (two-tailed)	.696	.079	.121	.005	.279	.260
SAQ total						
Pearson correlation	.079	−.390**	−.291**	−.113	−.149*	.291**
p (two-tailed)	.267	.000	.000	.129	.044	.000
PICTS t scores						
Current						
Pearson correlation	−.090	−.193**	−.104	−.156*	−.073	−.104
p (two-tailed)	.204	.009	.183	.033	.323	.183
History						
Pearson correlation	−.061	−.328**	−.242**	−.082	−.050	−.242**
p (two-tailed)	.386	.000	.002	.266	.499	.002
Mollification						
Pearson correlation	−.016	−.309**	−.142	−.194**	−.221**	−.142
p (two-tailed)	.824	.000	.068	.008	.002	.068
Cutoff						
Pearson correlation	.003	−.217**	−.114	−.108	−.040	−.114
p (two-tailed)	.971	.003	.144	.143	.593	.144
Entitlement						
Pearson correlation	−.121	−.279**	−.125	−.122	−.149*	−.125
p (two-tailed)	.088	.000	.110	.098	.043	.110
Power orientation						
Pearson correlation	−.080	−.159*	.033	−.079	−.096	.033
p (two-tailed)	.257	.032	.678	.285	.195	.678
Sentimentality						
Pearson correlation	−.088	−.278**	−.101	−.168	−.150*	−.101
p (two-tailed)	.215	.000	.196	.022	.041	.196
Superoptimism						
Pearson correlation	−.071	−.394**	−.143	−.116	−.089	−.143
p (two-tailed)	.317	.000	.067	.114	.228	.067
Cognitive indolence						
Pearson correlation	−.142*	−.289**	−.103	−.085	−.011	−.103
p (two-tailed)	.044	.000	.190	.251	.881	.190
Discontinuity						
Pearson correlation	−.107	−.114	−.140	−.104	−.037	−.140
p (two-tailed)	.131	.123	.073	.159	.619	.073
Problem avoidance						
Pearson correlation	−.134	−.140	−.083	−.133	−.036	−.083
p (two-tailed)	.058	.058	.289	.070	.628	.289
Interpersonal hostility						
Pearson correlation	−.041	−.184*	−.073	−.121	−.113	−.073
p (two-tailed)	.564	.013	.352	.100	.125	.352
Self-assertion						
Pearson correlation	−.027	−.285**	−.204**	−.086	−.054	−.204**
p (two-tailed)	.700	.000	.009	.241	.468	.009
Denial of harm						
Pearson correlation	−.092	−.362**	.002	−.195**	−.183*	.002
p (two-tailed)	.194	.000	.977	.008	.013	.977
Fear of change						
Pearson correlation	−.029	−.122	.028	−.079	−.022	.028
p (two-tailed)	.682	.099	.724	.284	.771	.724

Note: SAQ = Self-Appraisal Questionnaire; PICTS = Psychological Inventory of Criminal Thinking Styles.
*p < .05. **p < .005.

In addition, Mahalanobis distance was calculated to check for multivariate outliers. When exploring the four main groups on the PICTS scales, only 5 of 259 cases were found to be in violation of this test. Because this is considered a small number of outliers given the sample size, these 5 cases were retained (Pallant, 2005).

Primary Analyses

Comparing prison tattoos vs. no prison tattoos. A multivariate analysis of covariance (MANCOVA; age as a covariate) procedure examined group differences between inmate participants with prison tattoos, nonprison tattoos, no tattoos, and the college student group on the Current and Historical Criminal Thinking Content Scales from the PICTS (see Table 2). Results indicated a significant omnibus between-group difference on the two content scales, $F(6, 464) = 11.02$, Wilks's $\Lambda = .766$, $p < .001$. Follow-up univariate analyses and pairwise comparisons indicated statistically significant differences for both the Current, $F(1, 3) = 5.07$, $p = .002$, and Historical, $F(1, 3) = 23.27$, $p < .001$, Criminal Thinking scales as college students scored significantly lower than the three inmate groups on both scales ($p < .05$). In addition, inmates with prison tattoos produced significantly higher scores than the other two inmate groups on the Historical Criminal Thinking Scale ($p < .001$) but not on the Current Criminal Thinking Scale ($p > .05$). There were no statistically significant differences between inmates with no tattoos and inmates with nonprison tattoos on either scale ($p > .05$).

A second MANCOVA procedure examined the four participant groups with respect to the eight criminal thinking scales (i.e., Mollification, Cutoff, Entitlement, Power Orientation, Sentimentality, Superoptimism, Cognitive Indolence, and Discontinuity). Results indicated a significant omnibus between-group difference on the eight criminal thinking scales, $F(24, 681) = 4.146$, Pillai's trace $= .382$, $p < .001$ (see Table 2). Follow-up univariate analyses, with a Bonferroni corrected alpha level of .006, indicated that college students scored significantly lower than the three inmate groups on the Sentimentality ($p < .001$) and Cognitive Indolence ($p < .001$) scales. College students also had significantly lower scores than the prison tattoo and nonprison tattoo inmate groups on the Mollification ($p < .001$), Cutoff ($p < .002$), Superoptimism ($p < .001$), and Discontinuity ($p < .001$) scales. College students had lower scores than inmates with prison tattoos on the Entitlement ($p < .001$) scale. Inmates with prison tattoos had statistically significantly higher scores than inmates with no tattoos and nonprison tattoos on the Superoptimism ($p < .002$) scale. Inmates with prison tattoos also had statistically significantly higher scores on the Mollification ($p < .002$) scale than inmates with no tattoos. There were no statistically significant differences between any groups on the Power Orientation ($p > .05$) scale. There were no significant

Table 2: Group comparisons of PICTS scales

	Prison tattoos n = 81		Nonprison tattoos n = 75		No tattoos n = 52		College students n = 66		MANCOVA Significance	Effect size
Scale	M	SD	M	SD	M	SD	M	SD	F	Partial η^2
Content									11.02*	0.125
CUR	55.137	10.154	52.895	10.253	51.695	10.295	49.545	7.590		
HIS	57.684	10.310	51.781	10.322	49.782	9.720	45.563	7.541		0.127
Thinking style									4.146*	
Mo	51.780	10.644	50.109	9.759	44.565	8.084	45.166	7.968		
Co	55.260	10.798	52.656	10.738	51.347	9.698	48.370	8.485		
En	54.150	9.955	51.375	12.860	47.434	8.274	49.444	8.710		
Po	56.643	11.988	53.093	10.974	51.413	9.597	54.000	9.895		
Sn	52.342	10.562	50.250	10.518	45.195	10.258	38.777	11.055		
So	57.438	11.150	52.265	11.474	47.695	8.129	48.222	7.735		
Ci	55.506	9.254	53.718	10.345	52.217	10.610	48.333	7.640		
Ds	56.054	10.110	53.406	9.943	52.130	11.198	47.000	8.128		
Factor									5.589*	0.108
PRB	54.986	9.513	53.359	9.641	52.847	10.807	49.963	7.403		
HOS	53.863	12.742	52.515	15.304	47.608	9.846	50.290	9.717		
AST	56.794	9.991	51.937	10.341	49.760	9.090	46.818	7.060		
DNH	51.835	9.816	50.406	10.290	45.065	7.992	41.727	8.759		
FOC	53.561	10.345	53.375	10.589	52.521	12.667	47.200	8.161		

Note: Separate MANCOVA procedures assessed differences between (1) prison tattoo inmate group, (2) nonprison tattoo inmate group, (3) no tattoos inmate group, and (4) college students with tattoos group. PICTS = Psychological Inventory of Criminal Thinking Styles; CUR = Current Criminal Thinking; HIS = Historical Criminal Thinking; Mo = Mollification; Co = Cutoff; En = Entitlement; Po = Power Orientation; Sn = Sentimentality; So = Superoptimism; Ci = Cognitive Indolence; Ds = Discontinuity; PRB = Problem Avoidance; HOS = Interpersonal Hostility; AST = Self-Assertion; DNH = Denial of Harm; FOC = Fear of Change; Content = Content Scales; Thinking Styles = Thinking Styles Scales; Factor = Factor Scales. Values are based on T scores.

*p < .006.

differences between the nonprison tattoo group and the no tattoo group on any of the scales ($p > .05$).

A third MANCOVA procedure examined the four participant groups with respect to the five Factor and Special Scales (i.e., Problem Avoidance, Interpersonal Hostility, Self-Assertion, Denial of Harm, and Fear of Change). Results indicated a significant omnibus between-group difference on the five content and special scales, $F(15, 693) = 5.589$, Pillai's trace = .324, $p < .001$ (see Table 2). Follow-up univariate analyses, with a Bonferroni corrected alpha level of .010, indicated college students had significantly lower scores than the prison tattoo and nonprison tattoo inmate groups on the Self-Assertion, Denial of Harm, and Fear of Change ($p < .003$) scales. College students had significantly lower scores than inmates with prison tattoos on the Problem Avoidance ($p = .001$) scale. Inmates with prison tattoos had significantly higher scores than the other two inmate groups on the Self-Assertion subscale ($p < .003$) and higher than inmates with no tattoos on the Denial of Harm subscales ($p = .009$). There were no significant differences between inmates with nonprison tattoos and inmates with no tattoos on any scales ($p > .05$). There were no statistically significant differences between any groups on the Interpersonal Hostility ($p > .05$) scale.

Results of the analysis of covariance (ANCOVA; age as the covariate) procedure examined the four participant groups with respect to the Self-Appraisal Questionnaire Total score (SAQ Total). There was a significant omnibus between-group difference on the SAQ Total, $F(3, 238) = 63.426$, $p < .001$. Pairwise comparisons indicated that college students had significantly lower scores on the SAQ Total Score than the three inmate groups ($p < .001$). Pairwise comparisons also indicated that inmates with prison tattoos had statistically significantly higher scores than the two inmate groups ($p < .001$). There were no significant differences between inmates with nonprison tattoos and inmates with no tattoos ($p = .132$).

Results of the ANOVA procedure examined the three main inmate groups and total self-reported number of convictions. There was no statistically significant omnibus between-group difference on the total number of convictions, $F(2, 25) = 1.194$, $p = .305$.

An ANCOVA (time served on current sentence as covariate) procedure examined the three inmate groups and total number of self-reported disciplinary infractions. There was a significant omnibus between-group difference on the total number of self-reported disciplinary infractions, $F(2, 582) = 5.492$, $p = .005$. Pairwise comparisons indicated that inmates with prison tattoos had significantly greater totals of self-reported disciplinary infractions ($M = 8.04$, $SD = 15.620$) than inmates with nonprison tattoos ($M = 2.16$, $SD = 2.631$) and inmates with no tattoos ($M = 3.38$, $SD = 5.613$, $p < .010$). There was no significant difference between the nonprison tattoo group and no tattoo group ($p = .973$).

Comparing inmates with greater and lesser skin surface covered with tattoos. Results of MANCOVA procedures (age as the covariate) that examined group differences between inmates with greater and lesser skin surface covered with respect to the PICTS indicated no significant omnibus between-group difference for the Current and Historical Criminal Thinking Content Scales, $F(2, 121) = 2.319$, Wilks's $\Lambda = .963$, $p = .103$; the eight criminal thinking scales, $F(8, 115) = 0.892$, Pillai's trace $= .058$, $p = .526$; or the five factor and special scales, $F(5, 118) = 0.489$, Wilks's $\Lambda = .980$, $p = .784$.

An independent-samples t test was performed to compare the SAQ Total scores for inmates with greater and lesser skin surface covered. Results indicated no statistically significant difference in scores for inmates with greater skin surface covered ($M = 33.26$, $SD = 10.66$) and inmates with lesser skin surfaced covered ($M = 30.06$, $SD = 11.30$) on the SAQ Total score, $t(124) = -1.635$, $p = .105$. Another independent-samples t test was performed to examine group differences for the total number of self-reported disciplinary infractions and also indicated no statistically significant difference in scores for inmates with greater skin surface covered ($M = 7.07$, $SD = 15.82$) and inmates with lesser skin surfaced covered ($M = 5.06$, $SD = 8.04$), $t(111) = -0.828$, $p = .409$.

Comparing inmates with visible and nonvisible tattoos. MANCOVA procedures (age as covariate) examined between-group differences for inmates with and without visible tattoos and revealed no statistically significant group differences for the Current and Historical Criminal Thinking Content Scales, $F(2, 179) = 2.173$, Wilks's $\Lambda = .976$, $p = .117$; the eight criminal thinking scales, $F(8, 173) = 1.795$, Wilks's $\Lambda = .923$, $p = .081$; or the five factor and special scales, $F(5, 176) = 1.385$, Wilks's $\Lambda = .962$, $p = .232$.

Independent-samples t tests were performed to compare the SAQ Total scores and self-reported disciplinary infractions for inmates with visible and nonvisible tattoos. There was a statistically significant difference on SAQ total scores as inmates with visible tattoos produced higher recidivism risk scores ($M = 33.16$, $SD = 10.58$) than inmates with no visible tattoos ($M = 25.45$, $SD = 10.95$), $t(197) = -4.940$, $p < .001$. There was also a statistically significant difference between inmates with visible and nonvisible tattoos with regard to disciplinary infractions with inmates possessing visible tattoos receiving more disciplinary infractions ($M = 7.21$, $SD = 15.14$) than inmates with no visible tattoos ($M = 3.11$, $SD = 4.90$), $t(176) = -2.275$, $p = .025$).

Comparing inmates with antisocial and non-antisocial tattoos. Results of MANCOVA procedure (age as covariate) indicated no statistically significant differences between inmates with antisocial and non-antisocial-themed tattoos on the Current and Historical Criminal Thinking Content Scales, $F(2, 179) = 1.926$ Wilks's $\Lambda = .979$, $p = .149$, or the five factor and special scales, $F(5, 176) = 1.478$, Pillai's trace $= .040$, $p = .199$, of the PICTS. However, results of a MANCOVA procedure that examined the two inmate groups with respect to the eight criminal thinking scales indicated a significant omnibus group difference on the eight criminal thinking scales, $F(8, 173) = 2.042$,

Pillai's trace = .086, p = .044. Follow-up univariate analyses, with a Bonferroni corrected alpha level of .006, indicated that inmates with antisocial-themed tattoos scored significantly higher than inmates with non-antisocial tattoos on the Mollification (p = .004) scale. There were no significant differences between groups on any other thinking styles scale ($p > .006$).

Independent-samples t tests were performed to compare the SAQ Total scores and disciplinary infractions for inmates with antisocial and non-antisocial-themed tattoos. Results indicated a statistically significant difference in recidivism risk scores with inmates who had antisocial-themed tattoos producing a higher SAQ Total score (M = 32.05, SD = 10.71) than inmates with non-antisocial-themed tattoos (M = 25.90, SD = 11.28), $t(197)$ = –3.902, $p < .001$. In addition, inmates with antisocial-themed tattoos self-reported a greater number of disciplinary infractions (M = 6.95, SD = 14.78) than inmates with non-antisocial-themed tattoos (M = 3.03, SD = 4.51), $t(95)$ = –2.333, p = .022.

Discussion

Results indicated that inmates with prison tattoos appeared to harbor a greater commitment to the criminal lifestyle with an irrational perception of entitlement, or sense of power, that the other inmates and college students did not demonstrate. In addition, inmates with prison tattoos tended to blame others for their involvement in criminal activity, and minimized and rationalized the harm inflicted on others as a result of their own criminal activities (Walters, 1990), compared to inmates without prison tattoos and college students with tattoos. Immaturity is inherent in these thinking styles as they both capture an inability to accept responsibility for one's actions.

Inmates with prison tattoos were at greatest risk for recidivism as compared to all other groups (i.e., inmates with nonprison tattoos, inmates with no tattoos, and college students with tattoos); however, there were no statistically significant differences between the inmates with prison tattoos and inmates with nonprison tattoos or inmates without tattoos with regard to the number of criminal convictions. This finding may appear contradictory, as those who are at higher risk for recidivism have a higher number of total convictions (Holland, Holt, & Beckett, 1982). However, on further examination, inmates with prison tattoos had the highest average number of convictions (mean of 6 convictions, range of 5 to 7), followed by the nonprison tattoo group (mean of 5 convictions, range of 4 to 6), and the no tattoo group had the lowest average number of convictions (mean of 4 convictions, range of 4 to 6). Thus, although power likely limited the ability to detect statistical significance, practically it appears that on average, inmates with prison tattoos are likely to enter prison with a greater number of convictions than their counterpart inmates without prison tattoos and inmates with no tattoos.

Walters (1990) indicated that career criminals are generally well behaved during periods of incarceration. Unexpectedly, it was found that inmates with prison tattoos were more likely to act out and receive a greater number of disciplinary infractions than inmates without prison tattoos and inmates with no tattoos. Although this finding appears to contradict Walters' (1990) theory, of these three inmate groups, inmates with prison tattoos are the group of inmates that should be of greatest concern to correctional staff in terms of management problems and therefore staff resources.

There were no statistically significant differences between inmates with greater skin surface covered and inmates with less skin surface covered with regard to criminal thinking, recidivism, and number of self-reported disciplinary infractions. The tattoo literature explores differences between individuals with tattoos in a variety of ways, including the amount of skin surface covered. Given today's "tattoo renaissance" (DeMello, 2000; Langellier, 2001; Sanders, 1989; Velliquette & Murray, 2002) and perhaps greater societal acceptance of tattooing behavior (see television programs Miami Ink or LA Ink as well as tattoo magazines for examples of media interest), it is reasonable to suggest that the amount of skin surface covered with tattoos may be of little importance. This has been explored in the tattoo literature (see Vail, 1999), and people who choose to acquire tattoo sleeves, back pieces, or body suits can be perceived as simply "collectors" and not as pathological. Results of this study produced similar conclusions as inmates with greater percentage of skin covered were not statistically significantly different (i.e., criminal thinking, risk for recidivism, disciplinary infractions) than inmates with less skin surface covered.

Although tattoos may be more acceptable in today's culture, there remains a stigma within even the tattoo community that hands, neck, and head are to be left undecorated (Steward, 1990). For professional appearances as well as the avoidance of stigma, there has been a long-standing belief that tattoos should be limited to areas that can be covered by clothing (Steward, 1990). Although no group differences emerged with regards to criminal thinking styles in this study, inmates with visible tattoos evidenced greater risk of recidivism and institutional behavior problems than inmates with non-visible tattoos. It seems reasonable to suggest that visible tattoos may create problems (e.g., difficulties finding gainful employment) for inmates when they are released back into society.

Regarding criminal thinking, inmates with antisocial-themed tattoos scored higher than inmates with non-antisocial-themed tattoos on only one subscale (Mollification) of the PICTS; however, inmates with antisocial-themed tattoos were at greater risk of recidivism and were more likely to present as institutional behavior problems for staff than inmates with non-antisocial-themed tattoos. The decision to acquire tattoos that have antisocial themes (e.g., hostile messages, aggressive, vulgar, morbid, or demonic images, or dire circumstances, or images or themes of societal rules violations) may be diagnostic.

Of the endless possibilities of tattoo images, these inmates chose images that communicate anger, hostility, and vulgarity. It was expected that inmates with antisocial-themed tattoos would have thinking styles aligned with a criminal lifestyle; however, these inmates only evidenced increased likelihood for blaming others for their criminal involvement. Perhaps this tendency to blame others is connected to antisocial-themed tattoos in particular.

Results of this study have implications for psychologists in the criminal justice system, particularly when it comes to assessment or mental health/ institutional screenings. Taking note of inmates who have prison tattoos, visible tattoos, or antisocial-themed tattoos may help correctional staff identify inmates who may be more likely to present as behavioral problems. Planning could also occur during the initial screening assessment, as well as repeat assessments, to scan for newly acquired tattoos. These screenings could influence placements within institutions, that is, housing assignments. These inmates could also be targeted as inmates to direct toward any rehabilitation programming geared toward reducing recidivism and increasing chances of successful life changes following their incarceration (e.g., career and educational programs, family programs, counseling services). Additional planning efforts could include advising staff to be mindful and alert when working with similarly tattooed inmates, as well as the development of appropriate correctional management strategies to reduce institutional problems.

In addition, results of this study may be useful for those wishing to create a formal measure of tattooing behavior or in updating future versions of current instruments that include items related to tattooing, such as the Lifestyle Criminality Screening Form (Walters, White, & Denney, 1991). This instrument assesses for visible tattoos and body surface covered with tattoos. Given the results of the present study, assessing antisocial content and the presence of prison tattoos specifically may prove valuable.

A symbolic mechanism indicating changed beliefs and behaviors is to consider removal of prison, antisocial-themed, or visible tattoos. Tattoo removal programs are available outside prison (Bazan, Harris, & Lorentzen, 2002); however, tattoo removal programs within correctional settings may prove beneficial as well. Some inmates expressed regret regarding some of their tattoos in their responses. They, of course, would be excellent candidates for such programs and may find that the removal of such tattoos could result in a smoother and more positive transition into society.

On the other hand, institutional management of prison tattooing may also prove beneficial, particularly with reducing or eliminating prison and antisocially themed or visible tattoos. Such a program has been enacted in Canadian prisons (Krauss, 2005). Although results of this program remain to be determined, such programs offer promise. Tattooing programs also have the potential to reduce the acquisition of problematic tattoos that negatively affect inmates' positive opportunities upon release. An opportunity to acquire tattoos in a prison tattoo parlor could also be used as positive reinforcement of good behavior. In addition, institutional management of tattooing could greatly reduce disease transmission, a common problem in correctional facilities (Godin, Gagnon, Alary, Noel, & Morisette, 2001; Krebs, 2002; Rotily, Weilandt, & Bird, 2001).

Limitations of the study included being unable to obtain historical information (e.g., criminal history, disciplinary history) for each inmate, which affected the research questions that sought to explore the possible connections between tattooing and institutional behavior. Also, cautious interpretation of the ability to predict recidivism via tattoos is warranted given the results of the SAQ, a measure that purely captures recidivism sans items related to tattoos, were linked to tattoos themselves. There were also difficulties in accessing sick calls or any information related to health concerns because of the Health Insurance Portability and Accountability Act regulations. Although inmate self-report of criminal behavior, including institutional behavior, is reliable (Kroner, Mills, & Morgan, 2007) questions related to institutional behavior remain tentative. Because variables in this study, including tattoos and information assessed by the PICTS and SAQ, were based on self-report, it is possible that shared method variance may have contributed to the significant positive correlations that were detected. Another limitation was the lack of power necessary to properly analyze racial and ethnic differences.

Future research could examine tattooing behavior and its possible correlations with criminal thinking, recidivism, and institutional behavior in other regions of the United States and among different racial and cultural groups. In addition, future research may continue to explore the issue of gang, prison, and antisocial-themed tattoo removal. Removal of gang tattoos is a statement about leaving gang life (Bazan, Harris, & Lorentzen, 2002). Could the removal of prison tattoos similarly signify leaving a criminal lifestyle? More importantly, could tattoo removal lead to a change in criminal behavior and subsequently becoming a productive member of society? Some participants in this study indicated a desire to remove some of their tattoos as they harbored regret about some of their tattoo choices. Should a robust finding to these questions emerge, tattoo removal programs may be a meaningful way for inmates to make a lifestyle change.

Notes

1. The authors are appreciative of reviewers' feedback, which resulted in an improved manuscript. Of note, one reviewer was particularly concerned about the appropriateness of including a college student sample as a comparison group with an inmate sample. We appreciate the conceptual issues of comparing inmates, the majority of whom are antisocial and have likely had rather different life experiences than college students, the majority of whom are unlikely to have antisocial traits and who are unlikely to relate to a life of crime or prison life from firsthand experiences. In addition, the authors appreciate the limitations of using recidivism measures with a college student group,

the majority of whom had never been jailed or imprisoned. Nevertheless, we elected to retain this comparison group as a point of comparison and as a referent group representing individuals with a tattooing lifestyle that is noncriminal in nature.

2. The demographic breakdown of participants in the various groups (i.e., inmates with prison tattoos [$n = 81$], inmates with nonprison tattoos [$n = 75$], inmates with no tattoos [$n = 52$], college students with tattoos [$n = 61$]), inmates with greater skin surface covered with tattoos [$n = 67$], inmates with lesser skin surface covered with tattoos [$n = 62$], inmates with visible tattoos [$n = 83$], inmates with nonvisible tattoos [$n = 125$], inmates with antisocial tattoos [$n = 89$], and inmates with non-antisocial tattoos [$n = 121$]) is available on request.

References

Anderson, R. R. (1992). Tattooing should be regulated. *New England Journal of Medicine, 32,* 207.

Armstrong, M. L. (1991). Career-oriented women with tattoos. *Image – The Journal of Nursing Scholarship, 23,* 215–220.

Armstrong, M. L., Owen, D. D., Roberts, A. E., & Koch, J. R. (2002a). College students and tattoos: The influence of image, identity, family, and friends. *Journal of Psychosocial Nursing and Mental Health Services, 40,* 20–29.

Armstrong, M. L., Owen, D. D., Roberts, A. E., & Koch, J. R. (2002b). College tattoos: More than skin deep. *Dermatology Nursing, 14,* 317–323.

Baden, M., & Roach, M. (2001). *Dead reckoning: The new science of catching killers.* New York, NY: Simon & Schuster.

Bazan, L. E., Harris, L., & Lorentzen, L. A. (2002). Migrant gangs, religion, and tattoo removal. *Peace Review, 14,* 379–383.

Birmingham, L., Mason, D., & Grubin, D. (1996). The psychiatric implications of visible tattoos in an adult male prison population. *Journal of Forensic Psychiatry, 10,* 687–695.

Braithwaite, R., Robillar, A., Woodring, T., Stephens, T., & Arriola, K. J. (2001). Tattooing and body piercing among adolescent detainees: Relationship to alcohol and other drug use. *Journal of Substance Abuse, 13,* 5–16.

Buentello, S. (1992). Combating gangs in Texas. *Corrections Today, 54,* 58–60.

Butler, J. R., Trice, J., & Calhoun, K. (1963). Diagnostic significance of the tattoo in psychotic homicide. *Journal of Social Therapy, 14,* 110–113.

DeMello, M. (1993). The convict body: Tattooing among male American prisoners. *Anthropology Today, 9*(6), 10–13.

DeMello, M. (2000). *A cultural history of the modern tattoo community.* Durham, NC: Duke University Press.

Drews, D. R., Allison, C. K., & Probst, J. R. (2000). Behavioral and self-concept differences in tattooed and nontattooed college students. *Psychological Reports, 86,* 475–481.

Etter, G. W. (1999). Skinheads: Manifestations of the warrior culture of the new urban tribes. *Journal of Gang Research, 6*(3), 9–21.

Frederick, C. M., & Bradley, K. A. (2000). A different kind of normal? Psychological and motivational characteristics of young adult tattooers and body piercers. *North American Journal of Psychology, 2,* 380–393.

Godin, G., Gagnon, H., Alary, M., Noel, L., & Morisette, M. R. (2001). Correctional officers' intention of accepting or refusing to make HIV preventive tools accessible to inmates. *AIDS Education and Prevention, 13,* 462–473.

Harry, B. (1987). Tattoos, body experiences, and body image boundary among violent male offenders. *Bulletin of the American Academy of Psychiatry & the Law, 15,* 171–178.

Holland, T. R., Holt, N., & Beckett, G. E. (1982). Prediction of violent versus nonviolent recidivism from prior violent and nonviolent criminality. *Journal of Abnormal Psychology, 91*, 178–182.

Jankowski, M. (2004, September). Paños – Art behind bars. *Skin & Ink*, 30–33.

Koch, J. R., Roberts, A. E., Cannon, J. H., Armstrong, M. L., & Owen, D. C. (2005). College students, tattooing, and the health belief model: Extending social psychological perspectives on youth culture and deviance. *Sociological Spectrum, 25*, 79–102.

Krauss, C. (2005). A prison makes the illicit and dangerous legal and safe. *The New York Times*. Retrieved from http://www.nytimes.com/2005/11/24/international/americas/24bath.html

Krebs, C. P. (2002). High-risk HIV transmission behavior in prison and the prison subculture. *The Prison Journal, 82*, 19–49.

Kroner, D. G., Mills, J. F., & Morgan, R. D. (2007). Underreporting of crime-related content and the prediction of criminal recidivism among violent offenders. *Psychological Services, 4*, 85–95.

Langellier, K. M. (2001). "You're marked": Breast cancer, tattoo, and the narrative performance of identity. In J. Brockmeier & D. Carbaugh (Eds.), *Narrative and identity: Studies in autobiography, self and culture* (pp. 145–184). Amsterdam, Netherlands: John Benjamins.

Laumann, A. E., & Derick, A. J. (2006). Tattoos and body piercings in the United States: A national data set. *American Academy of Dermatology, 55*, 413–421.

Levy, J., Swell, M., & Goldstein, N. (1979). A short history of tattooing. *Journal of Dermatological Surgery and Oncology, 5*, 851–856.

Loza, W. (2005). *Self-Appraisal Questionnaire*. North Towanda, NY: MHS.

Loza, W., Conley, M., & Warren, B. (2004). Concurrent cross validation of the Self-Appraisal Questionnaire: A tool for assessing violent and nonviolent recidivism and institutional adjustment on a sample of North Carolina offenders. *International Journal of Offender Therapy and Comparative Criminology, 48*, 85–95.

Loza, W., Dhaliwal, G., Kroner, D. G., & Loza-Fanous, A. (2000). Reliability, construct, and concurrent validities of the Self-Appraisal Questionnaire: A tool for assessing violent and nonviolent recidivism. *Criminal Justice and Behavior, 27*, 356–374.

Manuel, L., & Retzlaff, P. D. (2002). Psychopathology and tattooing among prisoners. *International Journal of Offender Therapy and Comparative Criminology, 46*, 522–531.

Mills, J. F., Loza, W., & Kroner, D. G. (2003). Predictive validity despite social desirability: Evidence for the robustness of self-report among offenders. *Criminal Behaviour and Mental Health, 13*, 140–150.

Newman G. (1982). The implications of tattooing in prisoners. *Journal of Clinical Psychiatry, 43*, 231–234.

Palermo, G. B. (2004). Tattooing and tattooed criminals. *Journal of Forensic Psychology Practice, 4*, 1–25.

Pallant, J. (2005). *SPSS survival manual: A step by step guide to data analysis using SPSS for Windows* (Version 12). New York, NY: Open University Press.

Phelan, M. P., & Hunt, S. A. (1998). Prison gang members' tattoos as identity work: The visual communication of moral careers. *Symbolic Interaction, 21*, 277–298.

Post, R. S. (1968). The relationship of tattoos to personality disorders. *Journal of Criminal Law, Criminology & Police Science, 59*, 516–524.

Raspa R. F., & Cusack, J. (1990). Psychiatric implications of tattoos. *American Family Physician, 41*, 1481–1486.

Rotily, M., Weilandt, C., & Bird, S. M. (2001). Surveillance of HIV infection and related risk behaviour in European prisons: A multicentre pilot study. *European Journal of Public Health, 11*, 243–250.

Sanders, C. R. (1989). *Customizing the body: The art and culture of tattooing*. Philadelphia, PA: Temple University Press.

Steward, S. M. (1990). *Bad boys and tough tattoos: A social history of the tattoo with gangs, sailors, and street-corner punks 1950–1965*. New York, NY: Haworth.

Tabachnick, B. G., & Fidell, L. S. (2007). *Using multivariate statistics* (5th ed.). Boston, MA: Allyn & Bacon.

Taylor, A. J. W. (1970). Tattooing among male and female offenders of different ages in different types of institutions. *Genetic Psychology Monographs, 81*, 81–119.

Vail, D. A. (1999). Tattoos are like potato chips . . . you can't have just one: The process of becoming a collector. *Deviant Behavior: An Interdisciplinary Journal, 20*, 253–273.

Velliquette, A. M., & Murray, J. B. (2002). The new tattoo subculture. In S. J. Ferguson (Ed.), *Mapping the social landscape: Readings in sociology* (pp. 68–80). Mountain View, CA: Mayfield.

Walters, G. D. (1990). *The criminal lifestyle*. Newbury Park, CA: Sage.

Walters, G. D. (1995). The Psychological Inventory of Criminal Thinking Styles: Part I. Reliability and preliminary validity. *Criminal Justice and Behavior, 22*, 307–325.

Walters, G. D. (2006). *The Psychological Inventory of Criminal Thinking Styles (PICTS) professional manual*. Allentown, PA: Center for Lifestyle Studies.

Walters, G. D., White, T. W., & Denney, D. (1991). The lifestyle criminality screening form: Preliminary data. *Criminal Justice and Behavior, 18*, 406–418.

70

Something to Show for It:
The Place of Mementoes in
Women's Oral Histories of Work

Christine Wall

Introduction

This article was partly inspired by a visit to the home of a retired railway signalman, where signs of his former occupation adorned every room of his house, and the contrast between this and the homes of retired women teachers and bank workers which contained no obvious clues to their former occupations or workplaces. It emerged that this was not because these women had not saved any mementoes from work but because they had packed them away, out of sight in attics and cupboards, placing them, according to Anton Bachelard, in the realm of dreams and the past, rather than part of the present functioning environment of the house (Bachelard 1994). The visits made to these retired peoples' homes were part of the fieldwork of a three-year ESRC funded project on work and identity.[1] This article focuses on two women who participated in the study, a retired bank worker and a retired teacher and investigates what was kept, the ways in which work memorabilia is displayed or stored, and how this might illuminate social relations in the workplace and work identities.

Sociological studies in this area, focusing on workplaces and the social identities derived from these, rarely touch on the material culture of work. There are some exceptions, for example the role of artifacts and mementoes in the workplace has been touched on in the area of organization studies and

Source: *Management & Organizational History*, 5(3–4) (2010): 378–394.

work identity in Elsbach's study of the effects of hot-desking. She found that artifacts that were personally selected and prominently displayed on desks and workstations were important to an employee's core sense of self and their absence threatened workplace identities (Elsbach 2003). Susan Halford, in her research on the spatiality of workplaces and the effects on individuals and teams, has referred to Baldrey's suggestion that the personalization of work-spaces with photographs and artifacts is a form of individual resistance to the imposed restrictions of organizational space (Halford 2004). Lyn Pettinger has recently used material culture theory in her study of retail workers and the way they engage with, and arrange settings for, objects prior to their consump-tion, arguing against a simplistic definition of retail work as purely service work (Pettinger 2006). But there appears to be a lack of material written on work identities in relation to workplace artifacts and in the context of domestic, social space.

Workplace memorabilia, regarded here as artifacts and mementoes kept from workplaces and stored in homes included; tools of a trade, ephemeral leaflets and pamphlets, union mementoes, uniforms and badges, long service awards, gifts from colleagues, and photographs both formal and informal. Understanding these objects in relation to their place in the lives and homes of their owners and also in the context of the process of recording an oral history was helped by using insights gained from the disciplines of material culture studies, anthropology, and oral history. Material culture recognizes that the material existence of objects, their weight, texture, size, colour, and their mode of production whether handcrafted or mass-produced, articulate information about the social practices implicit in their production. Thus, it is possible to understand the role of objects as forming a bridge between mental and physical worlds (Miller 1987, 99) and as also having agency in that they stimulate social effects and social action (Gell 1998). This study considers the role of artefacts, not so much as cultural objects, but as an integral part of the telling of an individual life history.

Valuable observations into the mechanisms of the narration of identity in relation to objects are found in Janet Hoskins ethnographic study of the Kodi people of Eastern Indonesia. She found that 'more important, intimate and "personal" accounts of peoples' lives' were obtained when she asked them about objects (Hoskins 1998, 2). The stories told about domestic objects were a vehicle for selfhood and a reflection of the owners' life, told in a manner Hoskins terms 'a distanced form of introspection'. The society described in her study is extreme in the way in which objects are invested with great significance for representing both the collective past and for storing individ-ual biographical memory but has been useful to this research in relation to methodology and interpretation. Her definition of a biographical object as a personally meaningful possession as opposed to a public commodity, gift or heirloom echoes the work mementoes in our study. The objects saved from work examined in this article did not confer identity or status through the means of their attainment or consumption, they were not farewell gifts from colleagues or long service awards from employers but personally chosen and kept mementoes. As such they were also distinct from reminiscence objects used in eliciting life stories, which are usually manufactured commodities, often museum pieces, typical of a particular historical period. Hoskins work focused on objects that were hoarded and kept and how they facilitated a narrative of the self through the vehicle of the object, a method with strong similarities to the work undertaken here. In the context of an oral history interview Joanna Bornat points out that, 'identifying the dialogic and interrogative nature of oral history helps to remind us that participation involves agency and decision-making and that the interview is essentially an interactive process involving two parties, each with their own agendas and purposes' (Bornat 2001, 230). In this case the object introduced into the dialogic process of the interview became, in some sense, a third party in that it stimulated certain emotional responses and memories. It was however, under the control of the participant who chose when and how to present their memento into the ongoing interaction between interviewer and storyteller.

The personal testimonies recounted here are composed of memories of former working lives. As Maurice Halbwachs argued, the articulation of memory is also a dialogic process constituted through dialogues with members of social groups, for example family or occupational cultures (Halbwachs 1992). James Fentress and Chris Wickham's *Social Memory* follows on from Halbwachs in stating that 'one remembers one's childhood as part of a family, one's neighbourhood as part of a local community, one's working life as part of a factory or office community and/or a political party or trade union . . . and these memories are essentially group memories' (Fentress and Wickham 1992, ix). Further they contend that the act of remembering is articulated in the form of a narrative which in itself is shaped by the conventions and styles of a culture that are in the end social and historical, and this too defines the act of memory as collective. However, they are also alert to the problem of individual memory in relation to the social world and warn that a conception of memory prioritizing the collective past might 'render the individual a sort of automaton, passively obeying the internalised collective will' (Fentress and Wickham 1992, ix). The tensions between personal and public remembering, and its cultural, social and psychoanalytic interpretations have been investigated in great detail by numerous commentators.[2] For example the oral historian Alessandro Portelli's work on memory recognizes it not as a mere 'depository of facts', but as an 'active process in the creation of meanings' (Portelli 1998, 52). Thus people do not simply recall in some spontaneous fashion the contents of a life lived but are shaping and composing remembrance, reviewing it, constructing it in the light of subsequent experience, which involves relationships of all kinds. In the research project, which is partly described here, our interpretation of the testimonies we recorded relied heavily on the work of Raymond Williams, in particular because of his concepts of lived experience and structures of feeling, whether dominant, emergent or residual (Kirk and Wall 2008). Williams' recognition of the importance of individual lived experience, albeit constrained, limited and shaped by dominant, hegemonic ways of seeing, provides a space for individual dissent and struggle with formal and systematic beliefs (Williams 1977, 132). Anna Green has recently written an essential and succinct critique of the theories relating to memory arguing strongly for recognition of individuals' ability to engage constructively with competing ideas and beliefs (Green 2004). The oral histories of the two women recounted here demonstrate that their lived experience of the workplace lay at the centre of the stories they composed to illustrate their positions, as women and as workers, in relation to the changing organizational practices of their employers.

Methodology

The research underpinning this article dates from a recent ESRC funded study, part of the Identities Program, in which 109 work-life histories were collected from retired and employed bank workers, teachers and rail workers. The research was designed to cover three cohorts of workers: the first cohort, comprising people who had started work in the 1950s or 1960s, were retired workers, a second cohort were current, mid-career workers, and the third were relatively recent starters. Research participants were contacted through approaching the appropriate trade unions or via personal contacts. In total 109 interviews with 36 bank workers, 32 rail workers and 41 teachers were recorded.

Although initially the research approach had been to use 'semi-structured interviews' the researchers engaged on the empirical work, both trained in the techniques of oral history, decided against any questionnaire-based methodology and instead set about the interviews using a prepared list of prompts designed to elicit a work-life history.

Interviews have long been used in sociological research investigating organizational change and quotes and sometimes quite lengthy extracts from transcripts are frequently used to support the arguments of the researchers. Rosemary Crompton used the work history of 'Noreen' who entered banking in 1951 to illustrate the gendered institutional processes within banks resulting in distinct career routes for male and female entrants (Crompton, 1989). Shorter quotes from a number of interviewees where work-life histories were taken were used by Halford and Savage in their research on restructuring in banking and local government in the early 1990s (Halford and Savage 1995). However, our intent was to move away from conventional sociological methodologies and instead use two main approaches: oral history accounts combined with analysis of the importance of work memorabilia. This was in order to position the work-life histories gathered in the foreground of the research rather than as evidence for any particular theoretical argument or cultural script. Above all, and to paraphrase Joanna Bornat (2004) we wanted to present people's working lives in their own words so as to maintain their authority as eyewitnesses to occupational and organizational change over their life course and the unique perspectives made possible through the personal testimonies of those who have had time to reflect on the past. We asked participants in advance whether they wanted to bring or show anything that held some significance for them in relation to work and, where permitted, these items were photographed. At the end of the interview arrangements were made for the transcripts to be returned for comments but very few people took up this offer: both of the women interviewed here declined.

Interpreting the transcripts and photographs was of necessity multi-disciplinary and methods derived from oral history, visual culture, material culture and narrative analysis were used. Much of the memorabilia was visual, in particular photographs, both formal and informal, of former workplaces and colleagues. In some respects the method here was a variant on photo-elicitation interviewing (PEI) pioneered by Douglas Harper in the 1980s. Harper's approach was typically based on a small number of case studies enabling him to build up relationships with the participants over a period of time and use either researcher-generated images or archive photographs in the interviews (Harper 1987, 19). PEI has also been used successfully where photographs have been made by the participants themselves, and later discussed in the interview (Clark-Ibanez 2004, Mizen 2005). Our approach, in consideration of a large sample and with time for only one interview session with each participant was to ask people in advance whether they had any memorabilia of work such as photographs, certificates, farewell gifts or souvenirs, to bring to the interview. We let the point at which these memorabilia are introduced to the interview arise from the work history being told and at the instigation of the participant, usually towards the end, and where there was informed consent we photographed the participant with their possessions. In some cases photographs had been carefully placed in albums and so the telling of a work history was accompanied by the story told by the photo album (Kuhn and McAllister 2006). The power of visual imagery in producing and maintaining occupational and corporate identities has been analysed elsewhere but evidence for this was also found in the personal collections of the interviewees (Wall 2008, Heller, 2008). Interestingly, and unexpectedly, as it had not been written in to the research methodology from the outset, we found that some people retained an extensive range of artefacts from their working lives – from documents and photographs to large and small physical objects that were retrieved, legally or otherwise, and either stored or displayed in the home. However, of the many people who contributed the stories of their working lives to the project there were only a small number, 20 in all and only 7 women, where artefacts, usually photographs, were integral to the interview.

In retrospect, using oral history, objects and photography together, as a method, was unpredictable – sometimes taking photographs and recording didn't coincide, sometimes the photographs we took were of such poor quality they were unusable, sometimes issues of anonymity meant that the photographs could only be used as part of the field-notes, and at other times the introduction of a camera into an intense telling of a story seemed like too much of an intrusion. However, in a few cases it was extremely successful and part of its success lay in the fact that the interviewee gained control of the interview process, noticeably gaining in confidence in the telling of her history while handling the objects she had saved from work. Most importantly, our awareness of the dialogic nature of the interview led us to understand that these stories were, in many cases, only rough outlines of the deep complexities underlying working lives that were almost always precariously balanced between exploitation and fulfilment.

Memories of Work: Testimonies of a Former Bank Worker and a Former Teacher

For the women interviewed here, retirement entailed packing up and putting away work memorabilia out of sight. In relation to Hoskins' work on the agency of biographical objects it would seem that these women interviewed actively 'put away' their work identities on a return to home-based life. These items were then deliberately unpacked in the presence of the researcher as part of the telling of their work histories. Asking women to tell us of their working lives gave them the opportunity to talk primarily about the role of waged work, and its meaning, in their lives. Interpreting these testimonies gave rise to the finding that the majority of women we spoke to, unprompted and at varying points in the interview introduced the subject of work in relation to current or past family responsibilities despite the question itself not being asked. In the following examples both retired women described themselves as putting their families first and choosing work that fitted around their domestic responsibilities but their testimonies revealed the ways in which work intruded into their entire lives so that this imagined boundary between the two spheres of work and home was never impermeable.

Pam, Retired Bank Cashier Aged 67

Pam invited me to her home for the interview and had got ready some folders containing papers she had saved from when she had been in work that she had neatly stacked on the kitchen table. These she had retrieved from the attic ready for my visit. She gave a fluent and detailed account of her working life from the age of 16 when she left school in 1958, despite protesting when

I first approached her on the phone that she did not think she had anything to contribute to the research.

> So, we can start at the beginning then . . . My first job.

Pam had travelled up from Essex to the City for her interview in 1959:

> And it was daunting, because it was a huge, marble building, huge doors, and a man on the door to show you even where the lift was, and to take you up to your interview room. Loads of staff around; very formal.

She continued by describing those first years in the bank; starting in the machine room, and after three or four years progressing to the ledgers. These were handwritten with debits, credits and interest on accounts all calculated in her head without getting down off the high chair at the ledger desk and going to use the bank's one and only 'adding machine'. Later, as a counter cashier she described using a brass shovel to scoop up the coin, her own set of scales at the side of the till and wooden pots in which the coins were stacked. She remembered the French polished mahogany bank counter and contrasted this with the rough wooden chair at the ledger desk where she had to be careful as she got down in case she laddered her stockings. She described having to dress smartly and being scrutinized by the chief clerk from his desk surrounded by glass and positioned:

> Behind the counter, in a very prominent place, so that he could see all the office, in one view . . . He could see the backs of the cashiers, but the faces of the customers . . .

This first part of Pam's working life ended when she got married at the age of 23 and stayed out of the labour market for 16 years while she brought up her children. But her connection with the social world of the bank continued because she had married a bank manager and this involved attendance at a constant round of dinners for bank customers as well as civic duties such as charity work. She was also part of a large social group of bank employees who met for parties and theatre visits and this included children's parties so that the social world of the bank spilled over into all aspects of her family life. She returned to work as she put it 'by the back door' getting a job as a cashier in a local agency bank where, 'they didn't interview me or see me, or anything. They knew me anyway from social events . . .'.

She found that everything had changed. Even the money had changed because by then it was decimal currency, however she remained in work for another 15 years as a cashier because she 'didn't want to go any further'. She went on to say:

> No, I didn't want to go up any higher. One bank manager in our family was enough, really, I thought. And then we started to have to sell; products and insurance, and all sorts of other things, and then it became a chore.

Here Pam pinpoints the wider change in banking practice from 'telling to selling' and the point in her own working life when her job became 'a chore'. Pam was able to date this to the early 1990s, a time with a high turnover of staff, especially managers, the introduction of targets and the start of keeping records on clients – ostensibly for a database but also used as a means of targeting clients for specific products. This was also the time when computers were being introduced, but Pam and her colleagues, all older women, were denied training in the new technology by their young, male manager. Pam's understanding of her work role was based on the idea of banking as a public service where the customer was 'the most important person'. She described the younger workers as being able to meet the new roles expected of them because they had never known anything different.

> Because they don't know any different they can do it. And they can probably be trained to do it quicker and easier than we were. We always used to say, well you're either a saleswoman or you're not. And they would say, well you could be trained, you can learn. But I don't think you can when you get over 50. [Laughs]. I don't really think you want to. If you don't want to be a saleswoman, you won't be. If you'd wanted to be one, you would have been one when you were younger. And I think the youngsters that do come in now know that it's going to be a sales-orientated job.

But Pam's explanation also reveals a particular stance towards her job, an ethical stance. Using 'we' in the second line she aligns herself as part of a particular generation and gender, in opposition to the 'they' of the organization that wants to retrain her group in alignment with a changed set of company objectives. In her shift from first to second person narrative, a device often used in literary fiction, she repositions herself as narrator of her own personal story to a viewpoint where she can generalize from her individual experience to include a wider social group, including the listener, who acted in full knowledge and with agency in their choice of occupation. She, and other women like her, are still the same people that went into the job in the 1960s – it is the job that has changed.

At the end of this first part of her account of work Pam turned to the folders on the kitchen table next to her. She produced a photograph taken in the mid-1960s when she had been seconded as a trainer of new entrants to the bank, a post she held for few years (see Figure 1).

It was mounted in a white embossed folder with a printed signature at the bottom, the mark of a professional photographer and clearly belongs to the genre of class portraits where teachers are positioned in the middle surrounded by their pupils. It is also a corporately produced image, likely to have been published in a company magazine to demonstrate the bank's in-house training, and dates to a time of great tension between banking trades unions and staff associations. Pam gazed at this photograph without any comment. She is seated centrally surrounded by the young trainees and I prompted a response

Figure 1: Pam, seated centre, surrounded by new entrants to the bank c. mid-1960s

by admiring her suit. She told me her aunt, who was a 'tailoress', had made it: and that was all she had to say. I, in turn, was fascinated by the carefully composed postures of those young women seated in the front row, with their hands clasped in their laps and their knees carefully positioned, representing a wider set of social conditions that constrained and controlled what was appropriate in young women's behaviour in the 1960s. It is also a portrait of young people who have positively chosen the respectable occupation of banking, not part of the 'counter culture' of the 1960s so often used as a shorthand in cultural and historical accounts of that decade. Next she showed me some postcards, that had belonged to her husband, of the bank's training centre based in a large country house (see Figure 2). She commented:

> I went to an open day at [H], and saw some of the rooms, and the bathroom, which was attached to one of the rooms, which had one of the trainee managers, maybe, using it; the bathroom was as big as this room. [*swings arm out to refer to the size of her kitchen.*]

These residential courses were created for future male managers and had the dual function of training in bank procedures and also in the social skills necessary for the civic functions and dinners expected of managerial staff. But Pam, entering the bank in the 1950s when there were segregated career

Figure 2: Post-card of residential training centre

routes for men and women, had only experienced these training centres as a visitor on a guided tour. Throughout her account of her working life however, she seemed acutely conscious of how her spatial surroundings supported the organizational structure of the bank, mentioning the intimidating architecture of Head Office, the highly polished mahogany counter compared with the rough wood of her ledger stool and the careful positioning of the chief clerk's desk to enable surveillance of both cashiers and their clients. It was at this point that Pam turned to a large folder and said:

> I've got some assessments. This is when I started being fed up of the bank. I'd done the same job for 15 years and now they're starting to query what I'm doing.

She took out a stack of papers, which turned out to be her appraisal forms dating back to the 1990s. As she held these pieces of paper she gave an account of what had finally precipitated her into leaving and the way in which she did it.

> And this [appraisal form] would have been the last, probably towards the end, probably the last one I did. And this was at the point when the whole of the bank was being turned over, and everybody within the bank was having to be interviewed for their job. All the jobs were being re-invented, if you like, and we were all having to be re-interviewed for the job we wanted to do. i.e. the job we were doing. And at that point I decided I'd been sitting in the same chair for 15 years, and I really wasn't going to be

interviewed by somebody my son's age. And I, that's it, I'm away. So I then, this chappie was standing in for the actual manager at the time, a female manager who was on maternity leave, and he, I said to him, I'm not going to be interviewed for my job. You had to actually apply for your job. You had to do it on a computer, which we didn't know how to do, and you had to be interviewed just the same. So I said, I am not doing that. I am leaving. And he said to me, well if you're going to leave Pam, could you perhaps wait until after October, when we get a little bit straight and we get a few more staff in? And I said, no, I'm going. Bye-bye [laughing].

By saving these appraisal forms, 'And there was a lot of anguish went into these things' as Pam told me, the objects of so much pain and humiliation, perhaps she had regained some control over her past and over the cause of her resignation. The act of holding them in her hands prompted the story of how and why she left the bank, a story composed as a type of victory tale in which she managed to leave work on her own terms and with her dignity intact. These were important documents for her as was her first letter of acceptance by the bank telling her what her salary was going to be. When I asked if I could take her photograph she wanted to be seen holding this letter, an object of great personal significance but one that did not seem to transcend generations for, as Pam told me, her daughter couldn't understand why she still had it (see Figure 3).

Pam later sent me the photos of her last day at work. The content revealed much about that last job and her leaving story; the high-tech architecture of

Figure 3: Pam seated at her kitchen table holding her letter of acceptance for her first post at the bank dated 1959

the bank, the tools and apparatus behind the counter, the care with which her colleagues had decorated her position at the counter on her last day with balloons and banners, the farewell cards placed beside her work station, and the grin of the young male manager. Her final, and perhaps only, act of defiance was to leave on her own terms. After Pam's official retirement she went back to work as she put it; 'on the odd occasion to help them out, when they were desperate . . . I could just do a week, and then wave goodbye again'.

Brenda, Retired Teacher Aged 67

Brenda had also prepared for her interview by getting out of storage a box containing items she had kept from her working life as a teacher. She had referred to this in a phone conversation as 'evidence' of her life spent as a teacher otherwise, she said, 'there'd be nothing to show for it'. The major part of Brenda's working life had been teaching in, and eventually running, a pioneering unit for children who were unable to cope with mainstream school. Her commitment to these pupils was absolute, despite increasingly difficult conditions imposed by lack of funding, and re-organization within the education authority that employed her. The period of time covered by her working life also saw major government controlled changes in educational practice and policies. The child-centred philosophies of the 1970s and professional identities of teachers were compromised with the introduction of the National Curriculum and the use of inspections in the name of accountability. The continual battles with the education authority to ensure funding and the frequent changes of premises weighed heavily on Brenda and she 'jacked it in' and left teaching feeling bitter and cynical at the age of 58 but she returned to work for a different authority for a few years until she was 60. These final years were happy and fulfilling:

> . . . I went and worked for another authority for the last two, well, no, not, for, I think, three or four years, but up until I was 60. I left it when I was 58 and I went to work for [B] in their home tuition service . . . and so there were children there that were youngsters, adolescents, who were suicidal, who'd been in hospital, who had broken something, who had been excluded, whatever reason, who were out of school and I went to work there. And I have to say that the last two years, the last three years, rekindled my joy of teaching whereas I had become really quite crabby and disillusioned.

Many years in the profession had made her aware of cyclical fashions in pedagogy and how many of her practices and successes were unrecorded. As she put it:

> . . . they'll come up with a bright idea and then somebody will say, oh, that's a good idea and, you know, you hear these things. Well, we were doing that

20 years ago. Well, where is the evidence that you've looked at what we did and you've pulled out the good things that we did and you discarded the things that didn't work? There's never any evidence. It just goes like that and nobody ever seems to learn any lessons.

She told me that she sometimes wished she had trained as an architect because she liked planning, buildings and design, and also because as an architect she would have had tangible objects to look back on in retirement. Instead she said:

But what does a teacher have? A teacher has memories, a teacher . . . I mean, obviously I know what a teacher has: a teacher's got the new next generation but . . . I'm not saying it's not there . . . it's just that you don't see it unless they come back and say, 'Hi, miss'.

Throughout the telling of her story Brenda referred frequently to the spatial settings and architecture of the places that she was expected to teach in with a clear recognition of the importance of spatial design on children's behaviour. For example she mentioned the importance of entrance and reception areas, good visibility and space for non-teaching rooms. Perhaps most important, in terms of material culture, was her description of how to create a good learning environment.

And it was only by, by creating a very sort of, um, nurturing, um, primary school set-up in a sense that you could get these kids because the classroom was full of their paintings and articles and very much like a primary school classroom would be because that's the only room we ever had. So we made it a nice room. Um, because this is what these kids needed . . . they needed this space where they felt, ah, totally secure, safe, understood and, relaxed and then when you starting untying all those knots, then they'd learn. They won't learn otherwise.

This explanation of providing a suitable place for learning suggests that Pat's classroom was an extension of an ideal domestic setting and also places her in a relationship characterised by emotional commitment and caring, in effect, *in loco parentis* to the children in her charge. The personal care taken in welcoming often very frightened children into the classroom was extended to the design and arrangement of furniture and decorations: an engagement on her part with the materiality of the schoolroom in order to mediate the experiences of those children who associated school with fear and panic.

After over an hour of talking, and towards the end of the interview B started to take out folders of photographs from the box, carefully mounted into albums or individually framed (see Figure 4). As Brenda started to unpack her box of memorabilia she told me how important photography had been while working with these children, how she always had photographs of staff

Figure 4: 'Something to show for it': The mementoes of a working life spent teaching

and current pupils on the wall so that newcomers could immediately see who everyone was and also for some children who had never possessed any photographs of themselves. Although I was told I could not take photos of the children she had taught, as it 'wouldn't be fair' and she was still, decades later, very protective of them. However, I was allowed to photograph B while she remembered and narrated each individual child's story.

She then retold aspects of her story again through the agency of her memorabilia; giving the relationships she had described earlier material reality in the carefully packed mementoes and photographs she took out of the box. In a series of mounted and annotated albums she showed me an alternative family history that ran parallel to her own: mealtimes, Christmas parties, holiday outings, family groups – all belonging to the children she had taught. The interview carried on for another hour with some repetition as photographs reminded Brenda of different stages in her working life but also in some instances with greater emotion and more information. Particularly so when she found a photograph of the manager who had failed to support her fight to keep the unit open in the face of reorganization: 'that's her – she was the one!'. During the interview it emerged that Brenda had brought up her own two children while she was running the special unit, and how that had limited her energy for any activities other than work, except for being a member of a local choir, mainly because the work itself and the relationships with her pupils, took up so much of her energy.

> You couldn't help but do all sorts of other things for these kids. You weren't just teachers. I mean, I, [sighs], got kids out of prison and kept kids out of prison and that sort of thing. . . .

But she was also closely involved with the parents and families of the children she taught from whom she received, 'a lot of gratitude and respect'.

Conclusions

The stories told by the two women as they unpacked their mementoes revealed the intensity of their emotional involvement with their workplaces, both positive and negative. As Brenda unpacked the box of things kept from work she remembered the name, background and personality of every child who had passed through her unit. The stories she told me of their lives were a demonstration of not just her memory but the strength and depth of her feelings for her pupils and that particular part of her working life. In Pam's case the photographs of the social world of the bank elicited a distanced introspection and telling of her work history until the moment when she held the appraisal forms in her hand. There was then a change in her bearing and manner as she embarked with emotional intensity on a very different type of story, one of personal anguish and pain at the erosion of her self-esteem in an organization that had mistreated her. This former pain was transformed through the telling of a story that ended in a victory for Pam and the maintaining of her own personal dignity and work identity in relation to opposing organizational values.

Both women through the telling of their work-life histories achieved a sense of composure in relating final episodes of contentment after periods of persistent problems at work. For Pam this was achieved by returning post-retirement, to work on her own terms and for Brenda through working at a school where her pedagogical outlook was reaffirmed. In both cases the retrieval of memorabilia and the handling of these objects had released intense emotions about a past working life of which there was no longer any trace in their immediate surroundings.

Both women stated early on in their interviews that their work, after marriage, had to 'fit around' their domestic responsibilities implying a separation of the home as a core and the workplace as periphery. However, as they continued with their stories it became obvious that this had not been the case for either of them. In fact, both recounted the interconnectedness of work, family and community life: neither of these women experienced work and home as separate spheres. Fundamental to each account was the memory of 'lived experience' in the way in which both started work as young women with a particular set of ethical dispositions. These were held dear throughout their working lives resulting in them both having dissenting roles in relation to organizational change and, using Raymond Williams' formulation of 'structure of feeling', a residual position. Terry Eagleton has referred to a residual structure of feeling as an 'active element in the present' and that 'residual forms of culture stand in opposition or as alternatives to a dominant culture and formation which will not accommodate its values or needs' (Eagleton 2000, 123).[3] Both women lived through profound changes to working life as the dominant and hegemonic organizational cultures shifted during the 1980s and 1990s resulting in their residual 'structure of feeling', grounded in a particular way of approaching work, becoming functionally oppositional. However, Eagleton's formulations allow for the residual to become emergent, as part of a future that challenges the dominant culture of the present, a resolution that, on an individual level, was achieved by both women.

The methodology used here, where material culture and oral histories are combined as a base from which to analyse past workplace identities, workplaces and their connection to present selves, has the potential to add to existing sociological investigations to include the nexus of social relationships, both historical and current, that coalesce around certain objects. These artifacts, made and brought home, gifted and kept, or taken, breach the secrecy of the workplace and the privacy of the home, making permeable the boundaries between these two distinct social spaces frequently described in opposition to each other and as having distinctly dual characteristics. The homes of both women were full of evidence of their familial relationships, with grandchildren's photographs and drawings given prominent positions in kitchens and living rooms but, while reminders of their own former working lives had disappeared from the domestic environment, they had not been completely discarded but preserved in a few carefully chosen mementoes. Daniel Miller has suggested that the home is now, the single most important site for material culture studies (Miller 2001). The incorporation of this approach into women's histories of work and workplaces would appear to have the potential for making explicit the complex relationships women have with work over their life course and, where possible, making public the personal mementoes and narratives of working life.

Notes

1. Does Work Still Shape Social Identity and Action? ESRC RES-148-25-0038.
2. There is a very large literature on the interpretation of oral histories, the best starting point being the collection of essays edited by Robert Perks and Alistair Thomson, *The Oral History Reader*. The tensions between individual and collective memory and the social role of public remembrance are investigated in two further key works edited by

Katherine Hodgkin and Susannah Radstone in the Routledge Studies in Memory and Narrative series, *Contested Pasts: The Politics of Memory* and *Regimes of Memory.*
3. Thanks to John Kirk for pointing me to this and see also, Chapter 2 in John Kirk's *The British Working Class in the Twentieth Century.*

References

Bachelard, A. 1994. *The poetics of space.* Boston, MA: Beacon Press.

Bornat, J. 2001. Reminiscence and oral history: parallel universe or shared endeavour. *Aging and Society* 21(2): 219–241.

Bornat, J. 2004. Oral history. In *Qualitative Research Practice,* ed. C. Seal, G. Gobo, J.F. Gubrium, and D. Silverman. London: SAGE.

Clark-Ibanez, M. 2004. Framing the social world with photo-elicitation interviews. *American Behavorial Scientist* 47(12): 1507–1527.

Crompton, R. 1989. Women in banking: Continuity and change since the Second World War. *Work, Employment & Society* 3(2): 141–156.

Eagleton, T. 2000. *The idea of culture.* Oxford: Blackwell.

Elsbach, K. 2003. Relating physical environment to self-categorizations: Identity threat and affirmation in a non-territorial office space. *Administrative Science Quarterly* 48: 622–654.

Fentress, J., and C. Wickham. 1992. *Social memory.* Oxford: Blackwell.

Gell, A. 1998. *Art and agency: An anthropological theory.* Oxford: Oxford Univesrity Press.

Green, A. 2004. Individual remembering and 'collective memory': Theoretical presuppositions and contemporary debates. *Oral History* 32(3): 35–44.

Halbwachs, M. 1992. *On collective memory,* ed. and trans. L.A. Coser. Chicago, IL: University of Chicago Press.

Halford, S., and M. Savage. 1995, Restructuring organisations, changing people: gender and restructuring in banking and local government. *Work, Employment and Society* 9(1): 97–122.

Halford, S. 2004. Towards a sociology of organizational space. *Sociological Research Online* 9(1).

Harper, D. 1987. *Working knowledge: Skill and community in a small shop.* Chicago, IL: The University of Chicago Press.

Heller, M. 2008. Company Magazines 1880–1940: an overview, *Management and Organizational History* 3(3–4): 179–195.

Hodgkin, K., and S. Radstone, eds. 2003. *Contested pasts: The politics of memory.* London: Routledge.

Hoskins, J. 1998. *Biographical objects: How things tell the stories of people's lives.* London: Routledge.

Kirk, J. 2003. *The British working class in the twentieth century.* Cardiff: University of Wales Press.

Kirk, J. 2008. Coming to the end of the line?: Identity, work and structures of feeling. *Oral History* 36(2): 44–53.

Kirk J., and C. Wall. 2009. Resilience and loss in work identities: A narrative analysis of some retired teachers' work-life histories. *British Educational Research Journal* 19(4): 311–322.

Kuhn, A., and K.E. McAllister. 2006. *Locating memory.* New York: Berghahn Books.

Miller, D. 1987. *Material culture and mass consumption.* Oxford: Blackwell.

Miller, D., ed. 2001. *Home possessions: Material culture behind closed doors.* Oxford: Berg.

Mizen, P. 2005. A little 'light work'?: Children's images of their labour. *Visual Studies* 20(2): 124–139.

Perks, R., and A. Thomson, eds. 2006. *The oral history reader, second edition.* London: Routledge.

Pettinger, L. 2006. On the materiality of service work. *Sociological Review* 54(1) 48–65.

Portelli, A. 1998. Oral history as genre. In *Narrative and genre,* ed. M. Chamberlain and P. Thompson. London: Routledge.

Radstone, S., and K. Hodgkin, eds. 2003. *Regimes of memory.* London: Routledge.

Wall, C. 2008. Picturing an occupational identity: Images of teachers in careers and trade union publications 1940–2000. *History of Education* 37(2): 317–340.

Williams, R. 1977. *Marxism and literature.* Oxford: Oxford University Press.

71

'Goods, Chattels and Sundry Items': Constructing 19th-Century Anglo-Indian Domestic Life

Swati Chattopadhyay

Historians maintain that in the hypermasculine world of British colonial India, the Victorian ideal of separate spheres for men and women found an exaggerated expression in the separation of bungalow and camp/court (Metcalf, 1995; Macmillan, 1988). As a marginal figure, who often disturbed both the masculine image and the occupation of running an empire, the appropriate role of British women was limited to gracing the household, creating a semblance of 'home'. Such a reading of British domestic life in India also assumes that the domestic ideology used in Britain to shape a distinction between public and private spheres was not only applicable in the colonial context, but was even more distinctly articulated. At the same time, scholars recognize the importance of the trope of 'empire' that was applied to household management by the colonizers. The inherent contradiction between the notion of separate spheres and the application of a model of public administration to the household has not been adequately addressed. Examining novels and housekeeping guides written by English women, Rosemary Marangoly George has made the important argument that the English home in the colonies allowed British women a 'legitimate public domesticity' through which they could cultivate a modern authoritative self (George, 1993–4). While she accurately notes that such a space of authority was not available to British women in England, she does not interrogate the colonial mastery of the texts, presuming

Source: *Journal of Material Culture*, 7(3) (2002): 243–271.

that '[a]s with the Empire, the territory of the home is already secured for the English occupant' (1993–4: 108). In a provocative sentence, however, she observes that, '[c]olonial occupation allowed for the continued evolution of this domestic female subject even as it seemed to disrupt the ideological and material requirements of domesticity' (1993–4: 99).

In this article I wish to explore the conditions of this disruption in the realm of domestic life in colonial India. I argue that the voice of authority that George excavates from these texts was underwritten by a deep anxiety of loss and lack of control, and that an inquiry into material culture and everyday domestic life in the colonies help us unravel the mastery of the colonial text. It is precisely because the home in India was not 'secure', that authors of house-keeping guides attempted to shore up this insecurity by asserting a new set of values about material culture.

The gendered distinction between public and private domains in terms of bungalow and camp/court locates the spatial question at the center of colonial life. My argument proceeds on the assumption that any discussion of domesticity necessitates analysis of domestic space, and the manner in which the boundaries between public and private were articulated through architecture and social use of space. By examining architectural representations, 19th-century descriptions of Anglo-Indian life in Calcutta, housekeeping guides written by British women, and probate inventories of British residents of Calcutta, I suggest that the significance of a model of domestic life formulated on a fundamentally different premise from that of practices in England – on an overlap of public and private spheres – may be revealed in approaching the problem of domesticity in terms of its *spatial* dynamics.

It is useful to remember here that the notions of bourgeois public and private spheres that were applicable in England (see Davidoff and Hall, 1987) did not apply in India. Although the British attempted to institute some form of civil life in India, they did so without giving Indians citizenship. The only legitimate public consisted of the men (and women) who formed the ruling class.[1] Anglo-Indian civil society, however, was not based on a strict separation from the colonial state. Rather than bracketing status and professional affiliation as was expected in the *ideal* bourgeois public sphere in western Europe (Habermas, 1989), one's social status, measured in terms of location in the hierarchy of colonial service, was the most dominant premise for structuring social relations in the public sphere. What constituted public life, from the British point of view, was necessarily centered around the colonial administration and encompassed a small group of men and women, self-styled Anglo-Indians, who tried to shelter themselves from the activities of Indian town life.

The first principle of the Anglo-Indian home was to keep native India at bay. However, the Indian architecture of the houses, the native artifacts in the household, not to mention the multitude of servants that one was 'compelled to keep', made this impossible. The alternative was to negotiate such differences in the household by assigning objects, people, and tasks a specific place in a rationalized system. The principles of 'similarity' and 'difference' discussed by Thomas Metcalf in *Ideologies of the Raj* (1995), found a specific utility for negotiating foreign cultural norms within the household. The effort to distance oneself from native life allowed British women to overwrite the nurturing model of domesticity with a model of public life directly drawn from the pages of colonial bureaucracy. The insistent tropes of 'camp', 'march', 'parade', 'empire' used in describing home life, literally, militated against the nurturing, domestic role of women. Even the values of 'duty' and 'rationality' espoused by Victorian domestic reformers and laboriously articulated in English house-keeping books took on a different meaning in the colonial context. After all, only in the colonies could British women be reminded that planting a garden was not merely a matter of feminine accomplishment and pleasure, but a 'duty' of empire. Housekeeping guides written by women claimed a new subjectivity for English women devoted to the cause of empire. Instead of 'chattels' and 'helpmeets' they were to become caretakers of needy English men, and in so doing the guides suggested jettisoning certain aspects of English material culture. However, this model of housekeeping and imagination of subjectivity, because it was constructed for and by those who formed the upper echelons of the civil and military service, would not include those Anglo-Indian households and families who resided beyond the privileged pales. The new vision of colonial domesticity formulated in the last decades of the 19th century and most clearly articulated in the work of Flora Annie Steel and Grace Gardiner, was based on a re-imagination of gendered identities in both England and India. Such revision promoted prevalent notions of class and race to its advantage, and asked that English women rethink accepted material culture practices.

Anglo-Indian Household Norms

Elizabeth Tilyard lived at 22 Wellesley 2nd Lane with her husband James Tilyard. The 1857 Calcutta Street Directory indicates that she was a midwife, and her husband a pensioner and pew opener at the Mission Church. When Elizabeth died in 1859 her household was probated.[2] Her husband had passed away in the meanwhile, perhaps shortly before her death – the probate indicates a new mourning dress. In the four-page probate list we get a glimpse of her domestic life. The only property she owned was the small house they lived in. After her death it was rented out at the small sum of 25 rupees by her heirs.

Elizabeth's house, a part of a neighborhood of narrow, irregular lots, inhabited by Indians as well as Anglo-Indians, was modest in comparison to the larger houses in the city. It did not have a spacious garden for her to prac-tice principles of English gardening. Unlike her social superiors, she employed only three servants – a cook, a sweeper, and a *bheestee* (water carrier) who supplied water to the household. It is unlikely that Elizabeth had a flourishing business as a midwife; her name was not included under the heading of 'Surgeons and Midwifes' in the List of Trades and Professions. Also, it is unlikely that she and her husband expected to retire back to England; they could not afford the cost.

Elizabeth's household articles were almost all plain. In contrast with the inventories of John Graham and Robert Dunlop, two of her elite contemporaries, no adjectives such as 'extremely handsome', or 'brilliant' were deemed appropriate in describing her possessions. None of the pictures in her house were oil paintings, consisting rather of a collection of 'colored engravings' and 'polygraphic prints'. No piano or books were listed in her inventory, and most of the light sources in the house were oil lamps. Also, there were more 'native' artifacts than in those of her affluent Anglo-Indian contemporaries in the city. Although she did not have any fancy dinner services – just a lot of queensware and an assortment of long dishes and curry plates – she had a well equipped kitchen that bore evidence of attempts to cook British food and serve it in a 'proper' manner. With her few servants she probably had more privacy than affluent Anglo-Indians who insisted on the pageantry of servants. While Elizabeth could not escape from the 'native' elements in the way of her social superiors, in her own manner she cultivated a British identity and aspired to conduct a respectable household. It is this latter aspiration that would not have met the approval of elite women.

The notion of 'eliteness' in colonial India, and specifically in the context of Calcutta, deserves some clarification. British elite society consisted of those employed in the middling to higher ranks of the civil and military service. Wealthy planters and merchants sometimes gained admittance to this favored circle simply because of their wealth. For example, in late 18th-century and early 19th-century Calcutta, a few British merchants were wealthy enough to entertain at a scale that rivaled the Governor General's hospitality. Even then, the social elite of the services, many of whom had to stay in boarding houses for the purposes of economy, considered themselves positionally superior. Such rules of precedence were rigidly followed at formal dinners and dances, leaving no doubt in anyone's mind of the standings in society. During the first half of the 19th century, all of these men and women, nevertheless, shared a common understanding of the social significance of household artifacts. Only in the heyday of imperialism would housekeeping guides begin to impart a new understanding of material culture, emphasizing the intangible quality of material relations over the tangible dimension of material artifacts.

Visiting Calcutta in the mid-19th century, Colesworthy Grant was struck by the remarkable similarity among house plans (Grant, 1862). In fact, a three-bay pattern for residences was the most consistent plan throughout the 19th century (Chattopadhyay, 2000) (Figure 1).[3] The carriage port on the north, the hall in the center, a verandah on the south, consisted of the central bay, and the other bays accommodated a symmetrical arrangement of rooms, with bathrooms and store rooms at the corners. The largest houses in the town

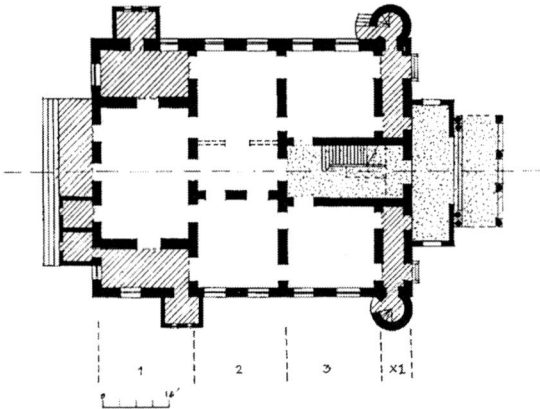

House on 3 Camac St.

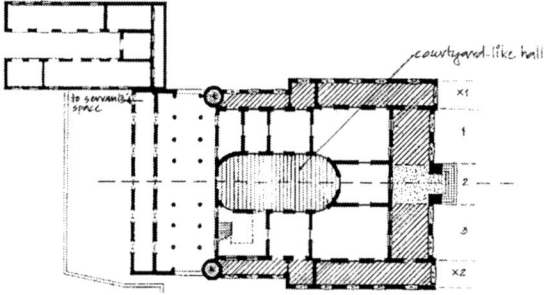

House on 1/1 Little Russell St.

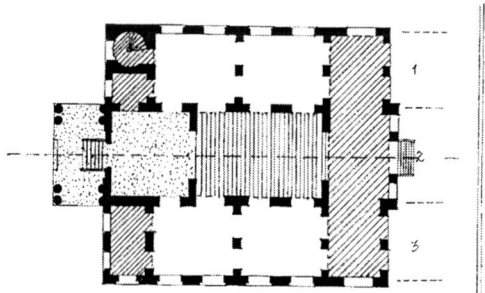

House on 23/24 Waterloo St.

Service spaces including bathrooms and servants' spaces

Main central space

Main entry

Source: Drawing by author.

Figure 1: Three examples of house plans in the 'white town' of nineteenth-century Calcutta

were located in spacious gardens after a suburban pattern. But much of what was loosely designated as 'white town' in Calcutta had small houses that abutted the street and stood cheek by jowl to commercial establishments. In small lots, where the three-bay plan could not be accommodated, only two bays were used. Even in this fraction of the standard plan the adherence to the 'pattern' was rendered visible. The details of house plans varied from one region to another, but most bungalows in up-country towns and cantonments were designed on a simple rectangular grid. Minnie Blane and her husband Captain Archie Wood's bungalow at the small station of Jhelum, in the 1850s, demonstrates such a variation in plan (Figure 2).

The key difference between the Anglo-Indian houses in Calcutta and their English counterparts was the multiple doorways between rooms that allowed for plenty of cross-ventilation, even if they sacrificed privacy. The lack of privacy compared with contemporary standards in England was a perennial source of displeasure among newcomers from England. The plans of the houses, modeled after Indian town houses rather than anything to be found in 19th-century England, refused to grant their residents a private interiority – the space of the 'intimate sphere' (Chattopadhyay, 2000). Also, the rooms, 14 feet to 20 feet high, were significantly loftier than English residences. Grant noted that in the typical Anglo-Indian house the hall opened onto four rooms which answered the purpose of 'parlour, dining, drawing and sitting rooms – titles, not generally, the first never heard in these latitudes' (Grant, 1862: 8).

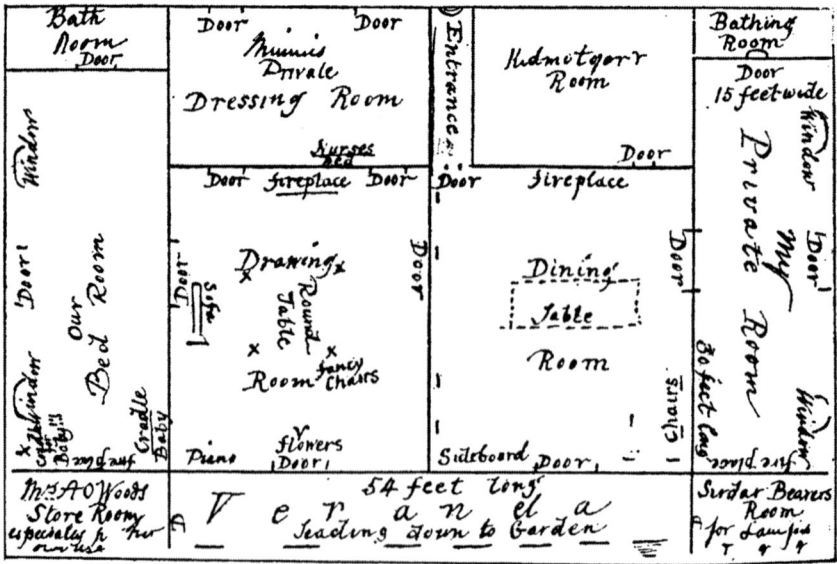

Source: Jane Vansittart (ed.) *From Minne, with Love, the Letter of a Victorian Lady (Maria Lydia Blane Wood) 1849–1861* (London: Peter Davies, 1974).

Figure 2: Plan of bungalow at Jhelum, Punjab, showing furniture arrangement

Source: Colesworthy Grant, *Anglo-Indian Domestic Sketch* (Calcutta: Thacker and Spink, 1862).

Figure 3: The 'Hall', in a Calcutta residence

If we are to take Grant's illustrations as reliable evidence, the hall would contain an assortment of armchairs, small tables, card table, piano, some pictures on the walls, a good number of wall lamps and shades, and a couple of table lamps (Figure 3). A mat on the floor and a fringed *punkah* (fan) complete the ensemble. Indeed the terms 'parlour' and 'sitting rooms' are absent from probates, but the room-by-room inventories clearly designate dining rooms, drawing rooms, bedrooms, *bottlekhanas*, bathrooms, writing room, and dressing room. The functions of writing room and dressing room were sometimes combined, or to put it another way, a room designated in a probate either as writing room or dressing room was used as a private chamber. The *bottlekhana*, an invention of Anglo-Indian culture, was a storage room, the function of which translated as 'pantry' in the English sense. As I explain later, the *bottlekhana* had special significance in the Anglo-Indian household.

Grant's typical residence was clearly an elite establishment, and the picture of material life conveyed in his description is closely replicated in the probates of three men who could afford material comforts. Three inventories – John Graham's (1859),[4] Robert Dunlop's (1859),[5] and Richard Clarke Bell's (1875)[6] – all convey the sense of polite households and uphold the accuracy of Grant's depiction, except that the type of furniture that adorns Grant's hall shows up in the 'drawing room' of these inventories. This is not surprising, because in 'lower-roomed houses' (that is, single-story houses), the hall was used as the drawing room. Only in very large houses could one afford to have a separate drawing room as well as a hall, and only in upper-roomed houses could the hall on the upper floor be used as a separate breakfast room. The hall's public location justified its use as a drawing room.

The commodious central hall(s) of these houses, in fact, posed a problem for the inhabitants. One had to buy a large assortment of furnishing at one shot to fill this space. For European residents in the service of the East India Company (or, later in the service of the British crown), most of whom were in the city for a short period of time, this was a predicament. Furnishing Indian houses after the English manner proved difficult due to the high cost of European furniture in India. When Belvedere House, one of the grandest houses in the presidency, was bought by the East India Company in 1854 with the intention of turning it into the Lieutenant Governor's residence, Lord Dalhousie, the Governor General, noted in a memo that the financial burden of the very large society in Calcutta would be lessened if the Lieutenant Governor did not have to pay rent and if he was provided with a furnished house (Buckland, 1901). The large household spaces in colonial Calcutta, with their exaggerated capacity to accommodate objects and furnishing, clearly demanded that prevailing policies as well as British material culture practices be reconsidered.

Anglo-Indian housekeeping guides recommended that an economic solution was to send all curtains, linen, and tableware from England and only buy the heavy furniture at the place of residence, typically, used articles sold by a predecessor. *The Englishwoman in India* suggested taking along a couple of fold up what-nots, and a pair of brackets (A Lady Resident, 1865: 22). The author of *Indian Outfits and Establishments* writing a couple of decades later suggested that furnishing all the rooms might have to wait. On arrival at her husband's station in an up-country town, she spent about Rs. 600 (60 English pounds) for the first round of necessary furniture purchase (An Anglo-Indian, 1882: 61–3). This cost would obviously be higher in large cities such as Calcutta.

Single men, unless holding a very high appointment, chose to stay in boarding houses or clubs to curb expenses. By the mid-19th century a large number of residences in Calcutta had been converted into boarding houses for these men and also for those with families. For those who had greater permanence in the city and could afford the cost, these large spaces became an opportunity to display wealth. In a rigidly hierarchical society where marked distinctions were made between those in the services and those considered outsiders – barristers, merchants, planters, and those associated with the railways, between civilian and military service, not to mention between Europeans, natives, and those of mixed Indian and European parentage (derogatorily referred to as the 'half-castes') – everyone knew each other's place. Consequently they did not balk at buying the whole lot of one's predecessor's furniture – the *toon* wood dining table that had 'seen the inside of most houses' in a town (An Anglo-Indian, 1882: 61). Standard furniture was to be expected in a house of a person belonging to a particular social station. Only the wealthy merchants and those in the highest civilian and military positions could have the luxury of elaborate and expensive furnishing to fill their equally elaborate houses. In such a context choice and arrangement of furniture became less a mark of individuality than a sign of Englishness, even when comprised largely of 'native' products.

John Graham, who lived in Calcutta with his family, although not in the highest ranks of the civil service, was well positioned, as assistant surveyor and chief draftsman in the Surveyor General's office, to reside with his family at 25 Park Street. The Street Directories suggest that in 1856 he had moved with his family to this fine address from his earlier residence a few streets away at Joratollah Street, possibly after a promotion. Although his office was only a few minutes walk from his house he owned two palanquins and a horse, but no carriages. His drawing room contained an assortment of armchairs, a couch, two mahogany card tables, two mahogany and two teak wood teapoys, eleven drawing room pictures, a painted *punkah*, a piano, circular piano stool, and four damask *purdahs* (curtains). In central hall houses it was typical to have *purdahs* in the doorways that connected the hall with the adjoining rooms. More than anything else this was done to give a comfortable 'look' to dining and drawing rooms, and not for privacy. It was necessary to drape the high doors and windows of the chief rooms in the house, the housekeeping guides claimed, 'otherwise you will never get rid of the comfortless unfurnished look' (An Anglo-Indian: 60).

To remedy the architectural dissimilarity of Indian houses from those in England, the residents were encouraged to evoke a sense of 'home' by carefully situating a few objects of English manufacture. When the latter was not affordable, they were asked to arrange them as one would in England: 'with a few pictures, photographs, brackets for odds and ends of china, japanese scrolls, having books and papers about, and a piano, a room could be made fairly pretty'. A few rugs on the floor, the housekeeping guides suggested, together with 'a covered mantelpiece board with lace and crewel worked border, and a glass in a plain velvet setting above it, with a few quaint ornaments about, will add much to the habitable look of an Indian room' (An Anglo-Indian: 63). The ideal of abundant velvet and lace, and the riot of heavy upholstery, bric-a-brac, and indoor palms, that characterized upper class Victorian homes, was usually pared down and took on vestigial form in India. In the colonial context the sparse trimmings acted as material presence associated with home comforts.

The advice about household furnishing available from housekeeping guides changed in the later part of the century. More and more cabinetmakers in Calcutta were producing European furniture and it was no longer as cost-effective to carry furniture from England. Indian rugs replaced Axminster and Brussels carpets in Anglo-Indian households. The inexpensive 'jail rugs', or Indian *dhurries* were considered quite 'tasteful' and appropriate because these could handle rough use. The author of *Indian Outfits*, however, recommended that buying a rug of good old design to 'take back home' was a good investment.

The possession of an expensive Indian rug as an index of status was more useful in England, as the security of one's social status was not as guaranteed at home as it was in India.

In tune with changing fashions in England, housekeeping books advised that heavy damask *purdahs* be replaced with floral chintz and cretonne. The emphasis on lightness and an unencumbered look was a relief to families who had to move frequently and could now seem to do well with less expenditure on household furnishing. But lightness had not become the norm for wealthy households in Calcutta even at the very end of the 19th century. Photographs of Belvedere House, the residence of the Lieutenant Governor of Bengal, taken in the 1880s and 1890s display lavishly furnished rooms with heavy upholstery, carpets, and studded with trophies, urns, and busts (Figure 4).

Many Anglo-Indian households in the early 19th-century city apparently distinguished between the appropriate decor for summer and winter, the heavier upholstery and thick carpets brought out during the winter months, replicating a practice common in Indian households.[7] But it is clear from Robert Dunlop's probate that sumptuousness in furnishing was prized as an obvious indicator of wealth regardless of the weather. The incessant care that these furnishings required in the hands of native servants assured the owners of their potential as symbols of wealth and status. Dunlop, an assistant in one of the

Source: Photograph courtesy British Library.

Figure 4: Interior of Belvedere House, late 19th century

agency houses in the city, shared his household with another gentleman. His inventory was made out in enough detail for us to know that the mahogany circular center table in his drawing room was of an 'unusually large size', and rested on a 'massive carved pedestal platform and side supports, the top measuring six feet in diameter and provided with a figured brand cloth cover'. He also had a matching pair of substantial mahogany side tables, and 'well made couches and chairs including a massive mahogany Victoria couch on castors having stuffed seat covered with crimson and white silk taboret also with protector and cushion'. The couch was accompanied by 'elegant mahogany frame Albert chairs' with silk taboret and spring seats.

In contrast, Richard Bell's household was simply arranged. The drawing room, for example, abided by the minimum prescription offered by guide-books. It was furnished with a small round table, three sofas, four drawing room chairs, one easy chair, one side table, one lamp table, a clock, three green *purdahs*, a glass flower stand, a clock, and the necessary indicator of polite society – a grand square piano. In addition, four oil portraits – family pictures – adorned the walls. The inventory also listed fireplace accessories – both luxuries and anomalies in the mild Calcutta winters, they were nevertheless looked upon as one of those endearing reminders of home. Rare in the more simple late 18th- and early 19th-century construction, fireplaces were added to these same houses when they were remodeled in the later part of the century.

The key material indicators of affluence in Anglo-Indian households were elaborate couches, a large number of matching chairs, the number and type of 'lustres' or lamps, and the number and quality of dinner services and table ware. As in England, the ability to afford several light sources at night was a sign of wealth (Milan, 1999).

J.H. Rivett-Carnac who arrived in Calcutta in 1858 noted that the typical Calcutta interior was 'early Victorian' with a good deal of Georgian (Rivett-Carnac, 1910: 36). Undergoing the tiresome ritual of house-calling expected of a newly arrived serviceman, he had the opportunity to survey the interior decoration of drawing rooms and halls within a relatively short time. It was this system of house-calling and having a large number of people for meals that meant that the decor of the public rooms in the house demanded special attention from the mistress. On one rare occasion, he found an interior that was 'light, cool, and graceful' without the necessity of steering 'between islands of massive couches and heavily upholstered chairs and colossal round tables.' 'It was,' he recalled, 'certainly unlike anything I had seen since leaving home.' What Rivett-Carnac was derisively pointing out was the unimaginative sameness of the household decor of his contemporaries, who favored well-established styles even when outdated.

While British residents attempted to keep their formal living spaces as 'European' as possible, Indian articles and modes of daily life were evident in the ostensibly private realm of bedrooms, bathrooms, and kitchens. All house-holds had some locally made articles of the less expensive timber such as jackwood and *sishu*, as well as cane, Chinese bamboo, and rattan *morahs* (low stools), easy chairs, and shelves. *Indian Outfits and Establishment* suggested buying the 'reasonably priced' wicker chairs and sofas in India, wadding them with cotton, and then dressing them in chintz to make 'very good easy lounges' (1882: 61). In affluent households these 'native' items were found in bedrooms, verandahs, bathrooms, and *bottlekhanas*. The nomenclature used for the objects in the private spaces was also often Indian. In Robert Dunlop's inventory we find 'brass *pickdannies* (spittoons) and 'sola bottle covers' in the *bottlekhana*, tin *pitarah* (trunk) in the dressing room and bedroom, 'glass *hookah* bottom with wooden *guttah*' in the writing room, *chillumchee* (water basin on wooden tripod), *morah*, and *gamlah* (basin) in the bathroom.

In some cases the Indian nomenclature found in probates could have been a function of Indians conducting the probate, but the frequency with which Indian words were used in daily life by Anglo-Indians is evident from journals, housekeeping guides, and novels set in the Indian colonial context. Every book on housekeeping supplied the reader with a glossary of Hindi/Urdu terms and their English translation. All of them went into the details of currency and weight conversion – Indian money to English pounds and shillings, and Indian weights of *seers* and *chittaks* to gallons, gills, and ounces. According to these authors, the smooth and efficient running of a household necessitated that women grasp the value of Indian money and the necessary bazaar rates, and match them with systems they were familiar with.

The housekeeping guides recommended that applied decor be minimized. Curtains were not typically hung in bedrooms, sometimes being replaced by paper cut-outs that gave the semblance of ground glass (A Lady Resident, 1865: 37). The authors advised that 'little besides the actual cot, above all no water, nor any clothes hanging up', should be allowed inside bedrooms, as they attracted insects, particularly mosquitoes. Making bedrooms pretty with crewel worked mats and draperies was discouraged in view of the trouble to keep them free of dust and insects.

The possibilities of dressing the household in English attire was attenuated not only by the climate and available furnishing, but the training imparted to native servants. Not surprisingly this constituted one of the most contentious aspects of Anglo-Indian domestic life. It was common to expect that wives of officers in the army or civil service would have to supervise 16 servants or more, and certainly no less than 10 even in reduced circumstances. All housekeeping guides complained about the difficulties experienced in procuring and training Indian servants. The extreme dependence on servants in every facet of housekeeping implied that the 'Englishness' of a household was necessarily mediated by the labor of Indian servants. This applied more to food preparation than any other aspect of daily life.

Mrs Clemons, who spent several years in southern India, noted that more dishes were served at the table than was the practice in England. The kitchen was not a part of the main house of the upper crust of European residents in

Calcutta or in other parts of the country. A part of the servants' quarters and outhouse, the kitchen, appropriately called 'cook room', was therefore more indirectly supervised and rarely visited. In fact, authors of the early guidebooks recommended that the less the lady of the house knew about these cook rooms the better (An Anglo-Indian, 1882: 68–9; Clemons, 1841: 187–9).

The passage of the prepared food from the cook room to the dining table was mediated by the pantry/storage or *bottlekhana*, and it is this space that supplies evidence of the elaborate aspect of foodways in these households. The contents of the *bottlekhana* varied a great deal from one household to another and clearly designated socio-economic status. Dunlop's inventory included a lot of Osler and Company's 'finest cut glass table ware', a set of Rodgers and Sons Table Cutlery with ivory handles, in addition to a large assortment of glass ware for liqueur, champagne, wine, and custard.

The range and number of dishes and serving utensils indicate that these households could entertain a large company at dinner without difficulty. In the beginning of the century it was common to host up-country guests or those newly arrived from England. Hotels were few and not considered respectable establishments until much later. It was apparently not uncommon to have anywhere between 10 to 25 for dinner, and thanks to the *khansamma* (cook) and a legion of servants even the simple menus were very elaborate by today's standards. It was common at this time to have 'Indian dishes' at the table, necessitating that the side dishes in a dinner set be renamed 'curry plates'. Moreover, many European men in their cohabitation with Indian mistresses or wives had adopted Indian food as a way of life along with other aspects of Indian home living. At a price one could get English canned food, however, even in the late 18th century.[8] In those households where one could not afford many of the pricey store-bought products or in some cases by choice, fresh cheese (the Indian style) was served at the table along with store-bought English cheese. Similarly preparing pickles and preserves, especially if one grew 'English vegetables' in the garden, was a cheaper alternative to the store-bought variety. All housekeeping guides advocated the planting of an English garden to ensure a steady supply of English flowers and vegetables for the table.

Foodways, however, took on a more English bent in the second half of the century. The more frequent passage of ships from England, and a substantially larger influx of those seeking fortunes in the East, meant that there was a critical mass of British men and women who desired a home-style menu; it is the presence of a large number of British women in India who accompanied their husbands that significantly changed the norms of domestic life. But in general the post-Sepoy Revolt (1857) era was marked by an avoidance of everything 'Indian', if one could. The author of *Indian Outfits* published in 1882 had to cajole her readers to consider Indian dishes in a menu. Of course what passed as 'Indian' at these tables was a peculiarly Anglicized version of Indian food – the latter made suitable for English tastes. Nonetheless, it was evident that even if one ate Indian-styled meals on a daily basis, formal dinners demanded that everything be English, even if it meant serving canned soup, canned salmon, canned peas, canned ham, and bottled fruit. Similarly, smoking *hookahs*, a habit most Englishmen and some women had developed during their Indian residence became more obsolete as the century progressed – being discarded as an obvious sign of Indianness. Consequently one is hard pressed to find one of these in the inventories later in the century such as that of Richard Bell. At the same time, we find housekeeping guides published in the last decades of the century urging their readers to acquire proficiency in the local Indian languages. Although, since the 18th century British colonial authorities had recognized the need for learning Indian languages, house-keeping guides regretted that Anglo-Indian women had not taken this idea to heart for domestic management even by the late 19th century. If the dignity and prestige of the household was to be upheld against all kinds of threats in a foreign land then acquiring knowledge of the language, customs, and habits of people was critical.

The Public World of Home

In *Colonial Masculinity*, Mrinalini Sinha notes that the white woman in India occupied a 'unique, yet contradictory, position in the masculinist colonial mythology' (1995: 46). To start with, the white woman was seen as a charming presence in a strange land. As a figure of veneration she was held up as the exact opposite of the sexualized Indian woman in *purdah*, and consequently, any real or imagined threat to the inviolable white woman was perceived as a threat to the entire British race. Anglo-Indian women were discouraged from socializing with Indian men of any class, or even pursuing philanthropic work, in case it brought them too close to native life. The legion of male servants (almost all servants were male) in the household continued to be a source of surprise and anxiety (Nugent, 1839: 123; Eden, 1872: 84–5). Paradoxically, much like the Indian woman behind *purdah*, the white woman in India was expected to be 'wholly absent from any kind of society', and yet represent a model of difference (Sinha, 1995: 46). Thus their social circle was limited to a small group of Anglo-Indians in which the hierarchy of colonial administration was paramount. Of course, this applied only to the women who were married to men holding middle to higher appointments in the civil and military services. While these elite white women were seen to need special protection from the lascivious gaze and wrath of Indian men, they were also considered the reason behind the increase in racial tension, and were perceived to be more racially prejudiced than their male counterparts (Spear, 1963; Strobel, 1987). No doubt this perception among British men had much to do with the fact that the presence of a large number of white women in India effectively changed the masculine culture of Anglo-Indian society (Ann Stoler, 1997: 351; also see Hyam, 1990). The presence of British women, more than any government authority, ensured that the practice of keeping Indian mistresses became rare among civilian and military ranks. The British women also frowned upon the men socializing with women of mixed race and on homosocial relations between British and Indian men. The feminine trope that was applied to Indian men, and to India in general, placed British women in a precarious role of carving out difference and sanctity.

Given the strictures of an overtly race-conscious society, the wives of British servicemen had little to do besides manage a household, and endeavor to make it a suitable locale for the obligatory socialization of the small Anglo-Indian circle. The unusual graceful decor of the drawing room that so impressed Rivett-Carnac on his daily round of social visits in Calcutta, not surprisingly, was attributed to the personality of the mistress of the household: 'exactly what her room had led me to expect . . . perfect hostess and accomplished lady' (Rivett-Carnac, 1910: 42). The housekeeping guides were conscious of this role expected of British women in India, noting that the drawing room and servants were indices of the 'character' of a mistress (Chota [Mrs Lang], 1909). But their advice exceeded the limited representation of graceful presence. Not merely symbols of English domesticity and feminine charm, their role was one of active management of the house and its compound – the very foundation of empire: 'We do not wish to advocate an unholy haughtiness, but an Indian household can no more be governed peacefully, without dignity and prestige, than an Indian Empire' (Steel and Gardiner, 1909: 9).

Why was it necessary to invoke the empire analogy in order to signify good household management? What was the mechanism that linked these constructs together? The 'unholy haughtiness' in the previous quotation was a reference to the idea of racial superiority that justified the authoritative treatment of servants, but it was undoubtedly also a desire to point out the equal responsibility that the women shared in the maintenance of empire. The common perception of the British woman in India as a self-indulgent, lazy figure surrounded by servants who ran the household – a predominantly male portrayal – was countered by the women themselves in the writing of housekeeping guides (Figure 5). These housekeeping books competed with cookbooks as well as commercial and medical guides authored by Anglo-Indian men. The latter had been in circulation since the early 19th century and the housekeeping guides sought to create an audience who would find a woman's advice more trustworthy. The authors unanimously acknowledged that domestic life in India required learning a new cultural system – weights and measures, currency, produce, Anglo-Indian social habits, foodways, daily and seasonal rhythms, architecture, transportation, language, and perhaps most critically, the management of servants. And yet they differed in their opinion of the degree to which British domestic practices had to be altered to suit this foreign context. Overall there appears to have been a shift towards a more rigid adherence to British customs later in the century, even when the physical artifacts of domesticity admitted more Indian manufactures. This change is evident in

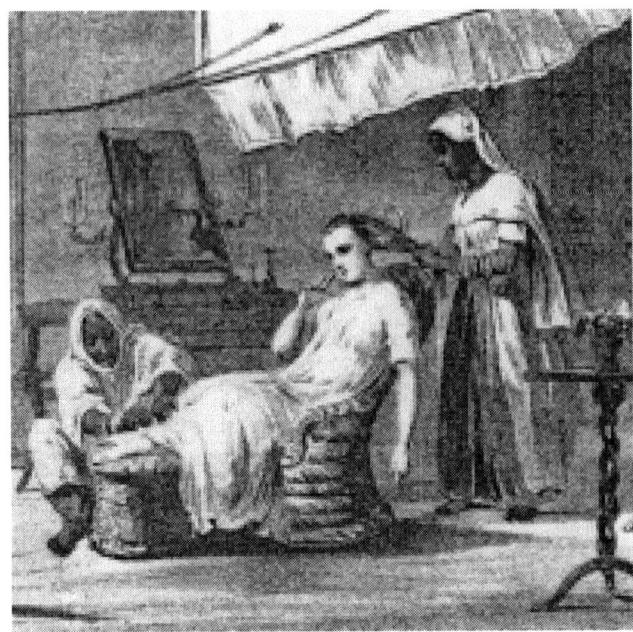

Source: G.F. Atkinson, *Curry and Rice for Forty Plates* (London, 1859).

Figure 5: The 'Magistrate's Wife'

Flora Annie Steel and Grace Gardiner's seventh edition of *The Complete Indian Housekeeper and Cook* (1909) which contained several revisions from earlier prescriptions. In enumerating what was to be expected in Indian domestic life, the authors of housekeeping guides, all of who were in India as wives of army officers, portrayed the social norms of the middling to upper strata of servicemen. In describing the responsibilities of running a household, appointing and managing servants, designing menus, and rearing children, the authors held themselves up as models to other British women who were attempting to negotiate the problematic terrain of race and gender.

Invariably represented as children, to counter any threat of sexuality, Indian servants loomed large in the discussion of setting up and managing households. The authors agreed that, given an opportunity, native servants would cheat ('as a rule they never speak the truth'), laze around, destroy property, and mismanage a household – over all 'they are a thoroughly undependable lot'. It was, however, up to the mistress of the house, to teach them honesty, work, and duty, and chastise them when necessary. But how could servants be punished for offenses if there was 'no hold either on their minds or bodies? – when cutting their pay is illegal, and few, if any, have any sense of shame?' The answer, to Steel and Gardiner, was obvious – 'Make a hold' (1909: 3). This was to be done by levying small fines for infringements and the money 'returned to imperial coffers' spent on small rewards for good service. Of course there was always the danger of impertinence given 'the way they treat their own women', and that they were more likely to listen to the master of the household rather than the mistress (A Lady Resident, 1865: 60–1). To deal with this impertinence, the women adopted the rhetoric and methods of the (male) colonial administration. The administrative analogy not only separated them from Indian women but it also emphasized their superior position to Indian men.

Since servants were the only Indian men they could legitimately converse with, in the worldview of British women, servants came to represent native men. Their first-hand knowledge of Indian life was largely drawn from their experience of ruling a household. The best way to keep this micro empire under control was for the mistress to set the example of routine, method, and tidiness (A Lady Resident, 1865: 5). And yet housekeeping books insisted that mistresses '(n)ever do work which an ordinarily good servant ought to be able to do'. Similar to the colonial administrator, the role of the mistress was to supervise and 'see that (the work) is done correctly' (Steel and Gardiner, 1909: 5–6). The objective was to inculcate the value of labor among the native population, in order for the English men and women to enjoy conspicuous leisure.

The first task of housekeeping, then, was the setting up of an orderly grid of spaces and tasks. The mistress had to know all the details of the hierarchy of servants, their job descriptions, and pay scale. Since the titles and responsibilities varied from one region to another the housekeeping books devoted an entire chapter to this topic. After discussing general methods of setting up the living spaces, the authors devoted considerable space to the rational organization and management of the store-room. This room, a part of the main household, was under the direct supervision of the mistress. It was the stage for daily disbursements of supplies and taking account of expenditure. The room was to be locked up, and in its efficient management was the key to running an orderly household.

In 1858 Minnie Wood, having newly arrived in India, wrote of dreading housekeeping as she could not communicate with the servants and needed her husband's attention in the morning to translate her orders to the servants (Vansittart, 1974: 68). It was exactly this kind of helplessness that Steel and Gardiner railed against in their advice to Anglo-Indian mistresses. Comparing the job of housekeeping with that of running an imperial office, they insisted on 'inspection parades'. Nothing in the household, they suggested, should be hidden from the eyes of the mistress, including the servants' quarters, kitchen, stables and fowl house. Opacity of language as well as visual opacity would have to be removed by learning Hindustanee and by visiting the 'back purlieus' every day as an integral part of the inspection parade when all servants were expected to be punctually in attendance in clean uniform. It was the responsibility of the mistress that these Indian men learn to become good servants dedicated to serve the empire. Underlying all these claims was the widely circulated notion that dirt and disease were endemic in India, and the natives accustomed to this environment were inherently squalid, immoral, and lazy. Such environmental determinism that equated architectural and spatial order with morality, claimed that a transparent visual order recognizable by British authority was the key to generating truthfulness among the native population. And this truthfulness among the natives was, in turn, necessary to British health and life. Consequently it was to this aspect that the mistress of the house needed to pay stringent attention. To facilitate supervision, Steel and Gardiner noted that servants should never be allowed to live in the town, but accommodated within the compound. This also necessitated that the head-servant be made responsible for bringing to the attention of the mistress any occurrence of disease among the servants and their families. The notion of the household as a barrier against the dirt and disease of India required that the mistress become the commander as well as medical officer.

That which remained incomprehensible could be made legible through rational ordering – checking weights of products bought and given out to the servants, laying down a grid of punctuality and specific duty for each servant, insistence on cleanliness, and by keeping of daily accounts. All grocery items and servants' wages were to be systematically recorded in account books. The author of *Indian Outfits* noted that a correct and strict system of accounting was even more necessary than in England:

> I settled my khansammas bill each day; some people do this weekly, but it is impossible to check off the items correctly . . . unless I made it a daily business, . . . You can keep a good check on the price of various articles the man buys by comparing the prices he charges you with those of the monthly 'bazaar tariff', a copy of which you must provide yourself with. The prices ruling in the bazaar are fixed by the master of it and the magistrate of the station, so that by comparing the list with your bills you will soon see if your man is endeavoring to cheat you or not. (An Anglo-Indian, 1882: 67–8)

First, the household's imperviousness against the public disorder of India, was overwritten by a clear recognition of the need to move beyond the confines of the compound and rely on the public authority of the bazaar master. The colonial public and private domains of authority tied together brought the home under the purview of public authority, inscribing it within a public sphere. Second, the wellbeing of a household was seen to be directly related to the protection against public scandal. The daily habit of correct accounting was necessary not just to keep a check on the servants but also to keep a check against over-extending one's budget, and a proof against accusations of bribery:

> It is perhaps a not sufficiently considered fact that all public servants in India are bound to keep written accounts showing their total receipts and expenditure. Apart, however, from the question of duty, there can be none as to the practical utility of being able at a glance to see how the money

has gone . . . It appears very desirable that at the outset married people should settle between themselves who is to undertake the duty [of keeping the purse and settling accounts]. For ourselves, we believe a woman to be far more capable of undertaking the somewhat irritating drudgery of detailed accounts . . . Men are apt to say, however, that a young girl entering on life can have no experience in such matters. True; therefore the sooner she buckles to the task the better, and with a very little help at first, and the usual monthly audit and consultation, there is small chance of failure . . . At the same time, even men are often woefully at a loss how to set about making a detailed record of expenditure. (Steel and Gardiner, 1909: 19)

Here Gardiner and Steel adroitly claimed the responsibility of keeping the purse from the men, by aligning finance management with domestic 'drudgery', and at the same time elevated this drudgery to a superior role. What is more, after assuring their readers that 'a young girl' can easily become accomplished in this task, despite what the men have to say, they turned the tables by suggesting that men were equally inept at keeping accounts, and in fact more so. Steel and Gardiner were urgently calling upon British women to recognize their own superior capacity and make that known to the men, who would otherwise refuse them a legitimate share of imperial power.

To ensure that inexperience or method did not stand in the way of keeping accounts for either men or women, the authors suggested a series of three forms (Figure 6). The grid and tabular structure of these forms resembled those used by the various departments of the colonial bureaucracy for presenting accounts and statistical descriptions. In fact, they suggested that these self-designed forms could be substituted by procuring an account book with similar tabular structure available from Thomson's College, Roorkee. The insistence on voluminous statistics in the colonial services was itself an attempt to grapple with the unfathomable nature of Indian culture (Cohn, 1987; Ludden, 1993). Grids for representing statistical data assured the authorities that the raw data of Indian life would be mastered if they could simply be assigned an appropriate location in that grid. These departmental forms transferred to the domestic context would perform the same goal of objective control of the household, in an attempt to overcome the difficulties of language, customs, and communication. Control over the gridded space of the departmental forms simulated control over material relations. Removed from the contradictions and lack of control over servants in the real world, the *representation* of order assured the colonizers of imminent mastery.

Two contradictory issues run through the housekeeping prescriptions: the foreign context of India and how every aspect of daily life had to be altered to suit this new environment, and the defiance with which they attempted to keep up English ideas of 'home'. For example, even after suggesting several points of difference in household management between England and India, they discarded the prevailing notion that rules of housekeeping need to be changed because of living in India:

FORM A.

Date.	Daily Memoranda, April 1881.	Dusters. Sent to the wash.	Given out to Khit.	Bearer.	Ayah.	Sahib.	Occurrences among Live Stock.	Grain Used. Gram.	Ardawa.	Bajra.	Dalli.	Fowls' mixture.	Linseed.	Date.	Eggs.	Loaves.	Milk.	Beer.	Claret.	Soda-water.	Lemonade.	Soap.	Cash Payments. Meat.	Sundries.	R.	A.	P.
4	Sunday	..	..	..	..	..	Killed 1 fowl	8	2	2	1	2	..	4	6	2	2	1	1	2	1	2	Beef 2/, fish 8 as.	Apples 2½ as., potatoes 3 as.	3	2	6
5	Dirzie absent	4 glass, 6 tea, 10 old, 10 new	15	8	5	4	Bought 4 ducks	7	2	2	1	2	1	5	5	3	3	1	..	2	...	..	Mutton 1/4	Suji 2½ as., tomatoes 2 as.	1	8	6
6	Carpenter half-day	..	..	..	..	..	Killed 2 chickens	7	2	2	1	2	1	6	11	2	2	2	1	4	1	..	Fish 6 as.	Tinning 1/4, peas 2 as.	1	12	..
7	Gave out tin of oil	..	..	..	..	..	Killed 2 ducks	7	2	2	1	2	1	7	4	2 & 12 rolls	2	1	..	1	1	4	Brains 2 as.	Maida 2 as., rice 3 as.	..	11	..
8	Engaged Kutbdin 10/	15	15	..	..	..	Bought 1 sheep	9	2	2	1	2	..	8	3	3	3	1	1	2	2	..	Beef 1/8, fish 8 as.	Oranges 12 as., Dall 1 a.	2	13	..
9	Gave out saddle soap	..	..	..	..	..	Bought 40 quail	9	2	3	1	2	..	9	2	3	2	1	1	3	1	..	....	Sago 4 as., spices 2½ as.	..	7	6
10	Horses shod	..	..	..	..	..	Killed 5 quail	9	2	3	1	2	..	10	2	2	2	1	..	1	3	..	Kidneys 4 as.	Lemons 5 as.	..	9	..

The Roorkee account book, costing Rs. 2, which can be had at the Thomason College, Roorkee, is recommended as a substitute for these forms.

Source: Flora Annie Steel and Grace Gardiner, *The Complete Indian Housekeeper and Cook* (London: William Heineman, 1909).

Figure 6: An example of the forms for the purposes of accounting recommended by Steel and Gardiner

There is no reason whatever why the ordinary European routine should not be observed; indeed the more everything is assimilated to English ways, the better and more economical will be the result. Some modification, of course, there must be, *but as little as possible* . . . Here as there, the end is not merely personal comfort, but the formation of a home – that unit of civilization where father and children, master and servant, employer and employed can learn their several duties. (Steel and Gardiner, 1909: 7)

In the late 19th century when it was considered by those such as Steel and Gardiner that household artifacts of British manufacture were not necessary, they insisted in an even more strenuous tone that British 'habits' be maintained. For these authors planting a garden after the English manner was not only a pleasure for the senses, and a 'rest for tired eyes', but in the dry northern country, 'a duty'.[9] The trope of duty – appropriately gendered – was certainly not new to Victorians, but in India it took on an unprecedented urgency.

What lay beneath this urgent call was the difficult recognition that the English 'home' in India was inherently a fractured notion – only in its absences, its lacks, did it gain identity. The very temporary nature of colonial life meant most Anglo-Indians did not have a permanent residence. Unless one was domiciled in India (and therefore regarded to reside beyond the pales of elite civilian and military life), or had a real-estate business (like some men did in early 19th-century Calcutta), Anglo-Indian residents did not buy houses. The rented houses were made comfortable for a short time but with the least effort. Housekeeping books repeatedly advised that cherished possessions, heirlooms, prized china, sumptuous furnishing – the very artifacts of material life with which Victorians surrounded themselves and measured their status – be left at home, in England. Steel and Gardiner encouraged the young housekeeper to 'go out armed with energy, hammers, tacks, brass nails, a goodly supply of Bon-accord Enamel . . . and then buy the old sticks at the bazaar . . . she shall have the prettiest house in the station, with nothing worth a button in it' (1909: 28). Certainly no housekeeper in England would be advised to relinquish material possessions in this manner. And as the probates indicate, certainly not all families heeded this instruction. But Steel and Gardiner's argument was that in India forming attachments with people or artifacts was a mistake. In its transient nature the home was interchangeable with the camp. As mistresses of the household the English women in India recognized that no matter how carefully they designed dinner menus and trained their servants, even in their own homes their position as mistress was only provisional. The hierarchy of colonial administration applied even within their households. Guests requested leave from the 'Burra Memsahib', the wife of the most senior official present, and not from the hostess. The household was merely an extension of the public world of administration, where all the rules and ceremonies of the latter applied.

The Indian home was incomplete, made so by long separations between family members, and a husband often away at camp or inspection. For those who could afford it, wives traveled to the hill stations to escape the heat of the plains during summer. Since it was considered necessary to send children above seven years to England, the absence of grown-up children was the norm. As Julia Curtis, an Anglo-Indian resident, noted with sadness, the women had the memories of their children as babies, they had their brief dutifully written letters, and their pictures: '[w]hatever homely things were left behind, one was always unpacked at each halt and put on the table in the tent, or above the fireplace in the rest house. It was the photograph of the child, or children at school in England' (Macmillan, 1988: 141). The woman had the option of either following the children home or staying with her husband. Steel and Gardiner found the 'increased facilities for "running home" on leave' to be responsible for 'breaking up' the Indian home (1909: 26–7). Either she abandoned her children or her husband, and consequently was left with the feeling that she was bound to fail either as mother or as wife (Macmillan, 1988). Since future rulers of the empire had to be reared at 'home' in England, 'home' in India could not be the place of permanent nurture. Those who defied this norm by keeping both parents and children together were accused of sacrificing their children's future and the future of empire for their own happiness.

Like the male heroes of Rudyard Kipling's novels who found solace in being immersed in government files, and needed the 'voice of fact' to confront chaotic India, Anglo-Indian women were asked to fill their days with work, even when they were not expected to labor in the household. Part of the objective of keeping detailed accounts of household expenditure, and even a complete record of meals served, including their cost, was to occupy their vacant time. There was always the suspicion that unless engaged in such chores women would fill their leisure hours with illicit pleasures (An Anglo-Indian, 1882; also see Steel, 1929: 122–3). Lack of work and physical exercise, even in the hot weather, the housekeeping guides claimed, was the cause of ill-health and moral decay. Without regular exercise one was sure to sink into the depths of lassitude peculiar to the natives.

Being asked to give up the role normally expected of mothers, the women found their duties expanded. The housekeeping books pointed out that what consisted of household duties in England were not the same as in India. Unlike English practice it was the women who were in charge of overseeing the stables and ensuring that the animals were in good health. Also, contrary to popular imagery, the women often had to 'march' over a thousand miles accompanied by small children and without their British male chaperones. In fact, rather than men being in charge of transporting the family from one station to another, it was the woman's responsibility. Reminding Anglo-Indian mistresses that 'solidities and fragilities are alike a nuisance,' Steel and Gardiner noted that families should not burden themselves with heavy or delicate furniture, because 'the safe transplantation of the necessities of life such as husband, children, books, and a piano, is generally sufficient strain on nerves' (1909: 28). This traveling household not only required supervision during packing and transportation, but a thorough knowledge of camping, the diplomacy to negotiate with villagers, and most importantly, the ability to plan ahead and keep the servants obliged. All the rules that governed the management of households were transferred to and tested against the outer world. And it was through this rhetoric of managing an empire – in which not only the natives but the needy English men and children required looking after – that Steel and Gardiner began to erode the masculine privilege of empire. The lacks and absences of the 'home' in India was to be utilized for a larger potential – generating an enlightened subjectivity for English women. If the few photographs or bits of lace and crewel work worked 'metonymically' to situate the idea of the 'original' home in the colonial context, the reintroduction of these material fragments in the mimicked home began to accumulate unintended meaning by being circulated in a new set of spaces, ideas, and actors. The insistence of the authors of the invariability of English ways – 'modification . . . as little as possible', and their professed immersion in the patriarchy of Victorian England through the 'formation of a home' with all its hierarchy, even when they recommended substantive changes in colonial housekeeping norms, was intended to recruit the value and authenticity of 'Englishness' to these challenges to patriarchy.

Resituating Material Values

To recognize the articulation of this new subjectivity it is necessary to return for a moment to Elizabeth Tilyard, who lived on the fringes of 'good society'. Flora Annie Steel and scores of memsahibs would have wanted to set themselves apart from the likes of the Tilyards. On her part, it is doubtful that she would find much to learn from the housekeeping guides.

The Anglo-Indian world that Flora Annie Steel and the authors of housekeeping guides inhabited was a distinctly different one from that of both the lesser fortunate, ordinary soldiers and their wives, and also those Anglo-Indians who had amassed considerable wealth in India. In concluding their section on 'Accounts' Steel and Gardiner reminded Anglo-Indian housewives that happiness did not reside in material possession: 'what is personal comfort? One thing is sure. In the multiplication of pots and pans, and the enlargements of the necessaries of life, lies anxiety and slavery' (1909: 22). Arcane methods of accounting were not only to keep this desire for proliferating material possessions at bay, but the mistresses were expected to derive consolation from such a mundane task because it cultivated a rational, progressive colonial mindset – requirements for managing empire.

It is doubtful that it escaped the notice of these long-term Anglo-Indian residents, that the planters and merchants such as Robert Dunlop and Richard Bell, as well as the families domiciled in India – at least those who made a good living but did not form the society of servicemen – often maintained more sumptuous homes than they did. Not surprisingly, those who were charged foremost with the duty of representing British pride had to disavow familiar notions of home life. The abdication of material possessions and therefore one's worth measured through them, was to be compensated by the satisfaction derived from the 'higher' duty of empire.

According to Steel and Gardiner, by surrounding themselves with superfluous material possessions, Englishwomen were perpetuating their own slavery. Visions of home-life in England here is referenced within the idea of women's uncompensated labor and sexual availability to the men in the household. It is their colonial experience, with its difficulties of procuring artifacts of English material culture, and possibility of masculine positioning, that suggested their freedom from 'domestic slavery', the only role that English men seemed to want for their 'chattels' and 'helpmeets'. By virtue of empire, domestic slavery could be transferred to the native servants. This transcription of the role of women that required abandoning material wealth provokes the question of what then were the legions of servants meant to slave for, if there was little that needed upkeep? It is here that the demand for routine and order among the servants reveals its significance. The limited material possessions, worth little in money, garnered new meaning as props around which labor was to be organized and displayed to testify to the British ability for producing an ordered empire. With the transference of household labor from the English women to Indian servants, the value of possessions was transferred from material artifacts to the bodies of the disciplined servants. Representation of power through the bodies of native servants was not a new conception. Scores of paintings since the 18th century had established such a mode of invoking colonial identity (see Chattopadhyay, forthcoming), but the gendered implication of this embodiment was revealed and explicitly articulated by Steel and Gardiner.

Once the tangible indicators of social superiority were rejected, British women were to aspire to the intangible dimensions of superiority measured through racial identity and expressed in the rituals of colonial bureaucracy. The army wife who was not expected to be 'anything except a decorative chattel' (Macmillan, 1988: 154) could be expected to find a sense of self worth if she were given the responsibility of the 'arduous', 'pioneering' task of ruling the 'empire of servants' with the hope of instilling habits for the benefit of the rulers of a future generation (Steel and Gardiner, 1909: 2). The abject submission that Flora Annie Steel expected from her servants – 'they love authority' – was not just a recitation of a common notion among British colonizers, but had another specific role in constructing domestic ideology in India. It helped to distinguish white women like her from the other white women who might wish to adopt the rhetoric of racial superiority – the wives of ordinary soldiers, railway workers, and petty entrepreneurs.

Speaking of the less fortunate British women in India, one Anglo-Indian resident described them as 'a poor feckless folk, their English physique enfeebled by the climate, and their moral fibre enervated by the unwonted possession of a servant or two' (Macmillan, 1988: 145). Once so much value had been placed on proper ruling of servants as the key responsibility of housekeeping, if the soldier's wife in town could also afford some of that privilege then the old class distinctions of home could not be maintained. Consequently, freedom from household labor could not be of the same import for all the classes. Besides, there was the danger that natives would perceive both mistresses as belonging to the same species of 'white' women. Working class white women – 'white, but not quite' – with their closer affinity to native life, threatened to lower the prestige of empire formulated on the basis of racial superiority.

Conclusion

We need to recognize the peculiarities of the colonial context, the anxieties of loss, as well as the liberation of being separated from England, before we can parse out the different dimensions of colonial domestic ideology. In its attempt to address the contradictions of race, class, and gender, colonial domestic ideology could never be identical to that of the metropole, nor could it be monolithically applied to all Anglo-Indian residents. The familiar rules for inferring status from material possessions were complicated in India by the intangibles of colonial authority, and by being introduced in new conceptual and physical spaces of encounter. The anxiety produced by the impossibility of the 'English' home in India was turned into an authorial plenitude by Anglo-Indian women in housekeeping guides that attempted to mask the discrepancy between the rhetoric of governance and experience of daily life.

Notes

1. In response to this assumption and the racial exclusivity that marked the spaces created to accommodate Anglo-Indian civil life, Indian men (and women) took it upon themselves to produce alternate spaces of social and political gathering. The formation of this Indian public sphere did not simply borrow the western European model either, but was heavily underwritten by notions of social responsibility that pre-dated the advent of the idea of the bourgeois public sphere. For discussions of various aspects of the Bengali public sphere, see Chatterjee (1993), Chakrabarty (2000).
2. 'Estate of Elizabeth Tilyard,' Inventories of Deceased Estates, Oriental and India Office Collection, British Library, L/AG/34/27/163.
3. I have discussed the meaning of colonial house plans of Calcutta in depth in Chattopadhyay (2000), having deduced the three-bay pattern from the documentation and analysis of 95 such plans.
4. 'Estate of John Graham,' Inventories of Deceased Estates, Oriental and India Office Collection, British Library, L/AG/34/27/163.
5. 'Estate of Robert Dunlop,' Inventories of Deceased Estates, Oriental and India Office Collection, British Library, L/AG/34/27/163.
6. 'Estate of Richard Clarke Bell,' Inventories of Deceased Estates, Oriental and India Office Collection, British Library, L/AG/34/27/182.
7. See Charles D'Oyly's drawing of the same room in summer and winter, Oriental and India Office Collection, British Library.

8. A 1784 advertisement in the *Calcutta Gazette* noted that since it only took the ship only four months, the products 'are all of superior quality' (Seton-Karr, 1864: 47).
9. This instruction also extended in informal ways to Indian families who occupied the rare 'privilege' of sharing space with the European community. Mira Chowdhury, a Bengali woman whose husband worked in a senior position in the railways, noted in her memoirs of how she and her husband felt obliged to plant a good garden because they were living among English families in the railway colony of Kanchrapara in Bengal. This was in 1927 and they were only one among two Indian families in that officer's colony. She also recalled receiving helpful advice from the English ladies regarding gardening and housekeeping. (Chowdhury, 1996 [1403 Bengali]: 221–2).

References

An Anglo-Indian (1882) *Indian Outfits and Establishment: A Practical Guide to Persons About to Reside in India.* London: L. Upcott Gill.

A Lady Resident (1865) *The Englishwoman in India.* Second edition. London: Smith, Elder and Co.

Buckland, C.E. (1901) *Bengal Under the Lieutenant Governors, Being a Narrative of the Principle Events and Public Measures During their Period of Office, from 1854–1899.* Calcutta: S.K. Lahiri.

Chakrabarty, Dipesh (2000) *Provincializing Europe: Post-colonial Thought and Historical Difference.* Princeton, NJ: Princeton University Press.

Chatterjee, Partha (1993) *The Nation and Its Fragments: Colonial and Postcolonial Histories.* Princeton, NJ: Princeton University Press.

Chattopadhyay, Swati (2000) 'Blurring Boundaries: The Limits of White Town in Colonial Calcutta', *Journal of the Society of Architectural Historians* 59 (2 June): 154–79.

Chattopadhyay, Swati (forthcoming) *Depicting Calcutta: Colonial Conflict and the Emergence of a Nineteenth-Century Modernity.*

Chota Mem [Mrs Lang] (1909) *The English Bride in India, Being Hints on Housekeeping.* Second edition. London.

Chowdhury, Mira (1996) 'Smritir Chhabi', *Aitihashik* 6 (2 Chaitra 1403 Bengali): 205–65.

Clemons, Mrs Major (1841) *The Manners and Customs of Society in India.* London: Smith, Elder & Co.

Cohn, Bernard (1987) 'The Census, Social Structure, and Objectification', *An Anthropologist Among Historians and Other Essays*, pp. 224–54. Delhi: Oxford University Press.

Davidoff, Leonore and Catherine Hall (1987) *Family Fortunes: Men and Women of the English Middle Class, 1780–1850.* Chicago, IL: University of Chicago Press.

Eden, Emily (1872) *Letters from India.* London.

George, Rosemary Marangoly (1993–4) 'Homes in the Empire, Empires in the Home', *Cultural Critique* (Winter): 95–127.

Grant, Colesworthy (1862) *Anglo-Indian Domestic Sketch.* Calcutta: Thacker and Spink.

Habermas, Jurgen (1989) *The Structural Transformation of the Public Sphere: An Inquiry into a Category of Bourgeois Society.* Translated by Frederick Burger and Thomas Lawrence. Cambridge, MA: MIT Press.

Hyam, Richard (1990) *Sexuality and Empire: The British Experience.* Manchester: Manchester University Press.

'Inventories of Deceased Estates', Oriental and India Office Collection, British Library, L/AG/34/27 series.

Ludden, David (1993) 'Orientalist Empiricism: Transformation of Colonial Knowledge', in C.A. Breckenridge and P. van de Veer (eds) *Orientalism and the Post-colonial Predicament*, pp. 250–78. Philadelphia: University of Pennsylvania Press.

Macmillan, Margaret (1988) *Women of the Raj.* London: Thames and Hudson.

Metcalf, Thomas R. (1995) *Ideologies of the Raj.* Cambridge: Cambridge University Press.

Milan, Sarah (1999) 'Refracting the Gaselier: Understanding Victorians Responses to Domestic Gas Lighting', in Inga Bryden and Janet Floyd (eds) *Domestic Space.* Manchester: University of Manchester Press.

Nugent, Lady Maria (1839) *A Journal of the Year 1811 Till the year 1815, Including a Voyage to and Residence in India, with a Tour of the Northwestern Part of the British Possession in that Country, under the Bengal Government.* London.

Rivett-Carnac, J.H. (1910) *Many Memories of Life in India, at Home, and Abroad.* London: William Blackwood.

Seton-Karr, W.S. (1864) *Selections from Indian Gazettes*, Vol. I. Calcutta: Military Orphan Press.

Sinha, Mrinalini (1995) *Colonial Masculinity: The 'Manly Englishman' and the 'Effeminate Bengali'* Manchester: University of Manchester Press.

Spear, Percival (1963) *The Nabobs.* London: Oxford University Press.

Steel, Flora Annie and Gardiner, Grace (1909) *The Complete Indian Housekeeper and Cook.* Seventh edition. London: William Heineman.

Steel, Flora Annie (1929) *Garden of Fidelity, Being an Autobiography of Flora Annie Steel, 1847–1929.* London: Macmillan and Co.

Stoler, Ann (1997) 'Making Empire Respectable: the Politics of Race and Sexual Morality in Twentieth-Century Colonial Cultures', in Ann McClintok, Aamir Mufti, and Ella Shohat (eds) *Dangerous Liaisons: Gender, Nation and Post-Colonial Perspectives*, pp. 344–73. Minneapolis: University of Minnesota Press.

Strobel, Margaret (1987) 'Gender and Race in 19th and 20th-Century British Empire', in R. Bridenthal, C. Koonz and S. Stuard (eds) *Becoming Visible: Women in European History*, pp. 375–96. Boston, MA: Houghton Mifflin.

Vansittart, Jane, ed. (1974) *From Minne, with Love, the Letter of a Victorian Lady (Maria Lydia Blane Wood) 1849–1861.* London: Peter Davies.

72

Self-Enhancement or Self-Coherence? Why People Shift Visual Perspective in Mental Images of the Personal Past and Future

Lisa K. Libby and Richard P. Eibach

Joan Didion's autobiographical play *The Year of Magical Thinking* portrays a traumatic period in her life. Describing the process of writing the play, Didion (2007) commented,

> I thought of [the character who would appear on stage] as "the speaker," or "she." I thought of myself as the witness, the watcher, the auditor, the audience. . . . It would be logical to assume that I adopted this distance to protect myself. It would also be wrong. The idea that whoever appeared onstage would play not me but a character was central to imagining how to make the narrative: I would need to see myself from outside. (p. B7)

Writing the play required Didion to integrate specific life experiences into a coherent story, and she suggests that reflecting on her past self from an external vantage point was crucial to this process. Didion's remark that she needed to see herself from the outside may be interpreted as a metaphor, but when thinking about life events – both past and future – people often picture those events in their minds and, on occasion, spontaneously see these images from the visual perspective an observer would have (*third-person*) rather than from their own visual perspective (*first-person*). This phenomenon has long been remarked on (e.g., Freud, 1907/1960; Galton, 1883) and more

Source: *Personality and Social Psychology Bulletin*, 37(5) (2011): 714–726.

recently verified by systematic investigation (e.g., Nigro & Neisser, 1983). However, the psychological function that imagery perspective serves is still under investigation.

The present studies speak to this question by investigating the determinants of imagery perspective. Specifically, we test whether use of third-person as opposed to first-person imagery is determined by a desire to disown a pictured event or by a focus on how the event relates to broader themes in one's life – one's self-concept. According to both hypotheses, shifts in imagery perspective reflect the function it serves in representing the subjective meaning of events. However, the hypotheses differ in their assumptions about the nature of that function. We evaluate the empirical basis for each assumption and conclude that evidence supports the hypothesis that a focus on an event's self-concept coherence, and not a desire to disown it, promotes use of the third-person perspective. Furthermore, given the commonalities in the constructive processes that support recalling the past and imagining the future (Addis, Pan, Vu, Laiser, & Schacter, 2009), we expect our predicted effect to hold regardless of whether the life events people picture are in the past or future. We report four studies that provide an empirical test and discuss implications for understanding the construction and maintenance of the temporally extended self.

Does Motivation to Disown a Pictured Event Promote Third-Person Imagery?

One hypothesis is that motivation to disown a pictured event promotes third-person imagery. This hypothesis follows from the assumption that third-person imagery excludes the self in the pictured event from the present self-concept whereas first-person imagery includes the pictured self in the present. This assumption frequently shapes assertions about the role that imagery perspective plays in psychological processes (e.g., Kenny et al., 2009; McIsaac & Eich, 2004; Sanitioso, 2008; Wilson & Ross, 2003). Most relevant to the present studies is an account that implicates imagery perspective in self-enhancement processes (Sanitioso, 2008).

This account starts with the assumption that imagery perspective serves as a cue to include pictured events in the present self (first-person) or exclude (third-person) pictured events from the present self. Based on this assumption, and in line with the idea that information produces assimilation effects when it is included in the representation of the evaluated object and contrast effects when it is excluded (Schwarz & Bless, 2007), recalling negative past events from the third-person perspective and positive past events from the first-person perspective should enhance the present self. Thus, this account proposes that people adopt the third-person perspective to picture negative events and the first-person perspective to picture positive ones in an effort to enhance the present self (Sanitioso, 2008). By this account, imagery perspective functions analogously to subjective perceptions of time: People have been shown to disown negative events by pushing them into the past and claim ownership of positive events by pulling them toward the present (Ross & Wilson, 2002).

Although some data appear to support this line of reasoning, other data cast considerable doubt. In evaluating the starting assumption that imagery perspective serves as a cue to include or exclude the pictured event from the present self, it is relevant to consider evidence from experiments that manipulate imagery perspective. Picturing an event from the third-person as opposed to first-person perspective can promote the exclusion of the pictured self from the present – for example, increasing perceived self-change since a recalled event occurred – but only when people hold a self-theory that defines the pictured self as inconsistent with the present. When people hold a self-theory that defines the pictured self as consistent, using third-person imagery promotes the inclusion of the pictured self in the present – for example, decreasing perceived self-change (Libby, Eibach, & Gilovich, 2005). These findings undermine the idea that imagery perspective directly cues the inclusion or exclusion of an event from the present self-concept.

Even if picturing an event from the third-person perspective does not necessarily exclude it from the present self, it is still possible that a desire to disown an event might prompt people to picture it from the third-person. In evaluating this possibility, experiments that measure imagery perspective are most relevant, and the support is mixed. One investigation tested whether an event's emotional impact, positive or negative, predicted the perspective people used to picture it. Such an effect would be expected, given self-enhancement motivation, if people shift perspective in response to a desire to include or exclude events from the present self. However, no evidence of an effect emerged (D'Argembeau & Van der Linden, 2004).

Another study directly manipulated participants' desire to claim or disown a past self and measured the perspective they then used to picture the event in question (Sanitioso, 2008). In this study participants either were led to believe that introversion or that extraversion was predictive of success. Then, they recalled and reported the perspective they used to picture an incident in which they behaved introvertedly. Participants were more likely to use the third-person perspective when they had been led to believe that extraversion was predictive of success. This result was interpreted as evidence that people shift perspective in response to the desire to disown (third-person) or claim (first-person) the pictured event (Sanitioso, 2008).

However, it was also acknowledged that the data did not rule out an alternative interpretation. The manipulation of beliefs about whether introversion or extraversion was predictive of success could have changed participants' present self-concepts before they pictured the introverted behavior. Thus, the effect of the manipulation on perspective could have been driven by the perceived consistency of the introverted behavior with the present self-concept

(Sanitioso, 2008). Indeed, other work suggests that inconsistency between present and pictured selves promotes third-person imagery (Libby & Eibach, 2002).

Furthermore, it is important to consider that although people are motivated to enhance the self, they are also motivated to achieve a coherent self-understanding (Swann, Rentfrow, & Guinn, 2002). Perceived inconsistencies represent a threat to self-coherence, but people can counter such threats by integrating the discrepant event with a broader life narrative, citing a turning point or trajectory of development that explains how the past self became the present (Ross & McFarland, 1988). According to another account of imagery perspective's representational function, it is just this way of thinking about an event that should lead people to picture it from the third-person perspective.

Does Focusing on an Event's Self-Concept Coherence Promote Third-Person Imagery?

We hypothesize that focusing on an event's self-concept coherence promotes third-person imagery. To understand the basis for this hypothesis, it is useful to consider the nature of event representations and of the self. Any life event can be understood in terms of the concrete details that define that particular situation or in terms of the meaning the event has in relation to the self-concept (Vallacher & Wegner, 1985). This distinction in levels of meaning corresponds with a widely recognized distinction between two facets of the self. William James (1890/1950) referred to these facets as the "I" and the "me." Many theories across philosophy and psychology converge on a similar idea, albeit using a variety of labels (see Gallagher, 2000). Here we use the terms *experiential self* and *conceptual self* to highlight the distinct bases of the two facets. The experiential self (i.e., the Jamesian "I") is the phenomenology of engaging with the immediate environment (Farb et al., 2007; Legrand & Ruby, 2009). The conceptual self (i.e., the Jamesian "me") is a framework of general self-theories about life themes, developmental trajectories, personality traits, and superordinate goals (Conway, 2005; McAdams, 2001; Ross, 1989).

The hypothesis that focusing on an event's self-concept coherence leads people to picture it from the third-person perspective follows from the assumption that imagery perspective shapes the level of meaning in event representations. According to this account (Libby & Eibach, in press), first-person images represent an event in terms of the experience of acting on and reacting to the environment – the basis for the experiential self. Third-person images represent an event in terms of its meaning in a broader context. General self-theories – the basis for the conceptual self – can provide such a context for autobiographical events. Experiments that manipulate perspective are most relevant to evaluating this assumption about the representational function of imagery perspective, and a variety of findings provide converging support.

For example, when people picture past events from their lives, first-person imagery produces more reliving of emotions evoked by experiencing the event than does third-person imagery (Robinson & Swanson, 1993). When people see actions depicted from a first-person as opposed to third-person perspective, areas of sensory-motor cortex are more active (Jackson, Meltzoff, & Decety, 2006). In addition, when instructed to picture a past event from the first-person rather than third-person perspective, people recall more details about their past emotions, physical sensations, and psychological states (McIsaac & Eich, 2002). Picturing a life event from the third-person perspective seems to cause people to analyze what the event means in relation to more general knowledge about themselves and their life. For example, compared to first-person imagery, third-person imagery makes people more likely to think about their pictured behavior in terms of personality traits, goals, and identities (Frank & Gilovich, 1989; Libby, Shaeffer, & Eibach, 2009; Vasquez & Buehler, 2007).

Thus, research that manipulates perspective suggests that imagery perspective defines the mental representation of a life event either as a specific experience (first-person) or in terms of its meaning in the context of their lives more broadly (third-person). If people's spontaneous choice of imagery perspective reflects this representational capacity, then manipulating the level of meaning that people focus on as they think about a life event should produce corresponding changes in the visual perspective people use to picture that event. Most relevant to evaluating this hypothesis are experiments that measure imagery perspective, and results are consistent.

In one study participants were more likely to picture an event from the first-person perspective if they had described their emotional experience of it rather than the objective circumstances (Nigro & Neisser, 1983). In another set of experiments, participants pictured themselves doing hypothetical actions. Participants were more likely to use the third-person perspective when the actions (e.g., voting, greeting someone) were described in terms of associated goals and traits (e.g., influencing the election by voting, showing friendliness by greeting someone) than in terms of concrete movements (e.g., voting by pulling a lever, greeting someone by saying hello; Libby et al., 2009). Thus, together, research that manipulates and measures perspective converges on the idea that the perspective people spontaneously adopt as they picture a life event should depend on whether they focus on the concrete experience of the event or on the event's self-concept coherence. Studies we report here tested this hypothesis directly.

Overview of the Present Research

Participants pictured past and future events from their lives and reported the visual perspectives they used. Studies 1 and 2 employed the phenomenon of self-change to investigate whether use of third-person as opposed to first-person imagery is determined by a desire to disown a pictured event or by a focus on the event's self-concept coherence. Studies 3 and 4 investigated shifts in perspective apart from self-change by directly manipulating whether participants focused on the experience of an event's concrete details or on integrating the event with a coherent self-concept. We predicted that, regardless of whether an event was in the past or future and whether it was positive or negative, adopting a coherence focus as opposed to an experience focus would make people more likely to picture it from the third-person perspective.

Study 1

Study 1 tested which of the two hypothesized determinants of imagery perspective could better account for a previously documented determinant: People are more likely to picture a past event from the third-person perspective if they believe they have changed since it occurred than if they do not (Libby & Eibach, 2002).

Because people are motivated to perceive self-improvement over time (Ross & Wilson, 2000), self-change will often be confounded with perceived negativity of the past self. Thus, the effect of self-change on perspective could be due to the use of third-person imagery to disown negative past selves and first-person imagery to claim positive ones. According to this account, if self-change is manipulated orthogonally to perceived negativity of the past self, then people should be more likely to picture an event from the third-person perspective if their past self is negative than if it is positive, regardless of whether or not they perceive themselves to have changed.

Alternatively, we propose that perspective varies according to whether people are focused on integrating an event with a coherent self-concept or are focused on the experience of the event's concrete details. When people believe they have changed they necessarily perceive an inconsistency between past and present selves. Inconsistency is a threat to self-coherence, but people can maintain coherence by linking the discrepant incident to a broader life theme that accounts for it (Ross & McFarland, 1988). Thereby, according to our account people should be more likely to picture an event from the third-person perspective if their past self is inconsistent with the present than if it is consistent, regardless of its valence. Study 1 orthogonally manipulated the valence and consistency of past selves to test this prediction.

Method

Participants.　Eighty undergraduates (56 female) participated in exchange for course credit.

Materials and procedure.　Participants were randomly assigned in equal numbers to complete one of four versions of a high school memories questionnaire, which varied according to a 2 (past-self consistency: consistent vs. inconsistent) × 2 (past-self valence: positive vs. negative) design.

In the consistent conditions, participants were instructed to identify an "aspect of yourself that has been an enduring quality of your personality since high school." It was specified either that this aspect be undesirable (consistent negative past-self condition) or desirable (consistent positive past-self condition). In the inconsistent conditions participants were instructed to identify "an aspect of yourself that you feel has changed since high school." It was specified either that this change be for the better (inconsistent negative past-self condition) or for the worse (inconsistent positive past-self condition).

Participants wrote about their chosen self-aspect for 5 minutes. Next, they recalled a high school memory related to this self-aspect – the enduring aspect of themselves (consistent conditions) or the way they used to be (inconsistent conditions). To elicit a specific autobiographical memory, instructions directed participants to recall an event that they were involved in or witnessed firsthand and that occurred at a particular place and time. Participants recorded a cue word identifying the event.

To measure perspective, the questionnaire introduced the distinction between first-person and third-person perspectives, explaining that memories are often accompanied by visual images and defining the two perspectives as follows:

> Some images you may see from the first-person perspective, which means you see the event from the same visual perspective that you originally did; in other words, in your memory you are looking out at your surroundings through your own eyes.

> Some images you may see from the third-person perspective, which means you see the event from an observer's visual perspective; in other words, in your memory you can actually see *yourself*, as well as your surroundings.

Because participants could have experienced multiple images of the event and some from each perspective (e.g., Huebner & Fredrickson, 1999), participants used a 10-point scale ranging from *entirely first-person* to *entirely third-person* to indicate the relative proportion of images experienced from each perspective.

At the end of the questionnaire, participants estimated the date of the recalled event, providing an index of its objective temporal distance. Participants also used a scale ranging from *extremely negative* (1) to *extremely positive* (10) to indicate their present evaluation of their recalled behavior, allowing for an additional test of the possibility that perspective is related to past-self valence.

Results and Discussion

Participants' ratings of the relative proportion of memory images viewed from the two perspectives were coded such that 1 corresponded to *all first-person* and 10 corresponded to *all third-person*. These values were submitted

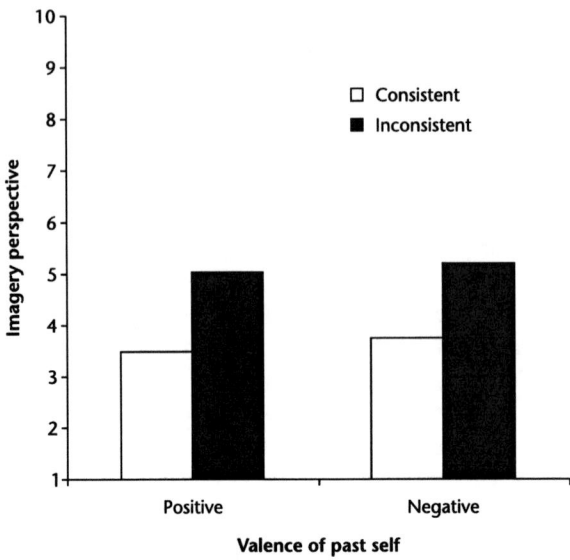

Note: Ratings were made on a scale ranging from *entirely first-person* (1) to *entirely third-person* (10).

Figure 1: Mean imagery perspective ratings in Study 1, depending on the valence of the past self and its consistency with the present

to a 2 (past-self consistency: consistent vs. inconsistent) × 2 (past-self valence: positive vs. negative) ANOVA. There was a main effect of past-self consistency, $F(1, 76) = 4.65$, $p < .05$. No other effect was significant, $Fs < 1$.[1] As we predicted, participants experienced more third-person imagery when their past selves were inconsistent (inconsistent–positive: $M = 5.05$, $SD = 3.12$; inconsistent–negative: $M = 5.20$, $SD = 3.52$) than when they were consistent (consistent–positive: $M = 3.50$, $SD = 2.82$; consistent–negative: $M = 3.75$, $SD = 2.94$), regardless of the past self's valence (see Figure 1).

We also looked for an effect of past-self valence using participants' ratings of their past behavior. Due to self-enhancement motivation, participants may have regarded their past selves more favorably when those past selves were consistent with their present selves than when they were inconsistent (e.g., Ross & Wilson, 2000), even if participants regarded negative past selves less favorably than they did positive past selves on average. If evaluation of past selves was thus confounded with self-change, then the previous analysis may obscure the role of past-self valence in determining perspective.

To investigate this possibility, we submitted participants' present evaluations of their recalled behavior to a 2 (past-self consistency) × 2 (past-self valence) ANOVA. There were main effects of both variables – past-self consistency, $F(1, 76) = 7.63$, $p < .01$, past-self valence, $F(1, 76) = 49.09$, $p < .001$ – as well as an interaction, $F(1, 76) = 5.55$, $p < .05$. Participants regarded their consistent past selves more favorably than their inconsistent past selves only in the positive past-self conditions, $F(1, 76) = 13.08$, $p < .001$, not in the negative

Table 1: Mean favorability rating of recalled behavior in Study 1, depending on past-self valence and consistency

| | Consistency of past self with present self | | | |
| | Consistent | | Inconsistent | |
Valence of past self	M	SD	M	SD
Positive	8.53[a]	1.37	6.33[b]	2.46
Negative	4.50[c]	1.79	4.33[c]	1.91

Note: Scale ranged from *extremely negative* (1) to *extremely positive* (10). Within rows and columns, means not sharing the same superscript are significantly different, $ps < .01$.

past-self conditions, $F(1, 76) < 1$ (see Table 1). This pattern does not match that observed for perspective, nor does it account for it: When including evaluations as a covariate in the analysis of perspective, the only significant effect was again that of past-self consistency, $F(1, 75) = 4.07, p < .05$, and there was no hint that evaluations predicted perspective, $F(1, 75) = 0.007, p = .93$.

The lack of evidence for an effect of past-self valence on perspective casts doubt on the idea that the desire to claim or disown pictured events directly determines imagery perspective. The fact that imagery perspective did depend on the consistency between past and present selves means it is plausible that imagery perspective varies according to whether people focus on the experience of an event or its self-concept coherence – if, in fact, people tend to direct their mental focus to self-concept coherence when they perceive inconsistency. Study 2 sought evidence to support this account.

Study 2

In Study 2 we asked undergraduates who judged their personalities as having changed or remained stable since high school to recall an event from that period. We predicted that those who believed they had changed, and thus perceived inconsistency between their present and past selves, would be more likely to picture the event from the third-person perspective and that a greater tendency to focus on the event's coherence with the self-concept would account for changed participants' greater use of third-person imagery.

The alternative idea that the motivation to claim or disown pictured selves determines imagery perspective suggests that imagery perspective functions analogously to subjective temporal distance. If this is the case, imagery perspective may be correlated with subjective temporal distance. Furthermore, to the extent that participants who had changed felt more temporally distant from the events they recalled, subjective temporal distance could account for their greater tendency to use third-person imagery. We expected this would be unlikely given the results of Study 1 and the evidence we reviewed in the introduction, but we included measures of subjective temporal distance in Study 2 to allow an empirical test.

Method

Participants.   Fifty-two undergraduates (39 female) participated in exchange for course credit.

Materials and procedure.   Participants completed a questionnaire distributed in stages. The first page measured whether participants believed themselves to have changed since high school or not. It stated,

> Over the transition to college there are some people whose personalities seem to change as a result of their college experience. However, there are other people whose personalities seem to remain pretty much the same over the transition to college.

Participants classified themselves as one type or the other. Then, depending on these self-classifications, they listed three things about themselves either that had changed or that had remained the same.

Next, depending on their self-identified status as changed or stable, participants recalled a high school memory related to either what they used to be like or to the enduring aspects of their personality. To elicit a specific autobiographical memory, instructions directed participants to recall an event that they were involved in or witnessed firsthand and that occurred at a particular place and time. Participants estimated the event date, providing an index of objective temporal distance, and then they described the event. The next page of the questionnaire presented two measures of mental focus, two measures of subjective temporal distance, and a measure of perspective.

The first measure of mental focus instructed participants to evaluate their written memory descriptions according to the extent they had focused on "what it was like to experience the event directly – e.g., describing the sights, sounds, smells you experienced; describing your thoughts and feelings during the event" versus on "analyzing the event – e.g., explaining the larger meaning of the event, what it says about your personality now or in the past, why the event happened, and/or what the consequences were or are." Participants used a 10-point scale ranging from *focused completely on what it was like to experience the event, not at all on analyzing the event* to *focused completely on analyzing the event, not at all on what it was like to experience the event.*

Next, participants completed a checklist consisting of 10 thoughts and feelings; 8 were used to compute a second measure of mental focus, and 2 were used to compute the first subjective temporal distance measure. Half the mental focus items (see the Appendix) were worded such that endorsing them signaled a focus on the self-concept coherence of the event, as opposed to the experience (e.g., "Thinking, 'why did I do that?'"), and the other half were worded such that endorsing them signaled a focus on the experience of the event, as opposed to self-concept coherence (e.g., "Feeling like you were living the event all over again"). The subjective temporal distance items were "Feeling like the event happened just yesterday" and "Feeling like the event happened ages ago." Participants indicated which, if any, of the thoughts and feelings they had while thinking about the recalled event.

Next came the measure of imagery perspective. Instructions introduced the distinction between first-person and third-person perspectives and asked participants to report their use of the two perspectives using the same 10-point scale described in Study 1.

After this came the second subjective temporal distance measure (adapted from Ross & Wilson, 2002): "Regardless of when events actually occurred in the past, sometimes they feel very far away, while other times they feel very close, almost like yesterday. As you think about it right now, how far away does the event you recalled FEEL to you?" Participants responded using an 11-point scale ranging from *like yesterday* (0) to *the very distant past* (10).

When the session ended participants used a scale ranging from *I've stayed exactly the same* (1) to *I've changed completely* (10) to evaluate the consistency of their personalities since high school. This was a check on participants' forced-choice judgments.

Results and Discussion

Participants were assigned to the changed or stable group depending on their own classifications. We expected most participants would naturally frame the development of their personalities one way or the other, but to identify those who might be ambivalent (and thus could not accurately be assigned to either group), we used the scale measure of self-change as a check on participants' forced-choice judgments. All but 4 participants provided compatible responses on the two measures, that is, rating themselves on the *changed* end of the scale (6–10) if they had identified themselves as changed on the forced-choice measure or rating themselves on the *same* end of the scale (1–5) if they had identified themselves as having stayed the same. The 4 participants with incompatible responses were excluded from analyses.[2] Thus, the final sample consisted of 48 participants, 29 in the changed group and 19 in the stable group.

Mental focus. The first mental-focus measure consisted of participants' ratings of their memory descriptions. The pattern of means supported our predictions: Participants focused relatively more on the coherence of the event with the self-concept if they believed they had changed ($M = 7.72$, $SD = 1.83$) than if they did not ($M = 6.47$, $SD = 2.91$). This difference was marginally significant $t(46) = 1.83$, $p = .07$. However, this was the one analysis in the studies reported here where the objective temporal distance of the pictured event was a significant predictor of a dependent variable when included as a covariate, $t(45) = 2.00$, $p = .05$. Controlling for the relationship between objective temporal distance and mental focus, the relationship between self-change and mental focus was significant, $t(45) = 2.41$, $p < .05$.

The second mental-focus measure was contained in the thoughts and feelings checklist. For each participant, we computed the proportion of mental-focus items on which he or she responded in line with coherence focus as opposed to experience focus (i.e., endorsed coherence-focused items and did not endorse experience-focused items). On this index (reliability: KR-20 = .80) values greater than .5 indicate a focus more on coherence than on experience, and values less than .5 indicate a focus more on experience than on coherence. Consistent with participants' memory description ratings, the checklist index suggested that participants were more coherence-focused when they believed they had changed ($M = 0.72$, $SD = 0.22$) than when they did not ($M = 0.25$, $SD = 0.20$), $t(46) = 7.37$, $p < .001$.

Subjective temporal distance.   The first subjective temporal distance measure was contained in the thoughts and feelings checklist. For each participant, we computed the proportion of subjective temporal distance items on which they responded in a manner consistent with feeling as if the event happened a long time ago (reliability: $\chi^2 = 7.76$, $p < .006$). Subjective temporal distance was greater when participants believed they had changed ($M = 0.74$, $SD = 0.32$) than when they did not ($M = 0.42$, $SD = 0.42$), $t(46) = 3.02$, $p < .01$.

The second subjective temporal distance measure was the rating scale. Again, subjective temporal distance was greater when participants believed they had changed ($M = 6.48$, $SD = 1.77$) than when they did not ($M = 4.11$, $SD = 2.64$), $t(46) = 3.74$, $p < .01$.

Imagery perspective.   As they were picturing their memory, participants used the third-person perspective more of the time when they believed they had changed ($M = 5.62$, $SD = 2.73$) than when they did not ($M = 3.68$, $SD = 2.38$), $t(46) = 2.52$, $p < .05$. This result replicates the findings of Libby and Eibach (2002) and Study 1.

Next, we investigated whether perspective was associated with measures of mental focus and subjective temporal distance. With both mental-focus measures, greater use of third-person imagery was associated with a bias toward coherence focus, as predicted (memory descriptions: $r = .35$, $p < .05$; checklist: $r = .46$, $p < .01$). With both subjective temporal distance measures, the sign of the correlations suggested that greater use of third-person imagery was associated with greater subjective distance, but the relationship was at best only marginally significant (scale: $r = .27$, $p = .06$; checklist: $r = .15$, $p > .3$).

Next, we created composite indices of mental focus and subjective temporal distance by standardizing and averaging the two measures for each variable. When both indices were used to predict perspective simultaneously, only mental focus was significant, $\beta = .56$, $t(45) = 3.76$, $p < .001$; subjective temporal distance: $\beta = -.07$, $t(45) = .50$, $p = .62$.

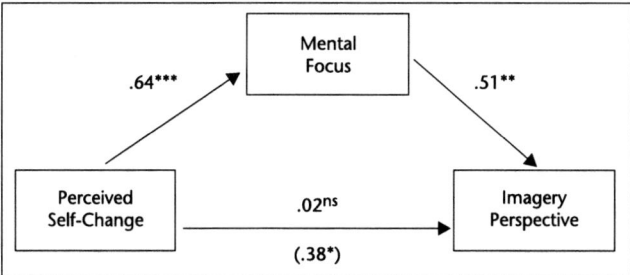

Note: Numbers on paths represent standardized regression coefficients. The coefficients along the path from perceived self-change to imagery perspective are the coefficients with (no parentheses) and without (parentheses) mental focus included in the equation. Perceived self-change was coded –1 for no change and +1 for change. The mental-focus index was coded such that higher numbers indicate more coherence focus and less experience focus. Higher numbers on the imagery perspective measure indicate more third-person imagery. Sobel $z = 2.69$, $p < .01$. *$p < .05$. **$p < .01$. ***$p < .001$.

Figure 2: Path diagram relating perceived self-change and mental focus to imagery perspective

Although this study design does not allow definitive conclusions about the causal relationships among the variables, a mediational analysis showed that the mental-focus measure accounted for the association between perceived self-change and perspective (Sobel $z = 2.69$, $p < .01$; see Figure 2), as we predicted.[3] An analysis using subjective temporal distance instead of mental focus as a potential mediator revealed no support for the idea that the greater subjective temporal distance of changed participants' memories accounted for their greater use of third-person imagery: Perceived self-change remained a significant predictor of perspective, $\beta = .32$, $t(45) = 2.00$, $p = .05$, when subjective temporal distance was included as an additional predictor, $\beta = .07$, $t(45) = 0.45$, $p = .65$.

In Study 1 participants used the third-person perspective more if their past self was inconsistent with the present than if it was consistent, regardless of whether or not including the past event in the present would be self-enhancing. Study 2 suggests that this pattern was not due to the effect of consistency per se but rather due to the effect of consistency on whether people focused on the experience of an event or its self-concept coherence. Although the recalled events felt more temporally distant if participants believed they had since changed, the relationship between subjective temporal distance and perspective was not reliable and did not account for the relationship between perceived self-change and perspective.

Studies 1 and 2 used the phenomenon of self-change to obtain evidence that perspective varies according to whether people focus on the experience of an event or its self-concept coherence. Studies 3 and 4 investigated this mechanism directly, apart from the phenomenon of self-change. These studies manipulated people's mental focus as they thought about life events, past and future, and tested the effect on perspective.

Study 3

Regardless of whether an event is in the past or the future people can focus on the experience of the event or its self-concept coherence. It is this difference in mental focus that we propose influences the point of view from which people construct visual images of events. Although there are certainly differences between recalling the past and imagining the future, both processes are constructive and appear to rely on a common core network for generating episodic event representations (Addis et al., 2009). Consistent with these commonalities, imagery is a hallmark of mental time travel in both directions (Brewer, 1996; Conway, Meares, & Standart, 2004), and visual perspective influences the level of meaning people perceive in actions, both when people recall the past and when they imagine the future (e.g., Libby et al., 2005; Vasquez & Buehler, 2007). Thus, if our hypothesis about the effect of mental focus on visual perspective is correct, focusing on the self-concept coherence of an event, as opposed to the experience of its concrete details, should promote third-person imagery regardless of whether the event is in the past or future. To test this in Study 3 we manipulated not only participants' mental focus but also the event's temporal position and measured the effect on perspective.

Method

Participants.   Eighty undergraduates (48 female) who attended their high school graduation at least one month prior to the study participated in exchange for course credit.

Materials and procedure.   Participants were randomly assigned in equal numbers to complete one of four versions of a questionnaire, which varied according to a 2 (temporal position: past vs. future) × 2 (mental focus: coherence vs. experience) design. Instructions either directed participants to describe their high school graduation (past) or their university graduation (future). In the coherence-focus conditions, participants were instructed to focus "on the broader significance of this event in your own life," defined as the meaning of the event in relation to personal characteristics and other life events. In the experience-focus conditions, participants were instructed to focus "on the concrete details" of the event, defined as the actions and sensory experiences involved. In each condition participants were instructed to refrain from focusing on the aspects of the event specified in the other condition.

After writing about the event for 7 minutes participants formed an image of that event and held it in mind while continuing to the next page, which introduced the distinction between first-person and third-person perspectives using descriptions from Libby and Eibach (2002). Participants indicated which perspective – first-person or third-person – they were using while picturing their graduation. They also reported the dates of their high school and university graduations.

Results and Discussion

We used logistic regression to predict perspective from mental focus (coherence vs. experience), temporal position (past vs. future), and their interaction. Mental focus was the only significant predictor (Wald $\chi^2 = 4.92$, $p < .05$; for all other predictors Wald $\chi^2 < 1$ and $ps > .65$). As hypothesized, participants were more likely to picture graduation from the third-person perspective if they focused on integrating that event with a coherent self-concept (past: 65% of participants; future: 55% of participants) than if they focused on the concrete experience of the event (past and future: 35% of participants; see Figure 3).

The temporally extended self stretches both into the past and the future, and for both directions focusing on the self-concept coherence of an event as opposed to the experience of its concrete details caused participants to be more likely to use third-person imagery. In this study, the event – graduation – was presumably self-enhancing, and participants should have been motivated to include this event in their present self-concept (Ross & Wilson, 2002), especially when they were directed to think about its meaning in relation to the self-concept. The fact that participants were most likely to adopt the third-person perspective under these conditions contradicts the idea that people

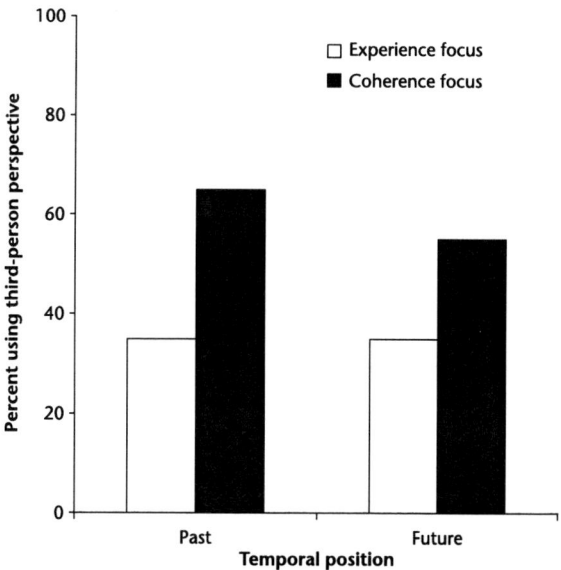

Figure 3: Percentage of participants using third-person imagery in Study 3, depending on temporal position of event and mental focus

use first-person imagery when they want to claim a pictured event and third-person imagery when they want to disown it.

Study 1 provides additional indirect evidence. Participants thought about either a past they should have been motivated to claim or one they should have been motivated to disown. This difference had no measurable impact on perspective, which instead depended only on the consistency of the pictured self with the present. We interpret this result to be a function of how the consistency of past selves influences the tendency to focus on self-concept coherence versus experiential details, and the results of Study 2 support this interpretation. Study 4 was designed to provide more definitive evidence by directly manipulating both the valence of a pictured event and participants' mental focus, then testing the effects on perspective.

Study 4

In Study 4 undergraduates imagined an important upcoming event – an interview for a desired position after graduation. They were either instructed to imagine the event unfolding according to a best-case or a worst-case scenario. We also manipulated their mental focus – either coherence or experience. To the extent that perspective depends on whether people desire to claim or disown the pictured event, participants should use more third-person imagery when they picture the worst-case as opposed to the best-case scenario. To the extent that perspective depends on whether people focus on the experience of an event or its self-concept coherence participants should use more third-person imagery when they focus on coherence than on experience.

Method

Participants. Fifty-six undergraduates (40 female) participated in exchange for $5 each.

Materials and procedure. Participants were randomly assigned to complete one of four versions of a computerized questionnaire, which varied according to a 2 (valence: best case vs. worst case) 2 (mental focus: coherence vs. experience) design.

First, participants briefly described the job or degree program they hoped to enter upon graduation. Next, they imagined that they had the opportunity to interview for this ideal position. Participants were either instructed to imagine this interview according to "a best-case scenario in which everything about the interview goes extremely well and you perform at your very best" or a "worst-case scenario in which everything about the interview goes extremely poorly and you perform at your very worst." In the coherence-focus conditions, participants were instructed to "explain what this interview would mean about you and your life," defined as the meaning of the event in relation to personal characteristics and other life events. In the experience-focus conditions participants were instructed to "describe what it would be like to experience the interview," defined as the actions and sensory experiences involved.

After participants had written about the interview they were directed to close their eyes and picture it. The next screen presented the imagery perspective measure, introducing the distinction between first-person and third-person perspectives similarly to Study 1. Participants used an 8-point fully labeled scale to indicate the proportion of images they experienced from each perspective as they had been writing about and picturing the interview. The endpoints of the scale were anchored at *all first-person images* and *all third-person images*.

The remaining questions were included for exploratory purposes or as manipulation checks. Participants completed the Positive and Negative Affect Schedule (Watson, Clark, & Tellegen, 1988). After this came a check for the valence manipulation: Participants used a fully labeled 7-point scale ranging from *very poorly* to *very well* to rate how well they imagined themselves performing in the interview. They used the same type of scale to rate how well they thought they would actually perform on such an interview. Next, they used fully labeled 5-point scales to rate imagery vividness and realism of the scenario. They used a fully labeled 7-point scale to rate how difficult it was to picture the event.

Next, as a check for the mental-focus manipulation, participants rated the thoughts they had when they wrote about the scenario. It was explained that they might have focused more on "what it would be like to experience the event directly – e.g., describing the sights, sounds, smells you would experience; describing the thoughts and feelings you would have during the event" or more on "analyzing the meaning of the event in your life – e.g., explaining its broader significance, what it would say about your personality and/or goals, how it would connect to other events in your life, and/or what the consequences of the event would be." Participants indicated the focus of their thoughts by choosing a point along an 8-point scale ranging from full focus on analyzing meaning to full focus on describing experience.

They then used 5-point scales ranging from *not at all* to *extremely* to rate their commitment to the career path that the interview represented, the likelihood they would follow this path upon graduation, and the extent of their preparation for the next step in their career path. Finally, they reported the month and year in which they would graduate.

Results and Discussion

One participant was excluded from analyses for failure to complete the questionnaire. This left 55 participants, with 12 to 15 per condition.

Participants' ratings of the proportion of images experienced from each perspective were submitted to a 2 (valence: best case vs. worst case) ×

2 (mental focus: coherence vs. experience) ANOVA. As predicted, there was no significant effect of valence on perspective, $F(1, 51) = 0.18$. The only significant effect was mental focus, $F(1, 51) = 4.81, p < .05$; participants used more third-person imagery in the coherence-focus condition ($M = 4.74, SD = 2.68$) than in the experience-focus condition ($M = 3.25, SD = 2.15$). This was true regardless of whether the interview represented a best-case scenario, which participants would be motivated to claim, or a worst-case scenario, which participants would be motivated to disown, $F(1, 51) = 1.29, p > .25$ (see Table 2).

We also analyzed participants' responses to the other questionnaire items using the same 2 (valence) × 2 (mental focus) ANOVA (see Table 2). Demonstrating the effectiveness of the manipulations, there was a significant main effect of valence on imagined performance, $F(1, 51) = 66.95, p < .001$, and a significant main effect of mental focus on the mental-focus manipulation check, $F(1, 51) = 8.45, p < .01$. The manipulations of scenario valence and mental focus also had significant or marginal effects on several other variables (see Table 2). However, none of these variables was significantly correlated with perspective ($ps > .25$), and the effect of mental focus on perspective remained significant when each of these variables was included as a covariate in 2 (valence) × 2 (mental focus) ANOVAs predicting perspective.

Table 2: Scenario ratings in Study 4, depending on valence and mental focus

	Valence							
	Best case				Worst case			
	Mental focus				Mental focus			
	Experience		Coherence		Experience		Coherence	
	M	SD	M	SD	M	SD	M	SD
Perspective	3.00	2.04	5.20	2.64	3.47	2.30	4.17	2.76
Positive affect[a]	3.46	0.71	3.04	0.67	2.84	0.51	2.98	0.69
Negative affect	1.46	0.49	1.47	0.68	1.45	0.41	1.98	0.92
Imagined performance[b]	*2.15*	*0.99*	*2.27*	*0.80*	*-1.67*	*1.29*	*-0.25*	*2.34*
Predicted performance	1.54	1.05	2.13	0.92	1.80	1.01	1.58	1.68
Vividness of imagery	4.62	0.77	4.73	0.88	4.87	0.64	4.33	0.78
Ease of imagery	1.46	1.20	1.07	1.34	1.33	0.98	1.00	1.35
Realness of scenario[a]	3.46	0.78	2.87	0.92	2.73	1.03	2.67	0.78
Mental focus	**2.54**	**1.13**	**4.53**	**1.64**	**3.87**	**2.17**	**4.83**	**2.37**
Commitment to career path[c]	4.00	1.08	4.47	0.74	3.67	1.05	4.17	0.84
Likelihood of career path	4.08	0.95	4.07	0.88	3.80	1.01	4.08	0.79
Preparation for career path	3.69	1.11	3.60	1.06	3.13	1.13	3.58	1.17

Note: Italic formatting indicates significant main effect of valence. Bold formatting indicates significant main effect of mental focus. Valence and mental focus did not significantly interact. Perspective and mental focus scales ranged from *entirely first-person/experience focus* (1) to *entirely third-person/coherence focus* (8). Scales for imagined and predicted performance as well as for ease of imagery ranged from *very poorly/extremely difficult* (–3) to *very well/extremely easy* (+3). All other ratings were on 5-point scales with endpoints coded 1 for the lowest level of the variable and 5 for the highest.
[a]Marginally significant main effect of valence, $p < .10$.
[b]Marginally significant mental focus by valence interaction, $p < .10$.
[c]Marginally significant main effect of mental focus, $p < .10$.

General Discussion

When people picture a life event, the imagery perspective they use varies according to whether they focus on integrating that event with a coherent self-concept (third-person) or on the experience of the event's concrete details (first-person). We found no evidence that perspective depends on whether people desire to disown (third-person) or claim (first-person) the pictured event as part of the present self. In Study 1, participants recalled events they should have been motivated either to disown or to claim. Imagery perspective did not vary according to this distinction but rather according to whether past selves were inconsistent with the present (third-person) or consistent (first-person). Study 2 suggested that the reason inconsistency promotes third-person imagery is that inconsistency promotes a focus on an event's self-concept coherence. Studies 3 and 4 provided direct evidence for this determinant of perspective. Both when recalling the past and when imagining the future, and regardless of whether or not the pictured event reflected positively or negatively on the self, adopting a coherence focus rather than experience focus made participants more likely to picture the event from the third-person perspective. Here we consider how these findings relate to other research on the self and event representations, and we discuss implications for the functional role of imagery in developing and maintaining the temporally extended self.

Relation to Prior Work on the Self
and Event Representations

The research reported here is concerned with different facets of the self and different ways of representing life events in memory and imagination. This creates points of contact with other lines of research that investigate these variables.

Self-awareness theory. Self-awareness theory (Duval & Wicklund, 1972) distinguishes between subjective and objective self-awareness, states that could be understood as mapping onto the two facets of the self we study here. Research in the tradition of self-awareness theory has focused almost entirely on the effects of experiencing one state of self-awareness or the other, and very little on the determinants of the two states (cf. Eichstaedt & Silvia, 2003), which is the focus of the studies we report here. Theoretically, objective self-awareness is proposed to vary according to gestalt figure-ground principles: When the self is the "smaller" area of the cognitive field, people should spontaneously experience objective self-awareness (Duval & Wicklund, 1972). This is proposed to occur when the self is distinct from a comparison set, which can consist of other people, nonsocial objects, or one's own past experience (Duval, Silvia, & Lalwani, 2001). Whereas self-awareness theory focuses on what causes the present self to become the object of awareness, the studies we report here concern what causes a past or future self to become an object in visual imagery. Yet, it is possible that the same principles apply.

We found that people were more likely to picture an event from the third-person perspective when that past self was discrepant from the present self, which initially appears to fit the principles of self-awareness theory. However, evidence suggested this effect was due to considering how the event related to the conceptual self, a process that promoted third-person imagery even when the recalled or imagined event was likely not discrepant from the conceptual self (e.g., graduation, successful job interview). It may be that considering a given event in terms of its coherence with the conceptual self causes the self in the pictured event to stand out as a figure against the ground of the conceptual self, even if the pictured self is not discrepant from the conceptual self. This would suggest an additional determinant of objective self-awareness. It is also possible that there are meaningful differences between objective self-awareness as it pertains to the present self versus past or future selves. Thus, further investigation of whether the factors that prompt shifts in imagery perspective also prompt shifts in self-awareness as operationalized by self-awareness theory would inform both that theory and an understanding of imagery perspective.

Construal level theory.   The manipulation of mental focus in our studies can be understood as varying the level of abstraction at which participants construed events. Construal level theory proposes that greater abstraction promotes greater psychological distance (Trope & Liberman, 2010). Other research shows that people are more likely to picture simple hypothetical actions from the third-person perspective if those actions are described in abstract as opposed to concrete terms (Libby et al., 2009). The present findings are consistent with this effect, demonstrating that it holds for complex events, regardless of their valence or temporal position.

However, whether use of third-person imagery necessarily reflects a feeling of psychological distance from the pictured event is a more complicated question. In the studies reported here perspective was not reliably associated with the subjective temporal distance of the event. And the results of the present experiments along with research reviewed in the introduction cast doubt on the idea that perspective functions to code the ownership of events, one of the proposed dimensions of psychological distance (Trope & Liberman, 2010). How or if third-person imagery varies in response to differences in felt psychological distance is an interesting question beyond the scope of this article.

Coping.   When it comes to coping with traumatic events, integrating those events into a coherent causal structure and highlighting the connections to larger themes and meaning in one's life can contribute to better outcomes (e.g., Taylor, 1983). One way to induce this sort of shift in understanding is to engage in expressive writing about the traumatic incident (Pennebaker, Mayne, & Francis, 1997). The effect of this procedure has been likened to a shift in perspective (Pennebaker, 1990), and the present findings suggest that expressive writing could produce a literal shift toward the third-person perspective in traumatic memories. However, the present findings also caution against assuming that spontaneous use of third-person imagery when recalling upsetting events necessarily reflects adaptive coping. Furthermore, the present findings suggest a potential moderator of the relationship between third-person imagery and coping as well as between expressive writing and coping.

For example, studies of trauma survivors have investigated the association between imagery perspective for traumatic events and recovery from them. In some cases spontaneous use of third-person imagery has been found to predict more severe symptoms of posttraumatic stress disorder (PTSD; e.g., Kenny et al., 2009). However, in other cases, this association has not emerged, and third-person imagery has even been found to predict better outcomes on some dimensions (e.g., McIsaac & Eich, 2004). The results of the present studies suggest one reason for this mixed pattern of results. If perspective varies according to whether individuals focus on the experience of an event or on integrating it into a coherent sense of themselves as a person, then whether use of third-person imagery is associated with better or worse outcomes should depend on the framework that individuals use to integrate the traumatic event with their self-concept.

In some cases individuals focus on a traumatic experience as defining a negative central organizing theme in their lives, and this tends to be associated with more severe PTSD symptoms (Berntsen & Rubin, 2007). However, individuals are often able to make sense of traumatic events in ways that preserve well-being (Bonanno, 2004). And evidence suggests that it is when this sort of framework is used that focusing on the broader meaning of a traumatic event in one's life has positive outcomes (Taylor, 1983). Thus, use of third-person imagery may predict worse outcomes among those who adopt a maladaptive understanding of an event's meaning in their lives but predict better outcomes among those who adopt an understanding that restores control and self-esteem. By extension, this analysis suggests that whether or not expressive writing predicts better outcomes in the wake of an upsetting experience may also depend on the way in which individuals perceive the upsetting experience to fit into a coherent concept of self. These possibilities represent intriguing questions to be addressed in future research.

Imagery Perspective as a Tool in Event Representation

In addition to these ways in which the present results connect with and diverge from other investigations of the self and event representations, they make a unique contribution by demonstrating the role of visual imagery. In cognitive psychology imagery is widely recognized as a representational tool (e.g., Reed, 2010). The present experiments help make the case that imagery serves a representational function in social psychological processes as well.

We found that the perspective people used to picture life events varied according to whether people focused on the events' meaning in relation to the self-concept (third-person) or on the experience of the events (first-person). Alone, this variation in imagery perspective might be interpreted as epiphenomenal, and thus as serving no purpose in psychological processes. However, given that the effect also works in the opposite causal direction, as reviewed in the introduction, it seems more plausible that variation in the use of first-person versus third-person perspectives reflects their representational function. According to this account, first-person images define an event in terms of the experience of acting on and reacting to the environment whereas third-person images define an event in terms of its meaning in a broader context. If this is true, then when people picture life events as they think about them, the visual perspective of those images may play a role in maintaining a certain construal of the event.

In the present studies participants were explicitly prompted to think about past or future events to investigate the determinants of visual perspective in mental imagery. However, there are many instances in everyday life in which people spontaneously evoke thoughts of life events. For example, people use memories of past events to ground a sense of personal identity (Singer & Salovey, 1993), and people think about past and especially future events during episodes of mind wandering (Smallwood, Nind, & O'Connor, 2009). Given the pervasive role of subjective construal in social psychological processes (Griffin & Ross, 1991) and the prominence of visual imagery when people think about life events (Brewer, 1996; Conway et al., 2004), imagery perspective may play a role in shaping the dynamics of a wide range of social psychological processes.

Conclusion

The present findings speak most directly to the role of imagery perspective in defining the two facets of the self. It has been suggested that the experiential self represents a primitive awareness shared with other animals, whereas the conceptual self is uniquely human (Gallagher, 2000). Humans have a notion of the self as a coherent entity persisting across time from the past to the present into the future. One process contributing to the construction of this conceptual self is the creation of an overarching framework linking specific life experiences to beliefs and theories about themes, trajectories, and goals that define the self across time (Conway, 2005; McAdams, 2001). The studies reported here demonstrate that focusing on these connections causes people to use third-person imagery, both when recalling the past and imagining the future. Given the bidirectional nature of the relationship between imagery perspective and the level of meaning in event representations, the present findings suggest that picturing events from the third-person perspective contributes to the construction and maintenance of a sense of self as an entity that extends in both directions across time.

Appendix

Mental Focus Items from the Thoughts and Feelings Checklist in Study 2

Feeling like you were living the event all over again
Feeling like you were transported back into the past
Feeling the same feelings you felt when the event was happening originally
Thinking the same thoughts you thought when the event was happening originally
Thinking, why did I do that?
Thinking of ways you could have acted other than the way you did
Feeling like your high school self was a different person
Thinking "that's not me anymore"

Note: Participants saw all items presented in plain text. Mental focus was scored as the proportion of items on which participants responded consistent with a coherence focus as opposed to an experience focus (i.e., responded by endorsing items here in roman text and not endorsing items here in italics).

Notes

1. Unless noted otherwise, including objective temporal distance as a covariate in this and subsequent analyses does not change patterns of means or significance.
2. The four participants who gave inconsistent answers initially identified themselves as having changed, but then rated themselves as unchanged.
3. We also tested an alternative model in which third-person imagery would account for the relationship between self-change and mental focus. Results were not consistent with this causal chain and provided only further support for our interpretation. When perspective was added to the model predicting mental focus from self-change, the effect of perspective was significant, $\beta = .34$, $t(45) = 3.05$, $p < .01$, but the effect of self-change remained significant, $\beta = .53$, $t(45) = 4.76$, $p < .001$. Thus, self-change relates to mental focus directly, independent of perspective. This supports the idea that the inconsistency created by self-change prompts people to focus on an event's self-concept coherence. The fact that perspective also predicts mental focus, independent of self-change, is consistent with research that manipulates imagery perspective (e.g., Libby, Shaeffer, & Eibach, 2009; Vasquez & Buehler, 2007). In that research, picturing events from the third-person rather than first-person perspective causes people to define those events in terms of their connection with more general theories about traits, goals, and identities, as opposed to in terms of concrete experience; the present analysis suggests the same. In conjunction with the main analyses in this study and other research, the present analysis is consistent with a bidirectional relationship between perspective and mental focus. However, together these analyses also suggest that in the case of self-change it is mental focus that initially prompts a shift in perspective and not the other way around.

References

Addis, D. R., Pan, L., Vu, M., Laiser, N., & Schacter, D. L. (2009). Constructive episodic simulation of the future and the past: Distinct subsystems of a core brain network mediate imagining and remembering. *Neuropsychologia, 47,* 2222–2238.

Berntsen, D., & Rubin, C. (2007). When a trauma becomes a key to identity: Enhanced integration of trauma memories predicts posttraumatic stress disorder symptoms. *Applied Cognitive Psychology, 21,* 417–431.

Bonanno, G. A. (2004). Loss, trauma, and human resilience: Have we underestimated the human capacity to thrive after extremely aversive events? *American Psychologist, 59,* 20–28.

Brewer, W. F. (1996). What is recollective memory? In D. C. Rubin (Ed.), *Remembering our past: Studies in autobiographical memory* (pp. 19–66). New York, NY: Cambridge University Press.

Conway, M. A. (2005). Memory and the self. *Journal of Memory and Language, 53,* 594–628.

Conway, M. A., Meares, K., & Standart, S. (2004). Images and goals. *Memory, 12,* 525–531.

D'Argembeau, A., & Van der Linden, M. (2004). Phenomenal characteristics associated with projecting oneself back into the past and forward into the future: Influence of valence and temporal distance. *Consciousness and Cognition: An International Journal, 13,* 844–858.

Didion, J. (2007, March 4). The year of hoping for stage magic. *New York Times,* pp. B1, B7.

Duval, T. S., Silvia, P. J., & Lalwani, N. (2001). *Self-awareness and causal attribution: A dual systems theory.* Boston, MA: Kluwer.

Duval, T. S., & Wicklund, R. A. (1972). *A theory of objective self-awareness.* New York, NY: Academic Press.

Eichstaedt, J., & Silvia, J. (2003). Noticing the self: Implicit assessment of self-focused attention using word recognition latencies. *Social Cognition, 21,* 349–361.

Farb, N. A. S., Segal, Z. V., Mayberg, H., Bean, J., McKeon, D., Fatima, Z., & Anderson, A. K. (2007). Attending to the present: Mindfulness meditation reveals distinct neural modes of self-reference. *Social Cognitive and Affective Neuroscience, 2,* 313–322.

Frank, M., & Gilovich, T. (1989). Effect of memory perspective on retrospective causal attributions. *Journal of Personality and Social Psychology, 57,* 399–403.

Freud, S. (1960). Childhood memories and screen memories. In J. Strachey (Ed.), *The standard edition of the complete psychological works of Sigmund Freud* (Vol. 6, pp. 43–52). London, England: Hogarth Press. (Original work published 1907)

Gallagher, S. (2000). Philosophical conceptions of the self: Implications for cognitive science. *Trends in Cognitive Science, 4,* 14–21.

Galton, F. (1883). *Inquiries into human faculty.* London, England: Macmillan.

Griffin, D. W., & Ross, L. (1991). Subjective construal, social inference, and human misunderstanding. In M. P. Zanna (Ed.), *Advances in experimental social psychology* (Vol. 24, pp. 319–359). New York, NY: Academic Press.

Huebner, D. M., & Fredrickson, L. (1999). Gender differences in memory perspectives: Evidence for self-objectification in women. *Sex Roles, 41,* 459–467.

Jackson, P. L., Meltzoff, A. N., & Decety, J. (2006). Neural circuits involved in imitation and perspective-taking. *Neuroimage, 31,* 429–439.

James, W. (1890/1950). *The principles of psychology, Vol. 1.* New York: Dover.

Kenny, L. M., Bryant, R. A., Silove, D., Creamer, M., O'Donnell, M., & McFarlane, A. C. (2009). Distant memories: A prospective study of vantage point of trauma memories. *Psychological Science, 20,* 1049–1052.

Legrand, D., & Ruby, P. (2009). What is self-specific? Theoretical investigation and critical review of neuroimaging results. *Psychological Review, 116,* 252–282.

Libby, L. K., & Eibach, R. P. (2002). Looking back in time: Self-concept change affects visual perspective in autobiographical memory. *Journal of Personality and Social Psychology, 82,* 167–179.

Libby, L. K., Eibach, R. P., & Gilovich, T. (2005). Here's looking at me: The effect of memory perspective on assessments of personal change. *Journal of Personality and Social Psychology, 88,* 50–62.

Libby, L. K., & Eibach, R. P. (in press). Visual perspective in mental imagery: An integrative model explaining its function in judgment, emotion, and self-insight. In M. P. Zanna and J. M. Olson (Eds.) *Advances in Experimental Social Psychology.* San Diego, CA: Academic Press.

Libby, L. K., Shaeffer, E. M., & Eibach, R. P. (2009). Seeing meaning in action: A bidirectional link between visual perspective and action identification level. *Journal of Experimental Psychology: General, 138,* 503–516.

McAdams, D. P. (2001). The psychology of life stories. *Review of General Psychology, 5,* 100–122.

McIsaac, H. K., & Eich, E. (2002). Vantage point in episodic memory. *Psychonomic Bulletin & Review, 9,* 144–150.

McIsaac, H. K., & Eich, E. (2004). Vantage point in traumatic memory. *Psychological Science, 15,* 248–253.

Nigro, G., & Neisser, U. (1983). Point of view in personal memories. *Cognitive Psychology, 15,* 467–482.

Pennebaker, J. W. (1990). *Opening up: The healing power of expressing emotions.* New York, NY: Guilford.

Pennebaker, J. W., Mayne, T. J., & Francis, M. E. (1997). Linguistic predictors of adaptive bereavement. *Journal of Personality and Social Psychology, 72,* 863–871.

Reed, S. K. (2010). *Thinking visually.* New York, NY: Psychology Press.

Robinson, J. A., & Swanson, K. L. (1993). Field and observer modes of remembering. *Memory, 1,* 169–184.

Ross, M. (1989). Relation of implicit theories to the construction of personal histories. *Psychological Review, 96,* 341–357.

Ross, M., & McFarland, C. (1988). Constructing the past: Biases in personal memories. In D. Bar-Tal & A. W. Kruglanski (Eds.), *The social psychology of knowledge* (pp. 299–314). New York, NY: Cambridge University Press.

Ross, M., & Wilson, A. E. (2000). Constructing and appraising past selves. In D. L. Schacter & E. Scarry (Eds.), *Memory, brain, and belief* (pp. 231–258). Cambridge, MA: Harvard University Press.

Ross, M., & Wilson, A. E. (2002). It feels like yesterday: Self-esteem, valence of personal past experiences, and judgments of subjective distance. *Journal of Personality and Social Psychology, 82,* 792–803.

Sanitioso, R. B. (2008). Motivated self and recall: Visual perspectives in remembering past behaviors. *European Journal of Social Psychology, 38,* 566–575.

Schwarz, N., & Bless, H. (2007). Mental construal processes: The inclusion/exclusion model. In D. A. Stapel & J. Suis (Eds.), *Assimilation and contrast in social psychology* (pp. 119–142). Philadelphia, PA: Psychology Press.

Singer, J. A., & Salovey, P. (1993). *The remembered self: Emotion and memory in personality.* New York: Free Press.

Smallwood, J., Nind, L., & O'Connor, R. C. (2009). When is your head at? An exploration of factors associated with the temporal focus of the wandering mind. *Consciousness and Cognition, 18,* 118–125.

Swann, W. B., Jr., Rentfrow, P. J., & Guinn, J. (2002). Self-verification: The search for coherence. In M. Leary & J. Tagney (Eds.), *Handbook of self and identity* (pp. 367–383). New York, NY: Guilford.

Taylor, S. E. (1983). Adjustment to threatening events: A theory of cognitive adaptation. *American Psychologist, 38,* 1161–1174.

Trope, Y., & Liberman, N. (2010). Construal-level theory of psychological distance. *Psychological Review, 117,* 440–463.

Vallacher, R. R., & Wegner, D. M. (1985). *A theory of action identification.* Hillsdale, NJ: Erlbaum.

Vasquez, N. A., & Buehler, R. (2007). Seeing future success: Does imagery perspective influence achievement motivation? *Personality and Social Psychology Bulletin, 33,* 1392–1405.

Watson, D., Clark, L. A., & Tellegen, A. (1988). Development and validation of brief measures of positive and negative affect: The PANAS scales. *Journal of Personality and Social Psychology, 54,* 1063–1070.

Wilson, A. E., & Ross, M. (2003). The identity function of autobiographical memory: Time is on our side. *Memory, 11,* 137–149.

73

Inner-City Children in Sharper Focus: Sociology of Childhood and Photo Elicitation Interviews

Marisol Clark-Ibáñez

Ten-year old Nanci sat on a stack of tightly packed clothing wrapped in opaque plastic near the front of a small, dimly lit warehouse. Her father worked in the back, ironing and assembling clothing. The darkness seemed to cool down the place on this hot summer Saturday in downtown Los Angeles. He came out occasionally to check on us, offering a tired smile and a nod of his head.

Nanci's thick chestnut-colored braids fell around her round face; this is the style she wore everyday for school. She excitedly looked over the photographs I had developed for her, exclaiming "oh no!" "cool!" and "hmmm" as she surveyed her own handiwork.

We were about to begin our photo elicitation interview. I settled onto my own bench of clothing to begin the session. I asked her to tell me which were her favorite images.

Nanci explained to me, "This isn't my favorite outfit, but it's the best photograph, like, in terms of the lights." She handed over the 3 by 5 picture.

I nodded my head in agreement, "Yeah, you're right. The lighting is good." I added slyly, "Nanci, you never told me about this!"

She giggled proudly, "Yeah, I do this a couple times a month. I'm pretty good!"

I knew Nanci as a fourth grade student at a charter school that emphasized high academic standards. Only after coordinating the time and place for her interview did I realize she was the daughter of a garment worker and that she sometimes worked with her dad in a warehouse. Now, after seeing the photos that Nanci took, I realized she was also a mariachi singer.

Source: Gregory C. Stanczak (ed.), *Visual Research Methods* (Thousand Oaks: SAGE, 2007), pp. 167–196.

I n her favorite picture, Nanci is dressed in a black suede *traje* or suit with silver *greca* (stylized floral embroidery) sewn up and down the outside of her pants legs and on the front opening of her jacket. Her black and silver *moño* (tie) puffed onto her chest complemented her large silver hoop earrings and framed her brightly painted red lips and black-lined eyes. Except for her makeup and her *banda* (sash) made of sparkly silver cloth, she wore the masculine costume, foregoing the fitted long skirt and cinched-waist jacket women typically wear.

Nanci's story illustrates the benefits and insights that I was hoping to discover in my photo elicitation study. First, the photo elicitation methodology allowed students to show me aspects of their lives that might have otherwise been hidden from an adult researcher like myself. I will spend much of this chapter elaborating on these aspects of photo elicitation. Second, photo elicitation helped me to uncover some of the institutional practices that might have served to perpetuate educational inequalities that might have otherwise not been revealed by just examining the school setting. I will briefly explain this here, as it will also illuminate the genesis of my study.

Nanci was an average student at a charter school in South Central Los Angeles. She had a sweet disposition and did her work but did not garner any special attention from the teacher or school officials. When I learned that she was an accomplished mariachi singer, I could not help but wonder why this extracurricular skill did not translate into valuable cultural capital and a better social ranking at school. I asked her teacher about it. Her teacher knew about Nanci's performances but thought her parents used Nanci for additional income. Rather than encouraging these performances, her parents should concentrate on her academic progress, Nanci's teacher felt. The teacher's judgment potentially cost Nanci any rewards, such as kudos given to students who play institutionally valued instruments, such as the violin or piano. For the study of schooling I was conducting at the time, the teacher's perspective on Nanci's extracurricular activities provided me with valuable insight to understand how the school's achievement ideology functioned (Clark-Ibáñez, 2004). However, I thought there was more to Nanci's story: It reflected a new and rich perspective about the complexity of inner-city children's lives. Without reviewing those photographs with Nanci on that hot summer day, I might never have seen this other world, segregated (and devalued) in her inner-city classroom.

How do we understand children sociologically? Previous research has discussed kids as *tabula rasa*, negating their agency (Jenks, 1996). However, I approach the study of inner-city children and their social worlds with the new sociology of childhood, a perspective that tries to understand children as active, creative, and important actors in their own right (Corsaro, 1997; Mayhall, 2002). This chapter explains how the use of photo elicitation interviews became critical to my understanding of kids in poverty and the way they viewed their own lives.

The Study

My current study of inner-city children emerged from my previous ethnographic study on inner-city schools (Clark-Ibáñez, 2004). When I began soliciting volunteers to participate in my study, I had already fostered relationships with the children through intensive participant observation in their classrooms for almost a full academic year. Through that year, I had established relationships with the kids and their families outside of the school setting as well. With parental permission, I took some students on weekend outings – we went to the beach or movies, drove through exclusive neighborhoods in Los Angeles (girls wanted to find actor Leo DiCaprio's house), and went to eat at fast-food restaurants. I also chatted with parents about school, life, diet, and work. I helped Spanish speakers fill out forms in English and accompanied teachers on student home visits. In short, I became immersed in the students' school and social lives for almost an academic year before I began the photography project.

Through my ethnographic fieldwork, I realized that many children had richly complex home lives, and I wanted to understand how this impacted their school lives. Nanci's case is just one example. Yet, once I began reading about the topics of children and poverty, I noticed gaps in the literature that did not capture the realities of the kids' social world outside of school – realities such as familial responsibilities, play, or peers.

Shortcomings in the Sociology of Childhood

Studies of children have several crucial shortcomings. They mainly tell about white, middle-class childhood because many times, these are the children to whom researchers have access (Adler & Adler, 1998). They study children in the aggregate and consider the effects of independent variables to understand children's experiences and likely outcomes. They study children in relation to other entities – motherhood, schooling, immigration, welfare system, racial segregation, and so on. They typically do not examine children's own lived experiences.

With the above factors at play, the literature does not address the subjective questions of what it is like to be poor, a minority, and a kid. A small group of publications, such as those that emerged from the California Childhoods project (directed by Catherine Cooper and Barrie Thorne) and Annette Lareau's (2003) *Unequal Childhoods*, provide insightful analysis into the lives of poor, working class, and minority children. Yet, in most of the current literature, multidimensional answers are largely missing because they tend only to highlight alarming (and real) issues such as the effects of violence, experiences related to schooling, or descriptions of abject poverty. Is this all there is to being poor and a kid?

Admittedly, several of my young participants recognized the local drug dealer's car; this curtailed their ability to play outside when the car stopped for a long period of time near their homes. I am not suggesting that researchers should downplay the stark realities of these kids' lives. Yet, my study revealed that tree houses, Barbies, and Tupac Shakur (hip hop artist) posters were just as relevant to children and their daily lives. Researchers have not been able to capture the quotidian aspect of their lives. By missing how kids negotiate mainstream media and material culture, studies create a static and staid frame of inner-city childhoods. Inner-city childhoods are framed as unidirectionally shaped by outside forces, disregarding the ways in which kids are shaping, creating, and negotiating aspects of their childhood experiences in an inner-city community.

In response to this gap, a growing number of researchers, such as Barrie Thorne, William Corsaro, and Jans Qvtrup, conceptualize children as collectively participating in society. To further elaborate this theoretical and analytical framework, it is useful to incorporate a methodology, such as photo elicitation, that allows researchers to explore and better understand the texture and complexity of inner-city kids' lives.

The Method: Choices and Children in Photo Elicitation

As I read the literature in search of this textured approach to children's lives, I also read more about photo elicitation as a methodology, and I thought this would be an ideal way to capture the tangible and intangible aspects of children's lives. In photo elicitation, the researcher introduces photographs to the interview context as a way to generate responses beyond the language-based conventional interview protocols. This approach is based on assumptions about the role and utility of photographs in prompting reflections that words alone cannot. Photo elicitation interviews, for example, can "mine deeper shafts into a different part of human consciousness than do words-alone interviews" (Harper, 2002, p. 23). Photographs can generate data illuminating a subject that otherwise may be invisible to the researcher but blatantly apparent to the interviewee (Schwartz, 1989).

There are a variety of approaches to conducting photo elicitation interviews. One of the first decisions that researchers must make is who will take the photographs.[1] Some researchers opt to take photographs themselves and present the images they captured to the research participants. This option allows the researcher to frame, select, develop, organize, and present the images to the interviewees based on their own research questions. For example, Harper (2001) used aerial views of farmland and historical photographs to interview farmers about their identity and community. (See Harper, 1987, and Schwartz, 1992, as additional examples.)

Using researcher-produced photographs is an excellent way to conduct theory-driven research. Toting a camera can help researchers better interact with the people they are studying (Collier, 1967; Schwartz, 1989), although it can take time (Shanklin, 1979). Once granted access, researcher-photographers may capture taken-for-granted aspects of the subjects' community or life that prompt discussion. In some cases, the interviewees alert the researcher to omissions and questions that later can be included in the interview protocol. Yet, photo elicitation in which the researcher makes the images may be limited by the researchers' interests and miss an essential aspect of the research setting that is meaningful to the participants.

In addition to the intrinsic biases of research questions, researchers must also be cautious of the tendency to capture the "visually arresting" images (e.g., homeless person asleep near a school entrance) rather than what might be meaningful for the interview subjects (Orellana, 1999). In documenting visual descriptions of South Central Los Angeles for my study, I noted my tendency to include images that, as an outsider, I found unique or beautiful (e.g., see Photos 1 and 2). However, for the children in my study, these images were unnoticed and "natural" elements of their environment; they lacked the significant meanings I may have imputed to them. For these reasons, I would not recommend the researcher-photographer approach for researching with children.

Given my framework conceptualizing children as active agents in their own right, I used a more inductive research approach where the researcher asks interview subjects to take their own photos to be used later as interview stimuli.

Source: Used with permission.

Photo 1: Pizza delivery man on bicycle

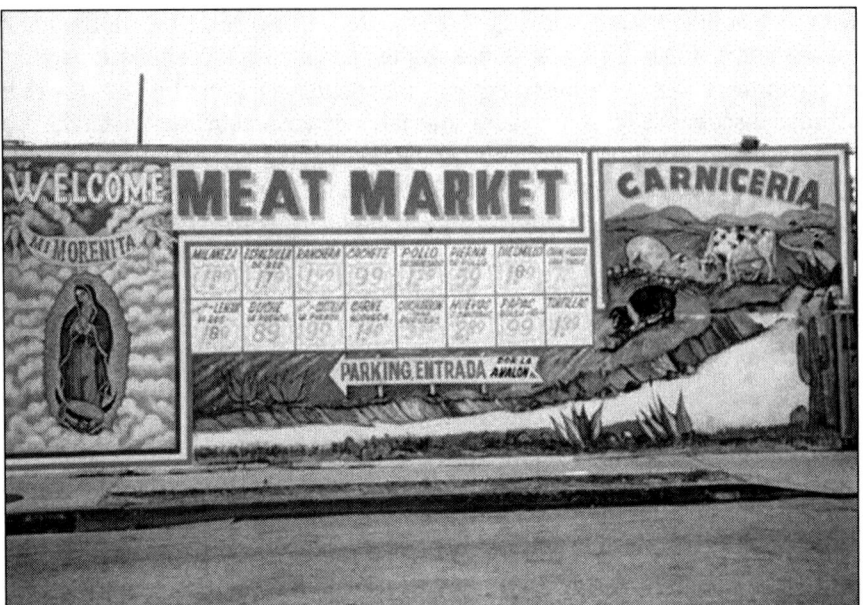

Photo 2: Virgen de Guadalupe mural on meat store wall

This is called an *autodriven* photo elicitation (Clark, 1999). Cindy Dell Clark reports that photographs taken by children captured and introduced content area that from an adult viewpoint might have been poorly understood (or even overlooked). I have found that, when adapted for the purpose of interviewing children, the autodriven photo elicitation becomes an ideal methodology to engage young people.

Previous researchers have outlined the limitations and problems of research with children (Adler & Adler, 1998; Thorne, 1993). Clark (1999) observes that researchers must have patience or sensitivity to work with children's pace, style, and playfulness. Conventional interviews are especially problematic for children. Clark (1999, p. 38) summarizes the following four challenges associated with interviewing children: children's level of linguistic communication, their cognitive development, the question and answer setting, and the accentuated power dynamics of the adult interviewing a child. Photos lessen some of the awkwardness of interviews because there is something to focus on, especially if the interviewee takes the photographs: They are familiar with the material.

Photo elicitation nicely intervenes along each of these challenges of conventional interviewing. First, in terms of linguistics, photo elicitation lets the children set the linguistic level in accord with their ability. The children decide what they want to say and how to do so. The researcher typically does not have a structured or complex interview schedule but rather lets the photographs and child's insights lead the way for conversation and sharing.

Second, in photo elicitation, children's cognitive development is matched with the type of information that may be elicited. Photography stimulates kids' memories in ways that are different from verbal-based interviews – ways that are potentially unknown to the researcher. Using photos can improve the interview experience with children by providing them with a clear, tangible, yet nonlinguistic prompt.

Third, because children lead the interview, the potentially awkward social setting created in the question and answer context all but vanishes. In particular, children may believe that if someone poses a question (especially an adult), there is a "correct" answer. I found that children were a bit confused when I asked them to tell me about their photographs, as if they had expected a more conventional interview. As illustrated in Nanci's interview, I usually found that asking an open-ended question – for example, Which one was your favorite? – was a good way to begin the photo elicitation session. Yet, once I made it clear that I wanted to know what they thought of their own photographs, they barely needed any probing at all.

Finally, photo elicitation disrupts some of the power dynamics involved with regular interviews. This is especially relevant in the cases where there are acute status, age, class, gender, or racial power differences (see Clark, 1999, and Harper, 1987, as examples). In my study, for example, when one of my participants, Silvia, went to Oregon for the summer to work in the fields with her relatives, she brought along her camera. For our interview that fall, I met Silvia at her home. She lived on a busy intersection in South Central Los Angeles and in front of an enormous electrical energy plant. Her mother hung back in the kitchen, and her little sister and brother sat in the living room with us, curious but quiet, during the interview. Image after image, Silvia became the expert. She explained how various kinds of farm machinery work, how tomatoes are grown and harvested, and how her relatives live (see Photo 3) – all topics, despite growing up in an agricultural area, that I knew nothing about and would not have been able to ask about in our interview had it not been for the visual data that Silvia provided. Photo elicitation can be a powerful tool to simultaneously gather data and empower the interviewee.

While it resolves the methodological challenges of working with children that Clark (1999) points out, photo elicitation has its own complications, which must be taken into consideration when working with children. For example, when the interviewees produce the images, researchers should be aware of differing definitions of what belongs in a photograph.

In my study, Victoria and her mother clashed over the concept of photographic content: Her mother thought what Victoria *should* use the camera to produce "important" images of her family and *not* the images she did produce of her friends and their clubhouse. In another example, Carla took photographs of her mother in front of the washer and dryer; during our interview, she revealed that her mother wanted her to take these. If children are producing images, researchers must understand that family dynamics of power and authority may affect their ability to take the photographs of their own choosing

Photo 3: Silvia's aunt and farm machinery

or to finish the project. In addition, these family interactions become another source of data. I learned about the household dynamics of the children's families and their effects on school assignments or homework.

The literature does not discuss children's inappropriate use of the camera. For example, in my study, Stanford's mother informed me that she caught him taking photographs of his naked sister, and so she destroyed the camera.[2] Photo elicitation allows the researcher into the interviewee's home and life through photographs in different ways and with different results than when the researcher is physically present. Because of this, photo elicitation practitioners grapple with issues of confidentiality and ethics on a case-by-case basis.

Photo elicitation is a powerful method, yet researchers must be cautious and thoughtful of their specific population's needs and capacities, especially in research with children. The choices and strategies that play to the strengths of children and the strengths of the method should be considered. With this in mind, the autodriven approach to photo elicitation can be an appropriate and successful methodology for studies of childhood or projects involving children.

Logistics of Photo Elicitation Interviews

Selecting photo elicitation for its methodological benefits within the interview process raises a new set of logistical considerations. Researchers must consider the overall financial cost, coordination of camera dissemination and retrieval, and time spent developing the photographs and conducting the interview. In terms of access, institutional support or insider connections are common prerequisites for conducting photo elicitation interviews (e.g., hospital in Clark, 1999; school in Clark-Ibáñez, 2004; community center in Orellana, 1999; kin in Schwartz, 1992). For interviewees, the addition of photographs may mean an additional layer of intimacy compared with regular face-to-face interviews; as a result, the researcher may find it harder to obtain permission from institutions or to recruit interviewees. However, unlike the researcher-photographer model, the potential for the interviewees to own a camera and the novelty of taking photographs for an outsider can help researchers overcome barriers to soliciting interviewees.

In my study, it took the last 2 months of the school year to obtain permission from parents, the school, and children.[3] Several parents helped me craft a permission form that would be clearly understood by other parents and that addressed issues such as costs, care of equipment, time commitment, reciprocation, and intended follow-up. I gave the following written instructions to the children who participated in the project:

> **What you'll do:** Take pictures of the people and the things that are the most important to you (e.g., family members, favorite places, toys – it's up to you!).This is a FREE project – it will not cost you or your parents anything.
>
> - This camera belongs to you! Remember to keep it out of the sun.
> - I will pick up the camera when you are done taking the pictures. I think a week should be enough time, but let me know if you need more time.
> - After the photos are developed, I will bring you the photos.
> - We will take some time to talk about the photos you took.
> - Call me with any questions: [my phone number]
> - Have fun!!

Reflecting on my study, I would now inform the children that they have the right to withdraw any photographs that they do not want to discuss. I learned this going through the photo elicitation process. When interviewees see the images, they may regret having taken some of them; if the researcher has already viewed them, this cannot be remedied. Therefore, the researcher should not view the photographs until the interviewee has had time to look them over and remove unwanted ones. Of course, the interviewees should be told in advance that this is the process.

Parents talked with me after school or called me at home to discuss the "camera project." Some wanted to be clear about the monetary costs to them (none), and others expressed anxiety about giving their children a camera for fear they would lose it. I explained to them that the children would be given "disposable" or single-use cameras, and I would have a few extras in case some children lost theirs. (I bought the cameras wholesale for $5 each.)

I gave the kids their cameras as soon as I received their signed permission slips. Although most children had never taken a photograph, they understood the basic principles of operating a camera and required little instruction. Most children completed the project within a week of receiving their camera. I developed double copies of their film at the local drugstore (about $8 per camera). Once the film was developed, I arranged an interview time and day with the child.

Viewing photographs gave other family members an incentive to be present; frequently, parents and siblings took part in the interview. Initially, I thought the participants might be shy about sharing their photographs in front of others, but most had arranged the interviews to include their families. This was no small feat because most parents worked two or three jobs each: many times, they alternated shifts so that someone could be home with the children. As I will discuss later, photographs elicited extended personal narratives that illuminate the viewers' lives and experiences, especially when viewed in a group setting (Schwartz, 1989).

The interviews lasted from a half-hour to 2 hours. Fifty-five children participated in the project, and 47 completed interviews. I spent three summer months exclusively conducting photo elicitation and then returned to Los Angeles for the rest of the interviews in the subsequent year. Most interviews took place in participants' living rooms, at the kitchen table, or on the front porch and in the backyard when it was too hot inside. I also conducted several interviews on Saturdays inside warehouses in the Los Angeles garment district, where kids helped their parents.

Making Sense of Image and Text

I am in the midst of coding the 959 images by using a semigrounded theory approach to see what categories emerge. I will also transcribe and code the kids' interviews to hear how they talk about their photographs. In my view, there is nothing inherently interesting about photographs; rather, photographs act as a medium of communication between researcher and subject. The photographs do not necessarily represent empirical truths or reality. In this sense, photographs used in photo elicitation have a dual purpose. Researchers can use photographs as a tool to expand on questions, and simultaneously, subjects can use photographs to provide a unique way to communicate dimensions of their lives.

The photo elicitation method can present a challenge of coding words *and* images.[4] Analysis may be difficult if the researcher must sift through the data from a lively group who viewed and referred to multiple photographs. People may talk over each other, it may be hard to identify which individuals are talking, or conversation may significantly shift themes. Careful and patient listening to the data, as required in other qualitative methods, is key in photo elicitation. The same attention to detail is required of the photographs. I numbered each photograph before the interview so that I could refer to the number throughout the taped conversation. This allowed me to identify the photographs by my cues on the audiotaping during the data analysis stage.

For initially understanding the visual data, I found it useful to draw on Doug Harper's (2002) three uses of photographs in photo elicitation. First, I used photographs as visual inventories of objects, people, and artifacts. Second, photographs depict events that were a part of collective or institutional paths (e.g., photographs of schools or images of events that occurred earlier in the lifetime of the subjects). Third, photos are intimate dimensions of the social. For example, photos of family or other intimate social groups, images of one's own body, and photos that connect oneself to society, culture, or history. It is important to add that a single roll of film may display multiple uses. For example, a child in my study took photos of her refrigerator and Barbies (inventory), her afterschool program building (institution), and portraits of herself and her sisters (social). After categorizing the images, I then could begin coding based on substantive issues, such as gender. I found that the significance of these images reflecting the textured lives of the children in this project arose at the intersection of these various levels of meanings and utility. While I favor the interpretive meanings of images throughout this chapter and the way that children can speak to and through them, I am not disregarding the empirical potential of photography as documentation discussed here. In fact, in this project, the two processes work hand in hand.

Visualizing the Texture of Inner-City Childhood

The kids' photographs and interviews revealed the day-to-day experiences of low-income urban children. The preliminary data presented in this chapter show the myriad experiences that shape these children's lives. My research gives priority to the voices and images of inner-city children and, thus, captures a complex social world that is deeper than images that are frequently used to characterize the inner city in popular media, such as gang activity, drive-bys, run-down schools, and cramped living conditions. Using photo elicitation was crucial to accessing the children's perspective about specific issues and experiences and uncovering their worldview in general. Photo elicitation, as a method, is good at giving children agency because the images and explanations mainly come from the kids themselves; this responds to the call from sociologists to allow for agency when studying children (Mayhall, 2002).

First, contrary to popular media, the children's photographs reveal more intimate and reflexive aspects of what we consider trappings of middle-class childhood. Students showed me their photos of the artifacts meaningful to them, such as soccer trophies, pop star fan books, and doll collection (see Photos 4, 5, and 6). While these artifacts could be found in middle-class homes,

Source: Used with permission.

Photo 4: James's trophies

Source: Used with permission.

Photo 5: Natalia's fan books

if you look more closely, they reflect indicators of poverty. The Barbie dolls shown here were bought at garage sales and the "99 Cent Store," and the fan books were checked out of the library. Look more closely at twins Lucia and Mariana's backdrop (Photo 7). Because there are so many people living in

Source: Used with permission.
Photo 6: Maria Sonia's Barbies

Source: Used with permission.
Photo 7: Twins Lucia and Mariana's stuffed animals

their home, they prop up mattresses against the wall during the day and lay them out on the floor as bedding by night.

Second, autodriven photographs showed me students' interpretation of material reality. For example, they inventoried any "big ticket items" they owned, such as a computer, Nintendo, or a television. The most common reason they gave for photographing these items was so that they would have a memory of it in case it was stolen or taken away. Indeed, within one year, several children did experience robberies of the very things they captured on film. However, most students did not own expensive items. After I developed the film and saw the items, I presumed the kids would discuss them with pride of ownership. Their tone as they described the items, however, was a melancholy pride: happy they owned it but anticipating its loss. This shows the importance of photo elicitation because the method allowed for the children to express *their* understanding of what constituted a potential everyday threat. For me, the images of everyday threat were the boarded-up illegally occupied homes, the bars on the windows and doors, and the constant police helicopter activity. For the kids, threat was symbolized in a more personal, intimate way.

Third, the kids took the most photographs of aspects of their social lives such as their friends, pets, and family parties (see Photos 10 through 15). To me, the images of the social contrasted with the image of the inner city in the popular media, as well as the academic perceptions of depression, fear, and fatalism in this environment. When listening to the kids explain these social photographs, I realized the power of the photographs to reveal much more about their lives. For example, one of my first interviews was with Janice, who took 38 photos of her new kitten (for an example, see Photo 16).

Source: Used with permission.

Photo 8: Ricky's computer

Source: Used with permission.

Photo 9: Antwon's television

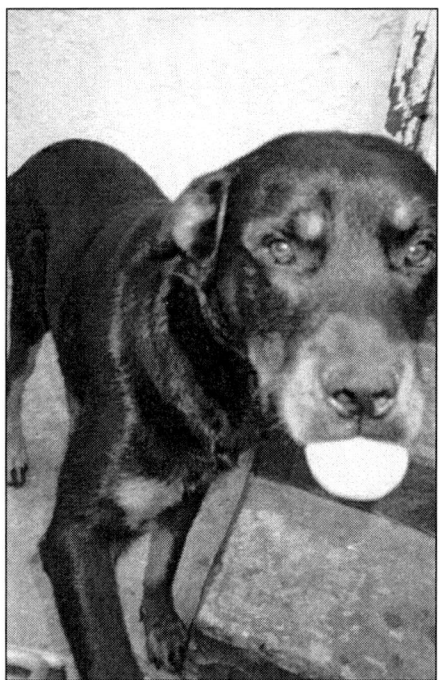

Source: Used with permission.

Photo 10: Tommy's dog

Photo 11: Sergio's siblings

Photo 12: Lorena's family cookout

I admit I dreaded this interview. What would we discuss besides her *gatito*? Janice still attended the school in my first study but had moved midyear to a slightly better-off community. For Janice, moving to a new community and not yet knowing anyone were factors in her strong attachment to her kitten.

Source: Used with permission.

Photo 13: Melodie's friends

Source: Used with permission.

Photo 14: Fernanda's birds

What became more important (and interesting) was the conversation about how her parents let her have the kitten after moving from Watts to Oak Park. For example, Janice explained that her family's slightly improved economic situation made it possible for her to have a kitten. Also, the images of the kitten

Source: Used with permission.

Photo 15: Phillip's family party

Source: Used with permission.

Photo 16: Janice's *gatito*

sparked Janice's memory of the pets she had in México, eliciting a detailed discussion about her immigrant journey from Mexico to Los Angeles.

Fourth, I am finding a gender difference in the position from which the photos were taken. Compared to boys, more girls take photos of the outdoors from inside. Boys as subjects of photographs and as photographers are more

Source: Used with permission.

Photo 17: David's photograph from the street

likely to be outside the home. Note how David has taken his photograph from the street (see Photo 17). Contrast this to the images from Jasmine, Julia, and Mercedes (see Photos 18 through 20) – all taken from within their homes. In the fourth girl's photograph (Photo 21), Pati's perspective is from within the home's second story. I could have simply coded the images

Source: Used with permission.

Photo 18: Jasmine's friends getting relief from the summer heat in the backyard

Source: Used with permission.

Photo 19: Julia's little sisters in the front yard

Source: Used with permission.

Photo 20: Mercedes has her friends pose in her backyard

Photo 21: Pati's view from the second story of her home

themselves – without the kids' explanations – to come to this conclusion. Yet, the interviews offered deeper insight about how girls and boys experience the special environment.

For example, Melissa showed me the photograph of a gigantic tree across the street, which she had taken from her front door (see Photo 22). She commented that it was her favorite tree. I asked her why. She explained, with tears filling her eyes, that she can only look at it and never really be near it. I probed, wanting to know why she couldn't cross the street. She told me that her dad makes her stay in the house and told her she would be deported to México if she is caught by *la migra* (Spanish slang for the Immigration and Naturalization Service [INS]). Indeed, INS vans did troll the community. With a rush of words, Melissa revealed that she was not documented, and neither was her mom, 20-year-old brother, or 16-year old sister. They all had to work so they needed to risk leaving the house. Melissa stayed at home alone until 8 or 9 P.M. each night. Thus, the tree was not just a tree (just as the kitten wasn't just a kitten) but rather a symbol of Melissa's immigration status, which restricted her movement. As in Melissa's case, immigration status may make a difference, but the trend to photograph from indoors held true for documented Latinas *and* African American girls, neither of whom have immigration issues.

Source: Used with permission.

Photo 22: Melissa's tree

In contrast, my photo elicitation interview with Toño confirmed that boys were "out and about" more than girls; he and his family provided insight about their experiences in the neighborhood. Toño took photos of his family in portrait and in action (e.g., his brother on a skateboard), his neighborhood, his afterschool care, and his favorite games in his room. As the family and I sat around the dining room table, the content of the photos spurred much conversation about the meaning of each artifact or action. What also occurred, especially when his father sat down at the table, was discussion of the graffiti (and the gangs it belonged to) that showed up in the background of the photos taken outside of the house and the day workers who also appeared in the photos taken outside (for an example, see Photo 23). Each family member who joined the conversation had a particular perspective and reality concerning these details that were inadvertently included in Toño's photos.

After viewing the photos, the family began to discuss the hardship of being *sin documentos* (undocumented or illegally in the United States) and finding work, as well as the trouble of having the gang members use their front driveway as a hangout. Relational and contextualized meanings emerged from the interview that may not have without the photographs. In this same interview, I was so focused on the "boys outside" photographs, that I missed the significance of the graffiti "tagging" of gang names and symbols (e.g., Grape Street High Rollers) in the background on which the other family members immediately focused. This early interview alerted me to other details that I might have otherwise considered background.

Source: Used with permission.

Photo 23: Toño's outside

Finally, the collaborative aspect of the photo elicitation interviews revealed dynamics in familial relationships. Many of my interviews with the children included their families and sometimes even their neighbors and friends. Sometimes, as in Toño's case, the family sessions were characterized by stories and insights building on one another. However, in other collaborative sessions, family tensions became apparent. Mostly, the kids and parents clashed over what the kids are doing when the parents are at work. For example, Melodie's mother laughed yet expressed dismay at hearing her daughter characterize the front yard tree as her "tree house" (no actual house is there, but she and her friends hung out in the tree limbs). She seemed somewhat embarrassed that she did not know the range of her daughter's play area because she was always working.

A clear conflict emerged with Victoria, a light-skinned, bright Latina and her mother. Victoria took her assignment very seriously and documented her social world in detail. She took photos of a secret club house, friends who dressed up for the "photo shoot," her little sister's chalk artwork, and the "blue line" train (taken by daylight) in front of her house that wakes her up at night (see Photo 24). In her lively interview, Victoria explained her photos and their meaning with passion. Her mother, who occasionally passed through the living room where Victoria and I sat for the interview, told her daughter that she was upset and "embarrassed" that Victoria did not take pictures of her own mother and father and "wasted" photos on her friends. Victoria countered that her mom goes to school and works two jobs; because she does not see her mother except at night and she could not figure out how to do the flash on her camera, she couldn't take her mother's photo. Her mother asked me

Source: Used with permission.

Photo 24: Victoria with best friends on first attempt at project

for another camera so that Victoria could take photos on their next family trip to Water World (see Photo 25). I agreed and gave them another disposable camera, and later, I conducted a second interview. In this case, the content of Victoria's first set of photos painted the creative and rich social life that Victoria, her sister, and their friends created when not in school. In addition, the conversation around the content also yielded data about Victoria's family dynamics.

In conclusion, while the categorical substantive findings are the stuff of sociological research, the process by which these emerge is where I found some of the most nuanced and intimate insights about inner-city childhoods. As I conducted interviews with children in South Central, I found that the data generated from photo elicitation interviews went beyond the normal scope of regular words-alone interviews. Photographs seem to allow the interviewees to reflect on related but indirect associations with the photographs themselves. In group settings, photographs serve to illustrate multiple meanings for the participants and sometimes reveal tensions among them. The most common experience conducting photo elicitation was that photographs spurred meaning that otherwise might have remained dormant in a face-to-face interview. The images may not contain new information but can trigger meaning for the interviewee (Collier, 1967; Schwartz, 1989). Although I have just begun to code the photographs and interviews to examine inner-city childhood, the data provide a rich perspective of "growing up poor" from the kids' own visual and verbal expressions, which go beyond solely pessimistic visions of urban blight yet are simultaneously shaped by urban poverty.

Source: Used with permission.

Photo 25: Mother-approved photograph of Victoria and friends at Water World

Rethinking Childhood

Theories on children currently examine the death (and for some the post mortem) of childhood. Researchers of this ilk examine (1) the effect of consumerism and electronic media, along with the corporations that produce these products and (2) the lack of "play" due to parental overscheduling of kids (Buckingham, 2000; Steinberg & Kincheloe, 1997). The kids in my study did take photos of consumer artifacts (e.g., Nintendo), yet when discussing their significance, it was clear that these products did not take an overwhelming role in or have a brain-numbing affect on their lives. Also, my participants showed through their photos that they have plenty of time to play. This gap (where empirical reality does not support theory) points to possible class or racial bias in the current theories that try to understand the nature of childhood. Whose childhood died? Researchers first must be able to understand the diversity of childhoods before declaring their death.

Using photo elicitation was crucial to accessing the children's perspective about specific issues and experiences and uncovering their worldview in general. Photo elicitation, used with other qualitative methodologies such as interviews or participant observations, can illuminate dynamics and insights not otherwise found through other methodological approaches. In addition, photo elicitation empowers the interviewees to teach the researcher about aspects of their social world otherwise ignored or taken for granted. When he introduced the methodology, John Collier (1967) wrote, "no type of fieldwork requires better rapport" (p. 51). I would argue that no type of fieldwork yields richer data.

Sociology of childhood scholars urge researchers not to view children as passive recipients of larger cultural processes and constraints. Photo elicitation can help address this concern. Jon Wagner (1979) writes that such methodology can benefit "social scientists interested in examining the connection between people's lives and the social and economic structures of the larger world" (p. 18). Indeed, the photographs of inner-city children reflected institutional, structural, and community understandings of their every day life. But more than that, photographs reveal the highly textured ways in which children negotiate these spaces and somehow once again become kids before our eyes.

When my interview with Nanci was finished, she kept her copy of the photographs and returned to work with her father. That day, I had another interview with one of her classmates, whom I was meeting in a nearby laundromat. As I drove away from downtown, I wondered about Nanci's life and future. Through looking at the corpus of photographs these children took, a part of me understands the kids' creativity and resiliency. Nanci embodies what is fascinating about children in the inner city. Through her images, she captured the intersection of play, work, culture, and dreams for a better future. The sociologist in me cannot ignore the structural inequalities and institutional processes that will shape their lives. However, at least in Nanci's case, I can report today, several years after the completion of my study, that she is still doing OK in school, still lives in South Central Los Angeles, and is still singing (see Photo 26).

Source: Used with permission.

Photo 26: Nanci the mariachi singer

Notes

1. Researchers also use historical photographs or the interviewees' family photo albums as interview stimuli.
2. This is the only time such an incident occurred in my study. However, students revealed that they took surprise photographs of their mothers, siblings, or friends. Thus, sometimes the cameras were being used for pranks and not for their intended use.
3. I obtained permission from the institutional review board at my home university to include the use of videos in the classroom and photography with the children. The review process took 6 months to complete. I wrote the board-required letter to the children and parents in my study in Spanish and English. Once in the field, I realized that parents did not understand the content of the official letter so with the help of several parents, I rewrote the letter maintaining its spirit but simplifying its language. I believed I would have done more of a disservice to the parents and violated the true goal of institutional review by giving them a letter they did not completely understand.
4. See Wagner (1979, chapter 10) for a terrific discussion of avoiding production and analysis errors using photo elicitation.

References

Adler, P., & Adler, P. (1998). *Peer power: Preadolescent culture and identity.* New Brunswick, NJ: Rutgers University Press.

Buckingham, D. (2000). *After the death of childhood: Growing up in the age of electronic media.* Cambridge, UK: Polity Press.

Clark, C. D. (1999). The autodriven interview: A photographic viewfinder into children's experiences. *Visual Sociology, 14,* 39–50.

Clark-Ibáñez, M. (2004). Lessons in inequality: A comparative study of two urban schools. *Dissertation Abstracts International A: The Humanities and Social Sciences, 64*(7), 2650-A.

Collier, J., Jr. (1967). *Visual anthropology: Photography as a research method.* Beverly Hills, CA: Sage.

Corsaro, W. (1997). *The sociology of childhood.* Thousand Oaks, CA: Pine Forge Press.

Harper, D. (1987). *Working knowledge: Skill and community in a small shop.* Chicago: University of Chicago Press.

Harper, D. (2001). *Changing works: Vision of lost agricultures.* Chicago: University of Chicago Press.

Harper, D. (2002). Talking about pictures: a case for photo elicitation. *Visual Studies, 17*(1), 13–26.

Jenks, C. (1996). *Childhood.* London: Routledge.

Lareau, A. (2003). *Unequal childhoods: Class, race, and family life.* Berkeley: University of California Press.

Mayhall, B. (2002). *Towards a sociology for childhood: Thinking from children's lives.* Maidenhead, UK: Open University Press.

Orellana, M. F. (1999). Space and place in an urban landscape: Learning from children's views of their social world. *Visual Sociology, 14,* 73–89.

Schwartz, D. (1989). Visual ethnography: Using photography in qualitative research. *Qualitative Sociology, 12*(2), 119–153.

Schwartz, D. (1992). *Wacoma twilight: Generations on the farm.* Washington, DC: Smithsonian Press.

Shanklin, E. (1979). When a good social role is worth a thousand pictures. In J. Wagner (Ed.), *Images of information* (pp. 139–157). Beverly Hills, CA: Sage.

Steinberg, S., & Kincheloe, J. (1997). *Kinderculture: The corporate construction of childhood.* Boulder, CO: Westview.

Thorne, B. (1993). *Gender play: Girls and boys in school.* New Brunswick, NJ: Rutgers University Press.

Wagner, J. (1979). Avoiding error. In J. Wagner (Ed.), *Images of information* (pp. 147–159). Beverly Hills, CA: Sage.

74

Video in Ethnographic Research

Sarah Pink

M any ethnographers and their informants produce and view video in their personal lives and professional work. However, until very recently video has been allowed only cursory mention in ethnographic texts on research methods. In the past, visual sociologists largely concentrated on photography, rarely considering the potential of video in the research process (Lomax and Casey 1998: 2). Visual anthropologists became interested in video in the 1980s, applauding new developments in video technology for the convenience, economy, durability and utility they offered. In comparison with film, which was used extensively in anthropological research in the 1970s (see Morphy and Banks 1997: 5), video was cheap and could record for a considerably longer period of time. During this period the potential of video was often harnessed to serve a scientific-realist approach. For example, Collier and Collier saw the idea that a video camera may be left running continuously for several hours as an advantage compared to the relative selectivity imposed by both the cost of film and the need to reload a camera more frequently (1986: 146). However, since the late 1990s researchers from different social science disciplines (such as social anthropology, sociology, queer studies) have begun to engage with video anew and as distinct from ethnographic film. This has meant exploring reflexive uses of video in ethnography, using video not simply to record data, but as a medium through which ethnographic knowledge is created. Simultaneously, technological developments, especially in digital video, invite new practical possibilities for video in research and representation. In Chapter 2 I discussed how particular cameras may be interpreted by video subjects, thus impacting on their strategies of self-representation. It is

Source: *Doing Visual Ethnography* (London: SAGE, 2007), pp. 96–116.

also worth reflecting on the design of the video technology used and how this affects the researchers' or video makers' strategies. In the 1990s Chris Wright described how the Sony PC7 digital video camera differs from more conventional cameras. In place of a viewfinder, the PC7 has a fold-out mini-TV screen that creates distance between the camera operator's eye and the camera, allowing the camera operator to see both the camera screen and the scene recorded. Thus the camera no longer follows the operator's eye butallows him or her a split vision, and to see and decide what is being recorded in relation to the scene in front of the camera (C. Wright 1998: 18–19). My experiences with a similar model, the Sony PC1E, in 1999, supported this and this design of digital video camera has persisted into the twenty-first century, now being more or less standard across a range of domestic and semi-professional models of the kind used in ethnographic research. Moreover, such technology changes not only the camera operator's view, but also what the video subjects see. Using the open camera screen of the video, the researcher can now maintain better eye contact with video subjects because the camera itself is not hiding his or her face. Video footage can also be viewed 'in the field' on this screen and listened to through the external speaker, with informants or people who have appeared in the video. In comparison with viewing playback though the camera viewfinder with headphones as one would have done using previous analogue technologies, this viewing context also allows researcher and informants to discuss the images during viewing. Video is of course not simply visual – it is an audio-visual medium and sound recording is part of video recording. In many instances the camera's internal microphone will be sufficient for the type of video methods discussed in this chapter. However, to achieve good sound quality, especially when not close up to the source of the sound, researchers might also consider using an external microphone and at times a radio microphone.

Ethnographers should develop a self-conscious approach not only to their relationships with the video subjects but also to how both relate to the camera, and to their different agendas regarding the video technology and recordings. In this chapter I discuss examples of using video cameras of different types over the past fifteen years or so. However, I write with the assumption that most contemporary video ethnographers will be using digital camcorders.

Defining Ethnographic Video

In the 1990s literature about ethnographic video and filmmaking there developed a tendency to distinguish between 'objective' research film or video footage and 'creative' footage produced for ethnographic filmmaking. This distinction was informed by debates in the 1970s and 1980s about the relationship between cinematography and scientific ethnographic film (see Banks 1992). Some (e.g. Heider 1976) argued that ethnographic film should be objective, unedited, not 'manipulated'; it should be guided by scientific, ethnographic principles, rather than cinematographic intentions. Such footage was intended to be stored as a film archive and screened to anthropological audiences; it was part of a project of recording an objective reality. During the same period others produced more creative, expressive films intended for public consumption. In particular, Robert Gardner 'distanced himself from realism' (see Loizos 1993: 140), producingfilms that used cinematographic and symbolic techniques that challenged the criteria set by Heider. Collier and Collier applied a similar distinction between 'research' film which 'is made to contain relatively *undisturbed* process and behaviour from which to develop information and concepts' and 'ethnographic' film that 'is usually edited to create a narrative selected by the filmmaker-producer' (Collier and Collier 1986: 152). They dismiss the possibility of using 'ethnographic' film for research purposes, claiming that the selectivity involved in its production makes it invalid as an observational record. These categories persist in recent work (e.g. Barbash and Taylor 1997) that regards research footage as objective data, 'raw material' and a scientific document. In this view creativity is not part of research as the ethnographer's intentionality must be scientific to be 'ethnographic'.

Here I propose three main criticisms of this approach. First, it is usually impossible or inappropriate to video-record people or culture 'undisturbed'; people in a video are always 'people in a video'. Moreover, like any ethnographic representation, research footage is inevitably constructed. Secondly, ethnographic knowledge does not necessarily exist as observable facts. In Chapter 1 I argued that ethnographic knowledge is better understood as originating from fieldwork experiences. Knowledge is produced in conversation and negotiation between informants and researcher, rather than existing as an objective reality that may be recorded and taken home in a note book, camera film or tape. Thirdly, and parallel to my discussion of defining ethnographic photography (Chapter 3), the question of the 'ethnographicness' of video footage does not depend entirely on its content or on the intentionality of the video maker, but its ethnographicness is contextual. In the broadest sense a video is 'ethnographic' when its viewer(s) judge that it represents information of ethnographic interest. Therefore video footage can never be purely 'ethnographic': a video recording that ethnographers see as representing ethnographic knowledge about an event and how it is experienced might, in their informants' eyes, be a video of a birthday party. This broad and contextual definition of ethnographic video invites the possibility for a range of different genres of video to be 'ethnographic'. This includes not only ethnographers' video footage, but (for example) home movies, events videoed by informants for ethnographers, indigenous videos made for self-representation to external bodies and documentary videos made through collaborations between researchers and informants as part of applied research (see Pink 2004a). None of these recordings are essentially ethnographic, but may become so when they are implicated in an ethnographic project.

Ethnographic Video and Local 'Video Cultures'

Ethnographers' uses of video benefit from awareness of how informants use and understand video technologies and representations. As Lomax and Casey noted from their experiences of videoing interactions between midwives and their clients, 'the camera . . . is socially significant given both its ability to preserve interaction for representation and participants' awareness of that ability' (1998: 6). However, reflexivity entails more than simply an awareness of how participants' interactions are affected by their 'camera-consciousness'. Rather, we need to firmly situate their self-awareness within the cultural and media contexts in which they live out their everyday lives. Moreover, an ethnographer with a video camera is a person with a video camera, the camera becomes part of its user's identity and an aspect of the way he or she communicates with others. It is not only cultural difference that influences the way video becomes part of a project, but in each situation the camera will impact differently on the relationships researchers develop with other individuals and the social roles they play. An individual ethnographer does not have one single and fixed identity as a video maker, but this will be negotiated and redefined in different contexts. To be reflexive ethnographic video makers need to be aware of how the camera and video footage become an element of the play between themselves and informants, and how these are interwoven into discourses and practices in the research context.

The complexity and variability of this researcher/filmmaker-informant relationship is demonstrated audio-visually in Braun's video essay, *Passing Girl, Riverside: an Essay on Camera Work* (1998), a reflexive text about video as 'a tool for cross-cultural research' (The Royal Anthropological Institute's Ethnographic Film Festival Catalogue 1998). Braun presents footage from three video projects he developed in Ghana, narrated with his reflexive commentary to represent the relationships he formed with the subjects of his research and video making in each project. The first part of the video discusses a short video recording of a young girl who passed by Braun's rooftop vantage point during a street festival. When she noticed that he was filming her, the girl performed to the camera, delighted at his attention, until, realizing that his interest in her had passed, she appears angry and disappointed. In his commentary Braun discusses the intentionality of video maker and subject. Reflecting on the power relationships and related ethical issues that are implied by such uses of the camera, his text provokes questions about the right of the researcher to film under such circumstances. In his next project Braun developed a collaborative relationship with his video subjects, this time members of a Ghanaian theatre company. He made a deal with the company to produce a series of commercial videos that they would sell in local villages. In return, they allowed him to travel with, and make his own documentary about, the group. This example demonstrates how the subjects of video may appropriate a video maker and his technology for their own ends. This entails a rather different power dynamic from that Braun experienced in his fleeting relationship with the young girl. Finally, Braun presents footage shot in the Ghanaian village in which he had lived as a child when his parents were missionary doctors. Here he negotiated his video making on yet another basis. His existing relationship with the local community enabled him to video freely and he shared his images by screening the footage for his subjects. These three examples show nicely how the video practices of one individual researcher can fit into local cultures and specific relationships with individuals in different ways.

Above I have noted how in Braun's second project he participated in producing local visual culture by making commercial videos for his collaborators. In most contexts of contemporary ethnographic research television, film and video form part of local cultural consumption, and often production too. An appreciation of local television and video cultures, and people's interpretations of media narratives and how these inform their understandings of video images, also support the use of video as a research method. I would not propose that media research *must* become a part of ethnographic work with video; each individual project will have its priorities and media may not be one of them. Nevertheless both public and domestic uses of television, video, film and internet are an important dimension of many local cultures and a growing area of ethnographic interest (see, for example, Hughes-Freeland 1997; Askew and Wilk 2002; Ginsburg et al. 2002; Rothenbuhler and Coman 2005). The emergent field of media anthropology (see for example) is developing an interdisciplinary approach linking the concerns of anthropology, sociology and media studies. Within this has developed a method that has been called media ethnography. This approach was earlier formulated as a departure from 'audience studies' and 'reception studies' in media analysis to propose a reflexive ethnography of media reception that focuses on how 'audience creativity' intersects with 'media power' (see Morley 1996: 14). However, media ethnography may now be said to be more generally an ethnographic approach to studying media forms and practices and their meanings within specific cultural contexts, individual narratives and social relations. This includes the possibility of going further than simply doing participant observation with television, video or film audiences and internet users to understand viewers'/users' individual and cultural understandings of media representations by extending this to also cover media practices such as commercial, public and domestic media production. Media ethnography can support ethnographic research with video by helping researchers to understand how their informants' interpretations of video cameras and 'ethnographic' video recordings are informed by meanings they invest more generally in audio-visual media practices and representations.

For example, a project by three visual anthropologists, Manuel Cerezo, Ana Martinez and Penelope Ranera, demonstrates the importance of sensitivity to media narratives and the meanings that informants invest in visual representations of themselves. The researchers were working with African immigrant workers in Spain. Since they had used photography quite extensively in the project, to the pleasure of their informants, they found their informants' reactions to their introduction of the videocamera surprising. Its presence displeased them and created moments of tension that were difficult to deal with (Cerezo et al. 1996: 142). Neither did the informants like the images of themselves in the video; while they admired its landscape scenes, they found themselves 'ugly' and 'poor' (1996: 143). The researchers situate these responses in relation to popular culture, pointing out that the immigrants, who work very long hours and have a low economic level, nevertheless return home every evening to watch television or videos. From the informants' viewpoint the video images of themselves on a television screen were images of poverty, they were permanently recorded images and could be seen by anyone (1996: 143). The informants' own gaze on the video images of themselves thus objected to the researchers' 'innocently' filmed video footage. This raised ethical issues that led Cerezo, Martinez and Ranera to argue that visual products like video should not be produced without their protagonists' permission. Their work emphasizes how important reflexivity can be in video research. The researchers' self-reflexivity and discussions with their informants about the video representations revealed how each of them had gazed differently on the video footage. By exploring this they learned both why the video images were problematic and how their informants interpreted images of themselves with reference to contemporary popular media culture. It is not only our informants' understandings of media representation that should inform our work as ethnographers, but also their understandings of media production practices – in both public and domestic contexts.

From 1999 to 2000 I undertook (with Unilever research) two video ethnography projects that explored aspects of the relationship between self-identity and the home in Britain and Spain. The research involved an in-depth interview of about one hour with each participant, followed by a 'video tour' of his or her home. The video tour entailed my informant showing me around the home while I video-recorded him or her. Guided by prompts, participants led the tour discussing with me aspects of the visual and material home, their feelings about it and treatment of it (further reading about this method can be found in Pink 2004b, Pink 2004c, Pink 2005: ch. 4). As the video tour method developed in the different sites and contexts of my fieldwork – that is, in the homes and personal narratives of different individuals – I realized that it was culturally embedded in specific ways. First, using a small domestic video camera (as described above) I was introducing a domesticated research technology that already fitted in the home. However, because this was also the 'latest' and smallest of the new domestic digital video cameras at the time, it aroused people's curiosity to hold and examine it. Secondly, all my informants in this research were conversant in video use. They had preconceived ideas about what to expect from and how to behave with a video camera. Although none of my informants had ever experienced a similar research exercise, each of our video recordings could be seen as a performance that had been informed by existingcultural and personal knowledge and experience about how one performs and communicates 'on camera'. Finally, the video tours are interesting because they show how each informant appropriated the video tour process him or herself by attaching it to a (usually subconsciously) chosen existing cultural narrative. For example, some informants developed the tour by taking the stance used to show a prospective buyer around the home, others used what I have called a '*Hello*! magazine' type narrative to communicate the idea of showing the home in a way that presents a lifestyle, and finally others linked the tour and the way that it encouraged them to reflect on their own personal trajectories to a counselling narrative. As such they were able to comment on both the material home, their embodied experiences of it and their self identities as we toured it. These performances and uses of narratives can be seen as an element of my informants' negotiations with me – since they also used them as mechanisms through which to select what they would and would not show me within the private space of their homes. They did not ever ask me not to video but at the same time took control over what I could and could not access through video (see Pink 2004c).

In contrast to working in domestic space, my experience of video-recording a public event in Northern Ireland in 1990 was very different. In this case I was carrying a large JVC semi-professional camera and was accompanied by a sound recordist with a professional-looking microphone. The video was part of an ethnographic project about migration from Belfast to London. We were to video-record the unveiling ceremony of a statue of William of Orange, just outside Belfast, and were developing a commentary on this event through interviews with George, the key informant, a migrant from Belfast to London, and interviews that he was leading. Once we had requested permission to film, with our professional-looking equipment we were ushered by the organizers into the enclosure reserved for television and film crews. Our presence with the camera developed various responses from people attending the event. One woman treated us as a source of public information, another interviewee gave well-considered responses to George's questions as if to a TV audience. In this case my collaboration with George involved negotiation over the planning and direction of the video. The other informants were in a sense also *his* informants. The ways we worked at the public event were also framed by our interviewees' and the organizers' interpretations of our activities, this being contingent on their own knowledge about video.

Knowledge that situates video technologies and representations locally can benefit ethnographic work and support collaborations with informants in a number of ways. This may include knowledge of local visual media and video culture, about local people's interpretations of video technology, reflexivity about the researcher's own role and informants' understandings of this. It is also useful to explore how video technology is made meaningful locally. This might involve examining the discourses through which video is discussed.

For example, is it discussed in relation to notions of, or exhibitions of, wealth or of scientific innovation? In what categories do local people situate video, such as popular culture, art, domestic activity or leisure?

The Potential of Video as a Recording Method

The approach I have advocated in the earlier chapters of this book is critical of the realist stance and of methods texts that limit the potential of video to recording focus group discussions and interviews to avoid losing important visual data and cues. Video is undoubtedly good for such visual note-taking, but such uses ought to be qualified with a rejection of the naive assumption that video records an untainted reality in favour of a reflexive approach that accounts for how video can become part of a focus group discussion or interview. This, combined with knowledge about the video or media culture of interviewees or focus group participants, should help the researcher to decide if video would be appropriate for that particular group, and how video could successfully be used in that specific research scenario. For example, when using a video camera to record midwife–client interactions, Lomax and Casey rightly acknowledge that 'the research is not marred by the necessary involvement of the researcher, but conversely, she is a contributor to the constitution of the interaction' (1998: 26). While their use of the tape is realist, they also use it as a device for reflexivity, noting that 'the involvement of the researcher in the interaction can be analysed and understood from the video text. The analysis, in turn, is informative about "normal" consultations; i.e. how midwives organise an overall structure of the visit' (1998: 26).

Video can be used for ethnographic diary-keeping (e.g. Holiday 2001; Chalfen and Rich 2004), note-taking (including surveys of the physical environment, housing, etc.) or recording certain processes and activities. For example, the sociologist Tim Dant, reflecting on his video research about the work practice of car mechanics, comments that 'Because of the capability of capturing the visible and hearable actions and interactions of people going about their ordinary life, it [video] would seem to provide a rich source of data for those social scientists interested in studying local social situations.' He goes on to suggest that 'The flow and pattern of life as it is lived is recorded and retained in the moving picture with sound to become available for close study and multiple replays' (2004: 41). Such uses are perfectly viable, although it is important to keep in mind that video materials of this kind should be treated as *representations* rather than visual facts. Moreover, their analysis should take note of the collaborations and strategies of self-representation that were part of their making. Nevertheless, this is not so much a limitation as an indication of the potential of video forethnographic research. In this chapter I focus largely on how video ethnography can be much more than visual note-taking, to explore how it is embedded in processes of knowledge production.

Getting Started

There is never any single 'right moment' to start using a video camera. In some cases video recording may become an element of a researcher's relationship with his or her informants right from the first meeting. For example, in my video ethnographies of the home in England and Spain video-recording was an unavoidable element of the fieldwork and was agreed with each informant from the outset. I introduced video as a matter of course as part of our interview process. In other projects, however, uses of video are negotiated on different terms. It may even be several months before the ethnographer considers it the 'right moment' to introduce video. Francisco Ferrándiz (whose work I discuss below) did not begin to use video in his research in Venezuela until he was already six months into the fieldwork, and then, as he notes, the 'most complex visual project had to wait a couple of months more' (1998: 26).

Similarly, video work with different informants may start at different times in a project as relationships between ethnographers, technology, images and different individuals develop at different paces and in different ways. For example, when I was shooting my masters degree project *(Home from Home)* in Northern Ireland, the grandmother of George, my key informant, was keen to be video-recorded talking with George in a conversational interview. However, initially, his mother did not want to participate. As the project proceeded, we continued to video-record interviews with various members of the family – an outing that George made with his nieces and some local public ritual events. Every evening we returned to George's parents' home where we were staying and viewed the SVHS footage through their video recorder and television. Although the SVHS images were not perfectly projected through the VHS recorder, we could see and hear enough to know we had the footage we wanted. George's mother also became interested, keen to see her grandchildren and other family members on video. As her interest and confidence in the video making increased, she volunteered to be interviewed.

Getting started is not solely a matter of finding the right moment but also involves technical procedures. This varies according to the equipment used but includes getting the camera out and setting it up, organizing sound recording and lighting. These procedures become bound up in the research process. For example, in their sociological research on midwife–client interaction, Lomax and Casey found that actually starting the videotaping 'became, in our research, a matter of some complexity and analytic interest' because 'even with specific arrangements, it is not possible to enter a person's home and set up camera without becoming interactionally involved' (Lomax and Casey 1998: 7). Similarly, when I interviewed people with video in their homes, I often collaborated with my interviewees to arrange that lights are strategically placed and switched on as we moved around video-recording. Here the technical demands of video-recording became a collaborative issue as both the interviewees and interviewer sought extra sources of indoor lighting.

Video and the Production of Ethnographic Knowledge

When we use video as a research method we are not merely video-recording what people do in order to create visual data for analysis. Rather we are engaging in a *process* through which knowledge is produced. Above I have emphasized the importance of understanding the cultural context in which one uses the camera. In this section I show how there is further variation in terms of what one might achieve through video ethnography. In part this is related to the different social and cultural settings of the different projects discussed below, and in part to the different research agendas video was engaged to support. In each of the projects referred to the researcher has taken a reflexive approach to the discussion of the methodology used in her or his work.

Learning to See

One of the opportunities afforded by doing long-term participant observation with a video camera is that one can learn not just about how other people do things but also become engaged in similar practices oneself. Where the practices one is learning about involve visual evaluation the camera can be an important tool. In Chapter 3 I discussed how I photographed the bullfight in ways that both followed the conventions of existing bullfight photography and under my informants' direction. Then by showing them these images, taking their criticisms of how I had *seen* (photographed) the performance and discussing what they *saw* in my photographs I came closer to understanding their visual knowledge about and criteria for evaluating a performance, performer and bull (see Pink 1997a). Through a discussion of her video research about cattle breeding in Northern Italy, Cristina Grasseni has suggested that the visual ethnographer might, by apprenticing her-or himself to their informants, develop what she has called 'skilled vision': the ability to see and thus understand local phenomena in the same way as the people with whom the researcher is working. Grasseni proposes that there is 'a parallel between the process of apprenticeship that a visual ethnographer has to undergo, and the process of education of attention that is required of anyone participating in a community of practice'. As such an ethnographer might learn to share 'an aesthetic code' (Grasseni 2004: 28) with her or his informants. In her own research, working with a breed expert Grasseni tried to 'develop an "eye" through an apprenticeship into looking at cattle'. As part of this process she used her video camera to keep a video diary, from which she showed footage to her hosts to comment on in such a way that this allowed her to compare her own way of seeing with theirs (Grasseni 2004: 17). Grasseni describes how when she first began to tour farms with a breed inspector she 'did not know what to point the camera at, because [she] could not *see* what was going on'. She realised that in order for what she saw to become meaningful she would need to learn 'to share the breeder's vision' (2004: 20). She began to use her video camera under the guidance of an expert who explained to her how to evaluate a cow.

> As a result of his Instructions, I started to look at the udders from underneath, lowering the camera to knee-height. I concentrated on the volume of the udder, trying to shoot from under the cow's tail to line up her teats. I also began to frame the cows mainly from behind, keeping the camera high above their backs to show the line of the spine and the width of the shoulders. (2004: 21)

The video camera was important in this exercise, since rather than simply looking at the cow as instructed, Grasseni video-recorded this vision; as she puts it, 'the camera functioned as the catalyst of my attention, tuning my eyes to the visual angles and the ways of framing the cow through the inspector's gaze' (2004: 21). As this example shows, video can be used as part of the process of learning to see as others do, in a directed way. Moreover this produces audio-visual materials that informants can then comment on to produce a further layer of knowledge. Grasseni situates these uses of video in relation to a theoretical understanding of vision. She argues that the idea of participant observation should be reformulated as not simply imitating what other people do, but (drawing from ideas of ecology) as a way of learning about how people's shared visions (or understandings) 'co-evolve' (2004: 28–9).

Collaboratively Representing Everyday Experiences

In other projects long-term fieldwork may not be a possibility, either due to the timescale allowed for the research or the nature of the subject. My own 'Cleaning, homes and lifestyles' project (developed with Unilever Research in 1999) was an exploratory applied video ethnography study that examined the relationship between people's self-identities, values, moralities, knowledge about housework, and the actual housework practices they engaged in, products they used and how they used them. We hoped to learn what domestic cleaning and the products used for it meant to people within the wider contexts of their lifestyles, homes and self-identities. I had six months to complete the research from beginning to the final report and presentation. There was no time for the immersion in my research participants' lives that forms part of long-term participant observation. This was for two reasons. First, I needed to complete the fieldwork within three months. Secondly, I was to study the relationships between 40 individuals, their lifestyles, homes and cleaning and the fieldwork was to take place in their homes. Short of living with each of them for several months I would be unable to participate in their everyday lives for extended periods.

For this study I developed a collaborative method, called the 'video tour', to achieve an in-depth understanding of the social and material worlds people

live in (see Pink 2004b). Therefore I only had one meeting with each informant in which we collaboratively set out to explore their homes using the video
camera. Whereas Grasseni sought to learn the 'way of seeing' of cattle experts,
and as such be able, using the camera, to imitate their practices herself, my
approach was to ask my informants to show me their homes and to describe
their practices to me on video both verbally and through embodied performance (see Pink 2004b, 2005). My meeting with each research participant
lasted between two and four hours. The research meeting involved two tasks.
First, a tape-recorded interview covering areas including their self-identities,
everyday lives, usual cleaning practices, moralities and values concerning dirt and cleanliness, knowledge about cleaning and definitions of clean and
dirty etc. The interview was structured by my checklist, but was focused on
allowing the research participant to talk and explain these areas her-or himself. It was a collaborative interview in that we worked together to enable the
research participant to define these areas of their lives. Secondly, the video
tour followed. This was a collaborative exercise that involved each research
participant working with me to represent her or his experience of everyday
life in the home and the routine practices this involved. Whereas in long-term
fieldwork we would wait for events to unfold over a period of time, here we
did not have that luxury. Instead we had one hour of video tape on which to
represent the research participant's life in her or his home. Therefore we very
consciously worked within a constrained time period to explore and represent
the home and to discuss the human and material relationships, sensations,
identities, emotions, memories, creativity and activity associated with the
research participant's life there. This included participants giving demonstrations of how everyday domestic activities were performed. They used their
whole bodies as well as words to show me what their lives and experiences
were like in their homes as I probed and guided the 'tour' according to the
objectives of the study.

Through this research I aimed to produce, with my informant, shared
understandings of their past experiences and current practices. To do so I had
to depend on our collaborations and to work with them to help them draw out,
reconstruct and represent the relevant experiences in a way that was meaningful to them, and to me. This produced a set of interview transcripts and
recordings and videotapes. Their content, which was at one level my audio-
visual representation of the research experience, included descriptions and
discussions of informants' past experiences, demonstrations of how things are
done, or of what has happened in a past situation, and explanations of knowledge and meaning, values and moralities. The other layer of knowledge was
based on my own first hand experience of the contexts in which the research
participants lived and experienced, gainedthrough the video tour. Whereas to
produce the knowledge represented on video my informants used their whole
bodies, to understand the research context I also used my own. This type of
video ethnography does not provide access to the level of experience and
shared knowledge that might be produced through the type of involvement in

people's lives permitted by long-term fieldwork. But it does allow us to explore collaboratively, and intensively, the visual and other sensory knowledge and experience that form part of people's everyday lives.

Handing over the Camera: Spontaneous Video

In Chapter 3 I discussed instances where informants have taken the camera into their own hands either to provide the researcher with photographs of him-or herself, or knowing that the researcher will give them copies, to produce the images of an event or activity that they want to have themselves. An interesting example of how this might also work in the context of video ethnography is demonstrated in Francisco Ferrándiz's work with Venezuelan spirit cults (1996, 1998). In this case also we see how video can provide a route to visual and sensory knowledge and, interestingly, how the camera itself was appropriated within a culturally specific activity. Situating the role of video in his fieldwork in relation to the cult's existing relationship with, and experience of, media representation, Ferrándiz pays particular attention to the way the video-recording developed through the intersubjectivity between himself and his informants. In some instances the video became a catalyst that helped create the context in which it was used, as in the case of a ceremony that was organized by his informants as part of the event of videoing it. However, of particular interest is that when Ferrándiz began shooting video, six months into his fieldwork, the informants with whom he was closely collaborating also took the camera to shoot footage themselves, each of them creating 'completely different visual itineraries of the same place' (Ferrándiz 1998: 27).

Ferrándiz takes his analysis further than merely the question of how different people created different video narratives of the same context. He forms continuities between the video making and the ritual activities in which his informants were involved; the visual practices of video-recording and the ritual practices coincided as people moved in and out of trance and in front of and behind the camera's viewfinder as the ceremony proceeded. In this research the video camera became part of the material culture of the ritual and its recording capacity an aspect of the ritual activity. Therefore Ferrándiz was able to learn about ritual practices both by observing the ritual uses of the camera itself and by analysing and discussing the video recordings that these uses produced.

Informants' Video Diaries

Above I have discussed a case where informants took the camera themselves. In other work, similar in ways to the photographic studies discussed in Chapter 3, researchers have given video cameras to informants, asking them to film their own lives. This use of video has a long history since Sol Worth and John Adair's (1966) 'Navajo Film Themselves' project which had as its main objective 'to ask the Navajo to show "us" (acknowledged researchers) how they saw themselves and their surroundings, or even better how they wanted to show themselves and their selves to outsiders' (Chalfen and Rich 2004: 19). Richard Chalfen (a visual anthropologist) and Michael Rich (a medical researcher) comment that the principle of handing the (now video) camera over to the research participants has been applied in a large number of studies across a wide range of disciplines. But, they note, few of these projects have been written up as academic studies (see Chalfen and Rich 2004: 19–20). One exception is Ruth Holliday's work on the performance of queer identities (2004).

Chalfen and Rich's own study was produced in the context of applied medical anthropology. Chalfen and Rich have developed a method called Video Intervention/Prevention Assessment (VIA) by which 'Young patients were instructed to follow a specified protocol to "teach your clinician about your illness" by using consumer model videocams in their homes, neighbourhoods, schools, work, church and events of their own selection. They could also make a series of diaristic "personal monologues"' (2004: 17). This means that 'VIA asks young people who share a medical diagnosis, such as asthma, obesity . . . to create a visual illness narrative, documenting their experiences, perceptions, issues and needs on video.' Developed in the form of video-taped diaries, these recordings represent the experience of illness from the patient's perspective. They provide a route through which clinicians, assisted by the analysis developed by the research team, might access patients' knowledge and understandings of their illnesses (2004: 18). This is seen as a way of creating better understanding and communication between clinicians and patients in a context where each may understand the illness in different ways. As such, Chalfen and Rich refer to this method as offering a form of cultural brokerage (2004: 20–2) (which is characteristic of applied visual anthropology work more generally).

As is often the case in applied visual anthropological studies, in this work it is not only the results of the research that impact on the lives of the participants, but also for the process becomes empowering (see below). Chalfen and Rich note that (in the case of a study of asthma sufferers) '[t]he process of self-examination had resulted in quantifiable improvements in patients' asthma status, possibly because of the cognitive dissonance between what they observed themselves to be doing and what they knew they should be doing' (2004: 23).

Collaborative/Participatory Video and the Empowerment of Participants

As some of the examples discussed above have shown, ethnographic video production may become interwoven with local video cultures. Suchwork is by nature collaborative in the sense that it involves the active participation of the informants in the processes by which knowledge is produced. It is indeed, as Banks (2001) has also pointed out, hard to imagine visual research that is not collaborative; however, there are of course different ways and towards different ends that video ethnographers and informants work together. One way to consider the question of collaboration is by asking what the various motives for participation in a video ethnography might be. In Chapter 2 I raised Engelbrecht's question: for whom do we make ethnographic films? Engelbrecht refers to documentaries that are edited and screened to anthropological and other audiences. But the question also applies to research footage: for whom do we shoot this footage when we collaborate with individuals and groups who also have an interest in the footage? Such collaboration results in ethnographers working with informants and participating in 'their' video culture, as well referring to other video cultures (for instance, video conventions in ethnographers' personal lives as well as in their academic discipline). Here I discuss two collaborative video projects that have produced research footage that was guided by the intentionalities of both researchers and informants, and also responded to the demands of academic and informants' video cultures. The idea of video as a medium that can be used to empower otherwise disenfranchised people has been developed in work on participatory development (e.g. White 2003). As the examples below show, this can also be applied to the use of video in ethnographic research that also serves academic ends (see also Pink 2004a, 2005: ch. 5).

Barnes, Taylor-Brown and Weiner (1997) have described a project to produce video tapes in which HIV-positive mothers recorded messages that would be viewed by their children after the mothers' deaths. The researchers' intention was to use 'the concept of "eternal mothering"' to provide 'a framework to study the interactive aspects of mothering and the significance of impending maternal death from a stigmatising illness' (1997: 7). They collaborated with each mother to produce a video document that she felt would represent her appropriately to her children once she was dead. Barnes, Taylor-Brown and Weiner follow Chaplin (1994) in attempting 'to replace the sociology *of* a topic with a sociology that emphasises less distance between verbal analysis and visual representation as data' (Barnes et al. 1997: 10), thus reducing the distance between the researcher and the subject.

Conscious of the positivist tradition that has informed their discipline, Barnes, Taylor-Brown and Weiner weigh up the 'experimental' restraints of their project, concluding that it offers limited opportunity for triangulation and noting how the presence of the camera and researcher may have affected the 'reality' recorded. However they argue that these limits are outweighed by the quality of the self-representation and narrative created by the mothers as 'the method offers the spontaneity and vividness of an uninterrupted stream of information from the individual, as the mother is allowed to talk without researcher intrusion in the form of questions' (Barnes et al. 1997: 13). The project departs from a scientific experimental stance by applying the feminist approach advocated by Chaplin (1994), whereby the knowledge is produced not about but for women, and the women themselves are situated 'at the centre of the production of knowledge' (Barnes et al. 1997: 13). They write, 'We acknowledge that there is no one single interpretation of social action that can claim to be definitive', and follow Chaplin's point that such representations do not convey singular meanings, but that '[i]n post-positivist and feminist philosophy the study offers a range of suggestions and an opportunity to construct a constellation of meanings about mothering' (1997: 14). They realize that they are dealing with:

> What mothers, within the contexts of their social worlds, select to represent of themselves to their children in permanent, structured, visual form, is interrelated to their attitudes about how mothers care for and protect their children, how their impending death from AIDS influenced their mothering and how stigmatisation from AIDS may be transferred from them to their children . . . their self-presentation. (1997: 21)

They saw this video tape as an empowering visual medium: it 'offers women, minorities, HIV-infected people, and other marginalised groups, an opportunity to reproduce and understand their world as opposed to the dominant representation depicted in the mass media' (1997: 27). Here the collaborative video research was situated in a particular cultural use of video that the mothers found appropriate to develop. Through it the researchers assisted the mothers in producing cultural documents that allowed them to develop simultaneously a sociological understanding of self-representation and experiences of mothering.

Contemporary visual ethnographers are working in contexts where power relations are complex. They involve not only the relations between researcher and informant but also with other institutions and individuals. The example above shows how collaborations with informants have contributed to their empowerment in more personal situations; in other projects ethnographers have used video in collaborative work to create both academic knowledge and to empower people who have lived through political conflict. Drawing Jean Rouch's notion of a 'shared anthropology', the visual anthropologist Carlos Flores discusses his collaborative video work with Maya Q'eqchi filmmakers in post-war Guatemala. Flores shows how a community-based video project he developed collaboratively with local Q'eqchi people simultaneously 'provided important ethnographic insights about an indigenous group and its transformations' and 'provided the communities with new mechanisms for sociocultural reconstruction and awareness after an intensely traumatic and violent period of civil war' (2004: 31).

Attaching himself to and initially adopting a participant-observer stance in an existing NGO video project, Flores began to learn that existing practices clashed with his own expectations of indigenous video: they seemed to represent a development agenda rather than focusing on traditional indigenous practices or the recent history of conflict, and were made in Spanish rather than local languages (2004: 35). When, in the next stage of his involvement, he began to contribute his own filmmaking skills and ideas, he encouraged them to take up these other themes, focusing on planting rituals in one video and conflict in another. As Flores's article shows, such collaborative work both opens up possibilities and is constrained in what it can achieve (2004: 39). His work also reveals that (like other work in applied visual anthropology – see Pink 2004a, 2005: ch. 5) it is not simply the final film document that is important, but rather the collaborative processes by which it is produced: it is through these processes that both new levels of engagement in thematic issues and of self awareness are achieved by participants and ethnographic knowledge is produced.

Viewing Footage with Informants: Interviewing with/Talking Around Video

Showing video footage to informants can also become part of a research project. In the examples discussed below this ranges from a formal video-recorded interview, during which the informant viewed and commented on video footage of an event in which he had participated, to much more casual screenings in which informants have become involved out of personal interest rather than by request. Whatever the context, the purpose of this method should not be simply to use video images to elicit responses from informants or to extract information *about* the images. Rather, viewing video with informants should also be seen as 'media ethnography'. This combines ethnographers actively discussing video images with informants and examining how they situate themselves as viewers of the footage. This means asking questions such as: How do informants' commentaries on video footage relate it to other aspects of their video/media culture? And what discourses do they refer to in their comments and discussions of the footage?

While studying at the Granada Centre at the University of Manchester, I collaborated with a fellow MA student to make a video about a Jewish family Passover meal. After shooting footage of the family meal, we asked our key informant to view and comment on this footage in an interview that was also video-recorded. This interview was held in his living room, where he sat by the video player, with a purposefully arranged array of family photographs and icons in the background behind his head. On viewing the 'ethnographic video' of the meal, our informant began to reflect on a range of related topics that were of ethnographic interest and served to contextualize the participants and the ceremony in religious, historical and kinship terms. In other instances interviewing or talking with video can become incidental to the project. When I was shooting the Belfast-based part of *Home from Home*, George and I viewed the footage in his family's living room most evenings. Other family members became keen to view and comment on these screenings of interviews and activities in which George and relatives were involved. I was able to learn more generally from their comments on the themes we were exploring in the video, part of which was concerned with why George had left to live in London and their views on this.

In some cases informants' responses to video can be surprising and may even change the direction of the research. Janet Hoskins describes how her research developed in tandem with her use of video in a project originally intended to be a study of ritual communication in the Indonesian island of Sumba. Hoskins screened video footage of past ritual events to the villagers who had participated in these activities. Treating the footage as a visual record of the rituals, she proposed to ask her informants specific questions about their activities. Their answers were to be used as data for her wider project that aimed to resolve cognitive problems concerning the sociology of knowledge and this distribution outside an inner circle of specialists (Hoskins 1993: 81). However, once she began to screen the video footage to her Sumbanese audience, she was struck by 'the feelings of discomfort, shock and sorrow' they expressed. Her research changed direction 'to explore issues relating to the filmic distribution of time' and 'the emotional responses to images of dead persons' (1993: 78). Situating her analysis of the responses to the film in terms of her knowledge of Sumbanese culture, Hoskins began to develop research about 'cultural perceptions of time' (1993: 80). Her video images of people who were now dead had accidentally disrupted the temporal and emotional process of mourning the dead that was so important to her informants.

Editing, distributing and viewing video footage with his informants was also an aspect of Ferrándiz's project in Venezuela (described above). Ferrándiz produced a tape when his informants asked to see copies of the video. He edited the footage to include expressive imagery by using slow motion to represent some trance sequences. The video was widely viewed and well received in the shanty town where Ferrándiz was working. The slow motion sections were to the satisfaction of his informants: 'it is important to stress the success of the use of slow motion, which seemed to embody with more accuracy the emotionality and fuzziness of the temporality experienced during the ceremonies, somewhere in the scales of trance, as opposed to the times where real time was used' (Ferrándiz 1998: 30). Viewing the video produced with informants can help researchers to work out what are and are not appropriate representations of individuals, their culture and experiences. These processes are represented audio-visually in Zemirah Moffat's reflexive ethnographic film *Mirror Mirror*. As part of the process of researching and making the film, Moffat involved the participants in a series of feedback sessions in different contexts: viewing footage of themselves individually on a laptop; viewing a rough-cut of parts of the film projected onto a stage that the participants usually use for performances in a bar; Zemirah Moffat's film *Mirror Mirror* explores queer identities in London. Embedded in the research and film making process is her collaborative and reflexive approach that accounts for

'Why ask Josephine?' © Zemirah Moffat 2006

both her own identity and part in the film and how the subjects of the film wish to represent themselves. As part of this she screened her footage to them in various contexts and edited their responses into the film itself.

In this scene the people represented in the film comment on a rough-cut they have viewed with Zem at the university. Their conversation, referring to the scene below, in which Zem cheekily asks Josephine if she likes her penis, is as follows:

Lazlo: It's really interesting, yeh because except for that moment, you're not playing with any of the tropes of gender questions.

Zem: Hope I've avoided them.

Lazlo: So it's curious, because you know everybody has the same prurient interests and everybody wants to know but that's not what you've been doing in the film so does it make sense, I mean especially without this information that she said you could ask her anything? Then there'd be a set-up for it, if we knew she'd given up control and you could ask her anything, and this is what you being perverse, basically, had decided to ask her, then I get it.

Maria: Yes!

Josephine: But I'd like this conversation to be cut in. [all *laugh*]

'Do you like your penis?' © *Zemirah Moffat 2006*
Here Zem makes herself a co-subject of the film

and then viewing and commenting on a rough-cut projected onto a screen in a university seminar room. In this case the participants, conversant about their own identities and active discussants of the process of representation and the extent to which the film was achieving its aims, continue to negotiate the way they are portrayed throughout the whole visual ethnographic and filmmaking process.

Ethnographic Uses of Digital Video

Technological innovations usually create or inspire new possibilities. Above I have noted how using digital cameras has changed ethnographers' perspectives on what is being filmed. Digital technology has also opened new possibilities for how video is used in research and representation and in creating continuities between these stages. I discuss this further in Chapter 8. Here I briefly consider how video, combined with other digital technologies, might be used in the research process. Above I have already noted how Zemirah Moffatt has screened her video tapes to the participants in her film video as part of the process of creating the film. Their comments have been fed back into the shooting and editing. However, little has been written about uses of digital video and other technologies as part of fieldwork. One example is a digital video research project designed by Fischer and Zeitlyn that has a brief similar to Hoskins's (see above) original research aims. Entitled 'Mambila Nggwun – the construction and deployment of multiple meanings in ritual', their research intends to use digitized video recordings of ritual to 'produce specific models of how collective representations of a specific socio-cultural ritual event are structured and distributed between participants and observers, and how these are accessed and used by people to solve problems in the present' (). In order 'to capture the many perspectives that contribute to the [ritual] event' the researchers use video in two ways: first, in existing fieldwork they have 'videoed segments of the event from as many points of view as possible, filming under the advisement [*sic*] of indigenous consultants'; secondly, they propose to 'select segments of this video . . . under the advisement [sic] of indigenous consultants, to prepare computer-based multimedia documents as an elicitation device for a range of participants and observers' (Fischer and Zeitlyn n.d.). Fischer and Zeitlyn's collaborative use of digital technology allows this project to stand out from most existing ethnographic research with video. This creates new possibilities for the representation, organ- ization and analysis of visual materials with the collaboration of informants in the field, as well as for the post-fieldwork organization and interpretation of materials (see Chapter 5).

Summary

In this chapter I have suggested a reflexive approach to video in ethnographic research that focuses on the question of how knowledge is produced through the relationship between the researcher and the subject of ethnographic video, the technologies used, and local and academic visual cultures. Recently, uses of video in ethnographic research have developed in tandem with new technologies, innovations and theoretical perspectives. Shifts from a realist approach to video as 'objective' reality to the idea of video as representation shaped by specific standpoints of its producers and viewers have encouraged the development of collaborative approaches to the production and interpret- ation of video images. The introduction of digital video and computer-based techniques seems particularly appropriate for the application of these methods and is forming the basis of future development in video research.

References

Askew, K. and Wilk, R. (eds) (2002) *The Anthropology of Media: A Reader*. Oxford: Blackwell.
Banks, M. (1992) Which films are the ethnographic films?'. In P.I. Crawford and D. Turton (eds), *Film as Ethnography*. Manchester: University of Manchester Press.

Banks, M. (2001) *Visual Methods in Social Research.* London: Sage.

Barbash, I. and Taylor, L. (1997) *Cross Cultural Filmmaking: A Handbook for Making Documentary and Ethnographic Films and Video.* London: University of California Press.

Barnes, D.B. Taylor-Brown, S. and Weiner, L. (1997) "I didn't leave y'all on purpose": HIV-infected mothers' videotaped legacies for their children', in S.J. Gold (ed), *Visual Methods In Sociological Analysis*; special issue of *Qualitative Sociology* 20 (1).

Cerezo, M., Martinez, A. and Ranera, P. (1996) 'Tres antropólogos inocentes y an ojo si parpado'. in M. Garcia Alonso, A. Martinez, P. Pitarch, P. Ranera and J. Fores (eds), *Antropologia de los Sentidos La Vista.* Madrid: Celeste Ediciones.

Chalfen, R. and Rich, M. (2004) 'Applying visual research: patients teaching physicians about asthma through video diaries', in S. Pink (ed), *Applied Visual Anthropology*, a guest edited issue of *Visual Anthropology Review*, 20 (1): 17–30.

Chaplin, E. (1994) *Sociology ond Visual Representations* London: Routledge.

Collier, J. and Collier, M. (1986) *Visual Anthropology: Photography as a Research Method.* Albuquerque, NM: University of New Mexico Press.

Ferrándiz, F. (1998) A trace of fingerprints: displacements and textures in the use of ethnographic video in Venezuelan spiritism. *Visual Anthropology Review*, 13(2): 19–38.

Ginsburg, F. Abu-Lughod, L. and Larkin, B. (eds) (2002) *Media Worlds: Anthropology on New Terrain.* Berkeley, CA: University of California Press.

Grasseni, C. (2004) 'Video and ethnographic knowledge: skilled vision and the practice of breeding' In S. Pink, L. Kürti and A.I. Afonso (eds), *Working Images.* London: Routledge.

Heider, K. (1976) *Ethnographic Film.* Austin, TX: University of Texas Press.

Holliday, R. (2001) We'e been framed – visualizing methodologies. *Sociological Review*, 48 (4): 503–21.

Hoskins, J. (1993) "Why we cried to see him again": Indonesian villagers responses to the filmic disruption of time'. In J Roliwagen (ed.), *Anthropological Film and Video in the 1990s.* Brockport, NY: The Institute Inc.

Hughes-Freeiand, F. (ed.) (1997) *Ritual, Performance, Media.* London: Routledge.

Loizos, P. (1993) *Innovation in Ethnographic Film.* Manchester: Manchester University Press.

Lomax, H. and Casey, N. (1998) 'Recording social life: reflexivity and video methodology'. *Sociological Research Online.* 3 (2), http://www.socresonline.arg.uk/socresonline/3/2/1.html

Morley, D. (1996) 'The audience, the ethnographer, the postmodernist and their problems', In P.I. Crawford and S.B. Hafsteinsson (eds), *The Construction of the Viewer.* Aarhaus: Intervention Press.

Morphy, H. and Banks, M. (1997) 'Introduction: rethinking visual anthropology', in M. Banks and H. Morphy (eds), *Rethinking Visual Anthropology.* London: Routledge.

Pink, S. (1997a) *Women and Bullfighting: Gender, Sex and the Consumption of Tradition.* Oxford: Berg.

Pink, S. (ed.) (2004a) Applied Visual Anthropology, a guest edited issue of Visual. *Anthropology Review*, 20 (1).

Pink, S. (2004b) *Home Truths: Gender, Domestic Objects and Everyday Life.* Oxford: Berg.

Pink, S. (2004c) 'Performance, self-representation and narrative: interviewing with video', in C. Pole (ed.), *Seeing is Believing? Approaches to Visual Research.* Studies in Qualitative Methodology – Volume 7. Oxford: Elsevier Science.

Pink, S. (2005) *The Future of Visual Anthropology: Engaging the Senses.* London: Routledge.

Rothenbuhler, E.W. and M. Coman (eds) (2005) *Media Anthropology.* Thousands Oaks, CA: Sage.

White, S. (2003) *Participatory Video: Images that Transform and Empower.* London: Sage.

Wright, C. (1998) 'The third subject: perspectives on visual anthropology'. *Anthropology Today* 14 (4): 16–22.